Samuel T. Gladding

Fifth Edition

the Creative *Arts* in Counseling

AMERICAN COUNSELING
ASSOCIATION
6101 Stevenson Avenue, Suite 600
Alexandria, VA 22304
www.counseling.org

Fifth Edition

the Creative Arts in Counseling

American Counseling Association

6101 Stevenson Avenue, Suite 600 • Alexandria, VA 22304

Associate Publisher • Carolyn C. Baker

Digital and Print Development Editor • Nancy Driver

Senior Production Manager • Bonny E. Gaston

Copy Editor • Kay Mikel

Cover and text design by Bonny E. Gaston.

Library of Congress Cataloging-in-Publication Data
Names: Gladding, Samuel T., author.
Title: The creative arts in counseling/Samuel T. Gladding.
Description: Fifth edition. | Alexandria, VA: American Counseling
    Association, [2016] | Includes bibliographical references and index.
Identifiers: LCCN 2015049584 | ISBN 9781556203657 (pbk.: alk.
    paper)
Subjects: LCSH: Counseling psychology. | Arts—Therapeutic use.
Classification: LCC BF636.6 .G625 2016 | DDC 158.3—dc23 LC
    record available at http://lccn.loc.gov/2015049584

To the good people of Decatur, Georgia,
who nourished my curiosity and creativity growing up;
especially to my former Decatur High School English teachers
Ann Lewis and Weldon Jelks, who encouraged me to write;
and to Walter McCurdy Jr. and Reid Crow at
the First Baptist Church, who taught me with
their stories and music.

also

To Jim Cotton, Robbin McInturff, Mariam Cosper,
and Laurie Smith at Adult and Child Developmental Specialists in
Birmingham, Alabama, from whom I learned
the art of good counseling.

∽

Contents

Preface

"Counseling is a professional relationship that empowers diverse individuals, families, and groups to accomplish mental health, wellness, education, and career goals" (D. M. Kaplan, Tarvydas, & Gladding, 2014, p. 366). In accomplishing its goals, counseling is a creative process, and counselors focus on helping clients make developmentally appropriate choices and changes. Effective counselors are aware of the multidimensional nature of the profession and choose from a wide variety of interventions when working with diverse populations. As a group, the creative arts is a sometimes overlooked aspect of counseling that can promote the best within the helping arena (Neilsen, King, & Baker, 2016). By its very nature, the arts foster different ways of experiencing the world and are enriching, stimulating, and therapeutic in their own right. When used in clinical situations, creative arts can help counselors and clients gain unique and universal perspectives on problems and possibilities.

In this fifth edition of *The Creative Arts in Counseling,* I concentrate on how the creative arts can be used independently and complementarily to enhance the counseling process on primary, secondary, and tertiary levels. Specifically, the following creative arts are examined:

- Music
- Dance and movement
- Imagery
- Visual arts
- Literature and writing
- Drama and psychodrama
- Play and humor
- Animal-assisted therapy, horticulture, and wilderness therapy

These arts share much in common. They are all process oriented, emotionally sensitive, socially directed, awareness focused, and applicable in numerous forms for working with clients over the life span. In addition, they enable people from diverse cultural backgrounds to develop in ways that are enjoyable as well as personally and socially enhancing.

Mental health providers such as counselors, social workers, psychologists, creative arts therapists, marriage and family therapists, psychiatric nurses, pastoral care specialists, and psychiatrists will find the content of these pages useful because of both the research and the pragmatic nature of the material covered. The material presented here comes from a variety of educational and treatment-focused work settings. Because of their systematic format, Chapters 2 through 9 may be especially helpful because they present a great deal of information in a relatively uniform manner. These chapters contain the following:

- Introductory background about the specific art form
- The premise behind using the art form discussed
- The general practice of using the art in counseling settings
- Unique use of the specific art with special populations, such as children, adolescents, adults, older adults, groups, families, and cultural minorities
- A summary
- Art-related exercises

Chapter 1 provides information on the history, rationale for, and benefits of using artistic methods in general; Chapter 10 highlights current trends in the use of the arts in counseling and includes additional resources. Together these chapters are bookends to those in between, enabling you to obtain a global view of the field, how it developed, and where it is going. Chapter 11 illustrates creative exercises in the different artistic domains covered in Chapters 2 through 9.

Creative Reflection boxes are distributed throughout the chapters to give you an opportunity and the means to reflect on your own creativity. They also, at times, demonstrate another way to incorporate materials and prompt you to a further exploration of your thoughts and feelings.

Overall, practitioners will find this book user friendly. Most of the ideas discussed here have been extensively field tested by experienced clinicians. By carefully reading this book, you will become better informed as a professional and be able to enhance your skills and effectiveness. The creative arts have much to offer the healing and helping professions and the clients who use these services.

New to This Edition

An old maxim states that a new book should never be written when an old book will suffice. That goes for revisions too. I could not agree more, which explains the 6-year time span between this edition and the previous edition. I would love to say that the fourth edition of this work is still up to date, but alas, it is not. The fifth edition includes 149 new references, which are mixed liberally with more classic texts and articles. By blending recent with more established findings, the best scholarship in the field of using the creative arts in counseling has been maintained and expanded.

Second, more than a dozen Creative Reflections have been added to the five dozen in the fourth edition of the text. These additions offer you an opportunity to "slow down" in each chapter and think about how the material you are reading applies to your life both personally and professionally. Through such a means, you can get to know yourself better as a clinician and as a person.

Third, Chapter 9, "Animal-Assisted Therapy in Counseling, Therapeutic Horticulture, and Wilderness/Nature Therapy," is new to this edition. Each of these approaches is examined in regard to its background, premises, general practices, and use with special populations. The chapter also includes a summary and related exercises.

Fourth, the subject index to this edition has been modified and updated to reflect the new content of the body of this work.

Fifth, all websites and addresses of creative arts therapy associations have been double checked and updated where needed. Some new ones have been added as well. Thus, you can easily access the latest research and conference information related to creative arts therapies.

Finally, 136 creative arts projects and exercises appear in Chapter 11. The creative arts are truly global and culturally relevant to counselors from multiple settings and backgrounds. This fact is reflected throughout this edition.

All of these changes have made the fifth edition of *The Creative Arts in Counseling* a thicker and more relevant text. This book is well organized, punctuated with examples, practical, and engaging while maintaining a scholarly base.

Enjoy!

—Samuel T. Gladding

Acknowledgments

Writing a book is similar to many other activities in life. Some say it is like having a baby and that the labor involved results in a newness that is breathtaking and well worth the time and nurture that went into the process. (My wife disagrees with this analogy and says being pregnant and then a mother is completely different. I imagine many other women would agree.) So I like to think of the process as similar to a good group experience. In productive groups, many people share valuable information and give you important feedback. In addition, groups usually occur over time. Psychoeducational and task groups help participants produce a product either directly or indirectly (and it is not a baby). Ultimately, the outcome is both an interpersonal and a personal experience. The group that has helped me formulate ideas, gather knowledge, and put together this fifth edition of *The Creative Arts in Counseling* contained some of the same individuals who helped me with the previous editions as well as a few new individuals.

First, I want to thank Carolyn Baker and the American Counseling Association Publications Committee for accepting my proposal for a fifth edition of this text. Carolyn kept me on task in a timely and professional manner. Next, I want to thank Dr. Richard Hayes for encouraging and supporting me to write this book initially. Without Richard's advocacy, I doubt this work would have ever been written. I also want to thank the reviewers and editor of the first edition of this text, Drs. Howard S. Rosenblatt, Stephen G. Weinrach, JoAnna White, and Elaine Pirrone. They were honest and straightforward in their appraisal of the manuscript and offered constructive thoughts that made this work far better than it would have been otherwise. In addition, I want to express my appreciation to Wake Forest University graduate counseling students—Katie Anne Burt, Dan Barnhart,

Michele Kielty, Debbie Newsome, Mary Beth Edens, Regan Reding, and Deborah Tyson, in particular—for contributing ideas and thoughts on counseling and the creative arts. Katie Anne, Dan, and Michele were especially helpful and industrious in locating the latest research on the creative arts and were meticulous proofreaders.

Finally, I am grateful to clients and colleagues over the years who have shared creative ideas with me and helped me to focus more on the importance of the arts in counseling. I especially appreciate the support of my wife, Claire, and our three children. They have humored me with jokes and goodwill while this book was in process. I am truly a fortunate individual to be surrounded with so much that is good, growth enhancing, and artistic.

About the Author

Samuel T. Gladding is a professor in the Department of Counseling at Wake Forest University in Winston-Salem, North Carolina. His academic degrees are from Wake Forest (BA, MA Ed), Yale (MA), and the University of North Carolina at Greensboro (PhD).

Before assuming his current position, he held academic appointments at the University of Alabama at Birmingham and Fairfield University (Connecticut). He was also an instructor of psychology at a community college and director of children's services at a mental health center, both of which are in Rockingham County, North Carolina. He is a Licensed Professional Counselor in North Carolina, a National Certified Counselor, a Certified Clinical Mental Health Counselor, and a former member of the North Carolina Board of Licensed Professional Counselors.

Dr. Gladding is the author of a number of publications on counseling, including *Becoming a Counselor: The Light, the Bright, and the Serious* (2009); *Counseling: A Comprehensive Profession* (2013); *Family Therapy: History, Theory, and Practice* (2015a); and *Groups: A Counseling Specialty* (2016). He is the former editor of the *Journal for Specialists in Group Work*. He has served as president of the American Counseling Association (ACA) as well as president of the American Association of State Counseling Boards (AASCB), the Association for Counselor Education and Supervision (ACES), the Association for Specialists in Group Work (ASGW), and Chi Sigma Iota (Counseling Academic and Professional Honor Society International). He has also chaired the American Counseling Association Foundation.

Dr. Gladding has received numerous honors. He is a Fellow in the ACA and the recipient of the ACA's Gilbert and Kathleen Wrenn Award for a Humanitarian and Caring Person and the Arthur A. Hitchcock Distinguished Professional Service Award. He has also received the Chi Sigma Iota (CSI) Thomas J. Sweeney Professional

Leadership Award, and the Association for Humanistic Counseling (AHC) Joseph W. and Lucille U. Hollis Outstanding Publication Award. In addition, Dr. Gladding is the recipient of the ACES Outstanding Publication Award as well as the ACES Leadership Award. Furthermore, he received the Lifetime Achievement Award from the Association for Creativity in Counseling (ACC), and the Research Award from the International Association of Marriage and Family Counselors (IAMFC). He is also a Fellow in ASGW and received this association's Eminent Career Award.

In 2008, the ACC named its Inspiration and Motivation award after Dr. Gladding. In 2015, ACA named its Unsung Heroes award after him.

Dr. Gladding has worked with counseling colleagues in Malaysia, Estonia, Australia, Singapore, Sweden, Austria, and South Africa and has been a Fulbright Specialist to Turkey and China. He is married to the former Claire Tillson and is the father of three adult children. He enjoys the arts, creativity, and humor on a daily basis.

Chapter 1

History of, Rationale for, and Benefits of Using the Arts in Counseling

Journey

I am taken back by your words
 to your history and the mystery of being human
  in an all-too-often robotic world.
I hear your pain
 and see the pictures you paint
  so cautiously and vividly.
The world you draw is a kaleidoscope
 ever changing, ever new, encircling and fragile.
Moving past the time and through the shadows
 you look for hope beyond the groups you knew as a child.
I want to say, "I'm here. Trust the process,"
 but the artwork is your own.
So I withdraw and watch you work
 while occasionally offering you feedback
  and images of the possible.

—Gladding, 1990b, p. 142

Counseling is a profession that focuses on making human experience constructive, meaningful, and enjoyable both on a preventive and on a remedial level. It is like art in its emphasis on expressiveness, structure, and uniqueness. It is also creative in its originality and its outcomes. Both are novel, practical, and significant.

This book is on the uses of the creative arts in counseling. The creative arts are frequently referred to as the expressive arts (Atkins et al., 2003). They are defined here as art forms, ranging from those that are primarily auditory or written (e.g., music, drama, and literature) to those that are predominantly visual (e.g., painting, mime, dance, and movement). Many overlaps exist between these broad categories. In most cases two or more art forms are combined in a counseling context, such as literature and drama or dance and music. These combinations work because "music, art, dance/movement, drama therapy, psychodrama, and poetry therapy have a strong common bond" (Summer, 1997, p. 80).

As a group, the creative arts enhance and enliven the lives of everyone they touch (Neilsen et al., 2016). Cultivation of the arts outside of counseling settings is enriching for people in all walks of life because it sensitizes them to beauty, helps heal them physically and mentally, and creates within them a greater awareness of possibilities (Jourard & Landsman, 1980). The arts help patients and clients by increasing self-esteem, increasing motor coordination and body control, providing relaxation, teaching coping skills, decreasing acting out behaviors, and developing awareness of emotions or underlying issues (H. Kennedy, Reed, & Wamboldt, 2014). "It can be said that . . . creative endeavors offer multidisciplinary ways to give voice to the human internal experience and to act as catalysts for learning about the self and the world at large" (Bradley, Whiting, Hendricks, Parr, & Jones, 2008, p. 44).

In counseling, the creative arts help to make clients more sensitive to themselves and often encourage them to invest in therapeutic processes that can help them grow and develop even further (A. Kennedy, 2008). As such actions occur, participants may give more form to their thoughts, behaviors, and feelings and become empowered. Aside from formal counseling sessions, "acts of artistic expression, in and of themselves, carry their own healing" (MacKay, 1989, p. 300). Involvement with the arts helps individuals recover from traumatic experiences and the stress of daily living. Thus, whether encountering the creative arts inside or outside of counseling, individuals who are involved with them usually benefit in multiple ways.

The possibilities encased of specific creative arts in counseling, singularly and together, are covered in various ways in this book. The processes and outcomes of using the arts in a therapeutic manner are addressed as they are related to specific client populations. Just as becoming a painter takes talent, sensitivity, courage, and years of devotion, a similar process is at work in counseling: The actual practice differs from knowledge of theory (Cavanagh, 1982). Csikszentmihalyi (1996) hypothesized that it takes at least 10 years for a person to be in a field before being able to master it. Thus, the 10-year rule for bringing talent to fruition seems to apply to artists, counselors, or anyone in refining their talent. Therefore, although the ingredients necessary to enrich counseling through using the arts are emphasized here, the effective implementation of these skills and processes will only come with practice on the part of the counselor—you!

The Nature of Creativity

When the creative arts in counseling are examined as an entity, it is crucial to initially explore the nature of creativity. This examination is prudent for two reasons. First, by knowing something about the nature of creativity, counselors may understand and better appreciate creative processes. Second, counseling, as mentioned previously, is by its nature a creative endeavor. Although the arts have much potential to help counselors in assisting clients, they are limited in what they can do unless counselors know how to use them creatively.

Creativity is an overused word that is sometimes talked about without being defined. It is a lot like kissing in that it is so "intrinsically interesting and satisfying that few bother to critically examine it" (Thoresen, 1969, p. 264). A central feature of creativity is *divergent thinking*, which is thinking in a broad, flexible, exploratory, tentative, inductive, and non-data-based way that is oriented toward the development of possibilities. Divergent thinking includes fluency, flexibility, originality, and elaboration in thought as well (Carson, 1999). Creativity and divergent thinking are associated with coping abilities, good mental health, resiliency, and couple/family functionality and happiness (Cohen, 2000; Csikszentmihalyi, 1996; Pink, 2006). According to Sternberg and Lubart (1996, p. 677), as an overall process, creativity involves "the ability to produce work that is both novel (i.e., original or unexpected) and appropriate (i.e., useful or meets task constraints)." It is positively related to spontaneity and negatively related to impulsivity (Kipper, Green, & Prorak, 2010).

In counseling and other helping professions, creativity combined with the arts frequently results in (a) the production of a tangible product that gives a client insight, such as a piece of writing or a painting, or (b) a process that the clinician formulates, such as a new way of conducting counseling that leads to client change. Creativity is a worldwide phenomenon that knows no bounds with regard to ethnicity, culture, gender, age, or other real or imagined barriers that separate people from each other (Koestler, 1964; Lubart, 1999). In addition, creativity can be preventative as well as remedial. Duffey (2015), a major advocate for the use of creativity in counseling (CIC), a term she devised, stated: "Creativity is as fundamental to counseling practice as the therapeutic relationship. In the best sense, the therapeutic relationship ignites creative problem solving, understanding, flexibility, and adaptability. In turn, this shared creativity deepens the counseling relationship."

Overall, creativity is a nonsequential experience that involves two parts: originality and functionality. A distinction can and should be made between "little-c creativity," that is, "everyday problem solving and the ability to adapt to change," and "Big-C creativity," that is, "when a person solves a problem or creates an object that has a major impact on how other people think, feel, and live their lives" (Kersting, 2003, p. 40). Big-C creativity is much rarer than little-c creativity. An example of Big-C creativity is formulation of counseling theories such as those devised by Sigmund Freud and Carl Rogers (Gladding, 2008). However, individual counseling mostly involves little-c creativity as counselors work with clients to find more productive and constructive ways of living. Regardless of whether it is Big-C or little-c, both types of creativity involve a six-step process (Witmer, 1985):

Creative Reflection

Many people find ideas coming to them at specific times of the day, such as early morning, or when they are engaged in certain activities, such as taking a shower. Think of when ideas are most likely to come to you. Keep a daily chart for a week of new ideas and the times in which they come. What does this activity tell you about yourself and what you need to be most mindful of in "finding time" to be creative?

1. *Preparation,* during which enough data and background information are gathered to make a new response.
2. *Incubation,* in which the mind is allowed to wander away from a task or problem.
3. *Ideation,* in which ideas are generated but not judged, a type of divergent thinking.
4. *Illumination,* in which there is a breakthrough in a person's thinking, a kind of enlightenment.
5. *Evaluation,* during which convergent and critical thinking occur. A part of evaluation is fine-tuning and refining thoughts or behaviors that have not been thoroughly considered.
6. *Verification/production,* during which an original idea becomes a new or refined product or action. In this last step, a person's life changes forever because it is impossible to see or be in the world again as before.

Although these general aspects about creativity are pertinent to counseling, the profession itself, through its theories, has even more specific ways of viewing creativity (Gladding, 1995). For example, the psychoanalytic viewpoint is that creativity is a positive defense mechanism, known as *sublimation*. From a gestalt perspective, however, creativity is an integrative process in which people become more congruent with themselves and their environments and thus try new behaviors. Imagery theorists, however, argue that creativity is a matter of envisioning mental pictures and implementing these pictures in reality.

Regardless of how it is seen, creativity is valued in society and in the culture of counseling. Through creativity, new, exciting, and productive ways of working, living, and healing are formulated and implemented with individuals, couples, and families (Carson & Becker, 2003).

History of the Creative Arts in the Helping Professions

Having explained the vital aspects of what creativity is and what the creative arts are, we can now examine in an informed manner the ways in which the creative arts have affected counseling. Many of the creative arts, such as drama, music, and dance, have had long and distinguished associations with healing and mental health services (Corsini, 2001; Westhenen & Fritz, 2014). Almost all art forms have been used since ancient times to help prevent distress and remediate internal and external strife. Some of their most notable contributions to mental health services are chronicled here according to broad time periods.

Ancient Cultures and the Arts

Ancient civilizations valued the creative arts for what they believed were their healing properties as well as their aesthetic properties (Atkins et al., 2003). For example, the ancient Egyptians, as early as 500 BCE, encouraged the mentally ill "to pursue artistic interests and attend concerts and dances" (Fleshman & Fryear, 1981, p. 12). The idea was that through such activities feelings could be released, and people were made whole again. Likewise, the ancient Greeks "employed drama and music as a means to help the disturbed achieve catharsis, relieve themselves of pent-up emotions, and return to balanced lives" (Gladding, 1985, p. 2). The connection and importance of music in the lives of the Greeks are symbolized in the Greek god Apollo, who was both the god of music and the god of medicine. The Greek philosophers Plato and Aristotle often talked about the effects of music and its importance to the health of the whole person (Peters, 2001). They advocated the

Creative Reflection

What art or arts were you first drawn to as a child? Think back to what attracted you to them. How has your experience since childhood influenced your thoughts, feelings, and experiences with the art or art forms that you initially found fascinating?

careful control of music to promote many moods from relaxation to excitement (Burkholder, Grout, & Palisca, 2015).

The early Hebrews used music and lyrical verse, too, in helping to develop integrated and healthy relationships. For example, when individuals, such as King Saul, were emotionally volatile, music served to calm them down (MacIntosh, 2003). Music was also used to remind the Hebrew people of the covenant relationship they shared with Yahweh (God) and with each other. The psalms, for instance, played a major part in worship and in creating a sense of community through religious rituals. At about this same time, in ancient Asian cultures, such as in China, music was emphasized as well. For example, Confucius loved music and believed that it was essential for a harmonious life (Y. Lai, 1999).

Similarly, the ancient Roman philosophers encouraged the public to use the arts to achieve health and happiness. Lucretius, Cicero, and Seneca "all spoke in different ways of the healing power of 'discourse.' Poetry, Lucretius said, could disperse the 'terrors of the soul'" (Coughlin, 1990, p. A6). A further belief among the Romans was that the study of humane letters could alleviate pain. Finally, music, cymbals, flutes, and other sounds were used by the Romans to dispel melancholy thoughts as well as to promote wellness (Peters, 2001).

Overall, ancient world healers saw power in the arts. They encouraged their followers to experience these forms of creativity vigorously. They believed that such a procedure had a significant positive mental and physical impact.

The Middle Ages and the Arts

In the Middle Ages (at least in Europe), magic and superstition replaced the arts in many quarters as the primary way to treat people who were emotionally disturbed. Yet even in these Dark Ages, the traditions and actual works of music, art, and literature were preserved in monasteries and were considered in the Judeo-Christian tradition to be a relevant part of the process of healing (Coughlin, 1990; Flake, 1988). For example, in medieval times, French monasteries used music to soothe the sick (Covington, 2001). Another interesting example of the use of the arts in the service of health was the treatment of the disorder known as Tarantism. This disorder arose in southern Italy and was believed to be caused by the bite of a tarantula. Healers thought that the only cure for this disease was music accompanied by the performance of a dance known as the tarantella (Coughlin, 1990).

The use of music, dance, painting, and literature as healing forces in African, Native American, and Asian cultures was even more widespread (Fleming, 1994). For example, African music developed into a form with strong, driving rhythms and choral singing that helped bind communities together. In addition, Asian, African, and Native American art in the form of paintings, jewelry, masks, and architecture flourished and helped give cultures and people in these geographical areas a distinctiveness. It was during this time period in the Americas that the arts became an integral part of Native American healing (Dufrene & Coleman, 1994). The use of metaphor and healing stories became especially powerful.

The Arts From the Renaissance Through the 19th Century

During the European Renaissance (starting in the 1500s), the use of the arts was emphasized in preventative and remedial mental health services, as it had been in ancient cultures. For example, in the 16th century, an Italian named Vittorino de Feltre emphasized poetry, dance, and games in the education of children and suggested the alternation of study and play in working with children (Flake, 1988). In the 1600s, "writers such as Robert Burton, author of *The Anatomy of Melancholy* (1621), talked about the role of the imagination in both psychological illness and health" (Coughlin, 1990, p. A9). One of his premises was that individuals who were imaginative and creative were more likely to be healthy. They could respond to both comedies and tragedies and thereby keep a better balanced and realistic perspective on life.

The integration of health and the arts was exemplified in the work of 17th-century physicians such as Tommaso del Garbo, who advised his patients that one way to avoid the plague was to keep a positive mind-set and to listen to music (Peters, 2001). His belief in the healing power of music was apparently a part of the culture of the day, as plays such as those written by Shakespeare demonstrate. Likewise, the poetry of meditation in 17th-century England arose at this time with an emphasis on health and wholeness. Poets such as Robert Southwell, John Donne, and George Herbert practiced meditation to become more sensitive to the images within themselves, which they then expressed in verse (Martz, 1962). Thus, concentration led to art, which led in turn to further exploration and discovery of the self.

By the time of the industrial revolution in England (18th century), the use of the arts in the service of healing had expanded. Reformers such as Philippe Pinel in France, Benjamin Rush in the United States, and William Tuke in England stressed the humane treatment of mental patients. A form of counseling known as *moral therapy* was begun. In this approach to treatment, individuals with mental disorders were sent to country retreats where they received individual attention including occupational training and special times of involvement in arts such as selected reading, music, and painting (Fleshman & Fryear, 1981). It was in this type of an environment that Vincent van Gogh, the famous Impressionist painter, spent part of his life as an adult. Overall, this approach proved to be beneficial but was quite time consuming and expensive. Thus, it was relatively short lived in Europe and the United States. Yet despite the brief lives of some forms of art treatment, the power and impact of the arts continued. Music, for instance, was seen as an adjunct to the practice of medicine in many cultures throughout the world (G. N. Heller, 1985). It is still valued in many medical settings, and soft, soothing music is often played in the background of physicians' offices, and surgeons may play music that calms and inspires them when they are operating.

Creative Reflection

Why do you think moral therapy has not been reinstated as a major treatment for those who suffer mental distress? How would you go about bringing this approach back? What changes would you make?

The Arts in the 20th and 21st Centuries

In the 20th century, the use of the arts in counseling increased significantly. One of the reasons was the work of Sigmund Freud. It was Freud who first probed the influence of the unconscious through the exploration of dreams and humor. His systematic way of treatment made it possible for others to emulate many of his methods, such as the inducement of catharsis. More important, Freud set the standard for incorporating artistic concepts into his therapeutic work.

> Freud found the fiction of Dostoyevsky, Sophocles, and Shakespeare, the sculpture of Michelangelo and Leonardo to be the inspiration for his theories. It was not his formal medical training, as much as his readings of *King Lear*, *Hamlet*, *Oedipus Rex*, and *The Brothers Karamazov*, that formed the cornerstone of his theories. (Kottler, 2010, p. 35)

The work of Carl G. Jung (1964), particularly his examination and use of universal archetypes, such as mandalas, also made the arts more attractive to researchers and innovators in counseling. *Mandalas* are symbols of completeness and wholeness, most often circular. As Jung (1933) stated, "The psychological work of art always takes its materials from the vast realm of conscious human experience—from the vivid foreground of life" (p. 157). Throughout his life Jung continued to draw and paint, portraying his dreams in writings and through illustrations that he sometimes carved in wood and stone. He felt that psychological health was a delicate balance between the demands of the outer world and the needs of the inner world. To him, the expressive arts represented an important avenue to the inner world of feelings and images. He came to see the unconscious mind as a source of health and transformation (Allan, 2008). Thus, through the influence of Jung, art and creativity became more valued as ways of understanding human nature in our culture.

In addition, the creative genesis of Jacob L. Moreno (1923/1947), the founder of psychodrama, fostered the use of enactment to work through pain and achieve balance. J. L. Moreno originated numerous psychodrama techniques to help clients become more self-aware and make insightful breakthroughs. All of his innovations have an artistic dimension, but among the most notable are the following:

- Creative imagery, in which participants imagine pleasant or neutral scenes to help them become more spontaneous.
- Sculpting, during which participants nonverbally arrange the body posture of group members to reflect important experiences in their lives with significant others.
- Monodrama, during which participants play all the different parts of themselves.
- Role reversal, during which participants literally switch roles with others. (Blatner, 1996)

Overall, a major reason for the growth of the arts in counseling during the 20th century was the power of the personalities who advocated for them. In addition to the writings of the theorists already mentioned, those of Abraham Maslow, Rollo May, Arnold Lazarus, Virginia Satir, Bunny Duhl, Peggy Papp, and Cloé Madanes emphasized the importance of counseling as an artistic endeavor and as a profession that can make a difference through the use of the arts. Research emphasizing the results of specific arts-related strategies and interventions also resulted in increased acceptance of artistic components in helping relationships.

Another important reason the use of the arts and artistic methods achieved prominence in counseling in the 20th century arose from the events following World War II. For example, veterans of the war were often in need of extended care for the traumas of combat. In addition to the traditional talk therapies, mental health practitioners began developing new approaches to working with those who were impaired. These included the use of some arts, such as drawing or painting, music, and literature. In this creative atmosphere, clients were helped to identify and work through pent-up emotions. Interest in the arts as an adjunct to traditional mental health practices thereby gained new recognition and acceptance. Furthermore, professional arts therapy associations were formed. Some of these, such as the American Dance Therapy Association, advocated using the arts in the service of counseling in a professional way.

Thus, out of the development of theories and the treatment of clients following World War II, arts therapies attracted more interest and gained more acceptance as unique and valuable disciplines. In the 1960s, universities began designing degrees in the arts therapies, such as dance and the visual arts. From the graduates of these programs came new enthusiasm and energy to develop standards and guidelines for practice. By the beginning of the 21st century, most art therapy associations either registered or certified their members as qualified practitioners and were attempting or had succeeded in making their members licensed as mental health practitioners in many states. Uniting many professionals in the field was the International Association of Expressive Arts Therapies (http://www.ieata.org/), which held conferences in many countries, including the United States.

Paralleling the growth of professional associations was a surge in the publication of periodicals dealing with the arts in counseling, such as *The Arts in Psychotherapy*. Likewise, the 1980s heralded an increased effort at sharing knowledge among mental health professionals interested in the arts. The National Coalition of Creative Arts Therapies Associations (NCCATA) was established in 1979. It held interdisciplinary conferences for arts therapists. The emergence of NCCATA signaled a formal and systematic attempt to foster communication between creative arts therapies groups and individuals interested in these groups. NCCATA also focused on being an inclusive voice to achieve legislative recognition for creative arts therapists (Bonny, 1997).

Then in 2004 a new association within the counseling world, specifically in the American Counseling Association, emerged. It was the Association for Creativity in Counseling (ACC). Led by Dr. Thelma Duffey at the University of Texas at San Antonio, the ACC quickly attracted members and began publishing the *Journal for Creativity in Mental Health*.

Rationale for Using the Creative Arts in Counseling

Along with the increased growth of creative arts in counseling has come the formulation of modern rationales for using them in the helping process. Numerous reasons beyond the fact that they have a historical precedent exist for employing the creative arts therapeutically. The Appalachian Expressive Arts Collective, comprising professors in a number of academic departments at Appalachian State University in Boone, North Carolina, has given many such motives. Among them are that these arts celebrate "connectedness, deep feeling, . . . intuition, integration, purpose, and the totality of the human experience" (Atkins et al., 2003, p. 120). This group and others have influenced the counselor education program at Appalachian State University to include a specific track on creative arts therapies in counseling. Other reasons the creative arts have grown in prominence in almost all helping professions follow.

The first reason for helping professionals to use the arts in therapeutic settings is that they are a primary means of assisting individuals to become integrated and connected. Often people who become mentally disturbed, such as those with an eating disorder, have a distorted view of themselves (Robbins & Pehrsson, 2009). They become estranged from reality, alien-

Creative Reflection

Reflect on how your interest in the creative arts has grown over the years. What art forms most attracted you 10 years ago? Five years ago? How has your taste in the arts broadened or deepened since you first became interested in them? What would you select as your three favorite art forms today (e.g., music, painting, photography, dance/movement, drama)?

ated from others, and thwart healing forces within themselves from coming into action. This type of estrangement is a phenomenon that Carl R. Rogers (1957) described as *incongruence*. It prevents growth and development. Many of the arts, such as dance, music, and poetry, have the potential for helping individuals become integrated and more aware of themselves. For instance, Robbins and Pehrsson (2009) found that poetry therapy and narrative therapy gave women with anorexia nervosa a voice (a catharsis) that helped them reclaim their individual power.

A second reason for using the arts in counseling involves energy and process. Most creative arts are participatory and require the generation of behaviors and emotions. Activity involving the expressive arts gives individuals new energy and is reinforcing because it leads somewhere. In many cases the input and output energy cycle involved in the arts is similar to that of marathon runners. Initially, runners use energy to cover mileage at a set pace. Later, after considerable physical pain, they experience what is known as a "runner's high," a feeling of renewal and energy that allows them to pick up the pace. After such an event, an analysis of what happened and how what was learned can influence their future as a runner take place. This type of reflecting and talking, especially with arts activities, can lead to new and usually improved functioning of the people involved.

A third reason for incorporating the arts in counseling is focus. There is an old African American saying that for people to achieve they must keep their "eye on the prize." The arts, especially those that involve vision, allow clients to see more clearly what they are striving for and what progress they are making toward reaching their goals (Allan, 2008; Lazarus, 1977). Other nonvisual arts such as those dealing with sound also encourage this type of concentration.

Yet a fourth rationale for using the arts in counseling is creativity. To be artistic as a counselor or to use the arts in counseling "enlarges the universe by adding or uncovering new dimensions" (Arieti, 1976, p. 5) while enriching and expanding people who participate in such a process. Thus, counseling as an art, and the use of the arts in counseling, expands the world outwardly and inwardly for participants. Better yet, the artistic side of counseling allows and even promotes this expansion in an enjoyable and relaxed manner.

A fifth reason for including artistic components in counseling is to help clients establish a new sense of self. Establishing this new sense of self is especially important in resiliency work in which clients are attempting to recover from adversity (Metzl & Morrell, 2008). At such times there is a need to engage in creative processes such as art or drama in order for the person who has been traumatized to gain a fresh perspective on life and himself or herself. Awareness of self is a quality associated with age. It usually increases in older adults (Erikson, 1968; Jung, 1933). This ability to become more in contact with the various dimensions of life can be sped up and highlighted through the use of the arts in counseling. The visual, auditory, or other sensory stimuli used in sessions give clients a way to experience themselves, whatever their circumstances, differently in an atmosphere in which spontaneity and risk-taking are encouraged within limits. Clients are able to exhibit and practice novel and adaptive behaviors. Thus, clients gain confidence and ability through sessions, and the arts assist them to "become" continuously (Allport, 1955).

A sixth reason for including the arts in helping, such as counseling, involves concreteness. In using the arts, a client is able to conceptualize and duplicate beneficial activities. For example, if writing poetry is found to be therapeutic, clients are instructed to use this method and media when needed (Gladding, 1988). By doing so, they lay out a historical trail so that they can see, feel, and realize more fully what they have accomplished through hard work and inspiration. Such a process allows their memories to live again and may lead to other achievements.

Insight is another potential outcome from and reason for the use of the arts and artistic methods in counseling. Two types of insight are most likely to result. The first is primarily that of the participants in counseling, that is, the counselor and client. In this type of insight, one or both of these individuals come to see a situation in a different light than when counseling began. For example, the client may see his or her situation as hopeless but not serious, or serious but not hopeless (Watzlawick, 1983). This type of focus makes a difference, for it is what people perceive that largely determines their degree of mental health or alienation (Ellis, 1988). In the second type of insight, mental health professionals in associations, for example, the American Counseling Association, gain new awareness into how they need to develop collectively. For example, they may recognize "that art often leads to science" and that balance is needed between scientific and artistic endeavors if the profession is to avoid becoming mechanical (Seligman, 1985, p. 3).

An eighth reason for using the arts in counseling centers involves socialization and cooperation. D. W. Johnson and Johnson (2014) compiled an extensive amount of information showing that cooperative tasks result in building rapport and establishing greater self-esteem and prosocial behavior. The arts are a useful means to promote these two developments and have been shown

Creative Reflection

Think of a time when you were positively influenced by participating in one of the arts. It may have been playing an instrument, acting out a part in a play, painting a picture, dancing, taking a picture, going for a jog or walk, or arranging flowers. What did you notice about your participation that made you feel or act differently? How unique or universal do you think your experience is compared with others who may have accidentally or purposefully engaged in an arts activity and found themselves better in the end because of it?

to provide a common ground for linking people to one another in a positive manner (Menninger Foundation, 1986).

A final reason the arts are useful and appropriate in counseling is that they are multicultural (D. A. Henderson & Gladding, 1998; Lewis, 1997). With regard to cultures, counseling, and the arts, it should be noted that different cultures and clients within these cultures have preferred ways of expressing creativity and artistic ability (Molina, Monteiro-Leitner, Gladding, Pack-Brown, & Whittington-Clark, 2003). Counselors are challenged to help clients discover what works best for them, when, and even why. Counselors provide a resource of materials and examples for clients to use in sessions. They can prompt the types of positive experiences that go with these resources while simultaneously becoming attuned to culturally preferred ways of dealing with problematic situations (Rossiter, 1997).

In different cultural settings, the arts may do any of the following:

- Draw people out of self-consciousness and into self-awareness by having them express themselves in a symbolic manner.
- Call attention to the process of expression as well as the universal and unique nature of strategies used in such a procedure.
- Provide a set of concrete experiences clients can carry with them to help them relate to others and themselves.
- Help clients develop new ideas and interests to use in relating to themselves and others outside of counseling.
- Bring clients together cognitively, behaviorally, and mentally by giving them experiences that link them with their past, their present, and their future.
- Help clients appreciate the beauty and wisdom of cultural backgrounds.
- Promote positive feelings and affect that can be tapped when celebrating and coping with life's highs and lows.
- Engender hope, confidence, and insight in persons who have never realized their potential for living life to the fullest.

Another way of summing up these components of the creative arts is to say they are likely to contribute to

- behavioral activation (a highly effective treatment for depression),
- self-efficacy/mastery,
- overcoming experiential avoidance,
- strengthening personal identity (an evolving process), and
- social connectedness (Neilsen et al., 2016).

Numerous studies, especially with children, show the impact of the arts in different cultures, such as those by Omizo and Omizo (1989) with Hawaiian children; Constantino, Malgady, and Rogler (1986) with

Latino children; Appleton and Dykeman (1996) with Native American children; and Woodard (1995) with African American children. The point is that there are multiple ways of using the arts in helping clients from different cultures and circumstances (Ishiyama & Westwood, 1992).

The SCAMPER Model as a Way of Becoming More Creative

Becoming professionally creative is important if counselors are going to be able to use the arts effectively. The creative arts may be expressed therapeutically in a number of ways, and the more ways clinicians know, the more effective they can be. One of the easiest ways to remember something about creativity and how the arts may be employed in counseling is to gain knowledge of the SCAMPER model. This model was formulated by Robert F. Eberle (1971). He devised a mnemonic device called SCAMPER as a way to cultivate and reward imagination and talent in children as young as 3 years old. His intent was to help them develop into healthy, mentally alert, and productive adults. Strictly defined, the word *scamper* means to be playful, as expressed in a hurried run or movement. However, the intent of the SCAMPER model is not on physical movement but on fostering imaginative and action-oriented strategies for being creative. The letters within the word stand for activities that may help people become more self-sufficient, more productive, and happier through learning to exercise one or more of these options in life.

In more recent years the SCAMPER model has been applied to the counseling arena to help counselors by providing a checklist of suggestions that can both prompt and stimulate them into formulating ideas in themselves and their clients (Buser, Buser, Gladding, & Wilkerson, 2011; Gladding & Henderson, 2000). The specific letters of **SCAMPER** and an example of each follow:

S = *Substitute:* To have a person or thing act or serve in place of another. By looking for something to substitute, you can come up with new ideas and better ways of living. For example, a person can use applesauce for butter in cooking.

C = *Combine:* To bring together, to unite to achieve a different product/process or to enhance synergy. For example, artistic movements, such as in dance, may come together over the course of a recital to make a performance.

A = *Adapt/Alter:* To adjust to suit a condition or purpose. For example, as people mature, they adjust to or alter life roles, such as being a parent.

M = *Modify/Magnify/Minify:* To alter, to change the form or quality; to enlarge, to make greater in form or quality; to make smaller, lighter, slower, less frequent. For example, in the movie *Gone With the Wind*, Scarlet O'Hara modified curtains in a window to make a new dress so she could look her best for Rhett Butler.

P = *Put to Other Uses:* To be used for purposes other than those originally intended. Think of what you could reuse from somewhere. For example, someone could use paperclips to make a necklace or a fishing hook instead of using them for their original purpose.

E = *Eliminate:* To remove, omit, or get rid of a quality in part or totally. For example, a person goes on a diet, practices thought stopping, or stops excessive talking.

R = *Reverse/Rearrange:* To place opposite or contrary to, turn around; to change the order in which an activity is done. For example, people may rearrange the emphasis they put on events in their lives, such as making failure more important as a time for learning and making success less important in this regard.

When one applies the SCAMPER model, innovative, artistic, and creative responses are often made in all aspects of life. For instance, in substitution, mild words may be substituted for harsh words to modify an angry situation. In the combining part of this mnemonic device, clients may be taught how to act as well as speak appropriately in learning to put together social skills. Likewise, in adapting, the counselor may help clients learn how to be more assertive or less boisterous in specific situations. In modifying, clients may come to realize that they have a choice as to how strongly to express themselves when they encounter others. A magnifying or minifying of their behavior will result in a change in the way they are seen by those around them. Similarly, if clients realize they may eliminate a behavior and get better results, they may do so and become more content. Thus, through hard work and effort, people may eliminate shouting or shyness if either causes them interpersonal problems. Finally, reversing or rearranging what people do can give them a whole new outlook on life. Therefore, clients who change their driving routes going places or daily routines in personal interactions may come to see their settings and colleagues in a whole new light or from a different perspective.

Creative arts techniques that come into play in applying the SCAMPER model are numerous. For instance, by substituting the words of a song, the emphasis may change, and clients may see what a difference

Creative Reflection

There are other ways to apply the SCAMPER model as a way of working with clients and as a way of reminding yourself how to be more creative. As you read this book, ask yourself in what way the exercises suggested here fit into the SCAMPER format. Be as specific as you can, for example, the exercise "eliminate."

new words make. So instead of "Mary had a little lamb," a substituting of words might be "Mary had a rock and roll jam." The difference is considerable. Likewise, in adapting a poem such as Portia Nelson's (1993) "Autobiography in Five Short Chapters" to be acted as a drama, people who usually read the poem may get a better feel for what the words really mean as they put them in motion. A way of emphasizing modification is to have a client draw a picture of a sun, a cloud, and a tree together (see Figure 1). Then, in a similar space, have the client again draw these elements in relationship to each other, but with one of the elements magnified or minified. In the process the client may come to recognize that he or she cannot change one thing in the environment without modifying another (*Sun, Cloud, Tree*).

Advantages and Limitations of the Creative Arts in Counseling

In my wrap-up of this introductory chapter, it is crucial to point out the pragmatic advantages of using the arts in counseling and also their limitations. Several pluses and minuses are mentioned in this last section, starting with those aspects that are most positive.

Advantages

A major advantage of using the arts in counseling involves playfulness. Almost all great leaders from Churchill to Gandhi have had a sense of playfulness about them that has helped them temper their reactions to serious moments and gain a clearer perspective on life (Erikson, 1975). As a group, most people who are involved with the arts are known for their liveliness and even mischievous ways even though they may be quite serious. There is a winsome quality about those involved with the arts that enables them to appreciate and create a type of cosmos out of chaos. This lightheartedness in the midst of serious tasks is enabling and life giving.

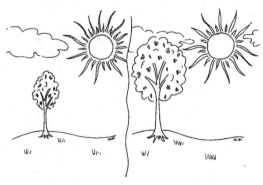

Figure 1   Sun, Cloud, Tree

A second benefit of using the arts in counseling is that such a connection often promotes collegial relationships (Arnheim, 1990). Many counseling theorists, including those who are existentialists, person centered, Adlerian, or gestalt, advocate this type of partnership. In healthy art and counseling encounters, professional barriers are broken down. In the latter, the ability of clients and counselors to more clearly understand and address present difficulties is enhanced.

A third advantage of including the arts in counseling is that such action usually promotes communication (Arnheim, 1990). Artists from Picasso to Stevie Wonder have talked about the universal language of artistic expression and the ability of the arts to convey information in a simple but direct way. Sometimes a picture or a movement is worth a thousand words. By sounding off musically, visually, or dramatically, clients are often able to help their counselors understand their predicaments better. Art can help outsiders, such as counselors, look on something that they have never been a part of and make them feel as if they had always been a part of it (Christenberry, 1991). As a result, these counselors become more sensitive and effective helpers as well as better communicators.

A fourth benefit of incorporating the arts in counseling is that artistic expression enables clients to recognize the multiple nature of themselves and the world. In other words, the arts allow clients to express themselves in multiple ways depending on the strengths they discover in themselves (Chan, 2001). This task of discovery may seem simple, but just as in the adventures of Carlos Castenada's (1972) character Don Juan, the complexities of life are not always easily learned or understood. Clients who have been struggling for identity may discover through their immersion in the arts during counseling that the depth as well as the richness of their lives is much greater than they initially envisioned. They may also learn for the first time, or again, ways they prefer to express themselves.

A fifth advantage of using the arts in counseling is their perceived objectivity. The arts are seen as neutral or even fun and therefore are not resisted.

> The use of the arts is a natural spin-off from the use of displacement material in other areas. Therapists, educators, theologians, and parents have used displacement materials for generations to help people focus on problems that they are too involved in emotionally to see clearly. (Guerin, 1976, p. 480)

A sixth benefit of using the arts in counseling is that these forms of expression allow, and even encourage, nonverbal clients to participate meaningfully in counseling relationships. "They are particularly well-suited for use in working with children and adolescents as they allow creative forms of self-expression for this developmental age-group that often struggles to put words to complex internal processes"

(K. M. Davis, 2008, p. 230). People who have been victimized or traumatized may be unable to verbally convey the events they have experienced because trauma is based on the visual and sensational nature of

traumatic memories stored in the brain, without translation into the narrative (Westhenen & Fritz, 2014). By using the arts, however, people may convey creatively and profoundly what is uppermost in their minds. The arts also encourage concrete thinkers and those of limited mental abilities to expand their horizons.

In addition, the inclusion of the arts in counseling gives the counselor one more tool to use in promoting diagnoses, understanding, or dialog in the professional relationship. When encountering extremely resistant or reluctant clients, counselors should use every means to bring about a mutually satisfactory outcome. The theoretical and technical aspects of the arts in counseling can make such a difference.

Limitations

The disadvantages of using arts in counseling must also be recognized, for they can cause complications if they are not acknowledged and dealt with properly. Not every counselor or client is a suitable candidate for such procedures. One of the chief limitations of using the arts in counseling is that clients who are artists themselves may not benefit from such an approach. In fact, according to Fleshman and Fryear (1981), "for artists, the use of the arts in therapy may be counterproductive" (p. 6). The reason for this phenomenon is that artists support themselves through creative expression, and to be asked to perform in a therapeutic setting may seem too much like work. In such situations, the use of arts in counseling becomes an obstacle to therapeutic progress.

A connected limitation of using the arts in counseling is that many artists (and some clients) may view counseling and activities associated with it as being nonartistic. Therefore, they may be less inclined to work on problems if the format is not highly structured and primarily cognitive in nature. For these individuals, using the arts in counseling may be distracting and frustrating.

A third reason that the arts are not always welcomed in counseling relates to popular misperceptions about the arts, especially links between creative arts and mental health. In the 17th century, Italian physician Ceare Lombroso linked creativity with mental illness. Even though such a connection is totally unfounded, the perception still remains and encourages reluctance on the part of many to participate in activities that are of an artistic or creative nature. To put in perspective the link between mental illness and art, British artist Toby Allen (http://zestydoesthings.tumblr.com/post/61131470551/the-real-monsters-are-reborn-upon-getting-so) has drawn pictures of how he perceives what he calls "mental illness monsters" such as depression or anxiety to look like. His hope is that his drawings will have the direct opposite effect of Lombroso and will give the intangibles of mental disorder some substance and make them appear more beatable as physical entities. He also hopes to reduce the stigma around mental disorders and make them more understandable. Figure 2 illustrates the emotion of "Worry." The creative task for

Figure 2   Worry

dealing with "Worry" is how to change "Worry's" expression and the behavior that goes with it.

On the opposite side of this reluctance, but with the same results, is the tendency of clients to avoid artistic enterprises because of an irrational fear that they will become too involved (Ellis, 1988). Such a response is typical of someone with loose ego boundaries and with obsessive-compulsive behavior habits, but it is also a feeling found in many other people. Some artists, such as Mozart, are reported to have worked at the expense of their health and that of their families. People who avoid the arts in counseling fear being placed in a situation with potential liabilities as well as possibilities.

A fifth drawback to including the arts in one's repertoire of counseling skills is that the techniques used may become arts and crafts, which are often seen as a much more mechanical and structured activity than procedures used in helping and healing (Gladding, 1985). It should be stressed that arts and crafts as typically practiced in therapeutic settings have limited goals and may be seen as busy work. Few problem-solving skills and innovative factors are used in arts and crafts as opposed to engagement in the arts. For example, crafts in counseling are usually associated with putting things together, such as assembling a basket, whereas the arts promote the production of something new and different. Crafts, on one hand, usually do not require much thinking. Instead, they instruct the participant to follow directions. The arts, on the other hand, involve the full use of one's imagination and often bring to the forefront latent talents and abilities.

A sixth limitation of using the arts in counseling is that clients may become too introspective, passive, or overcritical of themselves or situations. Such a posture leads to paralysis and inhibits growth born out of involvement. It is just the opposite of the active mental and physical involvement that Siegel (1986) described as an essential part of self-healing.

A seventh drawback to the use of the arts in counseling is that they may be used in nontherapeutic ways. Many art forms promote the expression of feelings and help persons get beyond the mere intellectual acknowledgment of situations. In helping clients recognize and express their feelings, especially the big four—anger, sadness, joy, and fear (Meier & Davis, 2011)—the release of emotions must be therapeutically channeled if clients are to realize more fully their own humanity (Warren, 1993). Catharsis in and of itself is of limited usefulness and may be detrimental to the health and well-being of individuals.

Creative Reflection

How do you think the limitations of using the creative arts in counseling can be overcome? Choose a limitation and plan a strategy for overcoming it. The strategy can include using a strength of the creative art.

A final drawback to using the arts in counseling is that they may be employed in nonscientific ways. The arts and sciences share four common attributes: "honesty, parsimony, duality, and insight" (Burke, 1989, p. 27). Honesty implies genuineness, authenticity, and openness of one's work. Parsimony is conciseness and straightforward simplicity. Duality is the ability to be simultaneously sensitive and tough-minded. Insight, as alluded to earlier, deals with the ability to understand old material in a new way. Whenever the arts are used in counseling without adherence to this common bond with science, practitioners face the danger that the results will not be therapeutic.

Summary

Counseling at its best uses an artistic quality that enables individuals to express themselves in a creative and unique manner. It is an activity that may be enhanced through encouraging some clients to participate in creative experiences, especially artistic expressions such as painting, writing, dancing, or playing (Atkins et al., 2003). These activities, if carried out in a nonmechanical and therapeutic manner, help people become more in tune with their emotions and form new, healthier relationships with themselves and others (J. D. Frank, 1978). The arts sensitize clients to untapped aspects of themselves and promote an awareness of uniqueness and universality. Ancient and modern civilizations have recognized this quality about the arts, and the tradition of using the arts in counseling is a long and distinguished one.

The creative arts in counseling are, as a group process, oriented, empowering, authentic, parsimonious, multicultural, and insight focused. They energize individuals and help connect them with positive aspects within and outside of themselves while fostering a new sense of self. By engaging in the playful, cooperative, and communicative dimensions of art, individuals recognize more clearly the complexity and simplicity of their lives. Similarly, counselors benefit from their involvement with the arts by being able to work with a greater variety of clients in therapeutic ways. Engaging in processes, such as utilizing the SCAMPER model of creativity, enriches counselors personally and professionally and helps their clients gain new perspectives or try different behaviors whether with the arts or not.

Although those who are professional artists, irrationally minded, and mentally unstable may not be appropriate for therapeutic treatment using the arts, many individuals are excellent candidates. It is to the advantage of everyone that professional helpers learn how to use the creative arts in counseling.

Exercises

1. When have you found yourself creative? What did the experience feel like? What art forms, if any, were involved?
2. Different creative arts have blossomed during specific time periods, for example, visual art during the Renaissance in Florence. Which of the creative arts do you like best? What time period is most exciting for you with regard to this art?
3. How do you think you might use the SCAMPER model in your counseling practice? Which activity associated with the model, for example "substitute," do you find most relevant to you?

Chapter 2

Music and Counseling

Harmony

The music of counseling varies in time
from the soft sob of weeping
to laughter's staccato.
Often the melody is found in the sound
of feeling in voices
and words rich in hope.
Within each session is a symphony
leading to inner harmony
and possibly new movements.

—Gladding, 1991d/2003

Music is a universal multicultural experience that can serve as a bridge to the development of new insights and behaviors (J. M. Brown, 2001; Silverman, 2008). It is most simply described as "the appreciation of sound" (Beaulieu, 1987, p. 13). Making music is a creative act as is listening in an active way. Both involve being sensitive and responsive to the cacophony of rhythm that occurs spontaneously in nature and purposely in human interactions (Schneck & Berger, 2006). On its most basic level, music is a nonverbal medium (Vanger, Oerter, Otto, Schmidt, & Czogalik, 1995). It has been used in various ways since the beginning of time to communicate and express feelings (Gfeller, 2002b; Silverman, 2008). Indeed, many civilizations and people have been defined by the types of music they developed, for example, classical music, and the part that music played in their lives. On a global level, some of today's popular music is significant in creating a sense of cultural identity, for example, hip-hop or rap.

Music sets up an atmosphere that is either for better or for worse. Stimulating background music seems to detract from the formation of initial counseling interactions, whereas soothing music seems to promote interaction (Prueter & Mezzano, 1973). A specific song or genre of music also may cue an urge to use substances among individuals who are addicted (Dingle, Kelly, Flynn, & Baker, 2015). On the other hand, music can be a power adjunct in reducing depression and generalized anxiety disorder (Esfandiari & Mansouri, 2014; Gutiérrez & Camarena, 2015). Overall, music can elicit a wide range of mental, emotional, physical, and spiritual responses.

Research on the effects of music is strong (Stephensen & Baker, 2015), and some studies indicate that music has the capacity to facilitate healing by influencing brain activity and creating and altering moods (Schweitzer, 2014). Music can facilitate the expression of emotions and reduce stress; it helps us tell our stories and process our experiences (Duffey, 2015). Music is used to capture attention, elicit memories, communicate feelings, and create a sense of community (Mandsager, Newsome, & Glass, 1997). It can help in the resolution of grief and abuse, increase intimacy between partners, be of assistance in identifying competing interests, and differentiate between people (Duffey, Lumadue, & Woods, 2001). Music is linked specifically with helping individuals convey thoughts and feelings, alter behaviors, and reduce unhelpful behaviors (Minor, Moody, Tadlock-Marlo, Pender, & Person, 2013). Simply put, music is the soundtrack of our lives. William Styron (1990), the author of *Sophie's Choice*, found music to be a lifesaver in his battle with depression and suicide ideation. His experience is not unique.

Many populations who have been the victims of abuse have developed distinct musical forms, such as African Americans' creation of spiritual gospels and the blues. This type of music has provided an outlet for their individual and collective expressions of pain (J. J.

Moreno, 1987). Other groups have created different sounds that express the essence of their experiences and perceptions. In the United States, the great diversity of sound includes rock and roll, bluegrass, hip-hop, rap, beach, jazz, country, clas-

sical, and big band music. Internationally, an even wider variety of sound exists, such as samba, reggae, and waltz.

According to Peters (2001), "Corporations such as MUZAK have made a business out of supplying background music to positively influence and regulate people's moods and behaviors in offices, businesses," and other environments (pp. 31–32). The influence of music in daily life is truly phenomenal. Even though people may not always remember lyrics, they seem to be influenced by "the beat, the rhythm, [and] the sound" of music they listen to regularly (A. White, 1985, p. 67). For many ordinary people, "music is the most significant experience in life" (Storr, 1992, p. 168).

Overall, music "allows feelings to be revealed that may not be defined in words" (Yon, 1984, p. 106). In essence, music "is a form of communication analogous to speech in that it has cadences and punctuation" (D. Aldridge, 1989, p. 93). For example, new age music, which makes use of long themes and slow tempi, expresses a sentiment and affect that cannot be translated into a verbal equivalent. Music is seen as a therapeutic ally to verbal approaches to counseling because it links people together and gives them a common denominator (Bonny, 1987; Rosenblatt, 1991).

In this chapter, I explore the multidimensional premise behind the power of music as well as the practical use of music in counseling. I distinguish between music therapy and the use of music in counseling. In addition, I explain and illustrate how music can be used with a variety of populations (e.g., from children to older adults) and in various settings (e.g., from clinics to educational environments). The use of music with other creative arts is also discussed.

Premise of the Use of Music in Counseling

Although all the creative arts help foster a link between the inner world of the person and outside reality, music "enhances this process by requiring time-ordered and ability-ordered behavior, evoking affective response and increasing sensory input. Music also requires self-organization and provides an opportunity for socialization" (Wager, 1987, p. 137). Music sets up an atmosphere. It can elicit a wide range of mental, emotional, physical, and spiritual responses.

Thus, music serves multiple purposes in helping individuals become more aware, able, confident, and social.

The importance of music to human health has long been recognized (Lingerman, 1995; Thaut, 2009). Throughout history, music has been used therapeutically. Hanser (1988) wrote, "The field of music therapy is based largely on claims of the sedative results music produces and the psychological impact of the musical experience" (p. 211). Documentation worldwide shows that music played a major role in healing and nurturing people from ancient cultures (Mandsager et al., 1997; J. J. Moreno, 1988b). M. E. Miller (1991) noted that "Homer recommended it to stave off negative emotions, and Pythagorus and Plato said a daily dose could improve one's general well-being" (p. 1E). Shamans have used "hypnotic and rhythmic music" (J. J. Moreno, 1987, p. 335) to help achieve emotional highs, a tradition that continues today in most cultures. Qualitative data support the importance of music and music therapy in meeting spiritual needs: Music and music therapy help participants feel closer to God and elevate their moods, especially when they are in hospital settings (Cook & Silverman, 2013).

Music and medicine were at one time strong allies because of their similar emphasis on wholeness. Indeed, in some countries, such as France, this connection is still strong, and "psychomusical techniques are regarded as excellent and privileged means of exploring dreams and ideas, the conscious and the unconscious, the affective and emotional worlds of the individual, and for provoking catharsis" (Owens, 1986, p. 302). In hospital settings, music may take one's mind off unpleasant experiences and promote spontaneous interactions. In addition, music is used worldwide to promote positive mental health, especially in psychiatric hospitals (Covington, 2001).

Music is both a passion and a diversion, and its uses in counseling are geared accordingly. Among persons for whom music is a central part of life (i.e., a passion), identity is strongly influenced by their shared values with select performers, writers, and other listeners. These individuals are usually quite willing to participate in counseling activities that involve music. In this type of situation, many of the words, sounds, and feelings these people embrace as their own actually originated with someone else and have been borrowed and incorporated by these people. The extent of music's healing and helping power in counseling is related to how deeply involved with it people are and what disorders or diseases they may be dealing with (Bruscia, Dileo, Shultis, & Dennery, 2009).

Creative Reflection

When have you or someone you know found a song or a piece of music to be comforting or uplifting? What piece of music was it? How was your mood altered? How do you feel about the music when you hear it now?

Because their identity is partially wrapped up in music, people with a passion for it are eager to be exposed to musical experiences. Therefore, counselors are usually more successful using music in working with these clients than they would be with those for whom music is only a diversion. For instance, a person of any age who likes music and who has lost a father may find Ashley Gearing's lyrical country song "Can You Hear Me When I Talk to You?" to be both cathartic and comforting (Mansfield, 2003). By being aware of the lyrics and melodies that clients have adopted and other complementary music, counselors who use music set up conditions that foster increased communication and understanding (Gladding, Bentley, & Flannery, 2003; Gladding, Newsome, Henderson, & Binkley, 2008; A. White, 1985).

In addition, music in counseling may be focused on the interests and tastes of clients. A musical approach may take the form of writing, performing, or listening to certain types of sounds selected by counselors. The idea behind this activity is to foster therapeutic expression by clients through having them participate in unfamiliar music-related experiences. For example, a client may play a new instrument in a predetermined way and make discoveries about his or her abilities never before imagined (J. J. Moreno, 1985). Similarly, ethnic music (i.e., music identified with a particular culture or subculture) may motivate "otherwise unresponsive mainstream music therapy clients into musical experiences through the exotic appeal of unfamiliar musical styles and approaches to music making" (J. J. Moreno, 1988a, p. 17). Even for clients who are unfamiliar with classical music, this genre can have a powerful effect. When carefully chosen and played softly, classical music "can be a tremendous aid in producing an atmosphere conducive to creative activity" (Nadeau, 1984, p. 68). Compositions by Schubert, Copeland, Strauss, Tchaikovsky, and Pachelbel, for example, can create an ambiance that encourages imagination and productivity.

A key in deciding on what music activity, if any, to choose is based on the goals of counseling (whether preventive or remedial) and the personalities of the individuals involved. For example, some individuals prefer classics by Beethoven, Bach, Brahms, and Mozart, and others opt for popular music by Third Eye Blind, Foo Fighters, Sheryl Crow, Jay-Z, Justin Timberlake, Taylor Swift, James Taylor, Coldplay, Ice Cube, and Jennifer Lopez. Still other individuals prefer energetic African- or Japanese-oriented group rhythms performed on drums, or traditional Indian and Asian music, which is helpful in stimulating imagery and fostering meditation (J. J. Moreno, 1988a).

Individual need is yet another crucial variable to consider in music-oriented counseling. For example, trauma victims need calmer types of music than those who are not so physically or psychologically distressed (McDonnell, 1984). Likewise, aerobic and exercise groups need and prefer rock, pop, and new age music (Gfeller, 1988). With regard to needs and music, it is helpful to realize that some clients need to be actively involved in making music (e.g., individuals who are depressed), but for others simply listening to music may be most beneficial (e.g., individuals who are anxious or manic).

Further, the decision about music activities is rooted in genuine sharing and self-disclosure about whether both parties in the counseling process are open to exploring this means of help. If the participants reach sharing and consensus, musical pieces used are likely to produce positive results because an atmosphere of trust and expectation is created. These qualities, along with the skills of counselors and the courage of clients to participate, ultimately dictate how powerful the musical experience will be. Well-chosen music conducted in collaboration with the client has the capacity to calm, relax, and help the client feel secure (Hodas, 1994; Owens, 1986). There is no substitute for personalizing the process.

Practice of the Use of Music in Counseling

The degree to which counselors and clients relate to each other when music is a part of counseling depends on whether music is used *as* therapy or *in* therapy (Bruscia, 1987). When music is used as therapy, the counselor is likely to take an active role, whereas during use in therapy the counselor's involvement may vary considerably.

Music Therapy

Music as therapy is usually known as *music therapy*. Techniques associated with music therapy are production, reproduction, and reception. *Production techniques* focus on emotional expression and creation of relationships through musical improvisation in which client and therapist create something musically new. *Reproduction techniques* involve client and therapist playing or singing precomposed pieces of music as well as learning or practicing musical skills. These pieces may be especially powerful in exploring memoires and relationships. *Reception techniques* involve the client listening to live or recorded music. These musical experiences may be used to focus on conscious awareness of the client's current mental state as well as to facilitate relaxation or pain management (Mössler, Assmus, Heldal, Fuchs, & Gold, 2012).

In music therapy, sound—whether played or listened to—often serves as a musical symbol of a symptom (McClary, 2007). According to the American Music Therapy Association (AMTA, 2010a), music therapy is offered as a degree in more than 70 American colleges and universities and is practiced all over the world. In addition, AMTA in 2015 formally defined music therapy as "the clinical and evidence-based use of music interventions to accomplish individualized goals within a therapeutic relationship by a credentialed professional who has completed an approved music therapy program" (AMTA, 2010b, "What Is Music Therapy?" section, para. 1). It is meant to effect positive changes in the psychological, physical, cognitive, or social functioning of individuals. As such, the process is goal directed. It may take one of many forms, but according to Peters (2001, pp. 6–8), music therapy has five main elements:

1. It is prescribed.
2. It involves the use of musical or music activities, for example, "singing, playing musical instruments, listening to music, composing or creating music, moving to music, or discussing lyrics and characteristics of songs or instrumental compositions" (p. 6).
3. It is directed or supervised by specially trained personnel.
4. It is received by clients from newborns to geriatrics.
5. It is focused on achieving definite therapeutic goals (e.g., physical, psychological, cognitive, or social).

In music therapy, clients improve their level of musical functioning while simultaneously accomplishing objectives related to new or improved behaviors in the areas of motor skills, academics, communications, social interactions, or emotions. The number of musically related activities (e.g., singing, playing in a rhythm band, playing "name that tune") that can be used to accomplish these goals is extensive (Schulberg, 1981). A main task for the music therapist is to be versatile and creative (Memory, 2002). Therefore, music therapists must be fluent and expressive in the language of music. Peters (2001) noted, "Technical musical skills needed by the music therapist include keyboard, guitar, and vocal skills; the ability to arrange, compose, and improvise simple songs and accompaniments; [and] proficiency in playing a variety of melodic and percussive nonsymphonic instruments and conducting skills" (p. 12). Overall, music therapists must be specialists in music and human behavior but must be generalists in their ability to apply this knowledge in various situations (Michel & Pinson, 2013). They must also be imaginative, intuitive, improvising, and intellectual (Bunt & Hoskyns, 2002).

According to Hadley, Hadley, Dickens, and Jordon (2001), music therapists do some or all of the following:

- Assess emotional well-being, physical health, social functioning, communication abilities, and cognitive skills through musical responses.
- Design music sessions for individuals and groups based on client needs using music improvisation, receptive music listening, song writing, lyric discussion, music and imagery, music performance, and learning through music.
- Participate in interdisciplinary treatment planning, ongoing evaluation, and follow-up.

To become professional music therapists, individuals graduate from specifically designed college curricula with a minimum of a bachelor of music (BM) in music therapy. Educational standards are established and approved by AMTA, which is the integrated organization formed from its predecessors, the National Association for Music Therapy and the American Association for Music Therapy. For a person to become a music therapist, AMTA requires successful completion of a specific number of coursework hours as well as supervised internships in approved programs of study.

Music in Counseling

Counseling that includes music in its overall structure is not nearly as encompassing or direct as music therapy, but it involves activities such as listening, performing, improvising, and composing that are beneficial for clients. Each activity has a population that profits from its use.

Listening to musical sounds in a deep and appreciative way is an art and a skill (Zorn, 2007). Such listening helps individuals to relax and learn, and directs their attention away from life stressors (Crabbs, Crabbs, & Wayman, 1986). Listening to music can help clients alter their mood by either reducing their anxiety or arousing their emotions. Listening also promotes the process of making music out of life and understanding more fully the rhythm and lyrics of songs. The latter case is sometimes referred to as audiotherapy (Lazarus, 2000). An interesting and effective way of listening to music is an intervention called *Mindful Music Listening*, during which clients with depression use mindfulness skills while listening to music to notice, label, discuss, and learn to manage their emotions (*Mindful Music Listening*). Possible advantages include greater client self-awareness and emotional regulation as well as a strengthened counselor–client relationship (Eckhardt & Dinsmore, 2012).

According to Hindu tradition, listening can occur on four levels. "The first is the level of meaning. The second is the level of feeling. . . . The third is an intense and constant awareness or presence, and the fourth is known as the 'soundless sound'" (Beaulieu, 1987, p. 13). Each of these levels is self-explanatory, except for soundless sound. It is really the rhythmic, punctual moments of silence within a composition of sound that make such a work predictable, safe, and enjoyable (Bonny, 1987). In addition to the four levels of listening, such an activity holds the power to stir up emotions in the unconscious. Song selection by clients is a kind of projective technique that reveals the needs of the unconscious for certain types of stimuli (Brodsky & Niedorf, 1986). By tracking the theme and tempo of music chosen, therapists can ascertain more clearly the emotional level at which clients are operating and thereby plan effective treatment interventions. They can also understand more readily what unique musical prescriptions, if any, might work for their clients (Hanser, 1988).

One way to help clients listen more intensely to music and the meanings they derive from it is to ask clients to bring in music on their MP3 players that reflects their emotional states. They may then be asked what part of the music speaks to them the most, for ex-

Creative Reflection

Ask three friends to tell you what music they listen to and how it affects them. What do they seem to listen to most: the rhythm, the melody, the lyrics? What music do you listen to and how does it affect you?

ample, the rhythm, the melody, the lyrics (if there are any), or some combination of the three (*Creating Emotional States*). At times the counselor can also provide music. In such a case, clients are asked to listen to the rhythm and lyrics of the music the counselor selects and to visualize a color that goes with it (Bradley et al., 2008). After the song is finished, clients may respond by talking about the experience or drawing or even moving to show what they got out of the exercise (*Counselor-Selected Music*). Bradley et al. (2008) have used such lyrical songs as "Don't Laugh at Me" (with regard to differences), "You've Got a Friend" (with regard to friendship), and "I Shoulda Listened" (with regard to ignoring good advice). In both client- and counselor-initiated listening activities, the music provides a springboard from which other life material is processed on either a verbal or a nonverbal level.

Another way of using music in counseling is listening to ethnic music. In this activity, clients listen to unfamiliar music (i.e., music identified with a particular culture or subculture other than their own). Clients then are asked to react to the music and talk about how the rhythm of the music is like or unlike the beat of their lives. This activity helps make clients aware of the rhythm of the life they lead as well as the rhythm of the life of others (*Listening to Ethnic Music*).

Performing music is a very personal experience with a powerful potential. It involves the musician, the instrument, and sometimes an audience. Through performing, individuals use music "as a means of communication, identification, socialization, and expression" (Siegell, 1987, p. 185). They introduce themselves in a way that is impossible to duplicate otherwise. Sometimes the music that is performed is relatively simple, such as becoming a sound within a group experience. At other times, it is elaborate and involves harmonizing many notes in a clear and distinct way. For example, drums have been used as an outlet for dealing with low assertiveness as well as anger (MacIntosh, 2003). It is the way they are played that makes a difference in the outcome.

Music was performed by employees of French mental hospitals as early as the 17th century for the treatment of melancholy. In the 19th century, music was elevated to an active form, as psychiatric patients organized choruses and orchestras (Owens, 1986). In the early part of the 20th century, music was considered an occupational therapy and focused on resocialization rather than healing. Throughout the history of musical performances, including today, clients from a variety of sites including mental hospitals and outpatient centers have benefited. Performing activates people to the realities of self, instruments, time, and others. Goldstein (1990) wrote, "The tempo of the song, the tone

Creative Reflection

Sound out on a table, a chair, or your knees what the rhythm of a typical or a special day is like for you. Include the sounds of getting up, going to work or class, eating lunch, afternoon activities, returning home, and finally going to bed. What did you notice about the beat or rhythm of your life? What would you like to change or keep the same?

quality of the singer, and the lyric content all provide indications of the feelings being expressed" (p. 120).

Improvising with music is best represented in American jazz, whether performed by clients or simply listened to. In improvising, musicians follow a plan to be playful as well as artful in their work with others. In a jazz band, for example, there are at least two parts: a rhythm section and a front line. "The rhythm section lays down the beat of the music. The front line instruments are responsible for the melodic lines and their interplay" (Barker, 1985, p. 132).

When counselors work with clients who are musically inclined, improvisation can be accomplished concretely by asking individuals to do variations on musical themes (Wigram, 2004). In these cases—and in others in which clients understand musical improvisation—individuals can play with their instruments and alter melodies (i.e., make them faster, slower, or more pronounced). The results of such transactions can then be discussed or in some cases left alone (*Improvsation*). In the latter situation, the process of creating and developing a relationship is seen as therapeutic in and of itself (Nordoff & Robbins, 1977).

Composing music is a creative act that puts composers in closer touch with their feelings. "It can be used as a way of promoting many of the healing qualities inherent in creative acts" (Schmidt, 1983, p. 4). It is empowering because it gives its composer an opportunity to arrange notes in a way that is unique and personal. Composing can also be self-enhancing in that it requires perseverance and discipline that become part of a person's self-concept after the event has occurred. For example, clients who play a musical piece representing their lives may be exhausted at the end from the intensity of the experience. However, such clients may also be quite satisfied with themselves for putting their feelings into sound and writing them down as well as playing them in an expressive and representative way (*Composing Music*).

Composing music need not always involve recognizable instruments. Instead, clients can be asked to tap, snap, click, bang, or hum to represent different emotions (Mandsager et al., 1997). A musical group of the 1960s, the Mamas and the Papas, had a popular record album titled *You've Got to Make Your Own Kind of Music*, which perhaps stresses the individualization of people, especially clients, in using themselves to create harmony both within and without. Composition promotes this creative emphasis, thereby proving useful to counselors who utilize music in treatment.

In actual practice, counselors may request or encourage musically inclined clients to compose a piece of music through which they can represent themselves, whether they write it down or not. At the next session, clients literally make music first and then talk about the experiences of composing and performing afterward. In some cases, musically inclined counselors may compose and play music to represent themselves to clients. Such a process, whether unilateral or reciprocal in nature, assists clients in realizing the universal power that a musical composition can generate.

Music in Counseling With Specific Populations

Music is used with a variety of populations—children, adolescents, adults, older adults—and in a number of settings—family/couple therapy, groups, hospitals/clinics, and educational environments. In this section, both the populations and settings are covered with regard to how music is used.

Children

Children, especially preschool-age and elementary-age children, seem to love music. They spontaneously sing, listen, or play musiclike instruments such as those found in rhythm bands. Children's natural affinity to music relates to a number of factors, including the fact that they may not have the vocabulary to express certain feelings without borrowing words such as those from a song that conveys such emotions (DeLucia-Waack & Gerrity, 2001). Regardless, the natural affinity of children for music can be used by counselors to promote fun, learning, good feelings, and bonding among children from diverse backgrounds (Crabbs et al., 1986). Songs can be used to "introduce a topic, begin a discussion, lead an activity, channel energy, suggest potential thoughts/feeling/new behaviors, or end a session with positive affect" (DeLucia-Waack & Gerrity, 2001, p. 280). Music may also be used to help foster changes in children who are developmentally delayed (D. Aldridge, Gustorff, & Neugebauer, 1995), who have been abused (Ostertag, 2002), or who are dealing with their parents' divorce (DeLucia-Waack & Gellman, 2007). In the last situation, music—as an intervention—has been found to be as effective as traditional psychoeducational methods in decreasing cognitive and social anxiety and many irrational beliefs.

Music is often a primary ingredient in teaching guidance lessons. One technique that works is the use of music to express feelings. For example, DeLucia-Waack (2001) wrote

Creative Reflection

What music and songs do you remember from your childhood? What memories, pleasant and otherwise, do you retain from that time? How do you think the music from your childhood has influenced your life?

a hands-on manual for counselors that offered them a creative way through music to help children of divorce learn new coping skills. Among the topics addressed were parental conflict and family relationships, anger management, divorce-related stress, custody issues, and court scenarios. Through music, children have been helped to understand and overcome the crisis of the divorce and develop in healthy ways. In another guidance approach, Gerler (1982) recommended that a counselor and music teacher work together to devise a game in which children are "teamed in groups of four and instructed to create musical ways to express feelings" (p. 63) without words or lyrics. In the case of fourth-graders who carried out this task, one feeling was assigned to each group, and they were directed to devise two or three musical ways to express this emotion. Responses ranged from forming a hum-and-sniffle quartet to represent sadness to using two pianos to convey an angry musical conversation (*Music and Guidance Lessons*).

Besides cooperative ventures with music teachers, counselors can work on their own to find and use music that gives their students experiences involving singing, composing, or playing an instrument (R. P. Bowman, 1987; Harper, 1985; Newcomb, 1994). Sometimes all three of these types of musical expression can be combined; however, usually one modality, such as singing or composition, is used more than others. Children find singing fun and often remember main ideas of lessons through incorporating them into songs (Crabbs et al., 1986). When songs are used in guidance classes, the following procedure is helpful (*Learning Songs in Guidance Lessons*):

1. Introduce the words of a song as a poem.
2. Chant the words in rhythm.
3. Practice chanting words for 3 or 4 minutes per class period until children memorize them.
4. After children know and understand the words, play the song (prerecorded music is fine to use).
5. Keep a double-spaced copy of the words before the children when they sing, with the verses separated from the refrain.

Outside of guidance classes, singing is also beneficial, especially for children who may have suffered trauma. This is because singing, besides being a natural behavior for humans in most cultures, may be "used as a self-help technique, a means of developing feelings of rapport with others, and a method of self-affirmation" (Mayers, 1995, p. 497). Singing a song repetitively, either alone or in a group of other children, can be ritualistic and hypnotic as well. It can alter breathing patterns and help in general relaxation.

In composition, children are encouraged not only to write but also to sing their songs. Mayers (1995) advised, "It is not necessary to teach the child to engage in this activity, only to direct the songwriting toward a therapeutic end. Children are capable of determining what they need, what words will be calming, what tune fits the mood" (p. 497). Through composing and writing their own songs, children learn to be more independent as well as creative. They also learn to be less anxious and feel a sense of empowerment. Mayers reported that children as young as 4 or 5 years can compose songs that are helpful to them in dealing with their situations.

Music is used with children in other therapeutic ways as well. For example, Hodas (1993) created a music tape titled *Stretch Yourself! Songs for Coping* that contains a variety of selections counselors can use with children who are having difficulty dealing with different forms of adversity. The song selections encompass a wide variety of topics, including sexual abuse, physical illness, suicide, the effects of war, and gender issues. Memory (2002) likewise chose music to use with at-risk children and teens. In dealing with special children populations, songs must be chosen with care. A well-chosen song can be quite powerful in helping children recognize situations and deal with them appropriately and constructively. Another way of breaking through children's shells of isolation therapeutically with music is by playing sounds familiar to them, such as internal body sounds (i.e., a stomach growling or a heart beating) or having them listen to neighborhood sounds (S. B. Baker, 1982). Once rapport is established in this manner, rhythmic activities and rhythm instruments such as sticks and tambourines can be used to engage these children and gradually draw them into social relationships with other children and adults (*Internal Body and Neighborhood Sounds*).

Adolescents

Music is popular with adolescents, and almost all teenagers listen to music as well as incorporate it into their lives (Kimbel & Protivnak, 2010). Young people almost invariably describe the positive benefits of engaging with music when asked to reflect on the relationship between music and health (McFerran & Saarikallio, 2014). Music is a particularly powerful source of social communication and social influence in this age group (Ostlund & Kinnier, 1997). At its best, music can be lifesaving, such as the lyrics on "How to Save a Life" by The Fray. Music can also increase pro-social behavior, for example, preventing HIV ("Music an Effective Tool," 2003). At its worst, music may become repetitive and stale or glorify violent behavior, which may

increase negative emotions and thoughts that can lead to aggression (A. Palmer, 2003). Popular music is both a reflection of and an exacerbating influence on attitudes, values, and behaviors (Bushong, 2002).

Most adolescents are deeply involved in music, such as playing a musical instrument, playing in a band, going to concerts, or identifying with major musical figures (Kimbel & Protivnak, 2010). For some, music is quite inspirational because it evokes "images of movies . . . in which movie characters triumphed over adversities" (Gfeller, 1988, p. 41). The fact that the website Spotify (www.spotify.com/us/?carousel=1) and its offsprings are largely listened to by an audience less than 30 years of age (and even the existence of such channels is known only to them) is further evidence of the importance of music in the lives of this age group. In addition, television shows such as *The Voice, American Idol,* and *America's Got Talent* focus on music and appeal to this age group as do games such as *Guitar Hero* and *Dance Dance Revolution* (Kimbel & Protivnak, 2010). Overall, the activities and events just mentioned plus the rhythm and words of Lil Wayne, Rihanna, Lady Antebellum, Black Eyed Peas, Drake, Tim McGraw, Ke$ha, and Lady Gaga speak to adolescent youth in unique and powerful ways.

For young adolescents, according to Wells (1988), "music therapy is helpful in bridging the gap between nonverbal and talking therapy. It aids in mastery and sublimation of thoughts and feelings, and it helps to facilitate ego development through success-oriented experiences" (p. 47). For older adolescents, participating in music therapy activities gives them a firsthand experience of the relationship between effort made and skill achieved in music performance. Adolescents in juvenile delinquency programs benefit from music therapy activities because they become increasingly aware of that connectedness between hard work and achievement (E. Johnson, 1981). Their self-esteem and self-expression may increase as well with a substantial decrease in hostility and disruptive behaviors (Rio & Tenney, 2002). Teens may also realize that playing a socially desirable music instrument such as the piano or guitar increases their acceptance among peers (Cassity, 1981).

In addition, adolescents are often interested in song writing and may wish to express themselves lyrically (Roscoe, Krug, & Schmidt,

1985). A song is generally considered to be a poem set to music (May-ers, 1995). To foster a preventative and therapeutic process, music therapists and counselors skilled in music can work with adolescents using a number of song-writing techniques, "including changing the words to familiar songs, filling in the blanks of edited familiar songs, vocal improvisation, adding new verses to known songs, parodying familiar songs, and using natural rhythms of speech as a starting point" (Goldstein, 1990, p. 119). Counselors who are musicians themselves may also use original music they have written to help adolescents explore difficult areas such as gender issues and sexuality (Hodas, 1991). In addition, school counselors and counselors who work with adolescents in other settings can utilize musical interventions such as music listening and sharing and using music in psychoeducational activities (*Song Writing*).

One interesting use of music in counseling at-risk youths, particularly inner-city African American adolescents, is rap music that has been transformed into "rap therapy" (T. Gonzalez & Hayes, 2009). Rap therapy (Elligan, 2004) is rooted in social learning theory (Bandura, 1977) and a cognitive behavioral model. Through it, "clients become aware of the association between personal lyric interpretation, their emotions, and at-risk behaviors. This awareness aids in their ability to be reflective and allows them to effectively problem solve" (T. Gonzalez & Hayes, 2009, p. 162). Like other counseling approaches, assessment and rapport are completed before any attempts at change take place. However, once these two stages of counseling are complete, clinicians work to help broaden clients' appreciation of other types of rap than those that dominate their lives and then through written exercises role play lyrics as well as engage clients to create and interpret their own lyrics. Finally, clients are encouraged to move into positive actions that are maintained through modeling and reinforcement.

Adults

Research has suggested that in addition to offering adults sounds to relax by, music enhances physical endurance, especially if "movement is rhythmically coordinated with a musical stimulus" (Thaut, 1988, p. 129). Therefore, adults who are athletes or who regularly exercise can enhance their efforts by coordinating their physical movement with certain sounds. These positive effects occur because music either distracts people's perceptions by causing them to selectively focus on pleasant stimuli or physically inhibits negative feedback transmissions (i.e., fatigue) because of the pleasurable electrosensory reactions it generates. Regardless, music is a prime ingredient in helping people physically and mentally maintain health or rehabilitate (*Music and Physical and Mental Health List*).

Another important function music plays in the lives of adults is by enhancing experiences for them. Childbirth preparation is often linked with relaxing and soothing music that makes delivery, recovery, and bonding stronger. The type of exhilaration that results makes intrapersonal and interpersonal relationships better. It promotes growth to the fullest (Maslow, 1968). Other marker events in the lives of adults are equally enhanced through music. As Virginia Perry, a counselor in North Carolina, wrote about a workshop she attended in which each session was introduced by music, "He sings, and I forget myself. We move, one through another, vibrating the resonances of soul. These connected hearts and voices remain beyond time and place" (personal communication, July 19, 1991).

Older Adults

"Music serves two primary roles in the lives of older people. . . . First, it evokes emotions, memories, and past connections in the person's life. Second, it can facilitate the enjoyment of shared interests and activities" (Duffey, Somody, & Clifford, 2006/2007, p. 52). Older adults benefit from participating in music. In fact, sharing a song can result in creating a therapeutic bond that affects the quality and longevity of life. For instance, in his "Creativity and Aging" study, Cohen (2005) followed a group of older adults averaging 80 years of age who participated in chorale programs at the Levine School of Music in Washington, DC, beginning in December 2001. After 2 years of comparing the music participants with a control group of similar individuals, Cohen found that the music participants

- reported better health and fewer falls;
- showed a slower rate of increase in doctor visits than nonparticipants;
- increased medication usage at a significantly lower rate than nonparticipants;
- showed greater improvements in depression, loneliness, and morale; and
- increased social interaction, whereas nonparticipants decreased interaction.

Overall, playing or making music with older persons has several goals, including the promotion of social interaction, the enhancement of self-worth, the encouragement of self-expression, and the recall of past events (Bruscia, 1987; Osborn, 1989; Rio, 2002). Ways of conducting sessions vary, and they may be carried out in a formal or an improvised manner. When such times are formally conducted, members of these groups follow more of a schedule, and their personal or interpersonal gains may become secondary to the achievements of the group as a whole. If the sessions are less formally conducted, however, more creativity and interaction may occur with less music.

In reminiscence or in present-oriented social groups, music may be the key to encouraging discussion of past or present feelings and thoughts about events, such as learning, romance, loss, and family life (Duffey et al., 2006/2007). Typically, music is initially played that revolves around a particular theme, such as the importance of home or family. Such an activity usually takes place after the group as a whole has warmed up by participating in a brief sing-along of familiar songs that include their own accompaniment of clapping and foot tapping. This approach has been found to be effective in helping reduce depressive symptoms in older people (ages 73 to 94 years) with dementia (Ashida, 2000) and has value in other older group settings too (*Reminiscence or Present-Oriented Social Groups*).

In a maximum-participation group, members select their own music and theme. In less democratic groups, most of the selections are made by the leaders with particular foci in mind. Songs such as Jerry Butler's "Only the Strong Survive" as well as Barbra Streisand's "The Way We Were" and early American ballads such as "My Old Kentucky Home" are used to set a tone and a mood that encourage talk and interaction after the singing has stopped.

Music may also be used with older clients to help them achieve better functioning in their movements. Rhythmic music, for example, acts as a stimulus for helping older patients with gait disorders improve the flow of their walk (Staum, 1983). In this process, the beat of the music serves as a cue for individuals in anticipating a desired rate of movement.

Creative Reflection

Music may help couples and families become more aware of themselves if it is created by them. In such cases, persons within these units make up sounds or play instruments that represent themselves as individuals within the couple or family context. Then they combine the sounds and try to establish a rhythm or beat with their spouse or family members. Ask your family or a family you know well to try to make musical sounds that represent them individually and as a unit.

Families and Couples

Music by itself may be beneficial to families or couples because of its ability to evoke feelings and promote cooperation. *Family-based music therapy* is a term used to describe clinical work with children and families (Pasiali, 2013). The primary therapeutic focus is on the facilitation of interaction and communication between family members to strengthen relationships. Shared musical experiences

Creative Reflection

The beat of drums often has an effect on people as they go about their daily routines. Find some drum music and see how it affects you and what emotions surface as you hear it.

during family-based music therapy provide a context that influenced a parent–child relationship. Feelings are often ignited or rekindled by playing music (Gladding & Heape, 1987). If a family or couple has experienced contentment or positive affect at a previous stage, the music of that time may spark memories that help individuals within these systems remember specific behaviors that were helpful in achieving harmony. Such events once triggered can aid the family or couple in getting unstuck from behavioral stalemates and positively reinforcing each other (*Music and Families/Couples*).

A similar method initiated by the counselor may be used in marital counseling. In such a situation, the counselor prescribes a song in which the lyrics represent issues brought forth by the couple. For example, Paul Simon's "Train in the Distance" is a song about yearning to live in a better time (J. Chapman, personal communication, November 19, 1994). The last verse of the song speaks powerfully to this point:

> "What is the point of this story? What information pertains? The thought that life could be better is woven, indelibly, into our hearts and our brains." Using that lyric as a cue, the couple is then asked to listen to the song at home, using it as a metaphor from which to initiate discussion of relevant thoughts, feelings, and issues. (V. Perry, personal communication, February 20, 1996)

Another way of working with couples is to involve spouses taking turns improvising on percussion instruments to depict musically what they perceive their typical pattern of communication to be. While one spouse improvises, the other writes thoughts that result from what he or she thinks the other is saying musically. The patterns for different feelings and times of communication are then discussed with the realization that some patterns of communication appear to be automatic and disruptive but that whatever the beat the pattern can change (Botello & Krout, 2008).

Groups

Most people in groups wish to be in concert with themselves and humanity. They are also looking to see where they fit in with others. Music provides an avenue for clients to assess themselves and others. Music can be especially powerful in a group at its beginning or end. Select music can help set an upbeat or a sedate tone when clients first enter the group room. For example, beginning a group through drumming is a "unique way to jump start conversations about group dynamics and each person's role in them" (Camilleri, 2002, p. 264). In addition, drumming may have an immediate mood improvement among those who participate in it and thus enhance the beginning of a group (Mungas & Silverman, 2014). Likewise, select music or music activities, during termination, can help instill in clients a sense of closure and can promote integration (Plach, 1996). Several song-books, such as *Rise Up Singing* (Blood & Patterson, 1992), contain a wealth of songs about subjects ranging from faith to friendships; they can be used to introduce music into a group at any stage, especially one that contains people from a wide range of cultural backgrounds (*Music and Groups*).

Hodas (1994) reported using music in a mixed group of European American and African American male adolescents to help the group handle anger, learn coping skills, and appreciate universal truths about human nature. In this group, varieties, some of which were even violent, were played. The group members came to realize through the music that when wrongs occur in society more constructive actions than revenge can and should be taken.

Stephens, Braithwaite, and Taylor (1998) used hip-hop music in an HIV/AIDS preventive counseling format with African American adolescents and young adults to educate these populations about protective factors for HIV. They contended that the overall implications of using hip-hop music in health promotion with African American youths are unlimited because this method makes use of culturally relevant materials to address the educational and health needs of the target community and is grounded in an approach that serves to stimulate cooperative learning based on peer-developed content. Moreover, the use of this medium can be applied to other health promotion activities, such as violence/harm reduction and substance abuse prevention, upon reviews of songs for appropriate content. In addition, hip-hop influences men's willingness to disclose emotion or even to inquire about counseling. Emotional writing, such as in hip-hop, has been a form of counseling suggested to be particularly effective with male clients (I. Levy & Keum, 2014).

Music also has a place in the healing and helping process with survivors of sexual abuse (MacIntosh, 2003). Through the use of music, spontaneity is evoked, and participants in the group become involved on a sensory and feeling level with the group or counselor. In the process, group members become fully present in a new way and become more involved in their relationships with others. Specific musical techniques used by MacIntosh (2003) include breathing and tone techniques, song writing in groups, and playing the drums.

Clients With Illnesses

Music functions in several therapeutic ways for clients with illnesses. Music can serve to promote closeness within families through group singing, lyric analysis, and reminiscences (Gilbert, 1977; M. E. Miller, 1991). This type of bonding enhances the quality of life for family members both inside and outside of the hospital and helps establish better communication patterns and firmer support systems (Fagen, 1982). In the process, anxiety and tension are lessened, and intimacy is promoted (Bailey, 1984; Slivka & Magill, 1986). In addition, religious faith may be increased through playing and singing religious music if the family is so oriented (*Music, Families, and Ill Member*).

Rider (1987) stated, "Music has the capacity to touch and bring to the surface emotions that have been repressed for years" (p. 117). Some chronic diseases such as cancer, rheumatoid arthritis, and coronary difficulties correlate with negative feelings such as anxiety, hostility, and depression. Fatigue appears to be an especially prevalent and undertreated symptom in cancer patients and cancer survivors. Select music, particularly violin, flute, and piano, can help clients in these and other tension-filled situations to relax more, especially if they are uniquely and individually selected for each patient (Fredenburg & Silverman, 2014). Therapeutic compositions may also be played universally. Music cited in the literature as instrumental in reducing anxiety include the Largo movement from Dvorak's *New World Symphony* and Brahms's *First Symphony* (Mandsager et al., 1997).

Music also can encourage healing by promoting catharsis and refocusing thoughts. For instance, G. Clarkson (1994) recounted the case of a young man with autism who, after several years of music therapy, began to communicate again. Likewise, in trauma-induced dissociative disorders, music may succeed where words sometimes fail because of its ability to reunite and integrate all parts of a client's total experience (Volkman, 1993). In addition, music therapy seems to be helpful in the recovery of breast cancer patients as they work to find and form new identities (G. Aldridge, 1996). In the process of making music, patients bring feelings into consciousness without any immediate verbal labels being attached to their emotions. This active intervention uses patients' strength and creativity to cope and maintain coherence in the midst of what might otherwise be chaotic transition. Further, music and music therapy in particular can have value in reducing physical agitation in participants with Alzheimer's disease (Jennings & Vance, 2002).

In addition to the direct use of music with those who have physical or mental disorders, music, as well as breathing, can be used in psychiatric emergency rooms to reduce the stress of clients and visitors in such settings (R. G. H. Miller & Spence, 2013). Overall, music has proved to be significantly effective in suppressing and combating the symptoms of psychosis and related disorders. However, investigating the effects between live and recorded music, between structured music groups and passive listening, and between classical music and nonclassical music is still something that needs to be done (Silverman, 2003).

Teachers, Teaching, and Supervision

Music can be used with teachers to help promote their mental health and avoid burnout. For instance, Cheek, Bradley, Parr, and Lan (2003) found that elementary teachers who participated in school-based counseling groups that used music therapy techniques in conjunction with cognitive behavioral interventions reported lower levels of burnout symptoms than teachers in school-based counseling groups that used cognitive behavioral interventions only. Forensic psychiatric patients also may benefit from cognitive behavioral music therapy, such as the song "Everything Changes," as a part of the multimodal treatment they receive. In music therapy sessions, music therapists deploy music in specific ways to elicit the reinforcement of appropriate behaviors in clients and help them experiment with new behaviors, adjusting incorrect thoughts, relaxation, and role playing. In other words, musical situations are created to stimulate patients to modify their behavior (Hakvoort & Bogaerts, 2013).

Music may also be used to punctuate and emphasize points in teaching a variety of materials. For instance, song lyrics provide students with a way to relate course material to their lives, "which helps to facilitate higher retention and comprehension of material" (Louden-Gerber & Duffey, 2008, p. 322). Thus, in learning about Enneatypes (a model of personality types), a student with Enneatype 3 (achievement) may come up with the theme song "Anything you can do, I can do better." Likewise, in an abnormal psychology course or a mental health center, song lyrics may highlight important concepts and provide concrete examples (Potkay, 1974; Schiff & Frances, 1974). Think, for example, of Don McLean's song "Starry, Starry Nights" about the life of Vincent van Gogh and how the melody and words of this work depict the difficulties of mental instability. In a similar fashion, the lyrics of Janis Ian's "At Seventeen" portray some of the transitions adolescents experience in forming their identities and establishing relationships with the opposite sex. The possibilities of using music as a background to understand thoughts and emotions throughout the life span and in different cultures are limited only by the imagination of instructors and their knowledge of different types of music.

Supervision may also be enhanced through bringing music into the process (Pearson, 2002). This procedure may be implemented by having counseling students listen to music outside of class that demonstrates certain concepts, or by bringing lyrical or nonlyrical music into the class that elicits specific emotions or ideas the instructor wants conveyed. For example, Jewel's "Pieces of You" is a powerful representation of hatred and fear associated with prejudice. Likewise, Dar Williams's "When I Was a Boy" portrays the process of gender role socialization and the losses involved for women and men. It fits well into discussions of social and gender identity development and how that plays into difficulties people may have that could bring them into

Creative Reflection

Try writing a four- or five-line prosocial lyric to music you already know. How easy or difficult do you find writing such lyrics to be? Do you think writing negative lyrics would be easier?

therapy. The point is that music can enhance supervision by helping sensitize supervisees to messages being sent through music that are a part of popular culture and that may promote health or pathology (*Music and Counselor Supervision*).

Music in Counseling
With Other Creative Arts

The ease with which music may be used in conjunction with textual or visual information contributes to its value as a highly flexible therapeutic medium (Gfeller, 2002a). Thus, music may be used with a number of creative arts to produce an effect it could not have alone. For instance, familiar sedative music plus imagery is more effective in reducing state anxiety among college students than just music alone (Russell, 1992). Music therapists may also consider utilizing social learning theory as a conceptual framework with existing research concerning social skills and communication when working with bullies and victims of bullying (Shafer & Silverman, 2013). In counseling, music is often connected with the creative arts of poetry, movement and dance, play, and autobiography and storytelling (e.g., LeLieuvre, 1998; C. B. Williams, Frame, & Green, 1999).

Music and Poetry
Poetic lyrics add to the rhythm message of music, although their impact varies (A. White, 1985). Lyrics often extend an understanding of what is important in clients' lives (C. O'Callaghan & Grocke, 2009). For example, adolescents are often influenced by the lyrics of rock songs. Such lyrics are detrimental when they are sexually explicit, violent, or exploitive in nature (Edwards & Mullis, 2001; L. Ray, Soares, & Tolchinsky, 1988). That has been the case with some of the recordings of 2 Live Crew and other rap artists and with some of the music produced by heavy metal artists (Took & Weiss, 1994). However, lyrics and music may be combined in a prosocial way, such as those by popular rock music artists such as Whitney Houston and her song "The Greatest Love of All," Don Henley and "Heart of the Matter," or Bette Midler and "From a Distance." Likewise, country performers such as Matraca Berg and Clint Black sing about growth through pain and convey a positive view of change in such songs as "I Must Have Been Crazy" and "Walkin' Away." These works sensitize listeners to words that promote the best within

Creative Reflection

Think of your life as a musical. Then make a musical autobiography reflecting the highs and lows of your existence. Include at least six songs. What memories are evoked from writing down and listening to this music? What song titles would you want to create to represent the next 10 years of your life?

and between persons. They provide "a nonthreatening device to stimulate . . . interaction" (Mazza, 1986, p. 297). It is important that counselors who use lyrical music listen carefully to the words as well as the melody of songs before advocating that clients try using the recordings therapeutically.

When music and lyrics are packaged together, the way they are expected to be handled therapeutically should be made clear. For example, an inspirational tape, such as Nancy Day's (1989) *Survivor*, which focuses on surviving and recovering from sexual abuse, may be one that counselors want clients to hear at specific times of the day when clients are likely to feel discouraged or depressed. Likewise, *If You Believe in You*, an audiotape by Dan Conley (1994), which describes the mixture of feelings derived from divorce, contains materials that should be used selectively. By prescribing music in this manner, counselors increase the chances of clients being therapeutically influenced. Developmental stages of people and families along with gender, ethnicity, age, and roles must be considered in the process (Gladding & Heape, 1987). Some music and lyrics are more appropriate for certain populations at specific times in their lives.

Music and Movement and Dance

Movement and dance and music complement each other. The action involved in moving to music, whether formal or informal, allows clients the freedom to express themselves in a way not possible in stillness. The awareness that follows can help individuals realize they are exerting themselves in ways they might never have imagined. The beat of the music makes such expression possible. Once clients have chosen new creative actions or danced in a set pattern, their awareness of self is never the same again. In a study jointly using music therapy and dance movement therapy with severely affected autistic adults, researchers found treatment to positively affect selective behaviors, emotions, and interpersonal interactions (Mateos-Moreno & Atencia-Doña, 2013). In other words, the combination of music and movement made a difference.

A healthy integration of sacred and secular music in fostering positive outcomes can be found today through the musical combinations of those who perform the blues and performers of religious music. Many blues performers have made this type of music their orientation to life after struggling to perform in the confines of churches. Their satisfaction with this arrangement has generally proved beneficial to them as well as to their audiences. They often move as they play, and their audiences sway in time with the beat of their sound, thus combining music, movement, and, at times, dance.

Music and Play

Music is used in play in a number of ways but primarily to set a tone or mood for an activity. One of the more integrative ways of fusing music and play together is music play therapy (J. J. Moreno, 1985). In this approach, a nondirective orientation is taken just as in play therapy, but the playroom is supplied with musical instruments instead of toys and traditional play therapy materials. Children with whom this approach is tried gradually become tired of randomly playing instruments and commit themselves to playing a tune either by themselves or with the counselor. In so doing, a structure is established to which these children become committed. This active setup can be manipulated for the overall benefit of the children.

Another way music and play may be combined is through improvised musical play, an intervention technique using improvised music and lyrics to encourage social play among developmentally delayed and nondelayed children in mainstream settings (Gunsberg, 1988). In such situations teachers make up simple songs using familiar tunes to describe what is occurring with the children, such as "Everyone is clapping their hands and being active." This encourages continuous interaction of the children and sustains "social play episodes lasting more than three times the expected duration" (Gunsberg, 1988, p. 178).

Music and Autobiography and Storytelling

A fourth way of using music with other creative arts is to do what is normally a literary task in sound or with sound in the background (Watkins, 1990). A music autobiography is one interesting literary task that can be done with sound. In this creative endeavor, participants represent their lives through sound. For instance, someone who has spent a lifetime living by the ocean may splash a hand in water with a certain rhythm; and someone who has lived in an arid region may clap rocks together in a unique way. Completing a music autobiography may also involve connecting bits of lyrical music together. The effect is particularly powerful if there are verses and a refrain, similar to what the rock singer Billy Joel did with his song "We Didn't Start the Fire" (*Music Autobiography*).

In storytelling, music may be used to enhance the background of the presentation. For instance, Painter (1989) recommended using classical music such as the first movement of Handel's Concerto for Harp and Orchestra in B-flat Major, the first movement of Bach's Suite for Harp, Mozart's Adagio and Rondo in C Minor, or the second movement of Wagenseil's Concerto for Harp and Orchestra as background music to stories being told to young children. Such pieces set a mood and stir up emotions that would not occur without such an accompaniment. Although Painter (1989) preferred the emotional nuances offered by classical music, other forms of music such as "Dixieland, swing, marches, ballet, solo instrumental, western, folk melodies, polkas, and novelty music" (p. 3) may also work to create an atmosphere for a story or the character in a story (*Storytelling and Music*).

Music and Film

Music, as indicated, has a long history in punctuating potent moments in films. John Williams has been especially prolific in composing music scores for such films as *Star Wars, Jaws, E. T., Indiana Jones, Jurassic Park, The Color Purple*, and *Schindler's List*, among others. A more recent development has been the origination of music videos. This medium, which became popular in the 1980s, at first simply depicted artistic impressions of song lyrics that featured recording artists. However, music videos have expanded and can be used for much more than simple entertainment. For instance, music videos can be used in empathy training, especially for counselors-in-training (Ohrt, Foster, Hutchinson, & Ieva, 2009). Such music videos as "When You're Gone" (Klasfeld, 2007) can be played to highlight loss and loneliness or "Concrete Angel" (Flanigen, 2002) to focus on feelings and features related to abuse. Thus, music videos "may serve as a medium for arousing emotional responses to a character that may represent future clients" (Ohrt et al., 2009, p. 329).

Summary

Music has a long history as a healing art. Throughout human history, music has soothed or inspired individuals. It has been a major impetus in the prevention and treatment of major disorders and minor problems. It has allowed persons to communicate in a universal, nonverbal way that has promoted identity, bonding, creation, and discovery. As William L. Schurk, sound-recording archivist at Bowling Green State University, observed, music is "not a lonely art form" (Rosenblatt, 1991, p. B7). Rather, it involves vocal, physical, social, and emotional responses. "Applications include improvising, recreating, composing, listening, [and] game or play activities" (Bonny, 1997, p. 70).

In this chapter the multiple ways music is used in counseling have been examined. Some professionals are music therapists, and other counselors use music in their therapeutic practice. Both types of individuals are helpful, but the background and emphasis of these two groups differ. In music therapy, practitioners place greater emphasis on certain procedures with specific difficulties and populations. Individuals who obtain the designation of music therapist are more skilled in music than counselors who occasionally use music therapeutically. Regardless of the counselor's designation, four ways that music may be used in counseling are through listening, performing, improvising, and composing. The choice of music in counseling depends on the needs of clients. Because music is so universal, it is appropriately used with children, adolescents, adults, older persons, groups, families, people who are ill, and educators/supervisors. The various ways this medium can be used are limited only by the creativity and skills of practitioners. Music is often combined with poetry and with movement and dance, which enhance its overall impact. In summary, music is a universal and versatile art that is of major importance to counselors who wish to promote catharsis, creativity, and communication abilities in a variety of clients and situations.

Exercises

1. On a daily basis, for at least a week, at specific times of the day, notice how you are feeling. With materials that are immediately available, such as pencils, pans, or books, make music by tapping, banging, or even humming in a way that best represents your mood. Record your sessions whenever possible and process these experiences with a colleague regularly. How could you use what you learned in this exercise with clients?

2. At the beginning of a group, ask participants to bring in music on MP3 players that express some of their feelings. Emphasize to the whole group that there is no right or wrong music for this task. As group members introduce themselves, have them use the music they brought in any way they choose. After introductions, discuss the variety of sounds and words within the group and what diversity, as well as sameness, can contribute to growth.

3. When working with people who primarily relate in a nonverbal manner, ask them to bring in music they like to listen to (from as many different sources as possible). Have them respond as they wish to the music, such as by drawing or dancing. Limit this exercise to about 15 minutes, and then process with them what happened as they listened or moved. What did they feel, think, and learn? What did they notice about their life with regard to the music?

Chapter 3

Dance and Movement in Counseling

Dance Street

Dance Street began before I was born
*   and I don't know where it will lead.*
Could be it will trail on forever
*   perhaps it will end with me.*
The street began in downtown Richmond
*   made of bricks, entitled "Dance,"*
*   for a man who bore the burden*
*   of fighting for a beaten people.*
When war ended he built again
*   cared for the "cause" but more its people,*
Moving with courage in the midst of strife
*   he left an ancestral legacy for the dance of life.*

—Gladding, 1991a/2003

Dancing is one of the oldest forms of art. It was first practiced by humans thousands of years ago, and we continue to use dance in a variety of ways: to communicate ideas and social norms, as a religious ritual, as a form of entertainment, and as a form of recreation. Before the invention of writing, dance was one of the most widely used methods for passing stories and ideas from one generation to the next. "Social" dances, such as square dancing and line dancing, are designed to create a sense of unity and cooperation among a group of people. They often form patterns, such as squares, circles, chains, and lines. "Joint" dance (a set of well-choreographed movements set to music and preformed either individually or in a group) and movement are known for their potential to promote social bonding in many cultures.

"Moreover, in making use of the interrelation of body, mind and spirit, dance also plays an important role in the healing rituals in many cultures" (Behrends, Müller, & Dziobek, 2012, p. 107). Thus, dance and movement are important dimensions of life. They are developmental, process-oriented, and cross-cultural types of expression (Chaiklin & Wengrower, 2016; Kampfe, 2003). They can also be transformational (Block, 2001). In the United States, classical ballet (e.g., *Swan Lake*), modern dance groups (e.g., Dance Theater of Harlem), Broadway productions (e.g., *A Chorus Line*), and specific recording artists (e.g., Michael Jackson, Taylor Swift) often give us pleasure through their grace, motion, and breathtaking performances. Likewise, we are entertained and enchanted with the dance and movement in some films, such as Bob Fosse's *Cabaret* and *All That Jazz*, as well as the individual and combined performances of actors such as Gene Kelly, Fred Astaire/Ginger Rogers, Bill Bojangles Robinson/Shirley Temple, and Richard Gere/Renee Zellweger/Catherine Zeta-Jones in movies such as *Singin' in the Rain*, *Top Hat*, *The Little Colonel*, and *Chicago* (Mitoma & Stieber, 2002).

In a similar manner, people worldwide are often moved vicariously or otherwise by different stimuli to take action on their own behalf or that of someone else. From ancient communities to modern times, individuals have recognized and revered the nature of movement and dance in the healing and helping process. However, the practice of dance and movement therapy varies according to the worldview of those who participate in it. Cultural sensitivity is called for in appreciating the many ways participants express themselves physically (Dosamantes-Beaudry, 1999).

Yet, as Hendricks (1982) noted, living "is movement, from the rhythmic motion of the tides to the life cycle of the human being. The way we move broadcasts our relationship to life. It is the bridge between what goes on inside and what we show the world" (p. 165). Although our movements may at times be "ugly, gut-wrenchingly choppy, and out of control" (Block, 2001, p. 117) as opposed to beautiful, inspiring, free-flowing, and seemingly effortless, they are ours, and they are important. It is not surprising that dancing is universal, because it links people together in ways other expressive forms of interacting cannot (Dingfelder, 2010).

Despite the importance society places on dance and movement, these two action-oriented artistic forms are often neglected aspects of counseling. That fact is ironic because "healers were movers until the age of the mind–body dichotomy, and ancient communities recognized and honored the healing power of movement" (Hendricks, 1982, p. 165). In many early cultures, dancing was considered as important as eating and sleeping and was directly associated with healing (F. J. Levy, 1988). Indeed, Stark and Lohn (1989) wrote that "dance was one of the [primary] ways in which people experienced their participation in a community" (p. 107). In societies that still follow an oral tradition, dance serves "as an instrument of consciousness and as a vehicle for mediating unknown forces, releasing pent-up emotions, and promoting individual transformation and communal inclusiveness" (Beaudry, 1997, p. 52).

The language of counseling is filled with dance and movement words and phrases, such as being "in step" or "out of step" with others, heading in the "right or wrong direction," "leaning toward a point of view," moving together like "poetry in motion," and "tap dancing around the issues" (Carkhuff, 2010). In addition, numerous counselors have backgrounds in and currently participate in dynamic endeavors that require coordinated movement and abilities, such as gymnastics, swimming, aerobics, dance, and jogging. Because a sit-and-talk model of helping is more conservative, expected, and easy to implement, counseling sessions are most often sedentary in nature. This staid model of reflecting and talking dominated traditional counseling theory and practice in the 20th century (Gladding, 2013). Counselors were not exposed to dance and movement in the therapeutic process, and they often failed as practitioners to make the most of the individual and collective abilities of their clients (Kottler, 2010).

In this chapter, I explore the multidimensional premise behind the power of dance and movement as well as the practical use of dance and movement in counseling. I distinguish between dance therapy and movement therapy. In addition, I explain and illustrate how dance and movement can be used with a variety of populations (from children to older adults) and in various settings (from individuals to groups or families). The use of dance and movement with other creative arts (e.g., music and art) is also discussed.

Premise of the Use of Dance and Movement in Counseling

Dance/movement therapy (DMT) is a widespread art-based form of psychotherapy for many somatic and psychic illnesses that has been developed since the 1940s with different orientations. It uses movement as a therapeutic tool "to further the emotional, cognitive, physical and social integration of the individual" (American Dance Therapy Association [ADTA], 2015). Research has found small but consistent effects with clients for the improvement of well-being, mood, affect, and body image over the past couple of decades through the therapeutic use of dance and movement (S. Koch, Kunz, Lykou, & Cruz, 2014). International research confirms that DMT is effective in working with oncology patients and patients with depression (S. Koch et al., 2014). Some people with Parkinson's disease who generally cannot move at all can walk in time to music (Dingfelder, 2010). Furthermore, dance and movement therapy is useful in the assessment of people suffering from schizophrenia and in evaluating parent–child interactions (S. Koch & Brauninger, 2006).

The use of dance and movement in counseling and therapeutic settings has been found to benefit clients in one or more of six areas:

1. Resocialization and integration within a larger group system
2. Nonverbal creative expression for emotional expression
3. Total self- and body awareness and enhanced self-esteem
4. Muscular coordination, broader movement capabilities, and tension release
5. Enjoyment through relaxation (Ritter & Low, 1996, p. 249)
6. Promotion of empathy and prosocial behavior (Behrends et al., 2012)

As an approach in therapeutic settings, dance and movement are premised on a number of theoretical assumptions (Best, 2000). The first comes from the psychoanalytic literature, through the implicit belief that the initial awareness of self is through the body (Freud, 1923/1961). It is further assumed that body movement (as a representative aspect of the unconscious) may inform the conscious mind of feelings and repressed influences that affect a person's life (Dosamantes-Beaudry, 2001; Feder & Feder, 1981). "Movement conveys truth" and "is the direct printout from the unconscious" (Hendricks, 1982, p. 166). In this tradition, dance and movement promote awareness and further "the physical and psychic integration" of people (Krueger & Schofield, 1986, p. 327). These avenues of expression help clients heal their fragmentation and alienation from themselves and others (Chaiklin & Wengrower, 2016; Levine, 1996; Thomson, 1997).

A second premise on which dance and movement in counseling are based is bodywork. There are many forms of bodywork, including

various forms of massage, rolfing, bioenergetics, yoga, Tragerwork, Lomi bodywork, and acupressure. They are all designed to help people dissolve psychophysical blocks in the body. Some are more physical in nature (massage), and others focus more on psychological blocks (bioenergetics). Direct manipulation of the body often triggers memories of old traumas and injuries or can produce a flood of feelings. (Weinhold, 1987, p. 7)

By working one's body through dance and movement, avenues of awareness that were previously closed begin to open up. Bodywork seeks to help people become more integrative (Brownell, 1981). It is especially effective with people who are closed to talking about their feelings.

A third rationale for incorporating dance and movement in the therapeutic process is based on developmental theory. Human behavior is initially dominated by physically oriented experiences. In infancy, movement is a primary way of communicating. "The bodily interaction between mother and infant is, in a sense, the first dialog. In harmonious relationships this physical give and take becomes a smoothly flowing piece of choreography, a perfect symbiotic dance" (Mohacsy, 1995, p. 33). Regardless of how rhythmic interpersonal relationships are, people pass through a number of different physical stages in life, each of which is characterized by distinct movement patterns.

A fourth rationale for dance and movement in counseling is based on gestalt therapy, which has recognized the potency of movement for many years (Payne, 2006). Fritz Perls and others involved in the formulation of gestalt therapy stressed that body movement is a primary method of experiencing feelings and promoting psychological growth (Meier & Davis, 2011; Perls, Hefferline, & Goodman, 1951). Perls probably overstated his case when he said, "Lose your mind and come to your senses." Nevertheless, this adage has value in reminding clients that through using all aspects of themselves they will make progress in working through personal issues. In movement and dance, the expressions of choice and change become visibly clear.

Further, the use of movement and dance in counseling is founded on social psychology and the interpersonal theory of Harry Stack Sullivan, which emphasized that personality is formed in relationship to others. The basis of movement and dance is to "establish or reestablish a sense of relatedness to self and to others" (Stark & Lohn, 1989, p. 107). In rhythmic movement, a person feels a "heightened sense of oneself (a flow of energy, a feeling of aliveness, and sense of well-being), [which facilitates] bonding and empathic response in the body with others" (Stark & Lohn, 1989, p. 107). Movement and dance are connecting arts that

Creative Reflection

When have you connected with someone else through movement or dance, for example, by playing a sport or being in a dance contest or recital? What do you remember most about the experience and how it affected or still affects you?

unite people with themselves and others by providing an integrative mind–body experience.

Practice of the Use of
Dance and Movement in Counseling

Dance and movement occur in many ways, and their impact is multidimensional. In purest form, dance and movement are initially expressed in physical movements. Indeed, the body is seen as the manifestation of one's personality, and any spontaneous movement is viewed as an expression of personality and health (Bunney, 1979; Dingfelder, 2010). Therefore, the way people move—from being "light on their feet" to being "mechanical and slow"—is an indicator of who they are and how they are generally functioning (L. F. Armeniox, personal communication, February 5, 1994).

The therapeutic emphases of dance and movement are multiple. "Dance and movement therapy allows for the treatment of complex psychological trauma (torture, rape, war experiences) and contributes to the healing process directly on a body level" (S. Koch & Weidinger-von der Recke, 2009, p. 289). Overall, dance and movement therapy has three main goals: physical, psychological, and social (Fleshman & Fryear, 1981).

> Physical goals may include releasing physical tension through activities and broadening one's movement repertoire. Psychological goals might include channeling one's self-expression in a meaningful way and helping a client adjust to reality. Social goals may involve getting a client to join a group interaction and to develop social relationships with others. (Gladding, 1985, p. 10)

The extent to which and how these goals are highlighted depend on the education and skill of counselors. Some professionals are specifically taught ways to use dance and movement therapy; others use this emphasis at selected times and in limited ways. In this section, different aspects of each tradition are examined, and populations with which movement and dance may best be used are explored. Dance and movement therapy affects changes in feelings, cognitions, physical functioning, social interaction, and behavior. Although they have much in common, dance and movement are also seen as distinct specialty areas.

Marian Chace (1896–1970) is considered to be the founder of modern dance and movement therapies (Sandel, Chaiklin, & Lohn, 1993). She

Creative Reflection

When have you found your body telling your mind something important, such as it is time to sleep, eat, or exercise? Do you tend to listen to such messages or ignore them? What is behind your reaction?

started her dance therapy work in the early 1940s at St. Elizabeths Hospital in Washington, DC and was a professional dancer before beginning her work as a dance therapist. Other pioneers who followed or were contemporaries of Chace included Mary Whitehouse, Blanche Evan, Liljan Espenak, Alma Hawkins, and Trudi Shoop.

Together, dance and movement therapists acknowledge "the intrinsic life forces in all people, the healing power of shared rhythms and expressed feelings" (Hendricks, 1982, p. 166). They believe in a reciprocal influence between a person's emotions and body movement. Changes in body movement can bring about positive changes in a person's psychic life and vice versa (S. Kleinman, personal communication, April 3, 1997). Despite these similarities, professionals in the fields of dance and movement therapy maintain many distinctions.

Dance Therapy

Dance therapy is the use of dance and movement as psychotherapeutic (healing) tools (F. J. Levy, 1988; Payne, 2006). Dance and movement therapists specialize in this area and have met educational and performance standards set up by the ADTA. The term *dance* is used by dance therapists to stress the "expressive movement and the integrating aspects of the rhythmic use of body movement" (Duggan, 1981, p. 229). Thus, dance therapy connotes the artistic nature of performance through movement and the use of music to promote rhythm and fluidity in this process. "Through dance one becomes more fully alive—physically, emotionally, intellectually, and spiritually. It opens a path toward one's higher self—a way to transcend the mundane" (Fisher, 1989, p. 15). Dance enables a person to cognitively process and overcome frightening events, feel one's physical self, analyze problems, find constructive solutions for everyday life, and improve one's body image and self-esteem (Bräuninger, 2012a). Music and music therapy are closely associated with dance and dance therapy.

Movement Therapy

In movement therapy, practitioners place less emphasis on performance and outside stimuli and concentrate more on feelings and senses. Therefore, movement therapy may include more improvisation and intuitive ways of acting (Kampfe, 2003). Through this approach people are trusted to act on their emotions and are encouraged in various ways to become more connected with their inner selves (Jacobs, Schimmel, Masson, & Harvill, 2016). The action associated with movement therapy is usually spontaneous, unrehearsed, and relatively brief. "The process of the mover [how the mover moves] is the focus of movement therapy" (Hendricks, 1982, p. 167). Drama and enactment techniques are closely allied with movement therapy.

Dance and Movement in Counseling

As previously noted, few traditional counseling theories have basic rationales that emphasize dance and movement as primary ways of clarifying or resolving problems. Nevertheless, dance and movement therapies consider such psychologically based authorities as Sigmund Freud, William James, Gordon Allport, Wilhelm Reich, Carl Rogers, Abraham Maslow, Alfred Adler, and Harry Stack Sullivan to have been influential in the development of their specialty (Chaiklin & Wengrower, 2016; Payne, 2006). For example, Liljan Espenak, a pioneer in dance therapy, based much of her work on integrating Adlerian concepts with the discipline of dance therapy. These Adlerian concepts included aggressive drive, inferiority feelings, social feelings, lifestyle, and first memory. The nonverbal emphases of other theorists have been especially valued by dance and movement therapists. The following examples illustrate how theories of counseling and movement are used separately or together.

The first example is gestalt therapy. It has two primary foci centered on movement. One focus is simply body language, in which the counselor and eventually the client concentrate on what different parts of the body are doing in conjunction with a client's verbalizations. A client may state that he or she is calm and relaxed while simultaneously making a kicking motion. The incongruence of these messages is pointed out, and the client is confronted with the inconsistency of verbal and nonverbal signals (Gladding, 2013). In the process, clients are encouraged to examine and own their personal feelings and behaviors more directly.

The other focus of gestalt therapy is the movement encouraged with the technique of becoming a dream (in which enactment of a dream event is carried out). In this process each part of a dream (e.g., people, event, and mood) is considered to be a projection of the self, and parts often represent contradictory roles (Perls, 1969). Dreamers are asked to become each part of their dream and to invent dialog and interactions between the various components regardless of how absurd such a process may seem. Through this technique opposite sides are expressed and become clearer, and the dream becomes the "royal road to integration" (Perls, 1969, p. 66).

A second example is social learning theory and family therapy, both of which focus on what many within these approaches call the dance: regular rhythmic interactions that enhance or impede one's overall functioning. Social skills and competencies through such a dance are emphasized with these perspectives. Selective dances are shaped and reinforced using the plethora of techniques derived from these traditions. The way individuals and family members generally relate to significant others in their lives determines how rigid, spontaneous, or healthy

Creative Reflection

What was the family dance like in your family of origin? What patterns kept repeating themselves?

their lives will be (A. Y. Napier & Whitaker, 1978). For example, in a social situation a husband and wife may constantly put each other down or compliment and encourage each other. As a result of these actions, their behavior will either be positive (spiraling up in a virtuous cycle) or negative (spiraling down in a vicious cycle).

Additional examples of how theories of counseling and movement are used separately or together are among atheoretical approaches, and these include a number of effective generic movement and dance experiences. Many of these approaches are associated with groups. For example, a movement activity that creates greater awareness for group members about the nature of conflict is known as home spot. In this nonverbal experience, individuals are asked to join hands or put their arms around each other's shoulders. Then they are to pick out a spot in the room to which they wish to take the group, without telling anyone. Finally, they begin trying to move the group toward the spot they have selected (Jacobs et al., 2016). The ongoing group dynamics are the primary focus of the exercise as group members struggle with issues of power and persuasion in a 2- to 5-minute time span. After the struggle that inevitably comes with the exercise, group members talk to each other about the specifics as well as the general nature of the dance they just went through and what it can mean to the life of the group and to their own individual lives (*Home Spot*).

Overall, movement and dance are actively practiced as a part of counseling because they

- get people moving around and keep them from becoming fatigued from sitting too long in one spot,
- provide a change in format and an opportunity to renew interest and energize,
- give individuals a chance to experience something rather than simply discuss it,
- help participants remember what they experience more vividly than words alone, and
- involve all people in a counseling experience or the total person that is the client in a way not possible otherwise.

Dance and Movement in Counseling With Specific Populations

Professional dance and movement therapists (and those who use these modalities in counseling) "work with all ages and populations—in psychiatric hospitals, prisons, geriatric residence programs, adolescent halfway house settings, special education programs, and private practice" (Hendricks, 1982, p. 166). A representative sampling of the settings and techniques used is presented in the material that follows; however, movement and dance are constantly being created and implemented. Those who prefer these active, art-based ways of working with clients must be innovative in their endeavors.

Children

A primary characteristic of many children is abundant energy, so the use of dance and movement with them is often accepted with enthusiasm. The idea of movement activities with children focuses on self-awareness. For instance, directed dance and movement therapy may help abused children exercise control over personal space and regain a sense of control and ownership of their own bodies (Goodhill, 1987). Movement and dance also help children gain an awareness of others. Several types of movement exercises can engage children and promote different aspects of their mental and physical health quite concretely (Chiefetz, 1977; Tortora, 2005).

Exercises for Physically Functional Children
Walking. In this activity, children walk in a circle at their normal pace and cadence. After they have a feel for how they walk, they are asked to walk faster than usual and then to walk in slow motion. Walking is then linked to feelings so that the children walk as if they were tired, happy, or sad. After this experience, children are instructed to act as if they were walking on or through different terrain, including a desert, a mountain, mud, ice, water, and even silly substances such as peanut butter, whipped cream, yogurt, and cornflakes. After the walk is completed (usually by pretending to walk through a grassy meadow), children and their leaders talk about what the experiences were like (*Walking*).

Locomotion. The idea of the locomotion exercise is to have children see how many different movements they can make to get from one place to another (e.g., jumping, running, and skipping). They can then combine movements and even do the same movements with a partner. Afterward, the feelings involved with these movements are processed (*Locomotion*).

Robot. In robot, children pretend they can only move or talk as a robot does. They become stiff-limbed and monotone. Halfway into the exercise they become human again. After the exercise they work with their facilitators and talk about the robot-to-human experience (*Robot*).

Exercises for Children With Disabilities
Movement and dance can have a therapeutic effect on children who are born with disabilities as well. One of the most dramatic examples of this impact is the use of movement with children who are born blind. In such cases, "the dance and movement therapist's highly developed communicative mode emphasizes sound, rhythm, and touch and helps the blind child find pleasure and safety in the

Creative Reflection

Think of the environments you are in every week. How do you move in each? How does your energy and movement differ in places you enjoy versus places you do not like?

natural expression of moving to- gether" (Kalish-Weiss, 1988, p. 108). Such experiences, which must be tailored for each child, are truly the essence of art.

Dance therapy treatment may be equally positive in outcome, as illustrated in the use of this process on a 12-year-old girl who had motor abnormalities,

Creative Reflection

When have you let your negative emotions out through movement? What movements have you found constructive in such a process? Which ones have proven negative? What do you do in letting your positive emotions out through movement?

mild mental deficiencies, and emotional problems (Lasseter, Privette, Brown, & Duer, 1989). The 1-hour, twice-a-week sessions of dance treatments over 18 weeks resulted in markedly improved motor de- velopment as well as enhanced self-esteem.

Adolescents

Dance and movement can be used preventatively and therapeutically with a wide range of adolescents (Anderson, Kennedy, DeWitt, An- derson, & Wambold, 2014; Block, 2001). Preventative dance and movement focus on helping adolescents explore "the radical changes in body image and awareness [they are undergoing] and the transient feelings of depersonalization this engenders" (Emunah, 1990, p. 103). Dance and movement therapy influences moods in adolescents regardless of gender, ethnicity, or diagnosis (Anderson et al., 2014). Dance and movement also lead to the expression of creativity within adolescents in healthy and actualizing ways (May, 1975). For example, it may help at-risk African American youth in developing socially ap- propriate skills and trust while having fun (Farr, 1997).

Therapeutically, dance and movement enable adolescents to express their conflicts in an active, behavioral form, which is often an easier form of communication for them than verbalizing what they are ex- periencing. Adolescents who are angry or confused can show their feelings in a safe and dynamic form by enacting them through dance and movement that can be accompanied by music. For clients with severe disorders, such as those with anorexia nervosa, body boundary exercises are used: Clients attend to the tactile differences "between their bodies and other objects in the environment" (Kaslow & Eicher, 1988, p. 180). Other movement- and dance-related exercises such as muscle relaxation, deep breathing, and centering also are helpful to this population, regardless of the problems they present.

Adults

Prevention

Dance and movement therapies are used in a number of therapeutic ways with adults. One of the most prominent is in prevention, and many adults participate in some form of dance or movement activity as a way to stay healthy and fit. Stress is reduced through dance and movement therapy (Bräuninger, 2012a). Although not formally considered "therapy," jazzercise and jogging are two movement trends that are therapeutic in their own right and have captured the attention of a large number of individuals. Jazzercise, which is valued for its group support dynamic and upbeat tempo, is a popular musically oriented way to exercise. Jogging is equally popular (Rosato, 2012). As a movement experience, jogging has been used in group counseling settings to help participants become psychologically as well as physically healthier (Childers & Burcky, 1984). In addition, many professional athletic teams hire dance specialists to help their players learn the agility and coordination essential to teamwork and individual performance.

Remediation

Dance and movement therapies may also be used in remedial ways, for instance, with women victims of child sexual abuse (Meekums, 2000; L. Mills & Daniluk, 2002). In such a setting, dance therapy especially helps clients reconnect with their bodies, play, be spontaneous, struggle constructively, connect with others, and experience a new sense of freedom. Dance and movement have also been used with adults who have depression. In a pilot study with working-age adults, people with mild, moderate, or severe depressive episodes improved their level of depression as well as comorbid anxiety (Punkanen, Saarikallio, & Luck, 2014). Dance and movement therapy have been employed as an intervention with trauma survivors as well. This therapy can help facilitate the reestablishment of trust, intimacy, social skills, and self-esteem, which are often destroyed in cases of relational trauma (Pierce, 2014). Dance and movement therapy have a positive impact on patients with breast cancer too, improving their quality of life and decreasing psychological distress.

Overall, dance and movement therapy can improve the quality of life for many adults suffering from stress in the short and long term. Social relations, global value, and physical health seem to improve significantly in the short term, and spirituality and general health factors seem to improve in the long term (Bräuninger, 2012b). For example, when used with obese women with emotionally eating problems, DMT statistically decreased their psychological distress and body image distress while increasing their self-esteem (Meekums, Vavernice, Majore-Dusele, & Rasnacs, 2012).

More formalized dance and movement therapies are helpful with those who have physical problems. For instance, ballroom dances such as Tango improve balance and coordination in patients with Parkinson's disease (Kiepe, Stöckigt, & Keil, 2012). Furthermore, in prison settings, dance and movement therapies have been used to enhance communication and interpersonal relationship skills (Seibel, 2008) and for the treatment of violence.

> This practice is based on the knowledge that engaging in the creative process is a deeply healing experience, one that can lead the individual toward new and profoundly different ways of expressing their innermost feelings of rage, frustration, confusion, and alienation. (Milliken, 2002, p. 203)

In addition, movement techniques may be therapeutic in other remedial ways. For instance, a client may address repressed anger and rage by hitting a pile of pillows or a foam rubber block with a tennis racket. To facilitate regression to an earlier age, a client may lie down on a mattress and kick. Likewise, in group settings, one group member may stand across from a client who is hitting or kicking (without actually touching or hurting anyone else) and role-play through various means the object of the negative intent (Wilner, 2001). In other words, dance and movement therapy and processes enable upset individuals to release their emotions in constructive, physical, and sometimes symbolical ways.

Bodywork
The use of bodywork with men and women has proved effective and is popular as well (Brownell, 1981). Although many forms of bodywork exist, it is defined here as any nonverbal activity in which adults actively participate. It makes use of props and gestalt-type experiences to help individuals become more aware of their body and emotions. Many individuals, particularly men, are able to release repressed feelings such as fear, anger, hurt, or joy. Women benefit from bodywork too. Through this method, they come to a clearer understanding of their own boundaries and are thus able to be more caring of themselves. Self and nonself distinctions gained through bodywork facilitate better intra- and interpersonal relationships (*Bodywork*). Likewise, dance therapy can help women reconcile the gap between inner experiences and external self-image and thereby facilitate a fuller integration of self (Meyer, 1985).

Older Clients
The use of creative movement and dance with older persons is an unexpected but pragmatic reality. Movement and dance activities have been associated with a number of improvements in this population (Pratt, 2004). For example, dance lessons involve becoming active, learning a new activity, and interacting with another through movement and friendly conversation (Haboush, Floyd, Caron, LaSota, & Alvarez, 2006). In older adults, dance and movement may also aid or help improve memory, alertness, reality orientation, judgment, personal insight, and acceptance (Ashley & Crenan, 1993). Further-

more, dance and movement with older clients have been found to help them become more tolerant, empathic, and open to one another and to enrich the quality of their lives overall (von Rossberg-Gempton, Dickinson, & Poole, 1999). In other words, dance and movement seem to have a positive effect on older adults.

Many older adults have the ability and willingness to engage in a number of movement activities, including simple dances, that benefit them physically and mentally. The exact nature of exercises chosen for members of aging populations depends on the physical well-being of participants as well as on the space and time available. Movement can include a number of activities that focus on such things as breathing (e.g., blowing soap bubbles), hand dances, nonlocomotor actions (e.g., bending a body part), enactment with props (e.g., moving a scarf to the flow of music), and exercises on the floor or in a chair (Fisher, 1989).

Even though older clients are not as flexible in their movements, the main limitation to working with this age population is the creative abilities of the dance and movement therapist or counselor. Dances, including aerobics, have proved useful to people in this age range (Atterburg, Sorg, & Larson, 1983; Lindner, 1982). The main emphasis of any movement or dance, however, should be on improving participants' self-esteem, physical well-being, socialization, and sense of accomplishment.

General Population

Jacobs (1992) devised a number of movement techniques to use in counseling with people of various ages. Jacobs stated that in using these techniques counselors may need to move either closer or farther away from clients at times to illustrate the movement/ dance going on in the therapeutic setting. In such cases, counselors should move with caution and inform clients of what they are doing either before or during the time they are moving. Four of Jacobs's general techniques, which are appropriate for clients over the life span, follow.

Evaluation of Progress

In evaluation of progress, clients are asked to stand up and position themselves according to how much progress they have made during counseling. A line is drawn representing where counseling started, and a goal line is also drawn, with clients placing themselves in between. Such a procedure may be especially powerful for clients who have become resistant to counseling or who are concrete thinkers and need to visualize their progress (*Evaluation of Progress*).

Feeling Pulled

The idea behind the feeling pulled technique is that clients often have forces in their lives that impede their progress in reaching goals. In this activity, a client is asked to start moving toward his or her goals with the counselor holding onto his or her arm and pulling him or her backward. The right amount of tug is agreed to by the client. The counseling session then turns to identifying what forces with what levels of power are inhibiting the client (*Feeling Pulled*).

Circles

When clients do the same thing over and over, they fail to make progress. In circles, clients are asked to walk around in the same direction a number of times to get a better feel for what doing the same thing again and again is like. It is hoped this realization leads to insight and new directions for the therapy (*Circles*).

Movement Between Chairs

The premise behind movement between chairs is that clients sometimes need to experience their vacillation with regard to decisions they have discussed but failed to make. In movement between chairs, clients are asked to simply move continuously between two or more chairs that represent decisions they could make. They are not to speak, unless they have something new to say at the end of bouncing back and forth between chairs, which should go on a minimum of 2 to 3 minutes (*Movement Between Chairs*).

Groups

When individuals enter a group, they often feel a great deal of tension. The other people are strangers, and everyone sometimes feels ill at ease about what to say or do. The ability of people to feel relaxed in the group and for the group to provide a structure that is supportive, safe, and predictable is crucial if members of the group and the group as a whole are going to function well (Gladding, 2016; Sandel & Johnson, 1996). In these situations some creative movement can help alleviate tension, break down barriers, and energize the group as a whole.

One way of promoting the formation of a group is called Train Station, which comes from Playfair (http://www.Playfair.com), an organization dedicated to putting fun back into the workplace. In Train Station, the group is divided in two. Half of the group is designated to be the greeters and the other half the passengers. The group is then given the following instructions: Each greeter has just received a phone call from a best friend from early childhood. It has now been a number of years since they saw each other, but the former best

Creative Reflection

Which of Jacobs's four techniques for adults do you think might be most effective overall? What makes you think so? Which of the techniques do you gravitate to most? Why?

friend is to arrive in a few hours at the train station in the city where the greeter now lives. After agreeing to meet the friend, the greeter is so excited that he or she hangs up the phone without thinking to ask what the person who called looks

like. Lacking this information, the greeter goes to the train station at the designated hour and decides that the best strategy to use in this situation is to move slowly but with enthusiasm toward the group of passengers now arriving. With arms waving, the greeters as a group move in slow motion as if running though a field of wheat toward the passengers, who all display similar behaviors. As each greeter gets to a passenger, looks are exchanged but then both realize the person he or she is exchanging glances with is not the right person; both then look away and toward another person in the immediate area who also turns out not to be the right person. This activity continues until all the greeters and passengers have passed each other, after which participants are given a chance to voice how they experienced the exercise. They are then informed by the leader of the group that nothing they ever do in the group will be as embarrassing . . . or perhaps as much fun (*Train Station*).

Another exercise suggested by Mintz (1971) to help a group experience a good beginning is known as Hand Dialog. In this exercise, two individuals are partners. They are seated and then instructed to improvise dances with their hands with one person initially leading and the other following. They put their hands together and may choose to keep their eyes open, but they are encouraged to close their eyes to get the full impact of this nonverbal experience. Participants may use their fingers, palms, or both in doing their dance. Likewise, they may use the front or back of their hands. After dancing with their hands for 60 to 90 seconds in one position, the leader instructs them to switch positions of being either a leader or a follower. Talking is reserved for after the dance has finished. Time is set aside for discussions between pairs, and then the group as a whole talks about feelings and emotions associated with what they have been through and how such affect is expressed nonverbally (*Hand Dialog*).

A similar type of movement dance that comes at the start of many groups, but can be implemented during the working stage of the group as well, is called Shadows. This exercise involves one person imitating another in a follow-the-leader style. Sometimes it is done in silence, but it is not unusual to have Shadows occur to music. The type of music chosen can help encourage interaction and break down inhibitions. After the event, participants talk about their experience in groups of two, four, eight, and then in the group as a whole (*Shadows*). Again, this type of movement opens individuals up to more awareness and gives them a common experience as a basis for sharing.

Families

The complex way individuals in families relate to each other is often referred to as the family dance (A. Y. Napier & Whitaker, 1978). In healthy families, "the partners do not need to hold on tightly . . . because they know they are . . . moving to the same rhythm" (Lindbergh, 1955/1975, p. 104). In dysfunctional families, however, members cling closely to one another and hesitate to let their members change, much less leave home (Haley, 1978). Thus, the results of family dances are either positive or negative. Healthy families move to resolve common problems and move toward final completion of themselves as a functional, working unit. Unhealthy families take steps to hinder the growth of persons within the family unit by keeping them developmentally delayed and stuck in nonproductive patterns.

Three family dance and movement exercises can assist families in distress. One is family choreography, which involves the whole family in a physical and mental experience. The other two are enactment and paradox, which are more artistic ways to help families move in harmony.

In family choreography, different members of the family stage a moment in time in the family's life. Then specific movements are given to each player and repeated until members of the family get a feel for the multiple interconnectedness of their lives (*Family Choreography*). This approach is well illustrated in the work of Papp (1982), in which married couples were assisted in acting out their patterns of behavior in this manner. The exercise resulted in a change in the couples' present actions and a potential metaphorical memory trace of what movements could be positive in the marriage.

In enactment, the counselor directs the family members to do a dance movement representing what they are stuck in, such as an inability to resolve arguments, and to show what happens during each step. This type of direction takes the involuntary nature away from the action in which the family members are stuck and places it in the hands of the counselor. Therefore, even if the family members do not resolve their disputes, their relationships with each other change. They have to try another (more positive) way of settling their disputes because of the power they have given the counselor to direct their old, nonproductive patterns (*Enactment*).

In paradox, a type of reverse enactment takes place. The counselor basically tells the family they cannot do something, such as change, or the counselor instructs the family to go slow. The results are either that the family obeys and moves differently under the counselor's direction or they rebel and change to resist the counselor's instructions (*Paradox*). Change in patterns and movement within the family are the end product.

Dance and Movement in Counseling With Other Creative Arts

Dance and movement in counseling can use techniques from other disciplines such as yoga (breathing techniques and different postures), classical ballet (emphasis on verticality), and even other partner dances such as Tango, Paso Doble, and Swing (with their focus on rhythmic synchrony) to connect people with their bodies, to anchor them physically to the ground, and to relate them to others (de Tord & Bräuninger, 2015). Dance and movement have many common elements with other creative arts. Fisher (1989) noted, "Shape, space, time, and force are used by dancers, artists, and musicians alike" (p. 51). On a specific level, dance is usually associated with the creative art form of music. After all, music provides a rhythmic background that can heavily influence the types and frequency with which persons engage in dance. Other art forms that have an influence on dance and movement are drama and art.

Dance and Movement and Music

> In many cultures the root word for music and dance are the same. It would be inconceivable for people in some parts of the world to remain motionless while music is played, or to move together rhythmically except with the support of music. (Chace, 1967, p. 25)

In the United States, the natural connectedness between dance and music is exemplified in society in a number of ways, including the following two sentences of a newspaper story about a college basketball team preparing to play in the annual National Collegiate Athletic Association (NCAA) tournament: "Some call the NCAA Tournament the 'big dance,' others the 'grand ball.' In either case, Wake Forest is ready to face the music" (D. Collins, 1991, p. C1).

Regardless of how it is portrayed, the linkage of music with movement occurs frequently when dance and movement are accompanied by rhythm and sound. One example is Project TOUCH, an intergenerational program between kindergarten children and residents of a geriatric facility (Mason-Luckey & Sandel, 1985). In this situation, the children and their older partners sing certain songs and move accordingly. Thus, in expressing feelings about fantasy and hope, the group sings the Texas folk song "Bluebird Through My Window" while standing in a circle holding hands. As the song is sung, a person designated as the bluebird flies

Creative Reflection

Have you ever thought of drama as movement or dance? What are your impressions now of drama as a part of movement or dance?

through the spaces (frames) made by the arms and finally lands within the circle and designates another person to become the bluebird.

Another example of music and dance pairing up is in the use of both to help homeless children learn problem-solving strategies (Straum, 1993). Although the combination did not produce significant results compared with more verbal methods, it did foster good participation and helped children to stay on task.

Dance and Movement and Drama

Dramatic activities that can be used as adjuncts to dance therapy have been outlined by D. R. Johnson and Eicher (1990). According to these practitioners, dramatic techniques are effective with adolescents in dance therapy because they mediate the threat of intimacy members of this population feel. Basically, the techniques work internally "by decreasing the ambiguity of emotional and feeling states" and externally "by providing a safer container for the aggressive drives stimulated by the intimate environment" (p. 163). Drama techniques such as labeling feelings, freezing action, and defining linear space can help unsure adolescents feel safe within themselves and secure with others.

Other successful dramatic activities include these exercises:

- *Adverbs.* One member of a group leaves the room, and the others decide on an adverb (a word ending in *ly*; e.g., *warmly*). When the member returns, he or she asks designated members to act out a task in a way that reflects the chosen adverb and tries to guess what it is (*Adverbs*).
- *Chair Game.* Group members decide on a famous person while one member of the group is gone. When that person returns, he or she is treated like the famous person by others in the group until he or she guesses that person's identity (*Chair Game*).
- *Areas.* The room is marked off into different feeling areas such as sad, bored, happy, and angry. Each member of the group spends time in these areas and tries to embody that emotion. Then members reassemble and talk about how each experience felt (*Areas*).
- *Environments.* The group breaks into two teams, and each creates an environment for the other, such as the surface of the moon or a tropical jungle. After going through or participating in the environment, the teams reassemble and talk about the experience and how it relates to their lives (*Environments*).

Overall, dramatic techniques such as these get adolescents moving in many directions and interacting with different people in novel ways. After adolescents have participated in dance therapy experiences, they usually are not intimidated and in fact may welcome opportunities to be more expressive and creative.

Dance and Movement and Art

When working with people with eating disorders, for whom perception of self is greatly distorted, dance and movement are sometimes combined with projective drawings (Krueger & Schofield, 1986). The idea in this treatment is to help clients to

- immediately visualize the movement experience they just had,
- give them a way to symbolize and objectify this experience in a drawing,
- depict current developmental issues that have arisen because of what they have been through,
- provide a concrete means (i.e., the drawing) to bridge the transition between nonverbal and verbal means of expression, and
- measure progress and change.

   Drawings are usually made at the end of each dance and movement therapy session, and the individual and overall affects of the drawings are analyzed by practitioners for patterns and symbols that will help create insight. Art and movement are also combined in the treatment of chemically dependent individuals. In this inpatient work, "concrete art and movement tasks are applied to parallel" (Potocek & Wilder, 1989, p. 99) each of the first four steps of Alcoholics Anonymous (http://www.aa.org). For example, in Step 1, in which addicts admit they are powerless over alcohol, participants construct with chairs the walls of a pit while despondent, self-absorbing music plays in the background. They take turns climbing over the walls and sitting in the pit in the midst of a darkened room. While there, they draw their feelings on a large piece of brown paper on the floor. In all four steps, similar movement and art exercises are expereienced with the intent of promoting abstract thinking and making intangible emotions clear.

Summary

Dance and movement therapy is a worldwide phenomenon, with dance and movement therapists living and working throughout the United States, Canada, Europe, South America, Asia, the Middle East, Africa, and Australia (ADTA, 2015). Dance and movement are physically demanding and energizing art forms. Their use in counseling varies, but in general they are used to help clients become more aware of their bodies, boundaries, and interpersonal relationships. They provide integrative ways of helping individuals of all ages and stages in life become more whole. They free people to move in ways that talk alone does not allow. Dance differs from movement in its emphasis on performance and music, but both stress that clients become actively involved in the therapeutic process. Through dance and movement clients are freed up to talk about their situations.

Some counseling theories, including psychoanalysis, gestalt, and social learning approaches, advocate and use dance and movement techniques. These procedures are more active with children than with older adults. Families and groups also use dance and movement, especially choreography, in ways that are unique and innovative. In movement, insight occurs and may be translated into ways of living a more productive life. Overall, dance and movement can be combined with a number of other creative arts, such as music, drama, and drawing, to enrich and enliven counseling sessions and to promote change and growth.

Exercises

1. Focus on your most physically active time of life. What did you learn from your body that now affects your practice as a counselor? For instance, are you more verbally direct when you are fatigued, or do you need a specific amount of exercise to feel mentally alert? Discuss your need or lack of need for movement with a colleague and notice how much structured or spontaneous physical activity plays a part in the life of your clients.

2. A dance is usually described as movement that is structured and usually performed on some level in public. What types of dances do you observe among clients and nonclients you know? How do such dances either get to the heart of issues or sidestep important issues?

3. Lead a milling-around exercise with a group of trusted friends or colleagues. In this exercise, individuals simply walk around and participate with others as instructed by the leader—by making or not making eye contact, by touching or not touching each other with shoulders or elbows. The idea is to assess how comfortable each member feels moving in a certain manner. The entire exercise is brief (about 2 to 5 minutes) and is processed with the group leader for as long as needed afterward (*Milling-Around*).

Chapter 4

Imagery and Counseling

An Image of Timothy

In my mind there's a picture of Timothy
and a vision of nonverbal memories.
Awakened to that awareness
I walk lightly and with joy
as a man having watched the birth of his son.
White clouds blow in the cool March air
but my sight is focused on a previous night
when new life and movement came into being
through the rhythmic cries of an infant.

—Gladding, 1991b/2010

"Images are a deep and universal psycho-neurological construct though which people process their experiences. Being central to human functioning, images contribute to the individual's sense of self, to the ability to remain oriented in the world and to pursue goals effectively in light of memories of past experiences and future problem solving based on them" (Sarid & Huss, 2011, p. 252). Conversely, imagery can be defined simply as "perception that comes through any of the senses—sight, smell, touch, taste, hearing, and feeling" (Kanchier, 1997, p. 14). Imagery is sometimes described as seeing with the mind's eye or as having an inner vision. It allows a person to create and, in essence, symbolically experience imagined results of behavior before an activity is performed (Manz & Neck, 2013). The use of imagery is one of the most powerful of human faculties. By using imagery, people can learn, rehearse, and solve problems (Myrick & Myrick, 1993). They can address present and future possibilities up to a point (Yaniv, 2014). Thus, imagery is a tool for working with and working through a person's environment and circumstances (Alvares, 1998). It is paradoxical: On one hand, imagery is passive, requiring little if any physical movement; on the other hand, imagery is complex in that those who practice it usually deal with a number of complicated matters that they must arrange or rearrange. Furthermore, imagery may be positive and inspire individuals to be more than they ever thought possible, such as a hero, or imagery may be negative, disempowering and marginalizing individuals. This latter type of imagery is often thought of as a "controlling image" and is pervasive in mass media where, for instance, women are pictured as sex objects or secondary to men (Hammer, 2009).

Imagery has an extraordinarily rich history in the helping professions (Achterberg & Lawlis, 1984; Utay & Miller, 2006). The ancient Egyptians and Native Americans used it (and in the second case still use it) as a way of helping. Many religious traditions including Christianity and Hinduism use imagery in their worship. In addition, traditional Chinese medicine has employed imagery in its service. Indeed, therapists and shamans in many cultures use or have used imagery, especially guided imagery, to promote positive change in personal and interpersonal relationships. Furthermore, considerable research supports the use of imagery in counseling and in allied health fields (Figley, 1986; J. Sommers-Flanagan & Sommers-Flanagan, 2015). For example, imagery has been found to be positively associated with the process of learning (Luria, 1968), memory (Arbuthnott, Arbuthnott, & Rossiter, 2001), relaxation techniques (Richardson, 1969), life meaning (Jung, 1953; J. C. Mills & Crowley, 1986), life enjoyment (Lazarus, 1977; Witmer, 1985), leadership (Neck, Stewart, & Manz, 1995), promotion of diversity (Russell-Chapin & Stoner, 1995), clarification of feelings beyond facts (O'Neill, 1997), and asthma relief, with an overall improvement in happiness, anxiety, and quality of life for the participants (Dobson, Bray, Kehle, Theodore, & Peck, 2005).

The titles and lyrics of popular songs such as John Lennon's "Imagine," Smokey Robinson's "It Was Just My Imagination," and the Buckinghams' "Imagine You and Me" emphasize

the significance of imagery in the life of people and its importance in promoting everything from peace to love relationships. Furthermore, the concept of the dream and envisioning a future is stressed in a variety of ways, such as in the words of the *South Pacific* song "Happy Talk" and the "I Have a Dream" speech of Martin Luther King Jr. The dream catcher symbol in American Indian tradition and the dream concept of life development for men elaborated on by D. J. Levinson, Darrow, Klein, Levinson, and McKee (1978) are also powerful conveyers of the potence and importance of vision. Almost all counseling theories and procedures depend to some extent on imagery (Gordon, 1978). It is a universal and natural modality for helping people engender, promote, or face change.

The two dominant types of images are visual and auditory, but there are as many images as there are sensations (e.g., sounds, touches, smells, tastes, and sights). Weinhold (1987) wrote, "Imagery is the language of the unconscious and, as such, it serves as a tool for bringing unconscious material to conscious awareness" (p. 9). Sometimes images spontaneously appear in the mind's eye without active, personal prompting, for example, free-association daydreams (Klinger, 1987). At other times, images are directed; that is, they are amplified or creatively enhanced like scenes in a Hollywood or Broadway production. Counseling usually focuses on elimination of unwanted spontaneous images that cause pain or distress and on promotion of directed images that help individuals relax and enjoy the inner and outer worlds in which they live (Witmer & Young, 1985, 1987).

In this chapter, I explore the multidimensional premise behind the power of imagery as well as the practical use of imagery in counseling. In addition, I explain and illustrate how imagery can be used with a variety of populations (from children to older adults) and in various settings (from groups to career counseling). The use of imagery with other creative arts (such as music and movement) is also discussed.

Premise of the Use of Imagery in Counseling

Several reasons exist for using imagery in counseling (Enns, 2001). A major one is related to what Bernie S. Siegel (1986) called a "weakness of the body: it cannot distinguish between a vivid mental experience and an actual physical experience" (p. 153). Therefore, in helping people help themselves, imagery may work as powerfully as actual behavior. This type of mental practice is seen most graphically among athletes and actors who imagine a winning performance and perform better as a result.

A second reason for using imagery in counseling is that it is an available resource that is already used in some form by clients. Almost all people carry mental pictures around in their minds, and tapping into these images has advantages (Ashen, 1977). For example, visual imagery can be used as a fast way of learning new material or remembering experiences, especially if affect is involved (Huss & Sarid, 2014). Visual images that contain emotional content are encoded in memory more rapidly and intensely than images devoid of emotional content. Through visualization, goals can be seen, and individuals can gain a clearer picture of themselves.

> A visual matrix is the building block of the most delicate and sophisticated information. Music notation is displayed visually; blueprints for buildings are visual guides; maps for air and space travel are visual; and computers have been designed to give visual readouts to maximize information provided to the user. (S. R. Lankton & Lankton, 1983, p. 327)

"Imagineering" solutions is a concept that designers and engineers use at the theme parks of Walt Disney; envisioning what they want a ride or attraction to look like or do sets the stage for imagining ways they can make the image real.

Auditory images such as voices are extremely valuable too. Milton Erickson, one of the leading pioneers in the counseling and therapy field, used to tell his clients and students, "My voice will go with you." This assurance made it easier for individuals to leave his sessions. It helped those he worked with remember what they had heard him say. It is common for people to remember auditory experiences associated with specific situations. Research on self-instruction indicates that those who give themselves auditory commands before performing an action do their tasks more efficiently and quickly than

Creative Reflection

When have you given yourself an auditory command? How did it affect the activity in which you were engaged? When have you seen others give themselves auditory instruction? What were the results?

those who are not prepared in this manner (Dattilo & Rusch, 2012; Ryan, Lynch, Vansteenkiste, & Deci, 2011).

Tactile (touch), olfactory (smell), and taste (gustatory) sensations are valuable assets in the art of counseling. Sometimes clients describe their feelings with regard to one of these senses, just as the minor character Marcellus in *Hamlet* does when he states, "Something is rotten in the state of Denmark" (Act 1, Scene 4). A phrase such as "I just want to get a handle on it" cues the counselor into the client's preferred ways of experiencing the world (Bandler & Grinder, 1975). Such information can be used to find images and therapeutic solutions that are agreeable to the client.

A third reason for using imagery, especially guided imagery, is that it is valuable for counselors and clients in "developing cognitive flexibility. It teaches people how to use their imagination as a tool for stimulating creativity and for loosening the tight grip of the so-called normal waking state of consciousness" (Weinhold, 1987, p. 9). Clients' former excuses for not taking action lose some of their power, and clients are seen as more capable than before. They have hidden mental resources that can be tapped and used to promote positive change. Their chances for breaking dysfunctional patterns are greatly enhanced, and their versatility in helping themselves is similarly magnified (Fisher, 1989; Kress, Adamson, Demarco, Paylo, & Zoldan, 2015).

A fourth reason for using imagery in counseling is that many client problems are connected directly to their images of self and others (Singer, 2006). One of the most graphic examples of this phenomenon is eating disorders (Justice, 1994). People with eating disorders almost inevitably have a distorted image of their body. However, concerns linked to images that individuals carry with them range from low self-concept and social ineptness to destructive game playing (Berne, 1964). Counselors who are image conscious and work with their clients from this perspective are much more likely to be effective than those who are not focused this way.

A final reason for using imagery in counseling is that it promotes a holistic approach to working with individuals by helping them connect their outside and inside worlds (Eisenstein-Naveh, 2001). Through imagery, many different aspects of one's personhood and environment can be examined and changed, if desired (Gawain, 1978). For instance, relationships, health habits, and talents may be assessed and modified appropriately by experiencing them in imagery form and then in real-life situations. The importance of imagery in counseling is well represented in the systematic and comprehensive perspective of Arnold A. Lazarus's (2000) multimodal therapy. In this approach, clients are assessed with regard to BASIC ID, an acronym in which each letter represents an area in life—behavior, affect, sensation, imagery, cognition, interpersonal relationships, and drugs or biology.

By working with people from this broad base, counselors are better able to identify difficulties that can be corrected and help their clients become more integrated.

Practice of the Use of Imagery in Counseling

Imagery is used in many different ways in counseling (Hall, Hall, Stradling, & Young, 2006). Sigmund Freud was among the first in the modern treatment of mental disorders to be concerned with imagery and its meaning, especially in dreams. It was Freud who emphasized the manifest (obvious) and latent (hidden) meanings of dreams and described dreams as the "royal road to the unconscious" (Freud, 1900/1953). It was also Freud who insisted his patients lie on a couch when trying to access their images, a position that modern research supports as enhancing the quantity and quality of images produced, possibly due to its association with relaxation, sleep, and dreams and daydreams (Sheikh, 2002; Sheikh, Sheikh, & Moleski, 1985).

Carl Jung expressed a great interest in symbols and images also, whether inside or outside dreams. He was particularly interested in images with universal qualities, which he called *archetypes* (e.g., the earth mother, the wise old man, the hero, rebirth). It was Jung's idea that certain images unite people with one another and with themselves. For instance, the *mandala* (see Figure 3), a Sanskrit word for "sacred circle," is a universal sign of wholeness and completeness that is embraced worldwide and that Jung thought was used in various forms as clients become healthier (Jung, 1968). He believed that mandalas denote a unification of opposites, serve as expressions of the self, and represent the sum of who we are. Indeed,

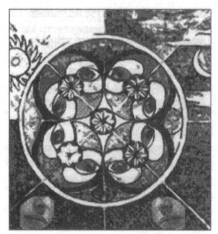

Figure 3 Mandala

Eastern cultures have used specific mandalas for visual meditation for many centuries. The Tibetan Buddhist Kalachakra, also known as the Wheel of Time, is probably one of the most famous mandalas and symbolically illustrates the entire structure of the universe. Circular forms are found at the prehistoric Stonehenge monument in England and the 13th century labyrinth at the base of Chartres Cathedral in France. Spiritual seekers have consistently created mandalas to bring forth the sacred through images and have evoked the circle in ritual and art making for the purpose of transcendence, mindfulness, and wellness. (Malchiodi, 2010b, para. 2)

In a research study examining the benefits of processing traumatic events through the creation of mandalas for people with posttraumatic stress disorder (PTSD), it was found that compared with a control group, individuals assigned to the experimental mandala-creation group reported greater decreases in symptoms of trauma at the 1-month follow-up (P. Henderson, Rosen, & Mascaro, 2007). There were no other statistically significant outcome differences. Yet, as these researchers pointed out, alternative modes of processing traumatic events (e.g., visually, symbolically) may serve individuals who are either reluctant or unable to write or talk about their experiences.

Outside of depth therapy, as espoused by these clinicians, imagery is embraced and used extensively by other counseling traditions, especially those based in humanistic and cognitive behavioral theories. The most outrageous way imagery is used is in the humanistic, existential family therapy approach of Carl Whitaker. In his work, Whitaker was known to fall asleep (leaving his cotherapist in charge), have a dream, and then share the images and experience of the dream with the family with whom he was working (A. Y. Napier & Whitaker, 1978). The art of this process is found both in the content and process of what Whitaker did. He gave the family a different picture of who they were and one with which they could not rationally argue. At the same time, he unbalanced the family unit by doing something unexpected and thereby enabled them to think and interact in a manner that was different from their routine.

In gestalt therapy, fantasy and imagery are used in some novel ways as well. Dreams are seen as the road to integration (Perls, 1969). As such, gestalt therapists encourage their clients to re-create and relive their dreams in the present. This procedure requires clients to become all parts of their dreams, and in doing so they must ask themselves such questions as, "What am I feeling?" "What do I want?" "What is my dream telling me?" (Rainwater, 1979). By enacting, questioning, and becoming aware of the many variables within dreams, individuals who work from a gestalt perspective become more integrated because they recognize and accept the polarities within themselves that they have previously projected onto others. With this acceptance, they are able to complete unfinished business in their backgrounds, such as unacknowledged grief, anger, or loss (Gladding, 1991f).

A similar way imagery is used in a holistic manner is exemplified by the humanistic psychologist Abraham H. Maslow (1991), who used imagery to help people gain a greater sense of gratitude toward others and the blessings of life. Maslow advocated imagining the death of someone for whom a person cares and thinking as vividly as possible about what would be truly lost and about what one would most grieve. After imagining in this way, the client's thinking would shift to how to conduct a complete good-bye and how to best preserve the memory of the person. Another technique he proposed was imagining oneself dying and in the process vividly seeing and saying good-bye to the people one loves best (*Saying Good-Bye, Getting Closure*). These techniques, Maslow stated, could prevent repetitive rumination or a sense of incompleteness, such as he suffered with regard to the loss of Alfred Adler with whom he had a slight argument shortly before Adler's death. Imagery of this type can promote health too.

Imagery is used in several ways in cognitive behavioral approaches. For example, in rational emotive hypnotherapy, emphasis is placed on here-and-now imagery of recent events and regressive imagery of remote events (W. L. Golden, 1986). In both cases, the use of imagery is emphasized as a way of understanding maladaptive thoughts and behaviors and devising strategies for changing them. Even more popular is rational emotive imagery, in which clients keep complete conscious control of their facilities (Maultsby, 1977, 1990). In this process clients are helped to create mental frames of reference for behaving rationally. They imagine themselves thinking, emotionally feeling, and physically behaving exactly the way they want to think, feel, and act in real life. When people combine rational emotive imagery with physical practice, they learn new emotional as well as physical habits in the shortest possible time (Maultsby, 1990).

In behaviorally based treatment, clients are sometimes asked to symbolically re-create a problematic life situation and then imagine it actually happening to them. "When clients have conjured up an image of a situation, they are then asked to verbalize any thoughts that come to mind, an especially useful way of uncovering the specific thoughts associated with particular events" (G. T. Wilson, 2011, p. 239). This particular technique is especially helpful during assessment to uncover thoughts associated with events of which clients may not be initially aware (*Symbolically Re-Create a Problematic Life Situation*).

Another use of imagery in counseling is found in systematic desensitization (Wolpe, 1958). In this therapeutic method, clients are requested to construct a hierarchy of different situations that trouble them, starting with those that

Creative Reflection

What do you think of Maslow's ideas regarding the use of imagery? How might you use either of his suggestions in helping yourself grow as a person?

are mildly disturbing and working up to those that cause major concern. They are then instructed to clearly picture each situation as they work up the hierarchy with the counselor and to simultaneously relax (*Systematic Desensitization*).

Creative Reflection

A Broadway play of the 1970s was titled *Don't Bother Me, I Can't Cope*. How do you think imagery can help people cope and be more productive in their daily lives?

The idea behind this method is that being relaxed and anxious are incompatible responses (i.e., reciprocal inhibition) and that clients can be taught to become relaxed in the presence of a situation that previously was bothersome. In other words, one emotion (relaxation or pleasure) is used to counteract another (anxiety), with imagery playing a major role in the process (McKay, Davis, & Fanning, 1981).

Imagery may also be used to cope with physical pain by incorporating pain into one's life rather than fighting it (Cupal & Brewer, 2001; Kleinke, 2002; Pincus & Sheikh, 2009). This type of incorporation can occur through dissociation (imagining the hurt outside of the body), fantasy (fantasizing that one is suffering for a good cause), imagining numbness, and focusing on sensations (studying what the feelings are like) (*Incorporating Pain Into One's Life Rather Than Fighting It*).

Two major outcomes of counseling occur in image form if treatment has been successful. The first is a change in self-imagery from a negative to a positive: Clients see themselves as more capable. The second change relates to coping images, which change from pictures of being out of control and helpless to images of being able and capable even in severe situations (Kress et al., 2015; Lazarus, 2000). Clients modify their outlook of themselves and function in a more healthy way when they see themselves differently.

Imagery in Counseling With Specific Populations

A number of client populations can benefit particularly from the use of imagery (Shorr, 2002). Imagery may help in working with individuals suffering from PTSD (Grigsby, 1987; Smucker & Dancu, 1999), career decision making (Hartung & Subich, 2010; Skovholt, Morgan, & Negron-Cunningham, 1989), self-injury (Kress et al., 2015), bulimia (Gunnison & Renick, 1985; Ohanian, 2002), difficulty in couple communications (Hendrix, 2008), and parenting problems (Skovholt & Thoen, 1987). Imagery may be used also in preventative and educational activities for children, such as enhancing self-esteem and reducing anxiety (Myrick & Myrick, 1993; Witmer & Young, 1987).

Counselors may benefit from using imagery and value it as a tool both for personal growth and for use with clients (J. Davis &

Brown, 2000). An excellent use of imagery in counseling in the 1980s was the Counselor of Tomorrow project sponsored by the Association for Counselor Education and Supervision (ACES), in which a film using numerous images helped professionals envision possible futures. Another has been the "20/20: Futures of Counseling" initiative in which 30 counseling associations in the United States came together to envision what counseling can be like in the year 2020. Counseling conventions, such as the American Counseling Association Conference of 1997, have even focused on minding counselor images and promoting counseling through the use of positive images. The following are some specific examples of the ways imagery can be used by counselors in working with clients at different ages and stages of life.

Children

Preschool children often feel they have little or no control over their lives, and they are often right. Directed imaging can be used to empower such children. One way it can be used is through imagining games, during which a teacher or parent reads a passage to children from a structured exercise book, such as Richard de Mille's (1967) *Put Your Mother on the Ceiling* or Joseph E. Shorr's (1977) *Go See the Movie in Your Head*. The children then visualize the scene. These types of imagery games at their best create divergent thinking, motivate and challenge children, and bring fun into the lives of those involved. They foster freedom in a constructive way not otherwise possible. When done properly, imagery games are always interspersed with reality-based exercises. Thus, they help promote within young children appreciation for imagery and reality (*Imagining Games for Children*). A useful book on the uses of imagery in counseling is *Imagery and Symbolism in Counseling* (Stuart, 1997), a comprehensive text that explores the therapeutic use of imagination and how myths, legends, and spontaneous images can be used in making feelings easier to work with and control.

For elementary school children with low self-esteem, imagery is valuable in enhancing their self-concept. One way this can be done is by having children look at themselves through the eyes of a special person (Childers, 1989). In this exercise, children pretend to be artists, and in this role they draw special people in their lives who love them. After the drawings are finished (just one drawing per child), the children pretend to be the special people whom they have drawn and to see themselves through loving eyes. Then they reassociate back into their own bodies and bring back with them loving feelings from the experience (*Through Loving Eyes*).

When using guided imagery with children in a school setting, Myrick and Myrick (1993, pp. 63–65) suggested five guidelines to make the experience enjoyable and productive:

1. *Create a scripted story.* A script helps the counselor to select the right words for an activity as well as to concentrate on creating a proper mood.
2. *Set the mood.* Setting a mood consists of two parts. First is introducing the activity to students. Second is helping students find a comfortable and relaxed position for participating in the imagery exercise.
3. *Speak softly and smoothly.* When the counselor speaks in a relaxed and soothing way, students are able to concentrate on the imagery, not the counselor.
4. *Bring closure to the guided imagery experience.* This can be accomplished in a number of ways, such as posing a final question or simply informing students that the imagery activity is about to come to a close.
5. *Discuss the experience.* If children are to benefit from an imagery activity, they need to be able to share their experiences with others. A discussion of what occurred may be directed by the counselor asking specific questions, or it may take a more open-ended format. The important point is that children get to air their thoughts and feelings.

Overall, imagery is a powerful and potentially effective force in working with children. Most children do not have a hard time imagining, and by tapping into this creative force, counselors can use it to promote growth and health within members of this population.

Adolescents and Adults

Much of the inner lives of adolescents and adults involve imagery too. For example, one summary of the literature reports that sexual fantasies are quite common in men and women from late adolescence through midlife and are rivaled only by problem-solving daydreams (Pope, Singer, & Rosenberg, 1984). Sexual fantasies may be used therapeutically to enhance a couple's sex life and overall relationship in the treatment context devised by Masters and Johnson (1970) or in other forms of couples, or even individual, counseling (*Relationship and Sexual Imagery*). Likewise, problem-solving daydreams can be used to help adolescents and adults anticipate and productively respond ahead of time to developmental situations they expect to face (*Problem-Solving Daydreams*).

With adolescents and adults, imagery exercises can be taught as a skill that can be used in the alleviation of depression (Schultz, 1984) and the modification of anger (F. F. Kaplan, 1994). With regard to depression, for example, people can be taught to imagine something that makes them angry and thereby gain control over the imaging process and the feelings associated with certain symbols. Similarly, they may learn socially gratifying imagery and positive imagery procedures and use these methods to temporarily or permanently combat depressive thoughts (*Depression and Imagery*). The use of imagery as a visual art form, especially in combination with verbal directive techniques, powerfully produces "more extensive and long-lasting improvements" (Schultz, 1984, p. 143) than most other forms of treatment. It enhances "the effectiveness of verbal cognitions in altering unpleasant moods" (F. F. Kaplan, 1994, p. 139).

Imagery can also be helpful in making transitions associated with immigration and living in a new culture. Toffoli and Allan (1992) found that guided imagery worked well with a group of adolescents enrolled in English as a second language class; it provided these teens with an opportunity to finish some of the unfinished business they had before immigrating to Canada. In this experience, students not only had a chance to relax and tap into their thoughts and memories but also were given an "opportunity to draw, write, and talk about their former school experiences and to learn about those of their classmates" (p. 140). A secondary benefit of this 16-session activity was that those involved enjoyed it "even when painful or negative feelings" were tapped (p. 140). Furthermore, language and writing skills improved during the process.

Overall, imagery seems to be highly correlated with the mental and physical health of adolescents and adults (Franklin, 2006). According to Rossman (1984),

> Imagery is receiving a tremendous resurgence of interest throughout the spectrum of the healing arts and is currently being researched in major medical centers and universities around the world in clinical situations ranging from the treatment of chronic pain to the management of patients with cancer. (p. 232)

The intensity of the public's interest in the positive and therapeutic use of imagery in health is reflected in the best-selling status of Bernie S. Siegel's (1986) book, *Love, Medicine, and Miracles.*

Older Clients

Both free and guided imagery can be especially powerful tools in working with older persons. Guided imagery exercises can be used to help those who are growing older take relaxed trips in time either to a place they long to go or back to a place they have enjoyed before (Fisher, 1989). These imaginary trips are followed with a process session. Individuals who have traveled in their minds come back to the counselor or a group setting and share their experiences in verbal or nonverbal forms, such as talking or drawing (*Relaxed Imagery Trips for Older Adults*).

Sometimes free imagery is used, too, in largely unstructured situations in which music may be played in the background and participants are asked to dance in their minds to the sound. After the experience ends, those who are mobile may act out what they envisioned, and the less physically agile may move their limbs to the beat of the music while remaining seated.

Focused visual imagery can also improve the functioning of older clients who have mild cognitive impairments. For instance, Abraham, Neundorfer, and Terris (1993) found that 46 nursing home residents (ages 71 to 97) made significant improvements in their cognitive abilities over a 24-week period when imagery experiences were used to help them. These researchers structured their focused visual imagery group around six themes: relaxation, protection (from anxiety and stresses that come with change), self-esteem, control (i.e., working out conflicts in symbolic form), energy (including strategies for increasing energy), and transition (e.g., dealing with aging, loss, and relocation).

> ## Creative Reflection
>
> Do you think structuring visual imagery experiences on the themes outlined by Abraham, Neundorfer, and Terris (1993) could be helpful to you or your clients regardless of your age? If so, how would you modify them to fit the people and environment you are in?

Groups

Using guided imagery in group settings appears to be a promising treatment that is empirically supported. For instance, Sklare, Sabella, and Petrosko (2003) found that guided imagery could easily be combined with solution-focused therapy to create solution-focused guided imagery (SFGI). The 44 group participants in their research study reported positive results from using SFGI to address a wide range of concerns ranging from negative behavior patterns, such as procrastination, to problems with serious health consequences, such as overeating.

As an intervention, imagery works well in a number of different kinds of groups and during distinct group stages. Different imagery exercises have been suggested to enhance group process in the initial screening and follow-up processes, and in the five-stage group model suggested by Tuckman and Jensen (1977) of forming, storming, norming, performing, and adjourning. In the forming stage, which is characterized by testing and dependency, group members may be given imagery tasks that are safe and connecting. They might be asked to describe themselves in the lines of a song or poem or by presenting their life to the group in historical photographs or a life roadmap. Likewise, in the adjourning stage, during which the focus is on closure and anticipation, group members may give each other good-bye gifts in the form of future visions for themselves and others (*Enhancing Group Process Through Imagery*).

Jacobs (1992) suggested a number of projective fantasies in group settings that he had found productive. Among his favorites is one he called Common Object. In this fantasy, members of the group are encouraged to imagine themselves as a common object, such as a piece of luggage or a ladder. They are then asked to describe what their lives would be like and how they would feel if they were indeed that object. For example, as a piece of luggage, a group member might have an active life of travel and feel both exhilarated and exhausted; as a ladder, a member might feel useful in helping others reach objects such as kittens in trees or leaves in a gutter. When talking about the common object, members are encouraged to stay in the present tense. They end up talking about themselves in many ways and seeing their lives differently as a result of projection and fantasy (*Common Object*).

Families and Couples

Family and couples work is wide open for the use of imagery. It is often employed in this type of counseling. For example, couple work imago (image) therapy is a method of using vision and enactment to help married people overcome obstacles to their relationship that are based on previous life experiences and expectations (Hendrix, 2008). This eclectic approach combines elements of psychoanalysis, transactional analysis, gestalt, cognitive therapy, and systems theory. It assists couples in seeing what they are doing and what they can do better. They are instructed to practice creating the new relationship they have envisioned.

Basically, imagery can encourage the following types of activities in couples work: (a) the collection of initial information, (b) decision making, (c) clarification of power and intimacy issues, and (d) preparation for future events (L. W. Hoffman, 1983). Imagery enlivens counseling sessions and helps make interpersonal relationships more interesting and memorable. Research by Morrison and Rasp (2001) has found that facilitated imagery is a successful technique for improving both partners' marital satisfaction. In their work, these researchers randomly assigned 20 marital couples (ages 23 to 66) to two experimental groups. Both groups received three sessions of structured marital enrichment, and one group also received three facilitated imagery sessions. Posttests were given at 1 month and 4 months following treatment. Couples exposed to facilitated imagery showed greater improvement on some scales of marital satisfaction and individual psychological functioning, and these improvements persisted at the 4-month posttest. In posttest interviews, couples reported that the primary benefit of the facilitated imagery sessions was insight into themselves and their spouses.

In working with families as a whole, guided imagery can increase awareness and the process of differentiation from a person's family of origin (Pare, Shannon, & Dustin, 1996). When guided imagery is combined with genogram work (i.e., drawing and analyzing a person's family tree), individuals are better able to access their conscious and unconscious thoughts regarding their families and themselves.

Health Care Workers

Health care workers are often exposed to stress-related visual images in their work, which over time can lead to stress-related symptoms such as elevated blood pressure, anxiety, and depression. To lessen the stress of these images and to reduce subjective discomfort levels (SUDS), Huss and Sarid (2014) worked with health care professionals to transform images they had by changing the elements of the images such as shape, color, size, and texture. This process was done nonverbally through harnessing the power of participants' creativity and imagination, thus giving individuals more control over these images and reducing their stress.

Career Counseling and Life Planning

The use of imagery, especially guided imagery and daydreams, has become more prevalent in career counseling and life planning since the 1960s (Skovholt et al., 1989). Some career-counseling material, such as Holland's (1985) *Self-Directed Search*, builds into the assessment process an examination of occupational daydreams (*Occupational/Career Daydreams*). It is the contention of certain researchers, backed up by theoretical, anecdotal, and empirical data, that although daydreams and fantasies do not guarantee a dream will come true, such processes are instrumental in helping individuals "contemplate new possibilities, try out new options, and make more informed life planning decisions" (Skovholt et al., 1989, p. 288).

When guided imagery is used in career counseling and life planning, it is a "structured activity in which the counselor provides guidelines to spur the imaginations of their clients" (Heppner, O'Brien, Hinkelman, & Humphrey, 1994, p. 79). Specific methods of how this procedure is carried out vary, but when possible a concrete representation of fantasies, such as a projected life map, should be created. The use of guided imagery is somewhat suspect because of a lack of strong empirical data on its overall effects. Nevertheless, the benefits of guided imagery in career counseling include (a) flexibility in thought, (b) emphasis on the promotion of divergent thinking and the generation of more career options, (c) safety of nonthreatening and inexpensive features, and (d) enjoyability and emphasis on considering nonrational aspects in decision making (Skovholt et al., 1989).

Imagery also may be used in helping counseling students make the transition from graduate to colleague status. Pearson (2003) suggested that in this process counselor supervisors set up a ritual in which students are guided through an imagery exercise that confirms that they are now ready to leave their graduate status behind and join the ranks of professional counselors. At the end of the imagery experience, they are presented with smooth stones that metaphorically represent their transition from rough neophyte learners to polished professionals. The stones are reminders of the words in the exercise and communicate to the new counselors that they are ready to embark on their professional journey (*Transition From Graduate to Colleague Status*).

Creative Reflection

When have you been through or used a ritual to make a transition in life? Did you use imagery? If so, what was the content of the imagery? If not, do you think imagery is something you might use with a ritual in the future? How?

Imagery in Counseling With Other Creative Arts

Because imagery is often a picture in a person's mind of an event or a way of being, it helps to make the image concrete. This way of representing imagery is best found in written, movement, musical, photographic, and artistic expression.

Written Expression of Imagery

One way to write about imagery is simply to keep a daily journal or log in which dreams, daydreams, and guided fantasies are recorded. Along with recording these events, it is important to note what reactions occurred with regard to the imagery. For example, individuals are reluctant to give up some fantasies, and certain nightmares make individuals sigh in relief when they awake.

In career counseling, written exercises can be used to help clients obtain a clearer picture of who they are and what they want to do vocationally. Kanchier (1997) noted, "Guided imagery can assist clients identify the kind of work and lifestyle they want" (p. 14), especially if it is combined with other career-counseling procedures. For example, in the Career Imagery Card Sort, clients are asked to sort 150 cards with career titles into five piles (Skovholt, 1981). During sorting, clients are asked to reflect on how the occupation matches up with their daydreams. Afterward, clients pick an occupation of high interest to them based on their daydreams and are taken on a guided fantasy of a day in that specific occupation (*Career Imagery Card Sort*). After the exercise is processed, clients continue to keep track of their daydreams about careers and discuss these unsolicited fantasies with the counselor in future meetings.

Imagery and Movement

Imagery and movement can be combined in many creative ways. One of the most dynamic is choreography, in which images of a family or situation (past, present, or future) are enacted in a repetitive way.

Family choreography (Papp, 1976) is an outgrowth of family sculpting; people in a family are arranged in various physical positions in space that represent their relationships to each other at a particular moment in time (Gladding, 2015a).

Family sculpting can be compared to an image one would get from a photograph, whereas family choreography is like a videotape. Both processes are nonverbal, so participants get to experience and see themselves rather than talk about their situations. Because of this nonverbal quality, a family and counselor are able to grasp members' experiences, boundaries, and alliances more easily and immediately (*Family Choreography*).

Imagery and Music

Visualization is sometimes promoted by the use of background music. Eastern European trainers of athletes have used the "largo movements of baroque instrumental music, with their strong, regular bass-line rhythms of about 60 beats per minute" to help athletes envision winning performances (Siegel, 1986, p. 153). Any type of music can promote mental imagery as long as the listener finds it relaxing. Guided imagery and music can also be used in the treatment of people with rheumatoid arthritis (Jacobi & Eisenberg, 2001/2002) and to enhance the performance of athletes (*Guided Imagery and Music*).

In addition to its physical impact, imagery when mixed with music may have a potent psychological effect as well. For example, a combination of music therapy and guided imagery is reported to have helped a small group of women in exploring and healing personal inner wounds (Ventre, 1994). Likewise, imagery has been included in the therapeutic repertoire for work with at-risk community college students (Schieffer, Boughner, Coll, & Christensen, 2001). Guided imagery and music have also been helpful with clients facing a terminal illness (Cadrin, 2005/2006). Furthermore, combining imagery and music has been found useful in working with older clients who have physical disabilities. Specifically, imagery and music have been used to help address a broad range of past, current, and impending future issues of older populations, including bereavement, sexuality, and the aging process. Carefully selected taped classical music that ranges in length from 4 to 12 minutes was a main stimulus for creating images in this situation (Short, 1992). The key to working with clients in this way is the care shown in choosing and using the right combination of music and symbolic images to achieve a desired effect.

> ## *Creative Reflection*
>
> Music has a way of evoking many images. What music creates the most images in your mind? Do you ever see yourself acting on these images, such as becoming stronger or more assertive?

An excellent journal for exploring more about the use of imagery and music is the *Journal of the Association for Music and Imagery*.

Imagery and Pictures

The importance of concrete imagery to reinforce or supplement abstract imagery has received a good deal of attention. Popular songs of the 1970s such as Jim Croce's "Photographs and Memories" and Ringo Starr's "Photographs" underscore the perception of how photography can aid in the development of pictures in the mind. Indeed, photographs and drawings have generally been found to promote learning in children and adults in many situations (Alesandrini, 1985). The ACES Counselor of Tomorrow project mentioned previously used photographs extensively in educating counselors about the future of the counseling profession.

Photographs are helpful as supplemental material, too, especially to show children an example of what they can image. Instructing children and adults on how to form internal mental pictures of specifics is equally effective. Several studies show that analogical (similar) and abstract (new and different) imagery can aid in learning and that the use of these verbal or written types of imagery should be more widely used.

In learning information and performing a new task, an analogical image would be most appropriate, but in representing something entirely new, an abstract image would work well. An example of how such imagery can be used in counseling is found in the Mailbox exercise I have devised. In this exercise, a client is instructed to take 12 to 24 photographs of a mailbox from as many angles as possible and then bring the photos to the next session mounted on poster board. When the assignment is completed, counselor and client discuss the task and examine the pictures. In this process the client usually discovers that just as a mailbox can be looked at from many angles, so can other situations. The client is then freed by this analogy exercise to devise novel images for his or her own life (*Mailbox*). Incorporating concrete abstract images that are related to earlier learning or that are completely novel can help clients become more mentally healthy by giving them a broader vision of situations and helping them master their environments.

Imagery and Drawing

Artistic expression of imagery can be displayed many ways. One is through having individuals draw in the air what they see in their minds. This technique, which may seem silly at first, helps clients put body movement to an image and reinforces their mental picture of it through simple motor movements (*Draw in the Air What You See in Your Mind*).

Another way to express imagery is to have people draw out their visions through lines of feelings (see Chapter 5). By setting down their images concretely, clients are better able to conceptualize what they are feeling and can therefore take positive steps to work on these matters. An even more artistic expression of imagery is to have a client draw images in a freestyle way and then process the experience and drawing(s) with the counselor. A good example of clients doing self-portraits in this way is found in the work of F. B. Newton (1976), who worked with college students to have them depict themselves in various moods over time. From the sketches, clients were able to talk about other important areas of their lives (see Figure 4).

Summary

Imagery is a popular concept in counseling with a distinguished historical past. It is well grounded in research and is becoming more used and appreciated as a powerful and effective helping tool.

Just as artists know when and how to time an expression to make the biggest impact, counselors who effectively use imagery therapeutically are aware of what to do and when. They imaginatively apply their skills in a deft and dramatic fashion as a preventive and therapeutic force.

Happy   Sad

Angry   Ambivalent

Figure 4 Moods

As this chapter has emphasized, almost all counseling theories make use of imagery. It is an extremely versatile art form. Furthermore, most of the other creative arts can be combined with imagery to make an added impact on clients and assist them in more quickly resolving their concerns. For populations ranging from children to older adults, imagery is an art that counselors can draw on to help clients understand emotional situations and provide appropriate services to their clients.

Exercises

1. Imagine that someone has asked you to demonstrate the most salient material you remember from reading this chapter. How would you do it? How could imagery help you complete this task even better?

2. Examine recent issues of the *Journal of Mental Imagery* and counseling periodicals such as the *Journal of Creativity and Mental Health* and the *Arts in Psychotherapy*. In what ways is imagery being used in helping? Are there predominant patterns for using imagery? Are there special populations for whom imagery is particularly effective according to the research?

3. What career images and senses are strongest for you when you reflect on yourself currently? What images about work did you have growing up? Are there wide differences between them and the realities of what work is actually like? Discuss this experience with a colleague.

Chapter 5

Visual Arts
and Counseling

Twilight

*When all my clients have left the office
I quietly turn off the overhead lights
and watch a lingering afternoon sun
silently spread gold-tinged hues
across my cluttered desk
and onto a wooden floor canvas.
That moment fills me with a sense of awe
for the calmness of light in the movement of life.
Walking in shadows I picture past sessions
and wonder if lives I so fleetingly touched
will dare to draw out personal scenes
with the brushstrokes of beauty and grace,
Where amid solitude and reflection
they may find hope and deeper meaning
in the clarity of stillness.*

—Gladding, 1975, p. 230; revised 2003

Art can be defined generally "as an arrangement or pattern of shapes and ideas which give form to the images that reside in the cosmos of objects" (McConeghey, 2003, p. 23). The visual arts include those processes within the realm of art that focus on visually representing reality symbolically or otherwise. They encompass a wide variety of media, including painting, drawing, coloring, photography, and sculpture (Malchiodi, 2012; Shechtman & Perl-Dekel, 2000). Knowledge of human history is often "a result of the work of the artist or artisans of particular times and cultures" (Nadeau, 1984, p. 62). It is through works of art that the health of a society is gauged. Through artistic experiences, individuals often experience more unified and meaningful lives, whether they are the creators or the observers (Maslow, 1991). For instance, Titus and Sinacore (2013) found that in certain contexts art-making can foster well-being in young adult women, suggesting that counselors can encourage art-making outside sessions to help clients enhance their mental health.

From prehistoric times, humans everywhere have tended to portray their world through visual means. Art exists "in every section of the world with a diversity that corresponds to the varieties of artistic experience" (McNiff, 1997, p. 38). Indeed, some visual arts, such as painting, are "as old as human society itself" (Vick, 2012, p. 6). Cave drawings, ancient Egyptian hieroglyphics, Turkish mosaics, and Impressionist paintings are but four examples out of dozens of the ways the visual arts bring form to feeling and concreteness to perception. Hieroglyphics, in particular, are an excellent demonstration of how pictures of objects, such as animals, trees, and birds, were first visualized as words and writing (see Figure 5).

Esman (1988) stated, "To Plato, the artist was one of those endowed by the gods with a 'divine madness'" (p. 13). Thus, the artist was both privileged and plagued. The first modern attempt to confirm or discredit the divine madness idea was initiated by the German psychiatrist and art historian Hans Prinzhorn (1922/1972), who attempted to scientifically study psychic forms of expression in art at the turn of the 20th century. Prinzhorn collected approximately 5,000 pieces of art from psychiatric patients all over Europe. He suggested that "expression is a basic psychic need for all people" (McNiff, 1997, p. 39). However, because his collection of art came from the mentally disturbed, a link between artistic expression and mental instability was created or reinforced in the minds of many.

Figure 5   Hieroglyphics

Much of Prinzhorn's influence was countered, however, by another of the early leading thinkers in the mental health field, William James, who was an artist before becoming a psychologist. James's artistic sensibility and experience "were critically important in the development of his psychologi-

Creative Reflection

When have you been emotionally moved by a piece of art? Why do you think the artwork had such an impact on you?

cal and philosophical thought" (Leary, 1992, p. 152). His background influenced the way he viewed human nature, which is one reason his view of human understanding has attracted the attention of many artists, humanists, scientists, and psychologists. James viewed art as a creative and productive human experience. Indeed, later writers such as Kottler (2006) have shown that creative artists who had mental disturbances, such as Ernest Hemingway and Virginia Woolf, have been helped to live healthier lives through the expression of their artistic ability.

Regardless of the ideas surrounding them, the visual arts have been instrumental in fostering the growth of culture and the mental health of people around the world. They often are a way to uncover hidden beauty and express identity (Dittmann, 2003). Shechtman and Perl-Dekel (2000) noted, "Art, like dreams, taps the unconscious and helps individuals to bridge their inner worlds, their covert conflicts and chaotic emotions with the reality of their environments in a nonthreatening, rather playful way" (p. 289). In addition, the visual arts frequently have a lasting effect that inspires and touches on universal themes, which arise from interpersonal encounters and individual struggles. Grace, beauty, harmony, balance, and rhythm are but a few of the underlying qualities expressed in visual arts (May, 1953). Though it may be true that "the way we perceive visually is directly related to how we think and feel" (Rhyne, 1973, p. 242), it is likewise true that visual stimuli within art can influence our thoughts and emotions. According to Jourard (1971),

> Human life can . . . be likened to the work of any artist, who, facing empty canvas or shapeless clay, transmutes it into pleasing forms. At first, the picture or statue exists only as the artist's imaginative experience. When . . . done, [the] private image is transformed into a public perception. (p. 92)

In this chapter, I explore the multidimensional premise behind the power of the visual arts as well as the practical use of visual arts in counseling (e.g., serial drawings and photography). In addition, I explain and illustrate how the visual arts can be used with a variety of populations (from children to older adults) and in various settings (e.g., from hospitals to educational environments). Unique visual arts, such as counselor drawings, are also discussed. The use of the visual arts with other creative arts (e.g., music and psychodrama) is highlighted too.

Premise of the Use of Visual Arts
in Counseling

The idea of using the visual arts in counseling and therapeutic set‑
tings is mainly the result of the pioneering work and writings of five
professionals: Margaret Naumberg, Edith Kramer, Judith Rubin,
Hanna Kwiatkowska, and Elinor Ullman (Good & Rosal, 1999;
Makin, 1994; Vick, 2012). Naumberg (1966), an educator, saw art
as an essential component of education while simultaneously view‑
ing it as a means of diagnosis and therapy. For Naumberg, art was
symbolic of the person behind the work (J. Rubin, 1980). Her ideas
were influenced by psychoanalytic theory. Naumberg's traditional
psychoanalytic view stressed that

> (1) art is yet another window to the unconscious, (2) insight is central to the
> process, and (3) treatment depends on obtaining the client's own interpreta‑
> tions of his or her own symbolic art images. Naumberg is responsible for the
> *therapy* in art therapy. (Orton, 1997, p. 256)

For Edith Kramer (1971), art was more a means of controlling,
managing, and integrating destructive impulses and conflicting feel‑
ings, especially in children. E. Kramer saw art as therapeutic in and
of itself. In her view, "the artistic process and products are ways to
release conflict, reexperience it, rechannel it through sublimation,
and resolve it" (Orton, 1997, p. 256).

J. Rubin combined qualities of both her predecessors. She saw
herself as an educator, and as such emphasized creative thinking and
flexibility as essential aspects of mental health. She stressed growth
in clients through artistic means (Makin, 1994).

Kwiatkowska made her major contribution to the field of art
therapy in the area of research and family art therapy. Vick (2012)
noted, "She brought together her experiences in various psychiatric
settings in a book [*Family Therapy and Evaluation Through Art*;
Kwiatkowska, 1978] that became the foundation for working with
families through art" (p. 9).

Elinor Ullman's most outstanding contributions to the field of art
therapy were as an editor and writer.

> She founded *The Bulletin of Art Therapy* in 1961 (*The American Journal of
> Art Therapy* after 1970) when no other publication of its kind existed. . . . In
> addition, Ullman . . . published the first book of collected essays on art therapy
> [*Art Therapy in Theory and Practice*; Ullman & Dachinger, 1975/1996] that
> served as one of the few texts in the field for many years. (Vick, 2012, p. 9)

Regardless of the particular theoretical viewpoint a professional
takes, the visual arts offer many mental health benefits for their users

(Nadeau, 1984). First, the visual arts tap the unconscious and help individuals express their covert conflicts nonverbally initially. Visual arts are closer to the unconscious because visual perceptions are more archaic than cognitive or verbal expression (Freud, 1923/1961). It is through such means that people realize and own the multitude of emotions that live within them. Art as a therapy or art therapy "is an integrative approach utilizing cognitive, motor, and sensory experiences" (Tibbetts & Stone, 1990, p. 139). At its core, it may be defined as a two-phase treatment: art creation and, over time, verbalizing this experience (Blomdahl, Gunnarsson, Guregård, & Björklund, 2013).

A second benefit of using the visual arts is that they symbolize feelings in a unique, tangible, and powerful way (Nichols, 2013). The visual arts, unlike talk therapies, assist people in picturing themselves or their situations in a concrete manner. For instance, abused children "typically portray the weather as disproportionate and/or excessive in size, and as falling on contents of the drawing" (Manning, 1987, p. 15). "Expressing one's thoughts through art is one way to externalize a distressing event and to prepare for healing and recovery" (Howe, Burgess, & McCormack, 1987, p. 35). Clients in such cases are more likely to be in a position to make changes depending on what they see. By using the visual arts in counseling, a visible trail is created.

A third benefit of using the visual arts in counseling is that they inspire and help people become more connected with the transcendent and growth sides of their personalities (J. C. Mills & Crowley, 1986). When clients can envision what they have accomplished over a period of time through paintings, drawings, and sculptures, or see what they could be, they are more likely to stay with the process of change until satisfied with their progress. Through the use of the visual arts, hope is created, as is a chance for new growth that might not be achieved through traditional verbal counseling. The visual arts in counseling help "increase self-esteem by facilitating self-awareness" (Tibbetts & Stone, 1990, p. 140). It is interesting to note that such self-esteem can come through even mundane artistic processes such as paint-by-number experiences or coloring in a coloring book in which individuals are moved as they complete their paintings or filling in pictures "to a deeper level of self-acceptance and self-awareness" (L. C. Rubin, 2000, p. 272). It is as if they were co-creating. Although coloring is usually considered an activity associated with children, adult coloring books (see Figure 6) have been found to lower stress levels (Santos, 2014).

A fourth benefit of using the visual arts in counseling is that many art tasks, especially those with children, are "usually perceived as nonthreatening" (Riley, 1987, p. 21). Yet, these tasks engage clients from the

Creative Reflection

When have you had the realization that a picture is worth a thousand words? What visual art form did it involve? What did you realize in the process?

Figure 6 Adult Coloring Book

very first session and help them identify goals for counseling. The arts are helpful also in revealing client problems that are sometimes difficult to talk about, such as family violence and sexual abuse (Brooke, 1995; Hagood, 2000; J. A. Rubin, 2010; Trowbridge, 1995).

An additional benefit of using the visual arts in counseling is that they can easily be combined with other creative arts such as movement, creative writing, and imagery (McNiff, 1997; Steinhardt, 1985). The flexibility of visual arts is outstanding, and the results can be kept mentally or physically as reminders of time and circumstance. Indeed, movements, visuals, and sounds can become elements of an art piece that transform a static representation into a living expression (Moon, 1997).

Practice of the Use of Visual Arts in Counseling

Visual arts are used in counseling throughout the life span (J. A. Rubin, 2010) and with special populations such as prisoners (Gussak, 2009; Meekums & Daniel, 2011) and individuals with PTSD (D. Avrahami, 2005). Although many people claim that they cannot draw, the visual arts appeal to numerous clients. Many standard psychological projective tests, such as the *Draw-A-Person* test (Machover, 1949) and the *House-Tree-Person* test (Buck, 1948), make use of clients' artistic abilities to express how they perceive and feel about the world. Other projective tests, such as the *Rorschach* and the *Holtzman ink blots*, also incorporate artistic forms.

In setting up situations for using the visual arts in counseling, counselors should provide the best quality art materials so that clients who might otherwise be intimidated by the use of these media will become more relaxed and creative (Makin, 1994; Nadeau, 1984). Other qualities important to visual arts counseling sessions are adequate space, quiet, freedom of movement, encouragement, and time. It is essential for those who assist in visual arts therapy to be patient too. Just as great art takes time, so does psychosocial change. It may take several sessions before clients begin to enjoy and benefit from visual arts experiences. Even more delayed at times is the ability of clients to integrate art into their lives in a productive way through owning what it symbolizes as a part of themselves.

Most counselors who use visual arts in their work have received special training. Those who earn a master's degree with a concentration in art therapy from a program approved by the American Art Therapy Association (2010) are eligible to become members of the association and apply to become art therapists registered through the Art Therapy Credentials Board. As professionals, art therapists work to set up conditions in which clients can explore underlying emotional issues and perceptions using a rich source of artistic materials and methods (Kaiser, 1996). Other professionals who do not want this credential compensate for the lack of overall training in using the visual arts by concentrating their practice on specific areas in which they are competent to work. Almost all clinicians who use the arts make use of perceptual strategies employed by the client artist, including negative spaces, relationships and proportions, lights and shadows, edges, and the gestalt or total product (McClure, Merrill, & Russo, 1994). As a group, visual arts practitioners participate in many activities (J. A. Rubin, 2010). The following sections provide some general examples of these activities.

Published Pictures

One way of introducing and using the visual arts in counseling is through making the most of already existing artwork. This approach arouses minimal anxiety, and it encompasses a variety of artwork that looks the way clients expect artwork to look. In addition, "there is an inexhaustible storehouse and variety of such images in this world: published pictures that appear in magazines, newspapers, and other periodicals, in books, on greeting cards and postcards, and as posters and art prints" (Comfort, 1985, p. 245). Published images provide an excellent basis for familiarizing clients with ways of understanding and communicating "how it feels to be a certain unique human being who holds an idiosyncratic worldview" (Comfort, 1985, pp. 245–246).

Body Outline Drawings

Another universal way visual arts can be introduced in counseling is through body outline drawings (see Figure 7). These drawings are made when a person lies spread out on a floor (sometimes known as spread eagle), and his or her body is traced on paper. After the drawings are completed, individuals can decorate them in any way they wish, literally and figuratively (Steinhardt, 1985). Sometimes in such an endeavor, people, especially children, reveal indirectly troublesome aspects of their lives that counselors can later discuss with them (*Body Outline Drawings*).

Serial Drawings

Serial drawings are portrayals or sketches of any object, such as a tree, an animal, or a scene, that is drawn by a client multiple times over

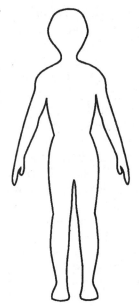

Figure 7   Body Outline

multiple sessions after the counselor initially requests the client to draw a picture. The idea behind the use of serial drawings is that through them, especially on a regular basis, clients will represent themselves and their problems symbolically. By working in a positive transference manner that involves a talk component to complement the visual element, a positive self-concept emerges, and behavior change occurs (Allan, 1978, 2008). This approach is Jungian and requires patience and an intuitive timing as to what to say or do and when (*Serial Drawings*).

Visual Journaling

A complement to serial drawing is visual journaling.

> Visual journals are essentially "art diaries." They often contain both images [usually drawings] and words. Like an actual diary, their contents may be rough drafts that may later become finished artworks. And like an actual diary, they are meant to document day-to-day experiences, activities, and emotions and are often autobiographical in nature. (Malchiodi, 2010a, para. 1)

Visual journals are instructive as well as therapeutic, as can be seen in the ideas and imagery of Leonardo da Vinci (see Figure 8).

Capacchione (2001) is one of the leading experts in visual journaling and has written a number of self-help books to guide readers through the process. Her work initially came out of her own painful and healing experiences, but it has far surpassed that now and is focused on wellness (*Visual Journaling*).

Research by A. Mercer, Warson, and Zhao (2010) has found that visual journaling decreases anxiety and general negative affect levels in medical students. Furthermore, there are indications that the regular practice of visual journaling can reduce heart rate as well as increase serotonin flow and immune cells (Malchiodi, 2010a), thus making this technique

> ## Creative Reflection
>
> Children do body outline drawings all the time in elementary school. You may have done one or seen one done and realize that most children enjoy this activity. Why do you think these drawings are less frequently done with older populations? How effective do you think they would be if they were done by and with more adults?

similar to the positive impact of journaling as found through the research studies of James Pennebaker (see Chapter 6).

Overall, visual journaling is taking off in some interesting directions. For example, altered books are visual journals that involve taking actual books and changing them in a variety of ways by drawing, painting, overwriting, or even destroying pages as a form of artistic self-expression. Rather than working with a sketchbook or journal with blank pages, the nature of the book itself provides a stimulus for creative journaling (*Altered Books*).

Clay

Being able to use a variety of artistic materials is essential in the process of employing the visual arts in counseling. Clay is one artistic substance that is too seldom used because of its bulk, weight, and

Figure 8 Drawing of Leonardo da Vinci Flying Machine

messiness. However, clay has a number of advantages. For instance, clay can help clients express themselves in concrete and focused ways. Working in clay can also promote cooperation between clients and counselors. It is a safe medium for many clients because they do not necessarily have to look at the counselor when they are making a clay object. In addition, individuals can use clay to regress or gain insight by manipulating, squeezing, and pounding it because it is so malleable (Makin, 1994). Working with clay may reduce anxiety and depression, lower defense mechanisms, and serve as an object onto which feelings can be projected (Atchison, 2001; de Morais et al., 2014). It is under the client's control, and some clients feel more empowered when working with clay than they do with many other visual arts materials.

Photography

Photographs are footprints of our minds, mirrors of our lives, reflections from our hearts, frozen memories we can hold in silent stillness in our hands—forever, if we wish. They not only document where we may have been but also point the way to where we might perhaps be going, whether we know it yet or not (Stevens & Spears, 2009). According to Weiser (1999, 2001), photography, or as she calls it, phototherapy, is a way to capture and express feelings and ideas in a visual-symbolic form across the life span. It has many similarities to art therapy and works "particularly well for people who find other visual arts too demanding or too risky to try" (Weiser, 2001, p. 13). Stevens and Spears (2009) stated,

> Phototherapy can involve tasks as basic as sending clients out to photograph something that has meaning to them, using family photos to elicit discussions of deep-seated memories and emotions, or viewing photographic exhibits. The goal is to facilitate a creative outlet, identifying things that have meaning to the client, and discovering a new skill. (p. 6)

Phototherapy can be utilized by almost any counselor and can be adapted to most theoretical frameworks (Ginicola, Smith, & Trzaska, 2012; Star & Cox, 2008). Phototherapy captures the therapeutic nature of images; it is concerned with taking, viewing, manipulating, presenting, and interpreting the image as a primary or supplementary form of counseling (*Phototherapy*). The basic techniques of using photography in counseling are related to relationships:

- Photos taken of the client
- Photos taken by the client
- Photos of the client by the client (self-portraits)
- Biographical pictures, which may or may not include the client, of groups of friends and family

Active phototherapy involves photos taken by a client that represent a feeling the client has or photos that the client thinks represent him or her. After being taken, the photos are scrapbooked or mounted on a poster board, and the counselor and client talk about them and ways change may come about. *Passive phototherapy* entails a client either making a scrapbook or mounting on poster board pictures that have already been taken. These pictures may be from a photo album or may be representative pictures from popular publications that show how life has been for the person.

Scrapbooks utilize either kind of photography. They incorporate "creative writing, journal entries, news clippings, poems, song lyrics, and other mementoes" in addition to photographs to give "voice and story to the authors" (K. Williams & Lent, 2008, p. 458). Scrapbooks are versatile and may be used in the present as a way of remembering specific times, or they may be used in the grieving process to honor and memorialize a loved one. Regardless of whether a scrapbook or a poster board is used, themes almost always become evident in working with photographs. If the photographs are used in a therapeutic setting, these themes may be discussed along with ways of altering them if appropriate.

A form of photography that is a multistep, participatory, action-research process is *photovoice*. It is conducted in small groups that focus on advocacy. Its ultimate goal is to influence systems and policy. It uses photographic images taken by people with little money, power, or status to enhance community needs assessments, empower participants, and induce change by informing policy makers of community assets and deficits. It brings together individuals with mental health needs, family members, mental health professionals, and researchers as equal partners in attempts to report the call for consumer-driven systems of care. With each photograph is a personal narrative about the object(s) in the photo and why what is represented needs to be addressed (Becker, Reiser, Lambert, & Covello, 2014).

Overall, photographs help "improve understanding and perception" of individuals, couples, groups, and families (Stevens & Spears, 2009, p. 10). Examining family photos may provide clues as to which family members are valued most, what successes and strengths a family or couple has, and what past issues have challenged or still challenge a family (Star & Cox, 2008). Taking photos can "give people a sense of achievement" (Stevens & Spears, 2009, p. 11), which can translate into higher self-esteem and functionality. In almost all procedures using photography in counseling, there is a project process, that

Creative Reflection

Of the art options just given (published pictures, body outline drawing, serial drawings, clay, and photography), which do you think you would be most comfortable working in? What is it about the medium that appeals to your senses?

is, an emotional response (Weiser, 1999, 2001). Such a process lets clients feel and see situations they are facing and talk about them (Loewenthal, 2013). Through affective, visual, and verbal processes, photographs can have a healing efffect, and they can stimulate clients and help them picture themselves in new ways (Morgovsky, 2003).

Visual Arts in Counseling With Specific Populations

The visual arts, like other art forms, cover the life span. They can be used in counseling with almost all populations because they are a powerful tool in communication. Indeed it is "now widely acknowledged that art expression is a way to visually communicate thoughts and feelings that are too painful to put into words" (Malchiodi, 2012, p. ix). Here, I examine the visual arts with regard to their use with children, adolescents, adults, older adults, and others.

Children

Art has been found to be an important outlet for children. It supports their expressive, cognitive, and affective ways of expression. Art-making in groups builds community and develops social skills. In addition, art-making supports creativity and divergent thinking as well as increasing student engagement in school (Ziff, Pierce, Johanson, & King, 2012). Research indicates that art can help young people reconcile emotional conflicts. In addition, when classroom interventions focus students on their creativity and expressiveness, creative arts therapies have been shown to improve children's verbal and creative thinking, reading comprehension, and, in particular, their self-perceptions of mastery and intrinsic motivation (Cortina & Fazel, 2015). Riley (1997) stated, "There is a way that children commonly share their stories with an adult, one that is both spontaneous and laden with content. They draw" (p. 2). By drawing and using art, children exert control in their lives and "cope with the challenges of daily living" (Finn, 2003, p. 159). The artwork that is produced is not as important as the impact of the process on the person doing the art. "The art work of children, when it is an expression of their simple and honest feelings, is almost always beautiful" (May, 1953, p. 190).

Tragically, children are many times the victims of abuse or mistreatment. In these situations, their art may reflect more pain than pleasure. In such situations, drawings help children and adults better understand what has happened and the child's reactive experience related to the abusive situation (Cohen-Liebman, 1999). Overall, children's art "is a safe way to 'tell' what has been forbidden to be talked about, a language of its own" (Riley, 1997, p. 2). Through art, children forge a vital communications link between themselves and helpers such as counselors. From that relationship, they may regain their health, resolve their grief, come to a constructive conclusion with their anger, find solutions, and build productive lives.

There are several ways to use visual arts to gather information from children about their mental health. One approach is through standardized psychological instruments (e.g., the Draw-A-Person and House-Tree-Person tests), but counselors tend to use more informal approaches in most situations. For instance, children may be asked to draw a circle and then to color different parts of the circle to represent various feelings, such as smart, dumb, good, or bad (Hughes, 1988). Drawing in such a manner helps children become more aware of how they see themselves and opens up concrete avenues for them to use in talking about their feelings (*Draw a Circle*). A second type of preventive approach that can be used by most counselors is to have children display feelings in sculpture, clay, or other art projects (Gerler, 1982). In this exercise, counselors team up with art teachers. The results may vary from ripped-up paper spread across the floor to represent anger; to a drawing of a sad face with paperclip tears to symbolize sadness; to decorated bags with string, ribbons, candy, and cotton balls pasted on to show happiness.

A third technique based on Jungian theory is the use of serial drawing. The idea behind a serial drawing, as already noted, is for a counselor to meet on a regular basis with a person, usually a child, and simply ask the individual to draw a picture (Allan, 2008). In this process, which takes place over an extended period of time (at least 10 sessions), a therapeutic alliance and rapport are developed between the counselor and the person, and a sanctuary where growth, development, and healing can occur is created as well (Jung, 1954, 1963). One variation of this approach is called Rosebush (see Figure 9; Allan & Crandall, 1986). In this exercise, the child is simply asked to draw

Figure 9   Rosebush—Healthy

a rosebush every time he or she meets with the counselor (*Rosebush*). The rosebush is symbolic of the child's mental health, and changes in the drawings indicate positive movement or distress within the child (D. C. Ray, Perkins, & Oden, 2004).

A fourth technique that can help counselors and children understand family dynamics more readily through art is family drawing and storytelling (Roosa, 1981). This procedure is used as part of a larger process for children under 10 years of age. It has four steps (*Family Drawing and Storytelling*):

1. Children draw their families, including themselves, on a sheet of white paper.
2. They make up a story of what the family is doing in the picture.
3. They draw on a separate sheet of paper any family member that may have been left out of the original picture (e.g., a divorced parent or a family pet).
4. After all of the drawings are photocopied and cut out, children (on a one-to-one basis) tell the counselor stories about small-group family interactions, using the cutouts as symbolic representations.

A final technique for working with children is the use of props. Schimmel (2006/2007) defined a *prop* as "any object that helps with counseling." She gave examples such as "a small chair, extra chairs, the whiteboard, and objects such as a soda or pop bottle, a dollar bill, a hammer, a filter, a shield, and Styrofoam cups" (p. 60).

Like Jacobs (1992), Schimmel demonstrated how props may be used like keys to help children unlock insight. For example, Schimmel used a dollar bill as a metaphor for self-worth. She has the child tell her what the dollar is worth initially and then crumbles the bill up, stomps on it, beats on it, and kicks it. She then unwads it and shows it to the child again, eliciting from the child how much the bill is worth, to which the child responds that it is still worth a dollar. The analogy becomes clear in the process: Even if the child is treated badly by a caretaker, he or she still has worth. The child is not worthless because of what someone has done to the child.

Overall, art in various forms functions for children as a medium for conversation, as an avenue for the expression of strong feelings, as a means for making metaphors visual, as a way of externalizing problems, and as a possibility for creating solutions (Mooney, 2000). Thus, "art in therapy helps children better understand themselves and how they function" in a family and in society (Orton, 1997, p. 261). "As children draw, paint, or sculpt, they are communicating their thoughts and feelings in a form of 'art talk' that the counselor can listen to and understand" (Orton, 1997, p. 261). Likewise, when using props with a counselor, children convey what they are experiencing and gain insight in return.

Adolescents

The use of visual arts for adolescents varies depending on their age and the situation that needs addressing. Visual arts have been used in community and school environments (Kahn, 1999) and have been found to have potency in both domains and in many treatment situations. They have been applied to treating sexually abused adolescent girls (A. Brown & Latimir, 2001), working with juvenile sexual offenders (Gerber, 1994), doing group therapy with a mixed group of teenagers (Rambo, 1996), assisting adolescents in crisis (Appleton, 2001), addressing adolescent depression (Riley, 2003), and even helping therapeutically with blind adolescents (Herrmann, 1995). In a Filipino study, Brillantes-Evangelista (2013) found that an eight-session art therapy intervention where abused adolescents drew and painted was significantly effective in alleviating their symptoms of PTSD, although it did not make a difference in treating their depression. Visual arts experiences range from those that are primarily preventive to those that are mainly remedial. Art materials used with adolescents include clay, paint, and photo equipment.

For young adolescents, structured art experiences related to counseling may be most appropriate. In fact, the National Career Development Association sponsors a positively directed program of this sort each year. It is a poster contest for children and young adolescents, for which they literally draw pictures of various careers and are encouraged through the awarding of prizes to think about their vocational futures (*Draw Pictures of Various Careers*). For older adolescents, a developmental approach may prove more useful, such as Appleton's (2001) model that defines four trauma stages (impact, retreat, acknowledgment, and reconstruction) and shows how four associated art therapy goals (creating continuity, building therapeutic alliances, overcoming social stigma/isolation, and fostering meaning) can aid in the movement from stage to stage.

Kahn (1999) also created a developmental, stage-by-stage model to use with adolescents. Her three-stage model is composed of Entry, Exploration, and Action-Taking. Specific questions and activities are related to each stage. In the Entry stage, art directives need to be open-ended and encourage teenagers to introduce themselves through their art. Appropriate directives include "Draw your neighborhood," "Tell me a story," or "Make a collage about who you are." In the

Exploration stage, self-expression is increased in an attempt to explore feelings, thoughts, and behaviors that might be problematic. Art directives at this stage might include such sentences as

- "Create a collage that depicts your understanding of why you are coming for counseling."
- "Draw how you see yourself in your group of friends, and then how you see yourself as an individual."
- "Choose a picture that represents your involvement in your academic work."

In the Action-Taking stage, art directives help adolescents set goals for change and elaborate on the behaviors they need to reach these milestones in their lives. Sentences are more specific at this stage and might include such art directives as these:

- "Draw one time when the change that you want to occur did happen, even if just a little."
- "Draw a bridge, representing where you are now and how you will be when counseling is completed. What are the obstacles in your way? What are the steps that need to be accomplished?" (*Draw a Bridge*)
- "Draw yourself in a scene 15 years from now. What goals will you need to reach during this time?" (*Draw Yourself in a Scene 15 Years From Now*)

Two other activities that have been devised for adolescents include photography and the painting of dreams.

Photography

Photo counseling or phototherapy methods appropriate for use with adolescents have been formulated by Amerikaner, Schauble, and Ziller (1980); Goessling and Doyle (2009); Gosciewski (1975); Hays, Forman, and Sikes (2009); Loewenthal (2013); Schudson (1975); and Weiser (1999). They include (a) active methods in which photographs are taken and talked about, (b) more passive processes in which already developed photographs are displayed and discussed, and (c) combined procedures in which photographs are mixed with artwork and other creative processes. In all of these procedures, the photographs serve as a catalyst to promote talking and help personalize the counseling process while promoting

Creative Reflection

When you were 15 years old, how would you have drawn yourself at age 30 or older? How accurate would that picture be if drawn today? What would have changed? What, if anything, do you think this tells you about project drawings by adolescents?

self-awareness and increased sensitivity. In the active photography approach, adolescents take pictures of themselves, their friends, and their environments. They may display the pictures in many ways, such as by mounting them on poster board or putting them in a photo album or scrapbook (see Figure 10). Through such a process and through their interaction with a counselor, adolescents describe their lives, including their feelings and plans for the future.

In the more passive photography approach, pictures that have already been taken are collected and displayed as adolescents reflect on the times these pictures represent. Both the counselor and the adolescent look for missing moments and significant themes that may be represented or absent. For example, I once used this procedure with an older adolescent and found that he had left out pictures of a significant portion of his life. When I inquired, he stated he had suffered a trauma at the beginning of that time, and it had taken him years to work through it. This omission gave me more material from which I could work to help him come to a final resolution regarding his trauma.

Finally, in the mixed category of photos and artwork, participants combine photographs with their own drawings, words, and even pictures from magazines and newspapers. This method has been used with teenage girls in the Southeast as a preventive procedure to help foster healthy dating relationships (Hays et al., 2009) and with at-risk students in the Northwest to enhance awareness and power (Goessling & Doyle, 2009). In both situations it proved to be powerful and educational.

Painting Dreams
In this visual arts approach, adolescents are encouraged to draw and paint troublesome dreams. In this way the covert nature of the dream becomes more overt, and adolescents who participate in this activ-

Figure 10   Photos Mounted on Poster Board

ity gain a mastery over the dream content. Especially helpful here is spontaneous painting, which can be akin to a dream and during which a person "abandons conscious control and allows the picture to appear" (Adamson, 1984, p. 37). A related activity that is not as threatening is *painting daydreams*. In such paintings, art becomes "fossilized consciousness, vibrating with the life it once contained" (Roje, 1994, p. 375). Yet, at the same time, the daydreaming process maintains a life of its own as visual representations continue to evolve (*Draw and Paint Troublesome Dreams and Daydreams*).

College Students

College environments expose students to a lot of different forms of art, but many students only see art in a distant and meaningless way. In contrast to this type of stale atmosphere are the healthy and innovative visual arts programs for college students sponsored by counseling centers. These programs for different groups at different times during the semester are collectively known as *art breaks* (Geller et al., 1986). The activities in art breaks are held on campus, usually require a minimum of 1 hour of time, involve minimal equipment, and are centered on an open group experience. They are designed to "(a) help students relax and release stress; (b) develop a sense of community through shared group experience; (c) air concerns about issues such as adjustment to college, roommates, and studies; (d) gain self-awareness; and (e) awaken creative energies" (Geller et al., 1986, p. 230). Sometimes themes are suggested by professionals working with students; often they are not. The same is true for discussion about what students create.

The following are some of the various forms that art breaks have taken:

- A group mural, in which long pieces of paper are hung on walls and various art materials are distributed and used (*Group Mural*).
- A clay piece group, in which students work in a structured small circle on individual clay pieces and then are encouraged by the group leader (an art therapist) to tell the group about their work and the experience as a whole (*Clay Piece Group*).
- Individual drawings of situations, during which pressures that have built up can be therapeutically released in a harmless and sometimes humorous way.

In art breaks the creativity of students is released and revealed. Feelings that accompany the expression of creativity are acknowledged as well, and healthy interactions with others are promoted.

Adults

Artwork reveals a great deal about adults, so using art as a part of a counseling treatment plan can be most beneficial (Oppawsky, 2001). For instance, the drawings of adults who are depressed show more empty space, less color, less investment of effort, and either more depressive affect or less affect than the drawings of well-functioning adults (Wadeson, 1980). However, as a group, adults are reluctant to use the visual arts outside of already published pictures. The reason is that most adults do not have refined artistic skills, and many feel embarrassed trying to express themselves in artistic ways.

Having adults draw or having a counselor introduce them to classic paintings can arouse feeling responses that may lead to reflections on issues they have repressed or want to talk about (*Classic Paintings*). Thus, visual art stimulation can help adults verbally reflect and/ or write about what is troubling or difficult in their lives using the created or viewed object as a starting place for fostering insight and promoting growth (Gladding, 2012).

The artwork of adults can also be useful to counselors working with this population in other ways. For instance, the use of art therapy with women who have cancer may help these women by enhancing their coping strategies, understanding their illness, promoting connectedness, and taking appropriate steps to deal directly with their disease (P. Baron, 1991; Borgmann, 2002). Unresolved grief may likewise be resolved through creating an image in a tapestry (Reynolds, 1999) (*Feeling Tapestry*). In essence, art therapy may address the emotional state of adults with life-threatening diseases and unresolved feelings while giving them coping skills that enhance and increase their perceptions of control and empowerment (Hiltebrand, 1999).

Art as a therapy may be used in adult rehabilitation too. Art may address many of the diverse cognitive, emotional, and functional needs of people disabled by strokes. Attention, spatial processing, sequencing, and planning seem to improve among those who persist in using art therapy. Use of the stroke-affected limb may increase. Several studies report improvements in social interaction and emotional expression as well (Reynolds, 2012).

Through prosocial means, counselors can use art to help adult clients function better regardless of their mental state or status. For example, the inclusion of arts in counseling an adult who is mildly mentally challenged has been shown to be positive in helping to reduce maladaptive behaviors and increase internal locus of control (Arnheim, 1994; Bowen & Rosal, 1989). Similarly, the visual arts can help adults plan their lives better. For instance, in career counseling, adults are often helped if they gain a sense of direction about where they have been and where they are going. At least two types of pictures can be drawn in such cases. One is in the form of a road map (see Figure 11) on which clients paint or draw their life path and career influences in the same manner that they map out directions to a specific destination (Liebmann, 2004). In this procedure, the person who draws the line may also pencil or color in any scenes or particular moments along the way (*Life Path and Career Road Map*). The idea

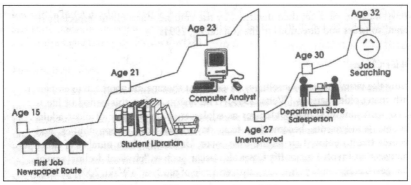

Figure 11   Career Road Map

in this visual art exercise is to give adults free rein to evaluate the factors that have most heavily influenced them and then symbolize these events and people in a form that allows them to see the past, present, and future all together. In such an experience, adults can get a feel for what may lie ahead if they do not think through their plans (D. Campbell, 1974).

The second type of drawing that can be used in such situations is known as windows (see Figure 12). In this experience, a person is asked to draw a window. She or he is then asked to draw scenery in the window, either looking from the outside in (i.e., interiors) or from the inside out (i.e., landscapes). The type of window drawn and the view are then discussed by the counselor and the client, especially with regard to issues and directions in life (Gladding, 1991f) (*Windows*).

Older Clients

Using the visual arts in counseling is an excellent therapeutic approach to use with many older people (Weiss, 1999). This period of life is filled with almost as many changes as adolescence, but usually with less stress as one becomes older (Greenstein & Holland, 2015). Several older adults become grandparents, are free from day-to-day work responsibilities, and are free to enjoy their leisure time more. Unfortunately, several other changes that involve major life losses also occur, such as "physical decline, sexual changes, changes in dependency status, and role of receiver" (Wald, 2003, p. 295). In both the areas of gain and loss, the visual arts can help members of this population. Indeed, history is filled with examples of aging

Figure 12   Window Drawing (Looking Out)

adults who combined experience with creativity, including such outstanding artists as "Michelangelo, Titian, Tintoretto, Hals, Picasso, and Grandma Moses" (Wald, 2003, p. 296). As a preventative and remedial force, the visual arts can take many forms, for example, pictures or models of remembered

> ## Creative Reflection
>
> When was the last time you drew or painted? How did it feel? What memories surface when you think of using a visual art medium? How similar do you think your thoughts are to those of clients you work with or might work with?

events from childhood, school, work, trips, holidays, and special occasions. Two other ways the visual arts can therapeutically enhance the lives of older adults are through photographs and memories and art on occasions.

Photographs and Memories

The use of old photographs is an excellent way to help older adults participate in the life-review process that is so important to fostering a sense of ego integrity (Myers, 1989; Sweeney, 2009; Weiser, 1999). The procedure used in introducing this activity can vary depending on the counseling setting. For example, if the counselor is employed in an older adult day-care center, he or she can ask members of the center to bring in photographs of their lives. However, the counselor may have to be more active and find some representative photographs if he or she is employed in an inpatient facility where clients do not have ready access to their personal possessions. In either case, the idea is to accentuate the positive and help clients in this process recall early memories and experiences while reframing negatives to promote self-esteem.

Art on Occasions

Art on occasions is the indirect suggestion of an older art therapist, Maxine Toch Frankenfelder (1988). She began an art therapy program at age 73 and upon graduation worked in a psychogeriatric day-treatment center. Her description of the experience reflects a great deal of versatility in using the arts. For example, in introducing art to her participants she began by drawing a mandala and then, within the mandala, drawing circles within circles, which she then colored. The group she worked with followed her lead and improvised too. On the occasions of members becoming ill, Frankenfelder had other members of her group make cards. At the termination of the experience, she had members draw the "saddest pictures they could imagine, but add a ray of hope. The images ranged from a weeping willow with a bit of sunshine to a Madonna and child" (p. 253). The pictures expressed sorrow in leaving the experience but hope for the future as well. Using the visual arts with older clients in this case was a way to therapeutically help them show care for others and at the same time care for themselves. That principle still remains true.

Hospitalized Clients

Only about 2% of hospitalized individuals in psychiatric settings spontaneously undertake artistic activities (Esman, 1988). Those who volunteer or who participate involuntarily are helped in several ways, most noticeably through the structure and control they gain in such endeavors. Through artistic expressions, hospitalized people are able to visualize their fears and feelings more clearly. They can then talk more concretely about the disturbing elements in their lives and ways they can overcome or neutralize them. Sometimes in this process clients draw themselves out as people and in the process devise strategies for becoming healthier.

Art therapy has been found to benefit patients hospitalized for severe burns who suffer psychological as well as physical trauma. Art can be of assistance at each stage in the recovery process (Russel, 1995).

Prisoners

A unique and effective use of the visual arts is emerging in the rehabilitation of prisoners (Meekums & Daniel, 2011). For example, the Saudi Arabian government has found that art therapy may disrupt the activities of those who promote violent extremism. Through art, the individuals can find refuge from past experiences and hardships and express anger through a safe medium that does not harm themselves or others. The government has used art therapeutically in helping to socially reintegrate ex-jihadists held in prisons (Alyami, 2015).

Although art may be a safe container for extremists' self-expression, working with those incarcerated for terrorist activities is demanding. Not only does it requires a deep knowledge of how art may be used therapeutically, but the professionals involved must understand local cultures and extremist populations and be willing to collaborate with other programs in the rehabilitation process. Adapting this program to other populations, such as destructive gangs, may not be effective due to the uniqueness of the Saudi culture. However, the success rate in this program is reported to be more than 85%, which is impressive and may lead governments and other groups to consider how art can be incorporated therapeutically in their own rehabilitation systems.

Groups

In addition to working with individuals using the visual arts in a therapeutic way, counselors may also use the visual arts in a group setting (Jacobs et al., 2016; Waller, 2012). According to Good and Rosal (1999), adding art may benefit a group by

- assisting in the formation, identity, and cohesion of a group by helping group members learn something about each other in a concrete form;
- helping to identify goals for group participation both initially and throughout the duration of the group;
- providing an additional avenue for communication of thoughts and feelings through drawings and pictures;
- supplying a means of viewing problems and issues from different perspectives;
- stimulating creative thinking and new ideas; and
- providing a historical record of the group's progress, including illuminating how the group stayed on task and the nature of group members' relationships with each other.

An example of the use of the visual arts in a group is an exercise called Balloons (Dansby, 2003). In this experience, each member of a group is given a sheet of paper with his or her name on it and a drawing of a bunch of balloons. Members of the group then pass their papers to the right around the group, and other members of the group write or draw a kindness or good quality about the person on one of the balloons. Members continue passing the papers and writing or drawing on them until each sheet is returned to its owner (*Balloons*).

Another group experience called Rainbow also has a visual art component (Dansby, 2003). In this exercise, a brightly colored rainbow is made with everyone in the group's name on a stripe. The group leader then focuses on the fact that everyone in the group has strengths and gifts that contribute to the beauty and uniqueness of the group. As each group member's name is read, other group members call out strengths of that person that are written down or symbolically drawn on that person's stripe by the leader (*Rainbow*). Both Balloon and Rainbow are excellent ways to end a group.

Families and Couples

Several structured ways exist to use the visual arts with families and couples. According to Riley (1987), "In the course of family therapy, a shared task such as a family drawing or mural" provides the counselor with an opportunity to "observe interactions, form a hypothesis about the family system, and plan interventions to alter dysfunctional sequences of behavior. By observing patterns of family behavior as well as the content of the art," counselors learn "about family members' relationships with each other and about the family system of which they are a part" (p. 21).

Creative Reflection

The balloon exercise requires only elementary skills as a visual artist. How do you think simplification would affect group members' willingness to engage in this activity? How might it affect your decision to use the exercise?

One way of working with families in an artistic endeavor is the Joint Family Scribble. Individual members of a family are asked to make scribbles and are then instructed to incorporate their scribbles into a unified picture (Kwiatkowska, 1967) (*Joint Family Scribble*). A second way is known as the Conjoint Family Drawing, in which the family is instructed to "draw a picture as you see yourself as a family." In this exercise, each member of the family draws a picture and then discusses the finished product with the rest of the family (Bing, 1970) (*Concurrent Family Drawing/Conjoint Family Drawing*). A variation of this type of drawing is the Conjoint Family Holiday Drawing, in which the family as a whole completes a joint drawing on the theme of a family holiday (K. Jordan, 2001). Often family members are surprised by the results of either type of drawing, and a lively discussion follows (*Concurrent or Conjoint Family Holiday Drawing*). A final variation of this type of visual art is the *Joint Couple Drawing*. It results in one of three outcomes. The "balanced style" is characterized by a coherent product, which is a result of the couple's ability to agree on one drawing subject and to work cooperatively. The "complicated style" is characterized by unconnected images without a common denominator, and the "disconnected style" is characterized by the absence of contact between the partners' drawings on the sheet (Snir & Wiseman, 2013).

A third way to use the visual arts with families is the Symbolic Drawing of Family Life Space (Geddes & Medway, 1977). In this procedure, the counselor draws a large circle and instructs the family to draw everything that represents aspects of the family, including members in relationship to each other, inside the circle. Persons and institutions that are not a part of the family are drawn outside the circle (*Symbolic Drawing of Family Life Space*). As with the other visual art exercises, the results of this procedure often get individuals within families talking to each other in new ways.

A fourth way to use visual arts with families is the Kinetic Family Drawing test. This is one of the most widely used projective methods in the world for evaluating an individual's perception of his or her family in context (Veltman & Browne, 2003) (*Kinetic Family Drawing*). In this test, an individual (often a child)

is asked to "draw everyone in the family doing something." In analyzing the drawing, the examiner looks for who is present and who is omitted or given a substitute. The size of the figures is important, as well as their position, distance, and interaction with one another. Special attention should (also) be given to the individual's self-portrayal. (Drummond, Sheperis, & Jones, 2016, p. 247)

As an instrument, research supports the use of the Kinetic Family Drawing test to predict and mediate internal problem behaviors of children (J. K. Kim & Suh, 2013).

A final way of using visual arts, especially with couples, is to use relational drawings (Rober, 2009). In this method, the counselor gives a couple the following homework assignment with an example:

> I would like each of you to make a drawing of your partner. Make your drawing in a metaphorical image, as you experience your partner. You can choose an animal, a house, a landscape, a person, whatever you find most appropriate to express how you experience your partner. . . . When you have made the drawing of your partner, you draw yourself on the same paper, also in a metaphorical image, as you experience yourself in relation to your partner. Let me give you an example. . . . Then I tell them that I might, for instance, make a drawing of my wife as a soccer ball. I then would draw this soccer ball on the paper and then I would ask myself, if she is a soccer ball, what would I be? Would I be the grass on which the ball rests? Would I be the soccer player kicking the ball? Would I be the pump inflating the ball? Would I be the goal? Or the referee? Then I choose an image, and I draw it on the paper. (Rober, 2009, p. 120)

When the couple returns, the emphasis of the session is on what happens around the drawings, not the drawings themselves. In particular, the therapist focuses on the clients' hesitations and the clients' surprises. The respectful dialog of the counselor with the partners about the drawing is central (*Relational Drawings*).

The main drawback to using visual arts with families is that members may feel these experiences are artificial and gimmicky and thus have no real-life value (Nichols, 2013). When such is the case, they experience a release of emotions within a session but no transferability of learning to situations outside.

Ethnic Minorities

Visual arts are not limited by color or class. People from all ethnic backgrounds and cultures can find meaning in visual arts. For instance, African American women have used visual arts as well as other creative arts, such as music, dance, imagery, and journaling, to transcend situations of oppression and to empower and self-nurture themselves (C. B. Williams et al., 1999). Likewise, Native Americans have used symbols in art to represent some of their feelings and to deal with these emotions in a safe and constructive way (Dufrene & Coleman, 1994).

In working with clients from cultures other than their own, counselors must understand something about the cultural heritage of their clients' visual arts. For example, counselors with a predominantly European background will have to become familiar with the more metaphorical use of imagery and color in Hispanic and Latin American arts. American Indian subcultures "may use stylized imagery to express events and feelings," making it "necessary for counselors to become familiar with art history and folk art of a particular cultural group through research, reading, and museum visitations" if they are going to be effective in working with such groups (Kincade & Evans, 1996, p. 106).

In addition, when working with clients who are culturally distinct from themselves, counselors must focus on two aspects of the experience. The first is their professional readiness. Counselors with an accurate and sensitive understanding of the cultures of their clients, as well as of their own heritage, will be more relaxed and ready to work artistically and therapeutically in an appropriate way. The second aspect of the experience counselors must focus on is the creative process involved in particular arts activities and what clients report learning or questioning from their experiences. Counseling using the visual arts will be successful with people from all ethnic backgrounds and cultures only as a result of thorough preparation and processing of experiences.

Counselor Drawings

The visual arts are not only therapeutic for clients in working through developmental and situational crises but also helpful for counselors either in working with clients to alter perceptions or in assessing various dimensions of their own personal lives. Milton R. Cudney (1975) was a leader in advocating for the use of counselor-made drawings. According to Cudney, pictures counselors might draw in sessions could help in understanding and objectifying counseling issues, increasing openness, promoting counselor–client conversation, and reaching nonverbal and nonreading clients. Cudney also believed that pictures could shorten the counseling process by clarifying problems and making them easier to address.

A way Cudney might work, and that counselor drawings continue to work, is to challenge a client's perception through a drawing (see Figure 13). For instance, if a client states that a problem is so large it cannot be overcome, and yet solid evidence shows the contrary, the counselor might draw two pictures. Both would be of a mountain, with the first mountain much higher and steeper than the second. The counselor might then say to the client that he or she hears the client describing the problem in terms of its overwhelming nature, like the first mountain drawn, but that the counselor perceives that the difficulty is much more like the second and has less of a slope. Such a challenge may

Figure 13 Client and Counselor Perception Problem

help the client think through how he or she is presenting a situation and modify his or her outlook accordingly (*Counselor Drawings*).

In addition to working with clients, counselor drawings may be helpful to the counselor in gauging his or her own mental health. For example, when drawing a picture of herself, Mary Beth Edens, a school counselor in Winston-Salem, North Carolina, came up with a wide variety of activities that helped her develop a strong self-concept. She titled her picture "Me!" (see Figure 14). In assessing her more difficult days, however, Edens found that she had self-defeating talk. She used

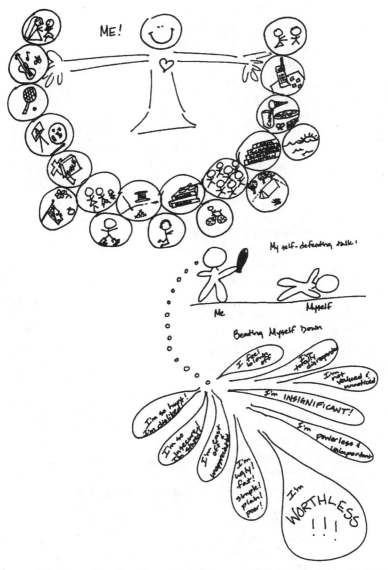

Figure 14   Drawings by Mary Beth Edens, 1995. Used with permission.

to put herself down. Her picture of how that talk affected her can be seen in the picture she titled "Beating Myself Down." The contrast between the two pictures is stark and significant. Edens found that through looking at the pictures she could remind herself not only of her strengths but also of ways she might sabotage herself if she was not careful. Her situation, while unique in the way it is depicted, is common to most counselors. As helping professionals we all have strengths to draw on, and as human beings we also have bad times that seem to deplete or temporarily defeat us. Counselor drawings can help us tap our abilities and understand our feelings.

Visual Arts in Counseling With Other Creative Arts

The visual arts can be combined in numerous ways with other creative arts in counseling. For counselors themselves, a book written and illustrated by the late Mary Joe Hannaford and her daughter Joey, titled *Counselor Under Construction* (Hannaford & Hannaford, 1979), graphically depicts what life is like when becoming a counselor, especially in the schools. In addition to this graphic approach, literature and words, music, and psychodrama are three primary ways of combining the visual arts with other creative arts.

Visual Arts and Literature/Words

One way to link the visual arts with literature is to have clients read a poem, a short story, or a novel and then have them draw main events or characters as they perceived them from their readings (*Visual Art With Literature*). This exercise may be exciting for preadolescents, adolescents, and adults. It gives them a paper trail of images by which to remember a story and an experience. It helps them visually remember main points in the literature that relate to them. Christenbury, Beale, and Patch (1996) compiled a list of fiction and nonfiction books published between 1990 and 1994 that are suitable for use with adolescents in this kind of bibliotherapy relationship. Such topics as illness and death, self-destructive behaviors, family relations, identity, violence and abuse, race and prejudice, sex and sexuality, and gender issues are covered by these authors in an annotated bibliography. For example, a book on the

Creative Reflection

Most counselors have never heard of counselor drawings. They are certainly the opposite of what most counselors and clients expect. Yet, they can be very effective. Think of a situation with a person, whether a client or not, and draw a representative picture of what you think that person's situation looks like.

list that deals with divorce and secrets is Willey's (1993) *The Melinda Zone*. After reading this work, adolescents draw what secrets or conflicts involving divorce look like, specifically with regard to the characters in the book and to themselves. Then comparisons and contrasts are made between the pictures while talking about them and the adolescents' similar situations. The latest adult version of such a work is *Self-Help That Works* (Norcross et al., 2013), which contains, among other things, descriptions of self-help books, autobiographies, and films around specific topics such as anxiety, drepression, and pain. Each work is rated as to its effectiveness.

Another way to combine art with literature is by having clients create an illustrated text about difficult situations they have experienced. This type of book shows feelings strongly but contains words as well (*Illustrated Text About Difficult Situations*). For example, participants could create a *Pain Getting Better Book* in and through which they can objectify their pain through drawings and simultaneously be helped to tap their inner resources (J. C. Mills & Crowley, 1986). This type of book both empowers participants and helps them discover the best within themselves.

Yet another way of combining art and literature is through writing and painting simultaneously. Either the words or the art can come first, but in the case of Harriet Wadeson (1987), it was words in the form of poetry about midlife that prompted her to paint. The result was a graphic and creative expression of the author–artist's perceptions about making the transition into another stage of life. The beauty of the experience was not only in the meaning it gave the creator but also in the symbols and guidance it left as a legacy for other women facing similar situations.

Finally, as previously noted, the visual arts (e.g., photography) may be combined with words to create an outcome more significant than either alone could do. This method is used by Goud (2010) in a self-exploration book of image–word combinations called *PhotoVerse*. Through PhotoVerse readers can see and be reminded of simple truths regarding their lives and life in general. The method used by Goessling and Doyle (2009) with at-risk adolescents also combines visual art with words. It seems especially strong because of the structured show, tell, and teach components. In this exercise, students were restricted in both time and number of images. However, they took interesting pictures that indicated to others what their lives and communities were like. The structure they followed is guided by the SHOWeD method of dialog, "which aims to take discussions from the concrete and personal level to critical analysis and social action" (Goessling & Doyle, 2009, p. 349). The series of questions is as follows:

S — What do you *see* happening in this photograph?
H — What is really *happening* in this photograph?
O — How does this relate to *our* lives?
W — *Why* do these issues exist?
eD — What can we *do* to address these issues?

Visual Arts and Music

A fun and exciting exercise for many clients is to have them draw images evoked by certain sounds in music. For instance, classical music may evoke placid scenes and flowing lines, and the staccato sounds in rap or disco may inspire action scenes or sharp, jagged lines (Fisher, 1989; Witmer, 1985). One way to draw to music is for clients to arrange music they like in a certain order and then draw to the music they enjoy (J. C. Mills & Crowley, 1986).

The visual arts and music may be used educationally and inspirationally too. Harter (2007) wrote, "Art and music share the ability to create sacred spaces, to honor the sacred in the everyday, in the broken, in the lost, to continually create new beginnings" (p. 178). They may document events and uplift spirits. A master of this procedure was Paul Fitzgerald at the University of Florida. Fitzgerald took photographs at professional meetings, such as the conventions of the Association for Counselor Education and Supervision, and at the end of the conference displayed slides of his photographs set to the beat of contemporary music by such individuals and groups as Bob Dylan, Elton John, Barbra Streisand, the Beatles, and Styx.

Visual Arts and Psychodrama

The visual arts usually are not combined with psychodrama due to the difficulty and challenge of linking these modalities together. However, in an experimental program involving termination and transition for a psychiatric day-treatment program, it was found that art activities could be used as a focus for role plays and psychodrama (Dallin, 1986). The nonverbal quality of producing visual arts served as a warm-up for enacting scenes connected with the act on a verbal level in psychodrama. The key bridge between the art and psychodrama experiences was having participants verbally process their art experiences before acting on them. Combining visual arts with psychodrama provides a way for clients to access multiple ways of knowing themselves: that is, seeing, hearing, and acting. In the process, they may more clearly experience themselves in different ways and take on new understandings of who they are.

Visual Arts and Meditation

In an intriguing study, S. Kim, Kim, and Ki (2014) investigated the effects of group art therapy, including breath meditation, on the subjective well-being of youngsters with depression and anxiety. Over a

5-month period, they conducted 13 sessions lasting 80 minute each with an experimental and a control group. Those who experienced art therapy combined with breath meditation were better off psychologically at the end of the research study when compared with the control group who experienced only art therapy to alleviate their depression and anxiety.

Summary

The visual arts have been a valuable asset to humankind throughout recorded history and even before. People represent their worlds visually, not just in their minds but in drawings, sculpture, and photographs. When individuals face and understand the concreteness of what they have created, they are often awakened to a new sense of self and a deeper understanding of their intra- and interpersonal relationships. The visual arts stir up feelings and open up possibilities. They serve as both a catalyst and conduit for understanding oneself in a larger world context (Gladding, 2012). The visual arts free clients to deal with issues they have not addressed by helping them work through the issues in a symbolic way and then by separating them from the issues and even the works of art they have created (Cohn, 1984).

In this chapter, several forms of the visual arts, including drawing, painting, clay work, sculpture, and photographs, have been examined with regard to their therapeutic use in counseling with a number of specific populations. Not everyone is artistic, but the visual arts lend themselves to being used in expressive as well as in already completed forms. The change that comes about as a result of employing visual art methods allows for versatility and is not necessarily tied to artistic ability. However, counselors must be cautious in their use of the visual arts with clients. Several ethical issues have yet to be worked out regarding these media, including issues related to confidentiality, documentation, ownership, and research (Hammond & Gantt, 1998). Nevertheless, the use of the visual arts provides a wide variety of possibilities for helping clients grow and develop through the creation of expressive forms.

Exercises

1. As an initial icebreaker in group or family therapy, spread a large sheet of paper on the floor and ask members to paint a cooperative picture with the materials you have provided, such as crayons or paint. After the group has worked on the project for about 30 minutes (tell them ahead of time how much time they have), have each member talk to you about the finished work and his or her part in it. Have members talk to one another during this time also. Try to link the feelings and experiences in the session project with parallel events in the group's or family's life. Be sure

to allow at least 90 minutes for this exercise so there is enough time to process what was drawn and experienced.

2. Make a mask of a feeling or mood you experience using a grocery bag as the main material (see Figure 15). Discuss with a friend or colleague the shapes, colors, and unique features of the mask. Then put on the mask and act in a way that you think represents the mask. Again talk to your friend or colleague about the way you acted and what insights you gained. Once you have completed the mask exercise, you may try it with clients when appropriate.

3. Aoki (2000) and Takata (2002) have reported on the widespread use of collages in Japan in psychotherapeutic settings since the late 1980s. Collages have been used in the United States (Linesch, 2001) and other countries too, for purposes ranging from family therapy to self-development. In this exercise, make a collage of your life showing its development up to now. Use photographs, pictures from magazines, words from newspapers, and other media in your construction. Allow 1 hour to complete the project. On a second day allow another hour to reflect on or refine your work. Present your collage to a trusted friend or colleague and talk about what you have learned about yourself and how you think you might use this method in therapy sessions.

Figure 15 Mood Mask

Chapter 6

Writing and Literature in Counseling

In Lines Through Time

In the morning light I write of you
   as my dreams fade to memories
   in the midst of winter's chill
      and the smell of fresh-brewed coffee.
In the noonday rush I think of you
   as I log frail thoughts into a dog-eared journal
      during silence preceding the joining of friends
      for lunch and the taste of fresh insights.
At home, past dusk, I read about you
   some words from my pen,
      some from more intimate and critical admirers.
At bedtime as I lie down
   my head dances with plans and emerging feelings
   as in your presence my life
      becomes more open like a book in progress.
I live with you in lines through time.

—Gladding, 1990a/2003

Counseling is a profession directly related to personal and societal health. As such, it is informed by numerous artistic traditions that describe human nature. One of the most powerful means of comprehending human life to the fullest is found in the written words of poets, novelists, biographers, therapists, and clients. In essence, counseling is an art and "a science of experience, not only from formal research and case conferences, but from literature. . . . Without Shakespeare's plays, Dostoyevsky's novels, or James's short stories, our knowledge of anguish and conflict would be hollow, our self-revelations would be one-dimensional" (Kottler, 2010, p. 35).

Sometimes troubled or stressed individuals have been able to help themselves through selectively or systematically writing or reading. Studies have shown that writing about oneself and personal experiences can improve mood disorders, help reduce symptoms among cancer patients, improve a person's health after a heart attack, reduce doctor visits, and even boost memory. The power of writing—and then rewriting—your personal story can lead to behavioral changes and improve happiness (Parker-Pope, 2015). For instance, *PostSecret*, an ongoing community mail art project started by Frank Warren, is a place where people anonymously mail their secrets on one side of homemade postcards that are then posted on the PostSecret website (http://www.postsecret.com/). The process offers catharsis for those who write and may offer identity with others and less isolation among those who read its posts. These procedures are done independently. Because all of the posts are anonymous, some individuals may write and rewrite their stories multiple times.

Many times, especially in a more formal setting, people need guidance from counselors on how to write or what to read. Such a service is provided by therapists such as Kay Adams through her journaling workshops (http://www.journaltherapy.com/). In both situations, the results have been manifested in the mending of broken spirits and the restoration of hope and wholeness. It is interesting to note that some of the primary writers and consumers of literature historically and contemporarily have been physicians, including John Keats, Anton Chekhov, A. J. Cronin, William Carlos Williams, Robert Seymour Bridges, Walker Percy, John Stone, and Rafael Campo (Barbour, 1991; Ingalls, 1997; Kolodzey, 1983). The connectedness between health, healing, and literature is significant. Indeed, not only physicians but "dramatists, poets, novelists, and diarists throughout the centuries have also made the link between emotion, disclosure, and health" (Wright, 2002, p. 286).

In this chapter I examine the premise behind and practices of reading and writing in counseling. Suggested methods for using these two traditions are highlighted. Although what is being done in the domain of the written word in counseling is being verified, systematically making the written arts more uniform in therapeutic practice is an area only now being addressed.

Premise of the Use of Literature in Counseling

The therapeutic use of literature as a healing tool in counseling is known by a variety of names. *Bibliotherapy, bibliocounseling, poetry therapy,* and *scriptotherapy* are the most common terms to describe the use of the written word in the therapeutic process. For simplicity's sake, the use of published literature in counseling is referred to primarily as bibliotherapy (from the Greek words *biblion* meaning "book" and *therapeio* meaning "healing"). Likewise, the process of having clients write is referred to as scriptotherapy (from the Latin roots *scriptum* meaning "thing" written and *therapia* meaning to "nurse" or "cure").

Regardless of what it is called, the concept of therapeutically using literature and writing "is as old as Aristotle's discussion of catharsis" (Hynes & Hynes-Berry, 1986, p. iii). Freud (1900/1953) credited poets and writers as being the first to discover the unconscious and bring it into awareness. Poets are able to experience some kind of "catharsis," "release," or even "therapy" through writing and performing. Performing poetry through such means as "Poetry Slams" has multiple benefits. Poets receive social support from others, overcome fears, share with others, feel listened to, are validated, and have continuous feedback that can be integrated into the growth of their work (Alvarez & Mearns, 2014). In any case, published literature, focused writing, and the spoken word have been used historically in a number of ways, such as working through grief, improving socialization, and increasing self-actualization (A. Berger, 1988; T. Bowman, 1994; Gold, 1988; Heninger, 1987).

Bibliotherapy

"In 1916 Samuel Crothers created the term *bibliotherapy* to refer to the therapeutic use of books" (Jackson, 2001, p. 289). As opposed to reading done for diversion or practical purposes, bibliotherapy is directed toward helping clients find solutions to their problems and concerns through directed reading. Jackson (2001) explained, "Through the use of bibliotherapy, the counselor can provide opportunities for clients to generate alternative thoughts, feelings, and actions, to learn new skills, and to practice new behaviors" (p. 294). Bibliotherapy helps people gain control over their lives and situations by identifying with others and finding unique and universal solutions. As a discipline, bibliotherapy subsumes not only texts for reading but audio and visual materials as well (Rus-Makovec, Furlan, & Smolej, 2015). As such, it provides both inspiration and solace (Riordan & Wilson, 1989).

A wealth of evidence supports bibliotherapy for a variety of treatments in many clinical settings (Chamberlain, Heaps, & Robert,

2008). However, in the world of bibliotherapy, there is a difference between "clinical bibliotherapy," which is implemented by a qualified counselor or therapist, and "developmental bibliotherapy," which "may be used by teachers and other lay helpers to facilitate normal development and self-actualization with an essentially healthy population" (Pehrsson & McMillen, 2005, p. 48).

Premises of Bibliotherapy

Bibliotherapy involves several nonexclusive premises. A first premise is that through literature the counselor can help clients realize more fully the multiple emphases behind counseling as a profession. Furthermore, participating in this process can assist individuals in making significant discoveries about themselves. For example, a great deal of poetry expresses subtle and overt psychological insights about life situations that are related to counseling themes (Chavis, 1986). By reading and discussing such material, counselors and clients may come to personalize aspects of the poetry into their own lives. In the process, they may "incorporate the Freudian insight about telling [their] story as it was, the Jungian insight of transforming it with a metaphor drawn from outside sources, and the Perlsian emphasis on the here-and-now action" (Gorelick, 1987b, p. 94). Counseling theories have a place in human growth and development, but that focus is sometimes de-emphasized. Literature, especially poetry, helps highlight the importance of counseling traditions in understanding life (Mazza, 2003). Poetic literature ranging from John Donne to Gladys Wellington emphasizes the many roads to client change and the difficulty and thrill of getting to and through life stages.

Another premise behind the inclusion of literature in counseling is that "true self-knowledge and a greater understanding of the world emerge" (Hynes & Hynes-Berry, 1986, p. 1). Clients realize that their problems are universal as well as unique. They learn that they share a connectedness with many other people across time, gender, culture, and circumstance (Duffey, 2015; Lerner, 1994). Such an experience gives comfort to individuals who may otherwise be naive or myopic in viewing their circumstances. For example, children may be unaware that other children face situations similar to theirs. Reading and discussing a book such as Joy Berry's (1987) *Every Kid's Guide to Handling Feelings* may be helpful in getting such children to talk about everyday emotions from love and joy to anger and jealousy.

Yet another premise for including literature in counseling is that more constructive and positive thinking and creative problem solving are generated (Watson, 1980). Reading literature is relaxing and enables participants to become more engaged in using imagery while mentally developing divergent and novel ways of resolving difficulties.

Levels of Bibliotherapy

Bibliotherapy is practiced on one of three levels: institutional, clinical, or developmental (R. J. Rubin, 1978). At the institutional level, those who receive treatment are generally distraught and often disturbed. Usually they are looking for information that can help them get better, and the material used at the institutional level is traditionally didactic and instructive. Such material can take many forms, such as general texts, for example, Jan Black and Greg Enns's (1998) *Better Boundaries: Owning and Treasuring Your Life*. Reading matter can also focus on how to deal with more specific disorders, such as Carolyn Costin's (2007) *The Eating Disorder Sourcebook*. The status of bibliotherapy in hospitals is reflected in the fact that The Joint Commission has approved this procedure as a professional modality (Lerner, 1997).

At the outpatient clinical level, people receiving bibliotherapy services have moderate emotional or behavioral problems. The material presented to them is usually imaginative (Riordan, Mullis, & Nuchow, 1996). Examples of imaginative literature can range from children's literature within a family context, such as Fred Rogers's (1998) *When a Pet Dies,* to practical guides, such as Drew Edwards's (1999) *How to Handle a Hard-to-Handle Kid*. In these types of literature, insight is gleaned from reading what others have done or thought about when faced with challenging situations or circumstances.

At the developmental level, the focus of bibliotherapy is on normal people and the multitude of everyday problems and situations they face. Therefore, the materials used are flexible and cover a wide range of emotions (Gladding & Gladding, 1991; Kelsch & Emry, 2003; Stanley, 1999). Judith Viorst's books for children and adults, such as *Alexander and the Terrible, Horrible, No Good, Very Bad Day* (1976) and *Necessary Losses* (1998), are examples of literature appropriate at this stage.

The Process of Bibliotherapy

At its best, bibliotherapy is interactive. It is "a therapeutic modality in which guided discussion of literature, other media material, and/ or creative writing by the participant or group is used to achieve prescribed therapeutic goals" (Rossiter & Brown, 1988, p. 158). The type of literature used and the way it is handled depend on the problems to be resolved and the thoroughness with which clients wish to achieve certain outcomes. Self-help, behaviorally based books such as Alberti and Emmons's (2008) *Your Perfect Right* and Bolles's (2016) *What Color Is Your Parachute?* often are prescribed by counselors because the results can be more readily measured than with works of fiction or inspiration (Riordan

---

Creative Reflection

What books, poems, or other writings have had an impact on you over the years? How? Why do you think these works of literature have had a long-lasting effect?

& Wilson, 1989). An important part of the bibliotherapeutic process is to personalize it so that materials are appropriate to clients with regard to reading level and situation handled. Therefore, to-the-point material in the form of articles from *Reader's Digest, Prevention,* and *Guideposts* may be appropriate for and prescribed to some clients, whereas such material would be unthinkable for others.

In the bibliotherapy process a triadic connection is fostered between (a) literature (the primary tool), (b) participants, and (c) facilitators (counselors or developmental specialists who help participants process the insights and knowledge they have obtained for real-life situations). A dual interaction occurs; participants' responses to a piece of literature are enhanced or expanded because of their dialog with facilitators (Hynes & Hynes-Berry, 1986). An example of this process at work is the use of prescriptive literature. This idea has been advocated over the years for a wide variety of human ailments (Perakis, 1992), but it originated in a concrete form when Jack Leedy (1985), a New York psychiatrist, started asking his patients to read specific poems in connection with certain disorders or problems. For insomnia, persons might read "Hymn to the Night" by Henry Wadsworth Longfellow, or for anxiety, the poem "I'm Nobody! Who Are You?" by Emily Dickinson (Kolodzey, 1983).

In a graduate counseling course on the creative arts in counseling where prescribed readings were assigned, researchers found that therapeutic reading opened doors for insight, action, connection, communication, building relationships, and growth as professional counselors (Bruneaua & Pehrsson, 2014). Some, if not all, of these qualities might occur in clinical situations, but the research has yet to be done. Overall, bibliotherapy is a popular way of working with clients. Research has suggested it will continue to be used and assessed even more in the future (Jack & Ronan, 2008; Riordan & Wilson, 1989).

Scriptotherapy

The term *scriptotherapy* is frequently used to refer to the process of writing in a therapeutic way (Riordan, 1996). In some circles, scriptotherapy is known as writing therapy (Wright & Chung, 2001). It is effective as a self-help and therapeutic approach to working with clients in the resolution of life difficulties, especially those that are unnoticed, denied, unresolved, or traumatic. It can promote personal growth and decreased isolation for populations that are vulnerable, such as adolescents living with HIV (Fair, Connor, Albright, Wise, & Jones, 2012).

Wright and Chung (2001) defined writing therapy as "client expressive and reflective writing, whether self-generated or suggested by a therapist/researcher" (p. 279). Writing enables self-expression, acceptance of feelings, and sometimes an increase in one's sense of spirituality.

Writing also may relieve pain and help clients deal with emotions on a cognitive and objective level (L. E. Mercer, 1993). Counselors and clients who use writing therapeutically create their own literature, which may be quite personal and insightful (L. Golden, 2001).

In addition to being a therapeutic release and relief, there may be secondary health benefits from writing (Lepore & Smyth, 2003). For example, writing about one's best possible emotional connectedness with a romantic partner is a promising clinical intervention for men whose restrictive emotionality often keeps them from visualizing, let alone having, more intimate relations with women. In a study in which male college students wrote 20 minutes a day, 3 days a week, for 4 weeks about how their lives would be different if they had the best possible emotional connectedness with a romantic partner, Wong and Rochen (2009) found these men reported a significantly greater decrease in psychological distress as compared with a control group of men who wrote about impersonal topics. Their research was built on James W. Pennebaker's (1990) work, which found that college students who wrote for 20 minutes a day, 4 days a week, about matters of concern to them stayed healthier than a control group whose members did not write. Furthermore, in an exhaustive review of the literature on writing as therapy, Pennebaker (1997, 2004) concluded that journaling about meaningful topics improved individuals' physical and emotional well-being, and that writing and talking about traumas were comparable as long as the topics were addressed meaningfully.

As a group, writers frequently begin expressing themselves in writing because of a problem they have had in their own lives. Their desire is to find a resolution through the written word. The result of their writing "consists of the deeper and wider dimension of consciousness" to which they are carried "by virtue of . . . wrestling with the problem" (May, 1969, pp. 170–171). Thus, what is produced is not only a literary and artistic work but also "genuine self-realization" (May, 1969, p. 172) that carries writers past innocence and into an existential dimension of life from which they can never emerge the same as before entering.

Ways of Doing Scriptotherapy

Clients often express a desire to keep a journal or write, but almost as frequently they end up not doing so. Kay Adams (1998) and Sandy Grason (2005) suggested a number of ways to help clients keep a journal. One of K. Adams's ideas is for clients to prepare themselves to write before they start the process. Preparation includes physically locating oneself in a space that is physically and psychologically conducive to writing and where there will be no interruptions. Once such a space is found, clients should go through any needed rituals, such as deep-breathing exercises or lighting candles, to further create a therapeutic mood.

One of K. Adams's (1998) favorite ways to get clients writing is called the 5-minute writing sprint. A timer is set to go off after 5 minutes, so the client does not have to continually keep track of time. Then the client begins writing about anything he or she wishes. The only rules are that the writing instrument has to constantly be in motion. If words do not come to mind, the writer should doodle or scribble on the paper in a flow that is similar to writing and that is continuous. When the timer goes off, the person stops writing (*5-Minute Writing Sprint*). This approach to writing is practical; most clients can find 5 minutes to devote to writing. In this exercise, I like to have clients write one day and read and reflect on what they have written the next. This practice helps clients stay motivated to write and gives them an opportunity to process what they are writing.

K. Adams (1998) also suggested that clients can be helped to learn how to write by doing a word cluster around a central word, such as *anger, anxiety,* or *distress* (see Figure 16). The word *anger* might lead to people, places, times, or situations that have been associated with this feeling in one's life. Ways of constructively dealing with the intensity of the emotion may arise as well (*Word Cluster*).

Clients can loosen up their writing skills (and their thought processes) simultaneously by writing a character sketch on someone they find interesting. When such an exercise is done, clients have a good opportunity to compare themselves with the admired person in a positive way (*Character Sketch*). Some therapists have found writing to be so empowering and effective that they tell their clients they must

Figure 16   Cluster Drawing "Anger"

write unless they like their therapist a lot, have plenty of money for therapy, have excellent insurance, and want to stay in therapy forever (L'Abate, 1992).

Other clinicians realize that writing is a way of taking care of themselves (E. K. Baker, 2003). These practitioners realize that through writing they may rid themselves of any toxicity that has built up over time in working with clients and also give themselves hope and happiness through words.

Forms of Scriptotherapy

Two forms of scriptotherapy that have become increasingly popular are therapeutic correspondence and rewriting personal stories (Riordan & Ketchum, 1996). *Therapeutic correspondence* is the writing of notes and letters by clients or counselors after a session. Such writing may take many forms, be done extensively, and follow a number of theories. For example, France, Cadieux, and Allen (1995) reported the case of a literary therapeutic encounter that lasted 5 months (15 letters).

The practice of therapeutic correspondence has been most noted and popularized on a clinical level by the narrative family therapists led by Michael White and David Epston (1990). These practitioners believed they should not write notes apart from those they would share with a family with whom they are working. Therefore, their clinical observations are often written in the form of letters that they send to client families. Session notes in the form of letters can stimulate client thought and help clients concentrate on particular issues. "Receiving a letter from a counselor may be a particularly meaningful experience for clients" (R. M. Hoffman, 2008, p. 346). Letters of this type can test the accuracy of perceptions as well (Riordan & Ketchum, 1996). Letters may also be used in counselor education settings to welcome students to a course; to focus on their strengths and contributions in between classes; and to summarize their development, give them feedback, and provide closure after a class ends.

In addition, letter writing may be used as an intervention to help sexual abuse survivors develop a sense of empowerment and control over their lives (Kress, Hoffman, & Thomas, 2008). In such a process, called Letters From the Future, victims of sexual abuse develop a future orientation in which they "perceive themselves as strong and competent individuals who possess the resources needed to manage the influence of past abuse experience" (Kress et al., 2008, p. 107). In doing so they externalize their problems, create new realities, and identify solutions to their situations. Then they write therapeutic letters to themselves that can be used during a session or afterward (*Letters From the Future*). The letters can take many forms, such as "strength through suffering," "personal accomplishment," "older, wiser self," and "rainy day" correspondence. Overall, the letters "serve as a vehicle to self-exploration and the creation of change" (Kress et al., 2008, p. 114).

Rewriting a story is an emphasis of solution-focused family therapists that is led by two prolific theorists–writers, Steve de Shazer and Bill O'Hanlon, as well as a social psychologist, Timothy D. Wilson. In the solution-focused family approach, counselors help clients find exceptions to the stories they tell or write. These exceptions are then examined and expanded to create new stories and break old, repetitive, nonproductive behaviors (*Rewriting a Story*). The idea is based on the philosophy of constructivism, which states that reality is a reflection of observation and experience, not an objective entity.

Creative Reflection

When have you used the word *all* in writing or describing a situation only to find out there were exceptions to what you were stating? How did it feel to have to modify your words? What exceptions do you see in the usual routine by which you live your life?

In T. D. Wilson's (2011) approach, writing forces people to reconstrue whatever is troubling them and find new meaning in it. Writing nudges people from a self-defeating way of thinking into a more optimistic cycle that reinforces itself. For example, students at a major university who were prompted to change their personal stories from those that were negatively based, such as "I am not as smart as other students at this college," to a more neutral or positive focus, such as "I am capable but I may need to study more," improved their grade-point averages. They were also less likely to drop out over the next year than the students in a control group who did not change their personal stories but instead received information on ways to study better. G. T. Wilson's approach is story editing: The facts and events do not change but interpretations of them do. It is empowering because of the internal locus of control people are given regarding the way they think.

Practice of the Use of Literature in Counseling

Literature is used in counseling in numerous ways. Five traditions are highlighted here:

1. Reading select prosaic works, such as novels, autobiographies, and self-help books
2. Reading select poetic works, such as classic or modern poems
3. Keeping a journal or writing an autobiography in whatever language form the writer wishes to use, such as telegraphic speech, poetry, reflective thoughts, or descriptions of events
4. Paying attention to the literary way clients express themselves in counseling, such as the use of select metaphors, and expanding these literary devices to create something new

5. Keeping a memory book, which includes narratives such as stories, anecdotes, and poetry as well as songs, photographs, and genograms

Prosaic Practices

Prosaic practices center on reading any type of literature, especially story-based literature in which the result is the formulation of new ideas, insight, recollections, or information (C. H. Lankton & Lankton, 1989). A number of different types of books can be read for either enlightenment or counseling purposes. Among the most frequently included works are short stories (fiction), biographies (nonfiction), self-help books, fairy tales, and picture books (S. T. Burns, 2008; Pardeck & Pardeck, 1993). Books that are selected to help clients should be chosen thoughtfully and with care. The age, stage, developmental level, and situation clients are facing need to be considered. Some books, however, have a universal appeal. For example, *The Wonderful Wizard of Oz* (Baum, 1900/2000), a children's book with adult themes about the meaning of life, is a work that can be used with people throughout the life span. This book, when read and processed thoroughly, can help participants in the bibliotherapy process become more attuned to themes about loss and identity in their own lives (Reiter, 1988). *The Wonderful Wizard of Oz* was once used successfully with a group of tornado victims in a counseling setting. Retelling the story served three purposes: to remember, to teach, and to motivate (Carmichael, 2000).

Stories that are novel, as well as those that are retold, are valued for their ability to release emotions in a cathartic way while conveying knowledge, instilling insight, making meaning, and preparing people for change and life transitions (Gladding & Wallace, 2010). Indeed, the majority of influential people in human history, from antiquity, such as Aesop, Homer, Confucius, Buddha, and Jesus, to contemporaries, such as Nelson Mandela, Garrison Keillor, and Maya Angelou, have been master storytellers.

Books that have been helpful for adults in prosaic but stimulating ways range from M. Scott Peck's (1978) *The Road Less Traveled* to H. Jackson Brown Jr.'s (2000) *Life's Little Instruction Book,* with a plethora of autobiographies and fictional stories sandwiched in between. For children, prosaic books may cover general subject areas, such as the importance of making decisions as found in Richard "Dick" Nelson's Stop-Think-Choose elementary and middle school novels such as *In the Land of Choice* (R. Nelson, 1997) and *Incident at Crystal Lake* (R. Nelson, 1996). Popular children's books such as the Harry Potter series may be more subtle in what they convey. The beauty of books, especially those that tell stories, is that they contain broad themes that can be discussed with a counselor. In addition to encouraging insight in the process of discussion, these books stimulate readers to write their own parallel or novel works and gain greater knowledge of themselves through the experience.

Counselors who need ready sources of self-help books, especially for adults, would do well to consult a resource such as *The Authoritative Guide to Self-Help Resources in Mental Health* (Norcross et al., 2013). Clinicians who wish to tailor literature to the developmental level and concerns of children and adolescents may find *The Best of Bookfinder* (Dreyer, 1992) and *Growing and Knowing: A Selection Guide to Children's Literature* (Trim & Gale, 2004) quite useful.

Poetic Practices

Poetic practices center on the use of poetry in the counseling experience. They include the use of metaphors, journal writing, letter writing, and ceremonies in health and mental health disciplines and have been widely reported in the professional literature (Mazza & Hayton, 2013). A group of counselor practitioners are certified by the National Association of Poetry Therapy (NAPT) to practice this specialization, which is being increasingly researched. Other professionals use poetry in their work occasionally but are not certified or registered by NAPT. The work of both groups may have considerable overlap, although training for a registered or certified poetry therapist is usually more thorough.

The term *poetry therapy* is descriptive of the use of a wide variety of poetry in counseling, especially by trained poetry therapists (Lerner, 1997; Stepakoff, 2009). The process of poetry therapy has five stages of action: entry, engagement, involvement, incorporation, and initiative (P. O. Heller, 2009). As a professional, "the poetry therapist is one who is committed to the appropriate use of language in the healing process" (Lerner, 1988, p. 120). He or she is not interested in the creation of great literature (although classic poetry such as that by Yeats, Keats, Shelley, Wordsworth, Tennyson, Dickinson, Plath, and Ferlingetti may be used). Rather, the poetry therapist is concerned with the proper expression of emotion. Thus, poetry that is written or used may not be exemplary, although such works are "vivid in imagery and emotional impact" and express universal feelings (Chavis, 1986, p. 121).

In choosing poetic works for counseling, special attention is given to form and content (Gorelick & Lerner, 1997). Poetic form focuses on the rhythm of a poem and how compelling, appealing, and appropriate it is (Hynes & Hynes-Berry, 1986). Kolodzey (1983) noted, "Verses tend to be clocked to a poet's body rhythms . . . and the poets we like best tend to be those whose body rhythms match our own" (p. 67). Content is the "what" within the poem that makes it appealing or repelling to particular audiences. For instance, didactic content is rarely embraced by poetry therapists or counselors who use poetry because it has a way of turning people off due to its preachy nature.

Poems that are most open to discussion have the greatest universal appeal (Lessner, 1974). In addition, the background of a poet can make a difference in whether the poem is pertinent or relevant to a particular population. For example, in using poetry when working with ethnic minority at-risk youths, J. Gardner (1993) used Native American poet Joy Harjo's (1983) poem "I Give You Back" to express wisdom and strength in resolving fear. The African American poet Lucille Clifton's (1991) poem "Whose Side Are You On?" has been used to describe the importance of community. In a Filipino study, Brillantes-Evangelista (2013) found that an eight-session poetry therapy intervention using the works of Filipino poets with abused adolescents was significantly effective in alleviating their symptoms of depression, although it was less effective in treating their PTSD.

Overall, using poetry selected for its capacity to generate discussion and exploration of cultural concepts, especially in a group setting, can be a productive, safe, and comfortable way to deal with emotions and experiences with multicultural and multilingual clients (Anser-Self & Feyissa, 2002). Such poems help these clients explore the past, present, and future; aid in developing an appreciation of life's wonders; bolster the clients' coping capacity when faced with life's potential barriers; and lead "to an acceptance and embracing of diversity while instilling hope, confidence, and a zest for life" (Anser-Self & Feyissa, 2002, p. 139). In recent years, poetry therapy has been used in working with those who have cancer, those who are addicted to substances, caregivers of patients (Heimes, 2011), and those who are depressed (Mohammadian et al., 2011).

Journals and Autobiographies

Keeping a journal (or log) of one's life or experiences about particular events (such as those that are stressful) is an excellent way to relieve tension and formulate a more controlled and logical understanding of taxing, tense, or traumatic experiences. Journaling can lead to emotional and psychological healing as well as learning over time. Although not appropriate for those with severe mental disorders, keeping a journal is a sound therapeutic approach for individuals of almost any age. Journals can be used across populations, theories, and settings. They record reflections on and feeling responses to present, personal experiences and can lead to greater self-awareness and growth, both during session and in between sessions (Hynes & Hynes-Berry, 1986).

Journals can be written in many forms, for example, the intensive journal process of Progoff (1975), the poetic reflections of Carroll (1970), or the therapeutic blogs (web logs) of Lent (2009). In groups, members and leaders may use logs and blogs to relive and reflect on experiences, become active in the group process, and give feedback to one another (Lent, 2009; Valine, 1983). One form of group writing is interactive journaling, in which members of a group share personal thoughts with other members in group counseling settings (Parr, Haberstroh, & Kottler, 2000). These types of journals allow group members to affirm and support each other altruistically and to deepen their understanding of self and others (*Interactive Journaling*).

The following are some of the other more common forms of journal work:

1. *The Period Log.* People are encouraged to define a recent period of their lives, reflect on their experiences and life events during that period, and record their feelings, impressions, and descriptions (*The Period Log*).
2. *The Daily Log.* This form of writing closely resembles a diary and serves as a running record of a person's subjective experience of his or her daily life (*The Daily Log*).
3. *The Stepping Stones.* The most significant points of movement in a person's life are listed in this type of journal. These points can help people see overall patterns and unconscious goals and motivations (*The Stepping Stones*).
4. *The Dream Log.* This log is used to keep a record of dreams and dream themes and patterns (*The Dream Log*).
5. *Twilight Images.* Thoughts and images that occur just before falling asleep are recorded in this type of writing (*Twilight Images*). (Weinhold, 1987, p. 10)

When a person keeps a journal, it is crucial that the material in it be reviewed on a regular basis so that reflection and insight can be used. A good method in such a review is to read journal entries every 2 or 3 days and spend the time that would normally be used in writing to reflect on what was written. Journaling may be an especially appropriate procedure for working with Asian Americans, whose cultural values are not to share issues about feelings or family relationships openly with a counselor, at least initially (Kincade & Evans, 1996). They are also useful in working with adolescents who may be hesitant to open up verbally in therapeutic settings (Utley & Garza, 2011). In such cases, the information written in the journal should be kept private and shared only if the client wishes to do so. Journaling may also be applicable for clients of any age who are not fluent in literary skills, because through journal writing these individuals have time to reflect and edit their thoughts. In some cases, an audiotaped journal may be used if the client is an auditory processor of information and lacks solid writing skills.

Writing an autobiography is usually a more formal and structured task than keeping a journal. A major advantage of writing an autobiography is that it lets a person express what has been important in his or her life, to emphasize likes and dislikes, identify values, describe interests and aspirations, acknowledge successes and failures, and recall meaningful personal relationships. Such an experience, especially for the mature client, can be thought-provoking, insightful, and a stimulus for action. On occasion, the experience can also relieve tension. (Gibson & Mitchell, 2008, p. 278)

There is no best method for writing an autobiography because each person's life is unique. Nonetheless, to be complete, an autobiography should include as much information as possible from as many different times in the client's life as feasible. Early childhood memories as well as current events add to the significance of such a work, and the more material that is included, the more likely that patterns will emerge and issues arise that can be discussed and resolved if needed (*Autobiography*).

Client Language and Metaphor

One of the main achievements of successful counselors is their ability to listen to and use the language of clients, a procedure known as *minesis*. This procedure often involves hearing clients' unique and universal metaphors and then using these figures of speech in select ways to build rapport and foster change. A metaphor is a figure of speech containing an implied comparison—expressing an idea in terms of something else (Meier & Davis, 2011). Clients from all cultural backgrounds use metaphors (Grothe, 2008; Myers, 1998). For instance, it is common for Native Americans to express themselves in metaphorical stories either verbally or in writing (Kincade & Evans, 1996).

Metaphors are powerful. In counseling they can facilitate self-awareness and cognitive reframing of a problem (Alvarado & Cavazos, 2006/2007). Through metaphors, clients' perceptions of themselves and their situations may change. In addition, metaphors facilitate communication, especially for indirect negative emotions that may be too painful to express directly (Shinebourne & Smith, 2010). Archetypal metaphors lend great power to this communication of ideas. These metaphors, such as light and dark, gain their power through the ability to be commonly identified by anyone, suggesting that clients will more often select metaphors of this type to convey their message.

> ## Creative Reflection
>
> Some of the most insightful literature ever written is in the form of journal entries and autobiographies, such as the *Diary of Anne Frank* (A. Frank, 1947/2003) or *Dare to Dream! 25 Extraordinary Lives* (Humphrey, 2005). Ask a reference librarian to help you locate books in this form or go online to find them. Try reading portions of one or more such works. What are your impressions?

According to Lyddon, Clay, and Sparks (2001), metaphors are central to at least five developmental change processes in counseling: (a) relationship building, (b) accessing and symbolizing emotions, (c) uncovering and challenging clients' tacit and unrealistic assumptions, (d) working with client resistance, and (e) introducing new frames of reference. Clients who speak in figurative language, especially metaphors, may weave a rich tapestry of tales focusing on such matters as being "wrapped up in rage" or "torn between two feelings." They may also give rich descriptions of themselves and their surroundings in a compact and emotionally arousing way, such as "he has a heart of stone" (McKee et al., 2003).

In some cases, counselors can help clients unravel or mend their situations by speaking metaphorically themselves to clarify or amplify what clients are saying. For example, a counselor might say to a client who is feeling helpless, "It sounds like you see yourself in quicksand and that you are going down fast with nothing to grab onto." Because of the different layers of sensory and informational meanings, metaphors are more likely to evoke an experiential response in clients than relaying adjectives alone (Levitt, Korman, & Angus, 2000).

When clients are struggling, relating to them through metaphor is an easy, effective way to elicit a response. In such situations counselors are primarily working to problem set, that is, literally to frame or reframe a problem so clients can deal with it. For instance, "a tidal wave of emotions" may be seen as "an abundant mixture of anxiety and depression." Then clinicians must work further with clients to use additional metaphorical language in select ways to solve problems so that clients do not become literally or figuratively stuck in the situations. For example, the "abundant mixture of anxiety and depression" can be weakened and controlled through exercise, role plays, relaxation techniques, preparation, and prescription medicines, which act as "barriers to the mixture becoming toxic or disabling."

Memory Book

The memory book is a way of passing on traditions, values, and norms from one generation to another (Pillay, 2009). It includes narratives such as stories, anecdotes, and poetry as well as songs, photographs, and genograms. Because of influences and advancements in technology, memory books can now be formulated digitally. Regardless of the form, these books have the potential to influence the well-being of their makers by getting them actively involved in this strength-based approach to collecting and recollecting events from life and communicating these in a healthy way to present and future generations, especially family members (*Memory Book*). The memory book can provide a tangible link to persons and their cultures. It may well be one of the most powerful ways of psychotherapeutically "working with clients and significant others who have terminal illnesses" (Pillay, 2009, p. 35).

Literature in Counseling
With Specific Populations

Children

Literature for children is usually written in the form of storybooks, fairy tales, and nursery rhymes (Bettleheim, 1976; Lerer, 2008). Often these works are unique in their simultaneous presentation of a story through words and pictures (Coughlin, 1991). They frequently have accompanying video- or audiotapes, and when that occurs children are exposed to the book content through a variety of stimuli. To be effective in using literature with young children, counselors may employ as many complementary media devices as possible.

Children's books are rich with characters that confront many of the same dilemmas faced by the children in our society (Nicholson & Pearson, 2003). Much of this literature focuses on teaching lessons "about how to handle most of the problems of childhood" (Guerin, 1976, p. 480). Numerous books help instill courage and deal with the mastery of fears in this population. Prime examples include Margery Williams's (1922) *The Velveteen Rabbit*, Maurice Sendak's (1984) *Where the Wild Things Are*, Beatrix Potter's (1902/1972) *The Tale of Peter Rabbit*, and Watty Piper's (1930/1972) *The Little Engine That Could*. Other texts, such as Dr. Seuss's (1950/1976) *Yertle the Turtle*, teach basic lessons about interpersonal relationships. Sometimes counselors can use familiar fairy tales, metaphors, and other stories in therapeutic settings to get children to open up without directly talking about their lives (Cowles, 1997). Such stories as Antoine de Saint-Exupéry's (1943) *The Little Prince* and the folktale about the *Ugly Duckling* are good examples of such material. In addition, a few television shows such as *Sesame Street* and *Reading Rainbow* promote books and reading materials that enhance children's cognitive, affective, and prosocial learning in a style that is appealing and digestible. An excellent source of 36 popular stories for elementary school children (i.e., kindergarten through sixth grade) is *Children Talking About Books* (Borders & Naylor, 1993). A useful Internet site for children's picture books is *Picturing Books* (http://pingb. picturingbooks.com/).

Young children seem to benefit from mutual storytelling (R. A. Gardner, 1971). In its original form, R. A. Gardner devised a verbal means by which a counselor and child client would tell a story together. The counselor would begin the story with a phrase, such as "Once upon a time," and tailor his or her initial remarks to parallel the present situation of the child. The story would then be turned over to the child to continue. The counselor would intervene only when the client becomes stuck or asks for help, at which point the counselor would add neutral descriptive material or ask a question

(*Mutual Storytelling*). The idea behind this activity is for the young client to really hear and attempt to resolve areas in life that are presently troubling. Kestenbaum (1985) and Hudson (2002), among others, have found this technique effective in highlighting issues in the lives of children and helping them work through these matters in a nonthreatening way. It seems effective for a wide range of ages.

Pehrsson (2006/2007) modified R. A. Gardner's method and worked with children in writing stories—a process Pehrsson referred to as "co-story-ing." The advantage to putting stories in a written form on paper is that they can be revisited and refined. Also, many children are not developmentally ready for talk therapies. Furthermore, insight sometimes does not come until after a story is written or talked about. In co-story-ing, there is a five-stage process that involves acceptance and affirmation of children's responses. The stages are preparation (gathering of materials), explanation (of what is to be done), composition (the actual writing of the story), ending-reflection (completion of the task), and expanding alternatives (where the story is revisited and altered if wished) (*Co-Story-Ing*).

Children of all ages benefit from writing. Young children, for example, begin to see themselves and their world more clearly through written exercises. They mature in the process, and writing "seems to proceed hand in hand with psychological growth, to reflect and enhance it, to deepen and extend it, and often to quicken the process" (Brand, 1987, p. 274). One way to help young children who have been sexually victimized is to have them create their own books of behavior rules for acting in certain situations (Strick, 2001). Another way to help them, especially in a group setting, is to have them make "paper bag books" from paper bags, usually the size of lunch sacks. Somody and Hobbs (2006/2007) outlined how to make such books and gave excellent illustrations of finished books in an article on using them with elementary school children from families experiencing high-conflict divorce. The details in their article are excellent and easy to follow.

Finally, children can be encouraged to write poetically about their lives and experiences. Such writing often results in gaining insight as children describe who they are and are not. For instance, in the following poem, a 10-year-old girl revealed how she pictured herself:

> I am the rain and not the river.
> I am a sunbeam but not the sun.
> I am a branch but not the tree.
> I am matter in motion but not the roar of the ocean. (Abell, 1998, p. 49)

Abell (1998) noted that writing poetry "can be an enriching component [for children] in their therapeutic experience" (p. 49).

Writing poetically is especially beneficial for academically inclined children (Hudson, 2002). As a means of exploring what it means to be human, writing poetry can add depth to human lives, even young lives. Although this type of writing may be free flowing and unstructured in many cases, a way to learn to write poetically about oneself and problems in everyday living is to use Kenneth Koch's (1970)

book *Wishes, Lies, and Dreams.* This text has illustrations and exercises that help children write poems about events and objects in their lives. Older children benefit as well. Journal writing also has been found to be therapeutic in helping children whose lives have suffered the turmoil of war (Costello, Phelps, & Wilczenski, 1994).

Adolescents

Adolescence is a time of turmoil in the midst of a search for identity. Therefore, literature serves a useful function in helping adolescents realize possibilities and meaning for their own lives. Biographies and autobiographies are especially relevant to this population. Such books as *Margaret Mead: A Life* (Howard, 1990), *The Rise of Theodore Roosevelt* (Morris, 2001), *Becoming Steve Jobs* (Schlender & Tetzeli, 2015), or *No Direction Home: The Life and Music of Bob Dylan* (R. Shelton, 2003) are excellent in giving teenagers insight into what they can be and how they can grow. Other works that deal with life difficulties, such as *The Kids' Book of Divorce: By, For, and About Kids* (Rofes, 1981) and *Don't Divorce Us! Kids' Advice to Divorcing Parents* (R. Sommers-Flanagan, Elander, & Sommers-Flanagan, 2000), can be helpful in gaining information on overcoming difficulties. These books offer perspectives on divorce and suggestions for coping from kids who have watched their parents go through it. As Pehrsson, Allen, Folger, McMillen, and Lowe (2007) noted, "A carefully chosen book can provide an effective means for healing preadolescents [and adolescents] experiencing divorce" (p. 412). In addition, novels such as Robert Cormier's *I Am the Cheese* (1996), *The Chocolate War* (1986), and *After the First Death* (1991) not only can be compelling as literary works but also can help students understand what is happening to them during adolescence (Monseau, 1994). In short, reading and discussing good literature in a directed way with adolescents and preadolescents is an excellent method for assisting them to cope and even thrive during this time of transition, challenge, and sometimes confusion from childhood to adulthood, especially with regard to family and society.

To obtain the most from bibliotherapy, adolescents and young children need to go through four distinct stages: identification, catharsis, insight, and universality (Kelsch & Emry, 2003). During the identification stage, adolescents intellectually identify with characters, situations, and settings found in various stories and participate in the story being read safely and vicariously. During the catharsis stage, adolescents become more emotionally involved in the story they are reading. They share the motivations, conflicts, and feelings with the character(s) with whom they have identified. Tension is released at the plot resolution. The end of this stage leads to the insight stage in which adolescent readers apply the outcomes of the story to their own lives. For instance, they may change their attitudes or behaviors in accordance with that of a certain character or characters. Finally, if bibliotherapy is successful, adolescents will reach the stage of universality in which they realize that their own issues are shared with others, and their empathy and sensitivity are enhanced. In this final stage, a connection is made with the larger world outside of the immediate one in which adolescents live.

Besides the traditional ways of helping adolescents develop, an interesting approach is to use a theme-oriented style of reading and writing fairy tales to assist them in thinking through problem areas in their lives. According to Franzke (1989), fairy tales can be used therapeutically in a number of ways, such as through modification, invention, acting out, or reading or reciting. For example, L. Hill (1992) used fairy tales such as Cinderella to treat persons with eating disorders. The model that L. Hill advocated has four phases: (a) identification with the fairy tale, (b) development of connection with the fairy tale, (c) introduction of conflict, and (d) problem resolution. "The fairy tale offers the client opportunities to experience novel thoughts, sensations, and behaviors by working with and through fairy tale figures" (L. Hill, 1992, p. 585).

Hoskins (1985) formulated an inventive example of a therapeutic fairy tale that clients create from the beginning. In this tale, which is appropriately used with adults as well as with adolescents, clients are asked to participate in a pretend experience for a limited time. Specifically, they are asked to image and then do the following:

1. Set up a scene far from the here and now in time and place.
2. Within this setting, include a problem or a predicament.
3. Include a solution to the problem that is positive and pleasing.
4. Write their story within a 6- to 10-minute time period.

They begin their tales with "Once upon a time" because that is how all fairy tales begin, but after this standard opening they are on their own. After the tale is written, adolescents share their stories either individually or in a group setting, depending on the counseling format. Particular attention is paid to how thorough the fairy tale is, the qualities of the main characters, the nature of the pleasing and positive ending and what it depends on (e.g., skill, chance, luck), and the type of language used in creating the story. It is stressed to participants after this exercise that the limited amount of time is symbolic of life in general; they do not have unlimited time to work on life issues (*Therapeutic Fairy Tale*).

Creative Reflection

What lyrics do you remember from adolescence? Are they still meaningful? What are significant events you associate with them?

By writing a therapeutic fairy tale, participants may get insight into their lives and find more universal meaning in their lives. They can recognize their own anxieties and fears as well as their own abilities to problem solve (S. T. Burns, 2008).

Another way literature is used with adolescents is through strategically discussing song lyrics and poetry related to life issues, especially careers. "Throughout the ages, poems and lyrics have moved people, and 20th-century youth have made lyrics a mainstay of their culture" (Markert & Healy, 1983, p. 104). Lyrics are generally user friendly for adolescents and can be used to reach them in a way that other media cannot. A particular area in which lyrical and poetic works are valuable is in career decision making. Song lyrics ranging from those of James Taylor's "That's Why I'm Here" to traditional songs such as "I've Been Working on the Railroad" address lifestyle and employment issues and can be arranged to fit particular groups with regard to ability, interest, and sophistication.

Adults

Adulthood is filled with opportunities and questions. The opportunities are especially prevalent in careers, and the questions are often difficult because they deal with making the most of limited time. As with adolescents, adults may find both comfort and direction in literature. Books that deal with midlife and beyond, such as *Thinking About Tomorrow: Reinventing Yourself at Midlife* (Crandell, 2007), *The Age of Miracles: Embracing the New Midlife* (Williamson, 2008), and *Darkness Visible: A Memoir of Madness* (Styron, 1990), offer wisdom and sometimes wit to those in the midst of life's journey. Some other top authors and books include *Why Marriages Succeed or Fail* by John Gottman (1995), *The Anxiety and Phobia Workbook* by Edmund J. Bourne (2015), *Feeling Good* by David D. Burns (1999), and *What to Expect When You're Expecting* by Murkoff and Mazel (2008).

Two annotated sources of self-help books and films that adults may find useful are *Self-Help That Works* by John Norcross et al. (2013) and *Read Two Books and Let's Talk Next Week* by Janice M. Joshua and Donna DiMenna (2000). Top-rated self-help autobiographies on Norcross et al.'s list include *A Grief Observed* by C. S. Lewis, *The Virtues of Aging* by Jimmy Carter, and *Breaking Free From Compulsive Eating* by Geneen Roth. Films that Norcross and colleagues have found that other therapists give high marks to include *Ordinary People, The Joy Luck Club,* and *Dead Poets Society.*

In addition to realistic stories and films, S. T. Burns (2008) recommended using fictional stories with adults to explore difficult topics in a safe and nonthreatening way: "These stories deepen awareness and increase problem solving skills" (p. 441). She recommended two free Internet sites for accessing stories. The first is the National Storytelling Network (http://www.storynet.org). The second is the website of D. L. Ashliman, a retired professor from the University of Pittsburgh, who created a page of folklore and mythological electronic texts (http://www.pitt.edu/~dash/folktexts.html). A third storytelling network, not directly mentioned by S. T. Burns, is the Healing Story Alliance, a special interest group of the National Storytelling Alliance (http://healingstory.org/). This site has excellent stories for adults and children on a variety of subjects, such as addiction and recovery, incarnation, domestic violence, and death. It is particularly oriented toward health care professionals and anyone who can see the benefit of a story as a tool in healing.

In addition, N. W. Brown (2006/2007) recommended using fairy tales in groups with adults where the tale is read and used for a springboard for meaningful discussion of unique and universal issues. N. W. Brown stated that fairy tales contain themes and issues such as fear of abandonment, sibling rivalry, and self-esteem that people of all ages hold as important. The agenda for using fairy tales in a group is for the leader to pick such a tale that contains existential or developmental issues. The leader reads it to group members, who have their eyes closed. Members then draw one or two scenes from the story that seem important to them. A leader-led discussion follows in which feelings and symbols are discussed and members describe how the fairy tale and its message are similar to what they are experiencing.

Two other scriptotherapy processes for adults are called writing the wrongs and writing the rights (Gladding, 1991f). In the first procedure, adults write out the wrong or disconcerting experiences they have had in life (e.g., unexpected death of a loved one, divorce, loss of physical or mental abilities). After the wrong has been described, clients write about the situation by not changing the facts but by simply writing out what they learned and how they have benefited or been made right (or better) from having had the unpleasant event (*Writing the Wrongs to Make Them Right*). Some excellent examples of this procedure appear in the October 1988 issue of the *Journal of Counseling & Development,* which was devoted to critical incidents in the lives of counselors. Another excellent example of this procedure is a brief article on loss and resolution by Sue Chance (1988) in which she interwove poetry, philosophy, and reality in a moving and dramatic way. The second procedure, writing the rights, is a parallel experience to writing the wrongs, except that it entails writing out the good or positive in one's life that was not from adversity and assessing what was learned from these experiences. In other words, this procedure focuses entirely on highlights in one's life. Lessons learned might include such things as "hard work pays off" or "if you treat people right, they will treat you right."

Older Clients

Writing is often quite therapeutic for older people. It is an ancient healing art found throughout recorded history. Wasserman (1988) noted that one of the best North American personages to exemplify this therapeutic resource was Nezahualcoyotl (1402–1472), king of Texcoco (a city located approximately 20 miles northeast of modern Mexico City). In his struggle with his own mortality, Nezahualcoyotl wrote poetry as a way of working through despair and finding purpose in life.

In more recent history, the life-review process has become a popular therapeutic tool in helping older clients (Garland & Garland, 2001; Haight & Haight, 2008). A life review involves having a person write his or her autobiography using family albums, old letters, personal memories, and interviews with others to gather and integrate life experiences into a meaningful whole (*Life Review*). Ideally, this effort produces wisdom and satisfaction while alleviating pain and regrets.

Another literary way of working with older adults involves reading works by those within their age range. Books such as Kenneth Koch's (1977) *I Never Told Anybody: Teaching Poetry Writing in a Nursing Home* and Marc Kaminsky's (1974) *What's Inside You, It Shines Out of You* illustrate the creative potential of older adults and their insightful wisdom. Furthermore, reading these works helps to sensitize older clients and those who work with them to facts and feelings about aging, and thus they assist in creating understanding and empathy as well as in providing enjoyment.

Further, in an experience that involves group work with older people, residents in nursing homes and other long-term care facilities can participate in reaction readings of poetry, during which they read poems aloud together as a group (i.e., a choral reading). They "then react to the content of the poems with their own knowledge, opinion, emotion, and imagination" (Asmuth, 1995, p. 415). In such an activity, residents become their own audience of their own performance. They are stimulated emotionally and intellectually. Furthermore, their self-concepts and cohesiveness as a group improve (*Reaction Readings*). Some examples of poems that have been found helpful in reaction reading include "Trees" by Joyce Kilmer, "They Have Yarns" by Carl Sandburg, and "Mother to Son" by Langston Hughes.

Groups

Groups are a popular setting for using literature. Creative writing exercises help heighten the use of language and emotion within a group (Wenz & McWhirter, 1990). Chavis (1986) observed that "At the present time, group therapy seems to be the setting in which poetry is most frequently used as a therapeutic tool" (p. 121). Psychiatric groups, which are usually open-ended and contain different people in each session, can use poetry and other literary works to generate a common bond at the start of the group session and to stimulate the expression of emotions. Self-help groups, such as Alcoholics Anonymous (AA), are settings in which other types of literature, for example, personal and inspirational stories focused on implementing the 12 steps of AA, are read. Usually poetry becomes a part of the group experience at the beginning or end of the process. In psychiatric and self-help groups, prosaic literature may be responded to throughout the process. In other types of counseling groups, however, literature is rarely referred to after the initial forming stage (Gladding, 2016).

Poems can be used at the beginning of a group as a catalyst. Lessner (1974) described this type of procedure. In her work with groups, she read nondidactic poems—such as those by Langston Hughes, Maya Angelou, James Dickey, or A. R. Ammons—to group participants after they have been through a series of warm-up exercises. Each person in the group is asked to identify with an image in the poem and then talk about this image with regard to how it represents him or her. For example, a person might identify with grass and talk about how his or her life is growing (*Poems as a Group Catalyst*).

Poems can also be used in closing by having group participants write couplets or lines and then link them together in an interactive way that results in a collaborative poem (Yochim, 1994). Such a procedure requires involvement by everyone in a receptive (listening and reading) and expressive (creating) way (Mazza, 1988). It is usually an effective way to terminate a group experience permanently or, in the case of open-ended groups, to close the group for that session (*Closing Poems*). Here is an example of a group poem:

> In the group today I learned
> to attempt strategies differently
> to be receptive to new ideas
> three ways to think outside the box (creatively)
> how powerful the arts can be
> the beauty and wisdom of learning together
> to experience differences and similarities
> creative new ways of thinking
> about myself and my potential
> Now I am moving on.

A way of helping groups grow through literature, especially through writing, is for case notes of group sessions to be shared with participants (Chen, Noosbond, & Bruce, 1998). In such a process, clients benefit

Creative Reflection

Have you found that writing out your thoughts and feelings helps you? What are the drawbacks to such a procedure?

by externalizing, personifying, and depathologizing other group members' problems. In addition, counselors benefit by increasing group trust because of their openness and giving group participants a chance to see group process more concretely.

Life Skills

Besides being used with specific populations, literature can be used in a guidance capacity to promote and foster general and specific life skills. One way to accomplish this is to utilize classic literary novels that deal with issues and problems of different age groups, such as those by John Steinbeck, Toni Morrison, William Faulkner, Anne Tyler, Oscar Hijuelos, Harper Lee, Ernest Hemingway, E. Annie Proulx, James Baldwin, Eudora Welty, and John Updike (Kelsch & Emry, 2003). The unique personal and universal developmental difficulties of primary characters in a particular book are discussed along with ways the characters handle situations. Different ways of resolving dilemmas are highlighted by a helping professional, and other literary examples dealing with similar themes are presented. In this way, individuals of any age can learn from the insights of literature and discussions with others, especially in a group setting. The result is that those who participate in such a process may become better prepared to face issues in their own lives. This lifestyle development approach complements and makes more relevant the theories of life development formulated by such well-known theorists as Erik H. Erikson (1968) and Carol Gilligan (1982).

Another way of promoting life skills using a reading approach is to have clients select relevant topics and chapters that deal with issues in their lives from a book such as Lerner and Mahlendorf's (1991) *Life Guidance Through Literature*. This text focuses on issues ranging from the establishment of personal identity to death as presented in novels, plays, short stories, and films. After reading, clients discuss their thoughts and struggles with the counselor as outlined previously in the bibliotherapy process. If a writing or scriptotherapy approach is chosen, it can take the form of writing poetry, which D. O. Bowman, Sauers, and Judice (1996) stressed as a way to anchor "insights into a context, physically as well as metaphorically" and thereby provide "a reference point for transforming experience" (p. 21).

Family-Life Guidance

An approach similar to life-span guidance literature is family-life guidance literature. Three different styles exemplify this focus. The first is found in *The Oxford Book of Marriage* (Rubinstein, 1990), which contains excerpts from different types of literature, from poetry to novels, that relate to the developmental stages of marriage, such as newlywed and midlife. A unique feature of this book is that it encompasses literature across many ages, civilizations, and cultures. It combines the best of the old with the best of the new.

A second focus is demonstrated by Chavis (1987), who took modern short stories depicting stages of family life and introduced the periods with a summary of the primary therapeutic issues involved. In this way an overlay is presented to readers before they read, alerting them to important elements to look for in particular passages. As in the life-span guidance approach, Chavis gave no answers but provided thought-provoking literature that stands on its own merits in addressing important family issues that must be successfully resolved. In this subtle, indirect manner, she helped counselors and the lay public gain insight and chart directions for their own lives.

The third focus in family-life guidance is the autobiography. Few have been written that focus on therapeutic issues, but among the best is Augustus Y. Napier's (1990) *The Fragile Bond*. In his book, A. Y. Napier discussed events of his own life that influenced his development as a professional and as a person. His book is unique in its inclusion of marriage and family life in so detailed and vivid a manner. It offers behind-the-scenes accounts and insight into the difficulties and successes of balancing a career with marriage.

Graduate Counseling Students

A unique way to help graduate counseling students resolve issues in their own lives involves having them write a 15- to 20-page family autobiography. They are instructed to describe the dynamics of their family of origin utilizing the terminology and theoretical rationale (Piercy, Sprenkle, & Wetchler, 1997) of major family theorists, such as Murray Bowen and James Framo. This type of assignment is biased in favor of students' perceptions of their families, yet it personalizes family theory and gives students an opportunity to think about issues within their own families.

Another way to help graduate counseling students is to have them read about the lives of noted professionals. Three resources in this area are *Journeys to Professional*

> ## Creative Reflection
>
> When have you been inspired by reading about the life of someone you have only met tangentially if at all? What is it about obituaries that are either uplifting or depressing?

Excellence: Lessons From Leading Counselor Educators and Practitioners (Conyne & Bemak, 2004), *Leaders and Legacies* (West, Osborn, & Bubenzer, 2003), and *Creating Your Professional Path: Lessons From My Journey* (Corey, 2010). These books highlight the achievements and setbacks of some of the most prominent counselors of the 20th century. The American Counseling Association newspaper, *Counseling Today,* along with the American Psychological Association journal *American Psychologist,* publishes current obituaries of leading figures in the helping professions too.

Literature in Counseling With Other Creative Arts

Many creative arts complement the use of literature in counseling. For example, words may be acted out in formal or informal dramas and, thus, may be seen as well as heard. Counseling approaches to working from a literary point of view may take the form of movement or dance, too, as individuals express in a dynamic motion the essence of poetic or prosaic words. In addition, some theories, such as cognitive therapies, become more dynamic when they incorporate poetic and prosaic exercises into their treatment (K. S. Collins, Furman, & Langer, 2006). Two of the most widely used ways of integrating literature with other creative arts in counseling involve music and visual arts.

Literature and Music

Music can be used in various ways with literature, and in some cases literature, especially poetry, is musical. It is next to impossible to recite a poem without some use of "rhythmic pauses, vocal inflections, and interline harmonies as in music" (Masserman, 1986, p. 61). In other cases, music is used to set a mood for a story or a poem or to heighten emotions. In these situations, instrumental or lyrical music may be played in the background before or during reading of literature (Ingram, 2003). Similarly, music may be played before a select writing exercise. In such circumstances, music helps stir up feelings and words that otherwise would remain dormant. An example of such a process is the playing of John Denver's song "Poems, Prayers, and Promises" as a backdrop for a writing exercise titled "What I Believe In" (A. Berger & Giovan, 1990) in which participants write about their most important values and how they are expressed (*Music and Writing*).

An auditory complement to literature need not always be musical. For instance, in conducting bibliotherapy, special-effects tapes, such as sounds of the wind, a waterfall, or a crackling fire, may be useful in setting an atmosphere conducive to reading or writing. Participants in a bibliotherapy session may also make music of their own (Hynes & Hynes-Berry, 1986). In the latter activity, clients either reflect in sound what they have experienced on the written level or anticipate what they believe will occur because of a story's title or the focus of a writing assignment.

Literature and Visual Arts

Visual arts serve a special function when combined with literature. In such cases, pictures are thousand-word representations that are either realistic or distorted. Self-portraits, free-form drawings, and classic paintings can be a prelude or a complement to writing assignments or other literary ways of expression that promote self-awareness and personal development (Creskey, 1988; Hageman & Gladding, 1983).

Drawing a personal logo and then describing it in a story is a creative and effective method for combining art and literature (Wenz & McWhirter, 1990). In this exercise, the logo is developed through playing with doodles until a symbol emerges that feels just right for the participant. Writing a story to accompany the art is similar to writing a therapeutic fairy tale as described previously (*Personal Logo and Story*). In hospice settings, terminally ill patients have benefited from the combined use of poetry and art (Hodges, 1993). In uniting these two art forms therapeutically, hospice residents have been able "to gather new thoughts and ideas, to reflect upon past memories and experiences, and to enjoy the fellowship of others" (Hodges, 1993, p. 28) who have truly understood and cared about them.

Another art and literature exercise is known as lines of feelings (see Figures 17 and 18). In this procedure, clients are asked to draw and color lines that represent their feelings about certain situations or people. The lines vary in length and shape, but often jagged, rough lines in red or orange are used to signify anger or discontent, and smooth, flowing lines in blues and greens are more often used to display calmness and contentment. After the lines are drawn, clients can expand on them by writing about what the lines represent, how it feels to draw them, or to whom or what they are directed (*Lines of Feelings*).

The use of modeling clay can also be helpful because of the hands-on experiences participants obtain from shaping it. Working in clay often gives clients a feel for life experiences that then may be expressed in

Figure 17

Anger

My anger speaks at times
and I am blind to the calm
in the valleys in between.
I want my anger to level out.

Figure 18

Content

When I am content my
feelings flow like waves on a calm sea.
I can see clearly. I am serene.
That is the way I am today
and want to be tomorrow.

writing. Likewise, photography can inspire reading or writing of the highest caliber and make the process of counseling more enjoyable and rewarding (Amerikaner et al., 1980). In short, music and visual arts contribute an added dimension to the main treatment modality of integrating literature into the counseling process.

Summary

Literature is used in numerous ways in counseling and with many different types of clients. Individuals gain insights and are able to release emotions through reading and writing exercises that are prosaic or poetic in nature. These processes are known as bibliotherapy and scriptotherapy, respectively, and are practiced on an interactive level. By participating in prosaic or poetic reading and writing activities, including keeping journals and creating autobiographies, clients gain a perspective on their lives that helps them establish meaning and purpose. By following the language of clients, counselors are able to offer them additional assistance for helping themselves.

Literature can be used in counseling with other media devices such as video- and audiotapes, pictures and drawings, and music. Storytelling may also be included and is quite effective with children as well as adults. For example, *Spinning Tales, Weaving Hope* (Brody, Goldspinner, Green, Leventhal, & Porcino, 2003) contains 29 children's stories from around the world that encourage conflict resolution, compassion, and sensitivity to the earth, and *The Healing Heart—Families* (Cox & Albert, 2003) provides powerful examples of the use of stories and storytelling in encouraging resiliency, empathy, respect, and healing.

When chosen properly, literature can offer life guidance for people of all ages. It depicts possible futures while energizing clients and offering them ways of integrating their experiences.

Exercises

1. Over the course of a week, reflect on the literature you have read or heard that has made a lasting impact on your life. Write down the titles and authors of these works and the age you were when you discovered them. Look for any age- or stage-specific patterns in your choices and how the literature you read or had read to you made a difference. After you have made your list, discuss this experience with a close friend or colleague. Invite that person to try the exercise also. Compare your experiences. What literature from both of your lists do you think might be helpful to others?
2. Examine recent counseling journals and American Library Association publications for articles on the therapeutic use of literature. What books and writings are recommended? How do these contributors recommend using literature in counseling?

Draw up a guidance lesson for a particular group you work with that makes use of ideas gleaned from your readings.

3. Consult a reference librarian in your local community about the literature currently being read. Survey these materials and think of ways you might incorporate popular works into your counseling sessions.

Chapter 7

Drama and Counseling

Without Applause

At 35, with wife and child, a PhD,
  and hopes as bright as a full moon
    on a late August night,
      he took his place as a healing man
Blending it with imagination, necessary change, and common sense
    to make more than an image on an eye lens
      of a small figure running quickly up steps;
Quietly he traveled like one who holds a candle
    to darkness and questions its powers,
So that with heavy years, long walks,
    shared love, and additional births,
He became as the seasoned actor,
    who, forgetting his lines in the silence,
      stepped upstage and without prompting lived them.

—Gladding, 1974, p. 586

Drama focuses on communication between people and the roles individuals take in their daily lives. It is literally everywhere in society whether on a formal or improvisational level (Blatner & Wiener, 2007).

> In therapy, as in all human activity, drama is both inevitable and necessary. It is inevitable because, during the human lifecycle, people are constantly confronted with dramatic changes, and it is necessary because all transitions occur as a result of more or less dramatic experiences-in-action. (Kedem-Tahar & Felix-Kellermann, 1996, p. 27)

Therefore, as Jacques eloquently remarks in Shakespeare's *As You Like It* (Act 2, Scene 7), "All the world's a stage." Roles vary as people develop and face new challenges at different times and in various situations.

Joseph Campbell (1949) took the view that much of human life and drama is similar to patterns found in myths throughout the ages. Unhealthy individuals often act out in rigid and stereotyped ways, for example, as placaters, distracters, computers, or blamers (Satir, 1972). In such roles they fail to be straightforward and honest with their thoughts and feelings. Through default they act in an uncaring manner, as do many characters on television soap operas in relationship to issues of intimacy (Lowry & Towles, 1989).

Healthy people, however, are able to change their behaviors in response to environmental demands. They are open and flexible and communicate in a congruent manner. Sometimes they become stuck and dysfunctional too, but in these cases they seek assistance. Drama or drama-related approaches to counseling, such as psychodrama or drama therapy, may be helpful to these individuals in gaining a "greater understanding of social roles" and a clearer perspective on their lives in "relationship to family, friends, and past life" (Warren, 1984, p. 133). In dramatic enactments facilitated by a specialized therapist, clients can "preview, review, and revise life roles" (Emunah, 2001, p. 99). In addition, interactive drama may open people up to their biases and awareness with regard to multicultural and diversity issues (Tromski & Doston, 2003). It is on the formal and informal use of drama, psychodrama, and drama-related techniques that the material in this chapter focuses.

The use of drama as a part of the healing process extends far back in history. One of its most important times was in 5th-century BCE Athens, where dramatic traditions originated and flourished for years. The tragic drama, the older of the Greek drama forms, "depicted the unthinkable and unspeakable in ways that allowed members of the audience to participate in the dual roles of sufferer-participant and empathizer-observer" (Gorelick, 1987a, p. 38). Dramatic productions dealt with the eternal struggle between individual strivings and realistic limitations and engaged observers in asking existential questions about self-identity and purpose in life. The works of Sophocles, Aeschylus, and Euripides are examples of dramas that fostered audience identification, catharsis, and insight in such a way that what was personally felt at the time of a performance "would carry over to personal life beyond the theatrical space" (Gorelick, 1987a, p. 40).

Even in modern times, dramatic art forms continue to be powerful and widespread. According to Landy (1997),

> The female shamans of Korea, the Taoist priests of China, the masked dancers at Owuru Festivals in Nigeria, and the celebrants at Mardi Gras in Louisiana and Carnival in Brazil, all enact a form of cathartic healing through assuming archetypal roles and working their magic. (p. 5)

Dramatic activities include rituals, plays, improvisations, storytelling, masks, puppetry, and festivals as well as theater performances. They are interactive, emphasizing relationships, emotions, communication, cooperation and imagination, in-context learning, and the give and take of interpersonal nonverbal cues (Guli, Semrud-Clikeman, Lerner, & Britton, 2013). The healing function of drama, theater, and dramatic activities is reflected in all cultures. Horwitz, Kowalski, and Anderberg (2010) wrote, "Today, therapists and scientists work with psychodrama and drama therapy, often describing theater as the art form closest to life itself" (p. 13).

Premise of the Use of Drama in Counseling

As a profession, counseling has many parallels with the type of drama practiced by the ancient Greeks and practiced worldwide today. One parallel is that in both endeavors, those involved learn to experience a whole range of emotions and to express them appropriately. Counselors and dramatists then and now practice being sensitive to the parts they are called upon to play and becoming attuned to those with whom they interact. Individuals involved in both processes become consciously aware that what they do and how they do it will have an effect on the audiences before whom they perform. In essence, people who practice these two professions become heavily involved in all aspects of life and experience life on its deepest levels (Friedman, 1984). They become role models in their search for deeper understanding. Their behaviors have either a positive or a negative effect on others with whom they closely deal.

Creative Reflection

When I was 15, I saw a production of *West Side Story*. I found it truly gripping, and it has been my favorite drama ever since. What dramas, either on or off the stage, have had an impact on you? How?

A second parallel in drama and counseling is timing (Okun & Kantrowitz, 2015). It is essential in both that events be timed to have a maximum impact. Friedman (1984) wrote,

> Good drama is not a function of clever words. And like all process, whether it is baking, gardening, or healing, it is a child of the experience of time. Time is the father of joy and pathos, tragedy and seriousness, irony and mischievousness, paradox and madness, and absurdity and love. Most comparisons of theater and therapy overlook this common organizing principle so essential to the flowering of human creativity. (p. 29)

In drama, impact moments are staged and involve three factors: the characters, the audience, and information about what is going to happen. Several incidents build up to a dramatic climax. Usually, the creation of such a scene is due to mystery (when a character in a story has information unknown to others), suspense (when someone else knows something is about to happen but a character is unsuspecting), and shock or surprise (when something happens that simultaneously surprises everyone; S. R. Lankton & Lankton, 1983). These scenes are staged—and timed—in such a way that everyone involved is aware of their importance.

An additional parallel is that in counseling, as in drama, certain dramatic movement is a natural part of the process. For example, family therapist Salvador Minuchin conducted family treatment as though he were a theatrical director, and he insisted that interpersonal enactments are essential for capturing the real drama of family life. In reality, counselors and clients may be in the midst of mystery, suspense, or even shock at times. At other times, less dynamic events occur. For instance, on occasion counselors withhold insights and ideas until they feel assured that clients will be able to hear and use this information to the fullest. Overall, drama and counseling often mimic each other.

A rationale for the use of drama in counseling is that life difficulties are reflected in counseling through dramatic means. Therefore, the language and action of counseling should be expressed in dramatic terms. This idea is most manifest in the theoretical underpinnings of transactional analysis. Clients enact the roles of parent, adult, and child by playing games such as "if only" and "kick me" and living by scripts that either enable or inhibit them in establishing healthy lifestyles (Berne, 1964). The most dysfunctional way individuals play games is through engaging in dramatic triangular interactions, in which all involved unconsciously agree to rotate among the three destructive positions of victim (the oppressed), rescuer (the savior), and persecutor (the punisher; Karpman, 1968) (see Figure 19).

Another rationale for using drama in counseling is that through enacting different roles clients will become more attuned to their full

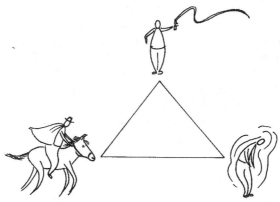

Figure 19 Karpman Triangle

range of feelings and become able to exercise all parts of themselves in an integrated and holistic way (Irwin, 1987). The idea behind this view is represented well in the work of gestalt therapy (Perls, 1969). In the gestalt approach, clients play many roles, some of which are more comfortable for them to enact than others. Ultimately, clients are introduced through role plays to those aspects of themselves that they have repressed or denied. Thus, role play and improvisation may be used as ways for clients to discover themselves and as assessment tools for clinicians to determine an individual's strengths and weaknesses (Forrester, 2000).

Yet another rationale for using drama in therapeutic settings is that through witnessing or participating in spontaneous plays or staged productions, participants gain insight into themselves by identifying with certain emotions that are expressed. For example, in improvisational theater, participants may change dysfunctional behavioral patterns, broaden the range of their displayed identities, and alter overtly serious and negative affect (Wiener, 2001). Thus, the focus of drama therapy is on changing the patterns and predictability of specific individuals or groups from those that are unproductive to those that are productive (Blatner, 1995; D. R. Johnson & Emunah, 2009). If all goes well, the level of feeling in particular persons is increased to the point that repressed or denied affect is recognized and eventually worked through as well.

For example, minorities are often stereotyped by majority populations and consequently have difficulties being treated as equals. The power of drama highlights such unequal and unjust action and can lead to greater sensitivity and fairness. *Guess Who's Coming to Dinner* (S. Kramer & Rose, 1967), a film about racial equality; *Coming Into Passion: Song for a Sansei* (Narita, 1996), a play about the stereotyping of Asian women; and *Dances With Wolves* (J. Wilson, Costner, & Blake, 1990), a film about the lives of Native Americans are three examples of dramatic productions that have made a positive impact on individuals in their audiences and society as a whole.

An additional rationale for using drama in counseling is that powerful drama, like effective counseling, is relationship oriented and based on a climate of creative spontaneity. In other words, methods and techniques are secondary to personalization and imagination. By reminding themselves that the elements of change and resistance are found in authentic people encounters, counselors can productively set the stage for newness. Such a premise is exemplified in the universal principle that "people hear you when they are moving toward you, never when they are being pursued" (Friedman, 1984, p. 29). Any dramatic approach to counseling or life includes both involvement and distancing (Snow, 1996).

Practice of the Use of Drama in Counseling

Several counseling traditions advocate either participation in or observation of dramas. The most notable are drama therapy and psychodrama, which share a common territory but are distinctive (Casson, 1996; Snow, 1996). In addition, drama is used in therapeutic settings in conjunction with gestalt therapy, rational emotive behavior therapy (REBT), and Adlerian counseling approaches (Gladding, 2013).

Drama Therapy

Drama therapy involves the "intentional use of creative drama toward the psychotherapeutic goals of symptom relief, emotional and physical integration, and personal growth" (D. R. Johnson, 1982, p. 83). It deals with hypothetical situations and uses projective techniques that tend to distance the performer from the material being enacted. MacKay (1987) stated that in drama therapy,

> the dramatic action part of the process is unlike traditional theatre performance in that the action is not scripted but improvised, a return in some ways to the earliest known forms of drama when the actor and the dramatist were one. (p. 201)

Through the enactment of fantasy and hypothetical situations, participants realize more fully the wealth of emotions within themselves and ideally translate this knowledge into their own life events. People who choose a drama therapist for treatment are generally open to, if not skilled in, acting (Landy, 1997, 2001). Many times they have developmental deficiencies, but they are usually not in a life crisis. "Drama therapy, as it is practiced today, is oriented specifically toward creative expressive learning of roles" (Kedem-Tahar & Felix-Kellermann, 1996, p. 34). "According to drama therapy, we are role players characterized by a certain range of roles, which dominate our behavior. . . . These roles manifest in concrete form and shape who we are" (Stahler, 2006/2007, p. 5).

Drama therapy consists of three stages: warm-up, enactment, and growth (Dunne, 1988). "The uniqueness of drama therapy is that it proceeds through role" and "through role-playing, storytelling, mask, and puppetry" (Landy, 1991, p. 39). Thus, drama therapy helps clients come in contact with internalized roles and allows the manifestation of these roles outward for a further extension of personal awareness.

Drama therapists registered by the National Association for Drama Therapy have a background in the theater. They are skilled in assessing the themes and potential impact of dramatic productions and hold at least an entry-level degree and preferably a master's degree from a college or university that offers a program in drama therapy, with at least an internship in this specialty before they begin practice under supervision (Emunah, 1989; Landy, 2006). Because of this education, drama therapists are able to help a wide range of clients, including adults with schizophrenia, children who are autistic and developmentally disabled, homeless persons, war veterans, and prisoners (Landy, 1997).

Psychodrama

The term *psychodrama* comes from the Greek words *psyche,* meaning "soul" or "spirit," and *drama,* meaning "action." Thus, psychodrama means "presenting the soul in action" (Kedem-Tahar & Felix-Kellermann, 1996, p. 27). According to Blatner (1997), the practice of psychodrama "involves the integration of imagination and action with verbal expression and self-reflection. Because it involves movement and speech, psychodrama, like drama therapy, can readily integrate the related creative and expressive modalities of dance, music, poetry, and art" (p. 23). The practice was originated by Jacob L. Moreno during the early part of the 20th century. He called psychodrama "a science which explores the 'truth' by dramatic methods" (J. L. Moreno, 1934/1993, p. 53). Through his observation of children, J. L. Moreno was convinced of the importance of spontaneity as part of the creative and vitalizing processes of life (Blatner, 1995). J. L. Moreno hoped to influence the mental health of mainstream society by forming a group of nontraditional actors into the Theater of Spontaneity in Vienna, Austria. Because of economic conditions, however, J. L. Moreno was forced to move his attention away from the masses to the treatment of the mentally ill and to move to the United States. By the 1960s, through his writings and workshops, he introduced psychodrama techniques to professionals in North and South America, Asia, and Europe (Hug, 1997). Psychodrama is very popular in traditional Chinese cultures today in Singapore, Malaysia, Taiwan, and China (N.-H. Lai & Tsai, 2014).

Psychodrama emphasizes encounters in the present. Individuals act out their problems or concerns in creative, spontaneous, and productive ways with a full expression of feelings. The emphasis in these circumstances is on the enactment of nonverbal events through which new realizations occur, thus enabling and empowering people in their growth and development. In these situations, it is vital that natural barriers of time and space be obliterated (Greenberg, 1974). Catharsis and insight must take place, too, through the total communication of feelings between individuals (J. L. Moreno, 1945). Research by Dogan (2010) shows that psychodrama has a positive effect with young adults. After a 12-week psychodrama program extending over 3 months, Dogan found that the 21 master's student participants improved in understanding themselves better; developing insight; gaining greater awareness of attachment styles; developing more self-confidence; improving their listening, empathy, and coping skills; and seeing life from a more hopeful perspective. Likewise, a 20-week psychodrama-based group of mentally healthy and mentally ill participants resulted in an increase in self-esteem for all involved and a decrease in their stigma of mental illness (Orkbi, Bar, & Eliakim, 2014).

Three phases occur within any psychodrama, similar to those in drama therapy: warm-up, action, and integration (Blatner, 1997, 2001). In the warm-up, everyone is emotionally and technically readied for the psychodrama by arranging the stage and engaging in affectively based activities such as sensory awareness (Blatner, 1995; J. J. Moreno, 1999).

In the action phase, the psychodrama is performed, with a protagonist assigning others within the group to various auxiliary ego roles of significant others or things in the protagonist's life (Gladding, 2016). Sometimes a protagonist is assigned to do a soliloquy. This person gives a monologue about his or her situation as he or she is acting it out. At other times, a monodrama (sometimes called an autodrama) technique is used, in which the protagonist plays all the parts of the enactment. A protagonist may be asked to literally switch roles with another person in the psychodrama, and through this role reversal he or she can gain insight into conflict as well. The protagonist may also be assigned the activity of watching from offstage while someone else plays his or her part (the mirror or mirroring technique). A final technique used in this action phase is the double or multiple double (in the case of ambivalence), during which a protagonist's alter ego helps express true inner feelings more clearly (Blatner, 2004).

In the integration phase, the protagonist is helped to process what happened in the psychodrama emotionally and intellectually. The counselor should emphasize understanding and integration so the protagonist can act differently if any similar situations arise (Gladding, 2016). Thus,

the essential process of psychodrama occurs not in the action itself, but more when the participants in the event can pause, stand back, perhaps consciously play out some alternative scenes and endeavor to respond to the problem with greater awareness and for the purpose of more authentic and inclusive effectiveness. (Blatner, 1997, p. 23)

Drama in Counseling: The Use of Cinema

Not all professionals who use drama in counseling are drama thera-pists, and not all use of drama constitutes psychodrama. Rather, drama can be infused in counseling in multiple ways, such as using videos and films to increase self-esteem (Powell, Newgent, & Lee, 2006), treat patients with eating disorders (Gramaglia et al., 2011), or teach important information. In the latter case, cinema may be used as a stimulus to edify graduate students on ethical concepts. Bradley et al. (2008) recommended such films as *Good Will Hunting, What About Bob?,* and *Mean Girls* for teaching ethics.

Another way to use films as a means to convey to counselors and clients the emotions and experiences of human life is through a pro-cedure known as cinematherapy (A. K. Newton, 1995; Powell et al., 2006; Sharp, Smith, & Cole, 2002). In this process of showing select movies and discussing them in general as well as specific ways, the power and potential of drama come to the forefront, and members of the viewing audience become aware of their own emotions as well as the possibilities for creating, influencing, or making changes in their lives. The depiction of common problems and the solution-oriented ending of many movies can remoralize and motivate people and may also provide a corrective emotional experience (Lampropoulos & Spengler, 2005). Films often have a more lasting effect than other means of communication and are time efficient, pleasurable, familiar, safer, and yet are social experiences as well (Lampropoulos, Kazantis, & Deane, 2004; Sheperis, Hope, & Palmer, 2003). They may exter-nalize problems couples and families are having and trigger positive changes as common difficulties, such as a leaving home or establish-ing appropriate parent–child boundaries, are discussed objectively and constructively (Ballard, 2012). It has even been found that some couples with strained relationships may improve as much by watching select movies that deal with issues they are facing in life as they would though participating in couples therapy (Rogge, Cobb, Lawrence, Johnson, & Bradbury, 2013). The key ingredient in such change is discussion by the couple of their impressions of the movie and how the characters and circumstances relate to their presenting concerns and what they could do differently now that they have seen the movie.

In teaching or guiding through the use of movies, counselors should be sure that films they select meet the following criteria as outlined by Dollarhide (2003):

- *Relevance.* The characters and/or plot should relate to the client's life.
- *Positive.* The story needs to have a positive message.
- *Appropriate.* The story needs to be at a developmentally appro-priate level.
- *Consistent.* Values should match those of the client watching.
- *Engaging.* Role models should be appealing.

Novice counselors and therapists can watch dramatic movies or even television series to help them begin to visualize as well as understand psychopathology (Wedding & Neimeic, 2014). Counselors in training may also learn about systems thinking (M. Alexander, 2000) and even learn about strategies to use in working with clients (Toman & Rak, 2000) through viewing films. *A Beautiful Mind, Who's Afraid of Virginia Woolfe?,* and *Ordinary People* are good examples of movies that depict the above three contributions drama in the form of film can make on individuals learning about mental and systems disorders and the process of therapy.

Using cinema with clients on a clinical level may take multiple forms. For example, Philip Guerin (1976), a pioneer in the marriage and family counseling field, included a number of movies in his work with families, such as Robert Anderson's *I Never Sang for My Father* and Ingmar Bergman's *Scenes From a Marriage*. He used these films to prod families into thinking about their own problems. In a variation on this technique, family therapist Frank Pittman (1989) used select dramatic scenes from movies as diverse as *Gone With the Wind* and *Steel Magnolias* to illustrate aspects of interpersonal relationships present on and off the screen. His intention was to emphasize the therapeutic interventions connected with such situations when they are dysfunctional.

Two of the most popular and useful books on using cinema in a variety of therapeutic situations are *Rent Two Films and Let's Talk in the Morning: Using Popular Movies in Psychotherapy* (Hesley & Hesley, 2001) and *Movies and Mental Illness: Using Films to Understand Psychopathology* (Wedding & Neimeic, 2014). The books explain how to use movies in therapeutic settings and include an anthology of therapeutic films that address a number of clinical issues, for example:

- family therapy (e.g., *The Great Santini, Parenthood*)
- couples therapy (e.g., *The Four Seasons, The Accidental Tourist*)
- individual therapy (e.g., *The Graduate, Bang the Drum Slowly*)
- psychopathology (e.g., *Rain Man, 28 Days*)
- vocational issues/occupational stress (e.g., *Erin Brockovich, Apollo 13*)
- meaningfulness in life (e.g., *It's a Wonderful Life, 12 Years a Slave*)
- sibling relationships (e.g., *Hannah & Her Sisters, Soul Food*)
- widowhood (e.g., *Message in a Bottle, Shadowlands*)
- transition to adulthood (e.g., *The Graduate, Breaking Away*)

Several excellent books and websites can be consulted to find films that are therapeutic. Among the older, but still relevant, books is *The Motion Picture Prescription* (Solomon, 1995). This text contains the names of more than 200 classic movies that counselors can use as adjuncts to help clients heal life problems. A follow-up to the pre-scription text with more current films is *Reel Therapy: How Movies Inspire You to Overcome Life's Problems* (Solomon, 2002). Cinema-therapy. com (http://www.cinematherapy.com/filmindex.html) and Therapeutic Themes and Relevant Movies (http://www.zurinstitute. com/movietherapy.html) both provide lists of useful films for discus-sion of difficult personal and interpersonal situations such as abuse, depression, couple relationships, stress management, anger, children, family issues, social issues, mental disorders, and anxiety.

To highlight values and decision making in life in both educational and community counseling settings, counselors can turn to movies of their own choosing that teach and challenge people's thinking. For example, *Fried Green Tomatoes* and *How to Make an American Quilt* may be shown to help women and girls develop a bond across genera-tions and encourage the sharing of stories and experiences (Bartlett, 2003). Among those I have used when teaching multicultural and diversity issues are *The Autobiography of Miss Jane Pittman, Brian's Song, Chariots of Fire, E.T.—The Extraterrestrial, The Elephant Man, Gandhi, Inherit the Wind, Judgment at Nuremberg, Mask, Pinocchio, Stand and Deliver,* and *To Kill a Mockingbird.* Counselors should view the films and decide what aspects they wish to highlight and why before using them.

In discussing the importance of drama in promoting mental health in schools, Sylvia (1977) pointed out five essential elements com-mon to both drama and counseling that may be used in the helping process: problem, choice, crisis, climax, and resolution. Problems may be presented in many ways, but usually a trademark of their ap-pearance in a play, movie, or a real-life situation is a certain amount of emotional discomfort or incongruence on the part of the people involved. For example, Hamlet is troubled by the sudden death of his father and the quick remarriage of his mother to his uncle. He agonizes over whether to pursue the matter further (choice) but eventually feels duty bound to the spirit of his father and confronts his mother, his uncle, and others involved by having actors perform a play paralleling his situation (crisis). The climax of the drama is the death of several leading characters, including Hamlet, and the final resolution is that the court in Denmark changes with regard to the primary players involved and its psychological climate.

When counselors use drama in counseling, especially a movie, care must always be taken to see that clients feel connected with this form of treatment and that they benefit from it. For instance, in enactments in a family unit, research has suggested that instead of having therapists tell clients what to do or say, families may do best when they are allowed to work out their own problems and test their own resources (Nichols & Fellenberg, 2000). However, movies can teach, too, and individuals, couples, and families may learn from watching dramatic interactions in films, especially if the behaviors shown are discussed with a counselor after viewing (Dermer & Hutchings, 2000). Films such as *The Story of Us* and *Pleasantville* take on new meaning when discussed immediately after being seen. Whether or not a medium such as a movie is used, drama in counseling will occur on covert or overt levels. It is up to the counselor in collaboration with clients to make the decisions that lead to or away from dealing with drama on a conscious level and modifying behaviors associated with dramatic displays.

Gestalt Therapy and Drama

Ever since its inception, gestalt therapy has emphasized drama techniques in its implementation (P. Clarkson & Cavicchia, 2014). *Gestalt* means the formation of an organized meaningful whole, and "the main thrust of gestalt therapy is to help people develop their faculties of awareness in order to make choices, determine their existence, and become self-sufficient. . . . Gestalt psychodrama reflects the existential, experimental, and experiential nature of Gestalt therapy" (Coven, Ellington, & Van Hull, 1996, p. 17). Some of the dramatic methods used in this approach include role playing, exaggerating, intensity, becoming aware of bodily senses, staying with feelings, and closure (M. James & Jongeward, 1971). In role playing, clients enact scenes or situations they would otherwise describe. For instance, in reporting dreams, clients are directed to role-play all aspects of their dreams (Perls, 1970). If clients have complaints, they are encouraged to exaggerate their discontent and put the complaint in perspective (*Role Playing*).

Regardless of what clients are working on, they are instructed to be aware of what their body is telling them as well as what they are saying. For example, a closed body posture in the midst of a conversation during which someone reports being open is a glaring contradiction. Therefore, while clients are focusing on themselves, they are reminded to stay with their feelings and not opt out of a situation by intellectualizing (i.e., head tripping). As a sophisticated actor knows how to feel a wide range of emotions and respond to them appropriately, so clients learn to become more attuned to their feelings and act on them accordingly.

The empty chair technique is unique in Perls's version of gestalt therapy (see Figure 20). It emphasizes that people should own their emotions. In this approach, which may also be used in gestalt psychodrama and in some other

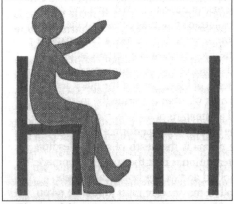

Figure 20 Empty Chair Technique

drama therapy settings, there is a hot seat for people who want to work and an empty chair into which troublesome emotions may be projected (Burleigh & Beutler, 1997). Individuals who choose to work will reflect and project emotions onto the empty chair as needed and talk

with the polar parts of themselves until some integrated resolution results (*Empty Chair*). Use of the personal noun "I" is encouraged in this and other types of transactions to increase a sense of personal responsibility (Coven et al., 1996).

REBT and Drama

REBT uses a number of behaviorally based and dramatic exercises to help clients become more rational and functional. Among the most dramatically creative is what is known as a shame attack. In this assignment, clients first mentally and then behaviorally practice, in role plays and in real life, a particular activity that they have always feared or dreaded (*Shame Attack*). The action might be as simple as going into a restaurant and asking for a glass of water, or it might involve pretending to faint in a crowd and trusting the best behaviors of those around to prevail in offering help. As in any drama, learning how to enact a certain part is difficult at first, but as practice continues the part becomes an integrated aspect of the personality until acting a certain way becomes a habit of the heart.

REBT combined with the action methods of psychodrama is also an efficient method of dealing with resistance when working with alcoholics and drug addicts (E. Avrahami, 2003). Role playing enables protagonists in REBT "to act, to rehearse their lives, according to different beliefs" (E. Avrahami, 2003, p. 212). In doing so, they are able to experience where distinct choices they might make in staging their lives would lead and see more clearly the end results of their beliefs.

Adlerian Therapy and Drama

Before Albert Ellis devised his theory and emphasis on the practice of integrating thoughts with behaviors, such as in shame attacks, Alfred Adler was stressing behavioral change through a process known as "acting as if" (Adler, 1924/1963). In this procedure, clients discuss how they would like to behave. Then they are simply instructed to act as if they were the persons they wish to be (*Acting "as if"*). This technique is usually met with protests because clients think they are being phony, but stress is lowered when individuals involved know they are simply acting and that their new behaviors in effect are no different from trying on new clothes to see how well they fit and feel (Mosak & Maniacci, 2011).

Drama in Counseling
With Specific Populations

Drama is used in different ways and at various levels of sophistication in counseling based on the age and stage of clients. It is critical that counselors be sensitive to developmental aspects of those with whom they work so that the drama work in which they engage will have a maximum impact.

Children

Preschool children live a life that is usually rich in fantasy and pretend (L. E. Berk, 2013). Getting them to act out dramas with toys or to talk to puppets is usually safe and fun for them and revealing for counselors (Hughes, 1988). Dramatic play in young children is related to creativity as well. Both involve alternative symbolic constructions and flexibility (Mellou, 1995). Therefore, children benefit in multiple ways through participating in drama activities.

One technique that has been successful with young children is the family puppet interview. Children make up stories about the family by using puppets (Irwin & Malloy, 1975). These stories usually highlight conflicts and alliances within families but may be of limited usefulness; asking direct questions is often more productive in obtaining information. Nevertheless, by using objects such as dolls or puppets familiar to children, the opportunity to learn or promote conflict resolution is maximized (R. K. James & Myer, 1987). In such situations, counselors must be sure to focus on issues at hand and not become too involved in manipulating the props or puppets (*Family Puppet Interview*). An alternative to using puppets is for clinicians to have children watch select segments of popular television programs such as *Sesame Street*, *Dragon Tales*, and *Daniel Tiger's Neighborhood*. Professionals who produce these shows frequently emphasize socially appropriate ways of dealing with troublesome situations of childhood, and after the shows have ended, children may benefit from talking about the situations in them.

A similar developmental opportunity for dramatic impact, insight, and growth is present with older children (ages 6 to 12 years). These children live between young childhood and adolescence (L. E. Berk, 2013). They often daydream and fantasize about their future. Therefore, drama techniques, such as role playing or staging guidance plays, are excellent techniques to use with this group (Feldman, 2008; N. S. Wilson, 1983). Children in this age bracket may enjoy writing and producing their own plays too. Such an activity helps them gain a perspective on their values and become sensitive to the way they handle complex problems or people.

An increasing number of scholars are realizing that drama therapies may be well suited to children diagnosed with autism spectrum disorder (ASD), nonverbal learning disability (NLD), or attention-deficit/hyperactivity disorder (ADHD). Several drama therapy programs are currently being used with these disorders. These programs have gained notoriety as treatments for social difficulties (Guli et al., 2013).

Yet another dramatic way of helping children in the middle years of childhood is by having them perform in plays that have already been written and that have relevance for them. For example, *Bullybusters* is a psychoeducational drama written for middle school kids with a message of "do not bully or let yourself be bullied" (Beale & Scott, 2001). Its enactment is reported to have reduced the incidents of bullying in the school in which it was performed by 20%. For counselors in need of a source for creative drama activities, especially for elementary school children, Renard and Sockol (1987) compiled a book containing guidance lessons for building healthy self-esteem. These lessons are based on dramatic activities, and each lesson contains the same format: focus, introduction, preparation, warm-ups and cool-downs, directions and activities, discussion, and summary. Likewise, Paul Rooyackers wrote two activity-filled books titled *101 Drama Games for Children* (1998) and *101 More Drama Games for Children* (2002). Each book is filled with acting and make-believe drama games that Rooyackers classified as appropriate for three categories: young children (6 and up), older children (9 and up), and teens to adults (12 and up). In addition, the time required (from 10 minutes to two 60-minute sessions) is given along with what, if any, props are needed.

Adolescents

Adolescents are often dramatic in their actions. Their participation in a number of ritualistic activities, such as sports or band, provides them with opportunities to play out parts of life in a highly charged and physical way and to keep their impulses in check. Drama can be used to assist adolescents in gaining greater control over their lives as well as in learning new roles (L. Nelson & Finneran, 2006). For instance, Shaffer (1996) used a psychodrama technique based on Shakespeare's play *Hamlet* to help middle schoolers learn to become more aware that what they do has an impact on others as well as themselves and that they have choices in what they do. Shaffer's approach works on both an experiential and a cognitive level. The adolescents first warm up (by reading or viewing a video version of *Hamlet*) and then examine the wants and needs of each character. This is followed by a role play in groups of three, in which one student plays the protagonist and is flanked by the other two students, whose roles are that of revenge and caution, action and inaction. In these role plays, which last for 15 minutes, each of the flanking actors tries passionately to persuade the prince (or princess) to choose his or her point of view. After time is called, the protagonist shares with the others in the group thoughts and feelings that emerged during his or her decision making. The process is repeated until each of the trio (and ultimately everyone in a group) has an opportunity to actively participate as the protagonist (*Hamlet Dilemma*).

Another way of working with adolescents, especially at-risk, disadvantaged, and marginalized adolescents, is to have them write their own play and then produce it before a live audience. Such an activity affords adolescents a healthy avenue for self-expression while providing an outlet for catharsis. It also opens up an avenue for better understanding of how adolescents see the world and some of the reasons for such a view (Bernstein, Ablow, Maloney, & Nigg, 2014).

Videotaped improvisational drama has been found to significantly increase the ability of adolescents to maintain internal locus of control (Dequine & Pearson-Davis, 1983). In most cases, videotaping therapy with adolescents helps them do one or more of the following: (a) receive instant feedback about their behaviors (especially in groups); (b) gain limited control over their therapy through operating some of the equipment, such as cameras and playback units; (c) deal with transference issues realistically because of being able to see their conduct; (d) overcome resistance to adults more easily because of a focus on equipment; and (e) become more involved in formulating their identities through objective observations of their behaviors, both verbal and nonverbal (Furman, 1990).

A formal type of videotaped drama is called Playback Theatre. It is a form of drama therapy that involves self-disclosure of audience members' personal stories. The disclosure is followed by an improvised dramatization of the audience members' stories by a director and players who have been trained in the art of improvisational theatre. Playback seeks to enter the world of tellers and artistically reflect the essence of their narrative through a moment-to-moment improvisation. It is through the artistic expression of the players' representation of the story that the audience can internalize their empathic feelings for tellers (*Playback Theatre*). Playback Theatre was developed to promote healing and social connection; it was not necessarily designed as a drama therapy intervention (Bornmann & Crossman, 2011).

When dramatic exercises are not videotaped, it is critical that a structured environment be set up in which adolescents still maintain a feeling of autonomy. This type of setting can be constructed by allowing adolescents to enact situations dealing with aggression, flight, conflict, and rebelliousness (Emunah, 1985). Using such a method avoids struggles between counselors and adolescents because primary issues are acknowledged in advance and dealt with therapeutically. Overall, adolescents, especially those who are prone to act out, benefit from drama therapy because of the differentiated tasks they are given and the role structures provided within each drama therapy session (D. R. Johnson & Eicher, 1990; Weber & Haen, 2005).

Adults

Adults may benefit from drama therapy in a number of ways. In women prison populations, drama therapy is quite effective in transcending the pain of incarceration (Moller, 2013; Trounstein, 2001). Likewise, drama therapy has proved powerful in helping female prisoners who are in addiction recovery to connect spiritually and psychologically to themselves, others, and a higher power through the use of "role play, improvisation, spontaneity training, storytelling, character development, mask work, and movement" (Stahler, 2006/2007, p. 3). In general, the use of drama in prisons is helpful in reducing rates of recidivism. In a classic study, Ryder (1976) reported a recidivism rate of about 15% for inmates who participated in a drama project he conducted. Such a rate is far below the national level. It has continued to be low in studies conducted in the 40 years since then.

Individuals who have suffered traumatic experiences may profit from drama therapy too. In these situations reliving the event in a safe environment through techniques such as those provided by drama therapy enables individuals to face their experience and introduce change into the outcome. For instance, drama therapy has been used successfully with Vietnam war veterans who have PTSD symptoms. It allows them to express their feelings openly and appropriately while helping them mend interpersonal relationships and become more integrated in society (M. James & Johnson, 1996).

Likewise, drama therapy is now being applied to group work with males who have been sexually assaulted (Mulky, 2004) as well as females who have been victims of sexual assaults. In men's groups, a safe room may be created and entered. In women's groups, face painting is sometimes used as well as dramatic enactments of traumatic situations to give form to feeling, create an empowering atmosphere, and facilitate healing (MacKay, 1989).

Women coping with alcoholic partners may also be helped by drama therapy through role-playing coping skills by using the Spouse Situation Inventory (Rychtarik & McGillicuddy, 1997). In this inventory, 24 representative problem situation vignettes that women of alcoholic partners confront are read individually by a woman who pretends that the administrator of the inventory is her partner. The woman pretends to say and do exactly what she would with her partner in the situation. Her response is evaluated, and in the process the woman has an opportunity to learn how effective her reaction is and what else she might say or do (*Spouse Situation Inventory*).

Marriage and family therapists have found drama techniques to be quite effective as well. Enactment is a major dramatic tool of most marriage and family counselors (Gladding, 2015a; Nichols & Fellenberg, 2000). Minuchin and Fishman (1981) noted that a counselor "constructs an interpersonal scenario in the session in which dysfunctional transactions among family members are played out" (p. 79) such as those involving yelling or fighting. In this scenario, the therapist can observe

> the family members' verbal and nonverbal ways of signaling to each other and monitoring the range of tolerable transactions. The therapist can then intervene in the process by increasing its intensity, prolonging the time of transaction, involving other family members, indicating alternative transactions, and introducing experimental probes. (Minuchin & Fishman, 1981, p. 79)

The drama, which occurs in presenting the problem and in finding successful resolutions, decreases the power of symptoms and empowers the family to be innovative.

Older Clients

Drama therapy has been used with a number of older people in specific conditions, for example, older adults with mild to moderate dementia (Jaaniste, Linnell, Ollerton, & Slewa-Younan, 2015). It has generally been found to improve their quality of life. Yet, drama therapy and the use of drama in counseling are just beginning to emerge in a sophisticated form for the older adult population.

One recent trend for working with older persons through drama is developmental drama therapy (D. R. Johnson & Emunah, 2009). In this approach, counselors work to help older adults who are disoriented or depressed to connect with their past and their present, and with each other, all in a positive way. A group format is used to implement this process, and group members are actively engaged in a sustained manner (D. R. Johnson, 1986). The developmental nature of drama progresses from greeting, to unison activities, to expression of group themes, to personification of images, to playing, to closing rituals. Members are encouraged to interact with their fellow group members and to recognize and own their emotions in structured exercises such as phoning home, in which a group member calls a significant person is his or her life and either resolves difficulties or expresses gratitude.

> **Creative Reflection**
>
> Try enacting a scene from your daily life. Get a friend or friends to help you if need be as you play the scene out with three different endings. Talk to yourself or to your friends about what you learned through this kind of enactment.

Families

Families are often the source of life's most dramatic scenes. Part of the reason is the presence of considerable affect among family members. Another reason is the physical proximity of family members to each other in space and time. Issues related to distance and closeness make families a forum in which drama is enacted passionately.

One dramatic way of helping families help themselves is through family sculpting (see Chapter 4). This drama technique originated in the 1960s from the work of David Kantor and Fred and Bunny Duhl at the Boston Family Institute. It was an attempt "to translate systems theory into physical form through spatial arrangements" (Papp, 1976, p. 465). In family sculpting, members of a family are asked "to arrange one another as a living statue or tableau" (L'Abate, Ganahl, & Hansen, 1986, p. 166). In this way, people are given the chance to actively and concretely convey their impressions of the family in a nonverbal yet potent manner by having different family members assume certain poses or postures. Sometimes their positioning is exaggerated, but the point is not lost on anyone as to how that family member and family dynamics are seen through the eyes of the person doing the arranging of the family as he or she sees them (*Family Sculpting*).

Family sculpting is a way of visualizing the closeness or distance experienced in a family as seen through the eyes of each member as he or she becomes a director of the sculpting (Gladding, 2015a). Because the process involves all members of the family unit, it enables the family to work with the counselor in a collaborative fashion. Sometimes sculpting is used to disengage family members from emotional experiences and "thus facilitate insight into the past and present situations" (Piercy et al., 1997, p. 57). At other times it is used to "bring about an affective experience that will unblock unexpressed emotions" (p. 57).

Sculpting is usually appropriate at any time during the treatment of a family because it stimulates interaction and promotes insight (L'Abate et al., 1986). At a minimum, sculpting should include the following:

1. Selecting a sculptor;
2. Choosing sculpture content (event, problem, or process);
3. Sculpting individual members of the family unit;
4. Detailing the sculpture;
5. Adding the sculptor into the scene;
6. Choosing to give the sculpture a descriptive title, a resolution, or a ritualistic motion;
7. Sculpting other relevant situations until a pattern emerges;
8. Deroling and debriefing all involved; and
9. Processing the results. (Constantine, 1978; L'Abate et al., 1986)

Initially, sculpting and psychodrama resemble each other, yet they are not the same. Foley (1989) noted, "The difference between sculpting and psychodrama . . . is that the latter is used to relive and resolve a traumatic event, whereas sculpting is more concerned with closeness and space as a means

of understanding emotional involvement" (p. 459). It is crucial that counselors who wish to use these techniques understand the advantages and limitations of each. Both processes may lead to change, but by design they address different aspects of life.

Drama in Counseling With Other Creative Arts

Drama has a natural connection with dance, music, art, and literature. Each of these arts complements the others in a way that highlights therapeutic aspects of change for counselors and clients.

Drama and Dance

Dance can be seen as drama enacted in ritualized and accentuated ways. For example, in Native American culture, dance is a dramatic way of invoking the favor of the spiritual world. In middle-class U.S. culture, dramatic exercises may help dance therapy participants become more relaxed and less resistant to the therapeutic process of change (D. R. Johnson & Eicher, 1990). Dance in such cases is an extension of drama and leads past itself and into greater self-awareness. Regardless of the circumstances, the techniques of drama and dance both focus on the integration of multiple aspects of people. Once individuals dramatically act out a role in a scene, they feel freer to express themselves in more nontraditional ways in dance, movement, or life.

Drama and Music

Music and drama share much common ground. For instance, music and drama both require self-organization and discipline to master lines and feelings. Music and drama enhance the process of helping people become more realistic "by requiring time-ordered and ability-ordered behavior" (Wager, 1987, p. 137). Each may complement the other, as is demonstrated in music being played in the background of a dramatic scene or dramatic enactments of musical compositions (such as those seen on music videos). As with dance, music accentuates drama. It increases the likelihood that participants and the audience will remember what they experienced.

Drama and Visual Arts

Art and drama are natural companions. In drama there is frequent discussion of drawing out a scene. On a concrete level, there is such an experience as pictorial dramatization, in which "clients draw pictures of an important moment, person, conflict, or fantasy. These pictures reveal inner feelings and give important data on self-esteem. Clients go on to act out short pantomimes or improvisational scenes based on the pictures" (Dunne, 1988, p. 141). In this method, people see and feel simultaneously. They become more aware of themselves and their environments (*Pictorial Dramatization*).

Drama and Literature

Literature and drama are combined in acting situations for which the script is already written, which is the case in plays and some poetry. This process may most powerfully occur when clients pantomime scenes that counselors create to parallel their lives (Dunne, 1988, p. 141). For example, the poem "Autobiography in Five Short Chapters" (P. Nelson, 1993), which is often read in addiction groups, may be enacted in such groups or in individual sessions with clients who repeat the same mistake over and over. The essence of the poem moves the client from falling in a hole in a street by accident to walking down another street. People who enact the poem or participate in such an enactment through supportive roles get a feel for what the poem is conveying in a greater way than through just reading it (*Enacting the Poem "Autobiography in Five Short Chapters"*).

For clients who are older or physically impaired, literature and drama may be united when these clients read and discuss tragic or humorous plays or movies such as those written by Eugene O'Neill, George Bernard Shaw, Luigi Pirandello, Langston Hughes, Tina Fey, and Neil Simon. In their discussions of these works, clients who cannot act out the scenes can imagine them or feel their impact and share these types of experiences with either the counselor or a therapeutic group.

Summary

The use of drama as either a primary or adjunct technique in healing and change has a strong historical tradition. Human drama is staged in both formal and informal ways. Insight into who we are as people is fostered through participating in drama-based experiences on many levels. Counselors share with dramatists the use of some techniques, such as staging, asides, scripting, and creating catharsis. The essence of what these two traditions share goes beyond technique to

a common impulse—an attempt to go beyond the everyday forms of communication to shift people's basic notions of themselves and their world. Both represent a revolt against the normal use of discourse . . . and recognition that communication is at least as much an emotional phenomenon as a linguistic one. (Friedman, 1984, p. 24)

Thus, from the ancient Greeks to today, we see a promotion of drama for the common good and sensitivity it instills and promotes.

In this chapter, the historical context of drama in counseling has been explored along with the parallels and processes that dramatists and counselors share. In addition, the primary types of drama found in traditional counseling approaches have been examined along with the groups most amenable to drama-focused treatment and ways in which drama may be combined with other creative arts.

Drama is an affective and effective approach to working with a variety of populations as long as the counselor uses theoretically sound methods (whether a drama therapist or not). In essence, "drama becomes a catalyst for real-life change, and real life becomes material for drama" (Emunah, 2001, p. 117). Treatment from this perspective involves creativity, openness, and a willingness to be authentic and empathetic. Like the last line of the poem that introduced this chapter, drama demands that counselors step up when they forget their professional lines and live their lives congruently, courageously, and transparently so that by example they help facilitate change in clients.

Exercises

1. Make a list of dramatic productions you have seen or participated in that have had a major impact on your life. Examine these dramas with regard to characters you identified with and emotions conveyed. Look at your own development as a person and the issues you faced then and now. What interconnections, if any, do you see?

2. With a trusted friend or supervisor, play the role of someone with whom you are having difficulty dealing. Enact the role of that person to the fullest extent possible through either dialog or behavior or both. After about 10 or 15 minutes of role play, process the experience and take special note of any changes in perceptions or attitudes that you have and any insights or feedback your friend or supervisor has to offer. Be especially cognizant about how you think of this person now that you have played him or her.

3. Videotape a session with colleagues or your own family during which you demonstrate the art of sculpting. As you and your participants review the videotape, stop it periodically and discuss what is occurring within you now as opposed to what you experienced during the actual sculpting. How different or similar are your thoughts and emotions in these situations?

Chapter 8

Play and Humor in Counseling

In Acceptance

She smiles gently on cool spring nights
that remind her of a youthful season
when children played quietly within small groups
and boys were speechless in her presence.
Amused, she laughs at recollections
letting the lines around her eyes
display the grace of older years
in the acceptance of fun and growth.

—Gladding, 1991c/2010

What did the math book say to the counseling book?
"I've got lots of problems!"

What did the counseling book say to the math book?
"I'm solution focused!"

∽

Play and humor are arts of the highest order; however, because of their lack of concreteness and structure, they are often underused, unappreciated, and sometimes misunderstood (Ness, 1989; Schaefer & Reid, 1986). Perhaps the reason for the neglect and confusion surrounding them is that counseling is considered to be serious work and is seen as quite the antithesis of fun and enjoyment. Yet, play and humor are multidimensional and flexible, and they are associated with creativity and the promotion of mental health and insight (R. A. Berk, 2002; Martin, 2007; Witmer, 1985). Therefore, it is important that clients and counselors learn to utilize play and laughter constructively in many situations, including counseling sessions.

Play and humor share numerous similarities, such as an emphasis on spontaneity, pleasure, and active mental or physical participation by those so engaged. Play and humor are also dissimilar. One of the distinguishing qualities of play is that it comprises many kinds of activity, linked by an attitude of nonliteralness and enjoyment known as playfulness (Liebmann, 2004). The most salient characteristics are these:

1. Play is pleasurable and enjoyable.
2. Play has no extrinsic goals; it is inherently unproductive.
3. Play is spontaneous and voluntary and freely chosen.
4. Play involves active engagement on the part of the player.
5. Play is related to what is not play. (Liebmann, 2004, p. 13)

A primary need of well-functioning human beings is play (Gladding, 1993). Counselors and clients often complain or confess that they do not incorporate play into their lives often enough. Winnicott (1974) wrote, "It is play that is the universal, and that belongs to health: playing facilitates growth" (p. 48). Too often, play in counseling is structured in the form of closed-ended activities such as board and card games (Crocker & Wroblewiski, 1975), whereas in more natural environments, play is open-ended in its content and implementation.

Humor as a unique art form combines the elements of reality and absurdity with surprise and exaggeration. Laughter is often accompanied by insight into the essence of what it means to be human (Arieti, 1976; Meggert, 2009). Allport (1955) noted that, at its best, "humor is a remarkable gift of perspective by which the knowing function of a mature person recognizes disproportions and absurdities" (p. 57). Comedians and cartoonists such as Mark Russell, Amy Poelher, Chris Rock, Amy Schumer, and Gary Trudeau (creator of *Doonesbury*) focus attention on specific political subjects that are absurd; generalists such as Jay Leno, Tina Fey, Whoopi Goldberg, Jerry Seinfeld, Jimmy Fallon, Eddie Murphy, Stephen Colbert, and Greg Evans (creator of *LuAnn*) concentrate on broader areas of human life that are fraught with imperfections. Depictions relayed by such artists remind us that "subjects for humor abound: our unfounded fears, endless primping, exaggerated story-telling, and inflated self-importance" (Burke, 1989, p. 281).

When individuals do not play or laugh enough, they become overly serious and mentally distraught (Ellis, 1977; Ellis &

Creative Reflection

What do you find funny? What do you do to play that does not involve competition? What do you need to do in both domains—humor and play—to live a more balanced life?

Dryden, 1997; Greenstein & Holland, 2015). The manifestations of this unhealthy behavior are displayed in uncontrolled anger, displacement, abuse, and depression—upsetting and unproductive states. Therefore, one of the primary tasks of counseling is to assist clients in learning how to play appropriately or be more playful with their words and actions, consequently having more fun.

In this chapter, I explore the multidimensional premises behind the power of play and humor as well as the practical use of play and humor in counseling. I treat each of these modalities separately and show how each may be used in counseling. In addition, I explain and illustrate how play and humor can be used with a variety of populations (e.g., from children to older adults) and in various settings (e.g., from groups to families). The use of play and humor with other creative arts (e.g., drama and the visual arts) is also discussed.

Premise of the Use of Play and Humor in Counseling

Play

The idea behind the use of play in counseling is that play has a non-literal quality about it, which, according to Liebmann (2004), "means it can be done in safety" and "without fear of real consequences. By representing a difficult experience symbolically and going through it again, perhaps changing the outcome, a child [or an adult] becomes more able to deal with the problems of real life" (p. 13). This type of activity, as described by Erik H. Erikson (1963) and seen in the dramatic play of children from age 2 years and older, is one way individuals master their environments, including person-to-person interactions (Smilansky & Shefatya, 1990).

The use of play techniques in counseling is based on many theories (O'Connor & Braverman, 2009). On one hand, behaviorists use play to help clients relax and learn to enact more adaptive behaviors. On the other hand, psychoanalytic theorists use play to try to foster insight and call unconscious conflicts into greater awareness (Cochran, 1996). Three of the dominant theories used in play are Jungian (Allan & Brown, 1993; Jung, 1964), Rogerian (C. R. Rogers, 1951), and Adlerian (Kottman &

Johnson, 1993). According to the Jungian viewpoint, the process of play and dramatization seems to release blocked psychic energy and activate the self-healing potential embedded in the human psyche (Allan, 2008). The Rogerian point of view likewise stresses the importance of self-expression and inner growth in a nonjudgmental environment (Axline, 1947, 1967). Adlerian theory focuses play on helping children understand the ways in

Creative Reflection

While at a university in Turkey, I was told that there were some visiting professors who were picky and refused to do what was expected. Instead of calling these professors "difficult," the faculty of the university labeled them "complex." The new name made it easier to accept and work with members of this population. When have you played with the art of reframing? How did it work?

which they gain significance in the world and make changes in the ways they act toward others. Thus, play in counseling is an active and integrated phenomenon that links mind and body together in a healthy way.

In addition to helping children and adults become more congruent and express themselves more clearly, play may also be used as (a) a means for establishing rapport, (b) a way of understanding family and peer interactions, (c) a tool for tapping unexpressed feelings, (d) an outlet for the safe expression of feelings, and (e) an effective method for teaching socialization skills (D. A. Henderson & Thompson, 2016). The annual International Play Therapy Conference and the Center for Play Therapy at the University of North Texas (Denton) focus on the multiple uses of play in therapeutic settings.

Essentially, the ability to play is connected with expanding one's imagination through pretending (Madanes, 1981). Pretending can be used throughout the life span. The art of make-believe allows individuals to see situations differently and to solve problems by reframing situations in a more positive light. Reframing does not change a situation; it simply describes the situation differently (T. M. Levy, 1987), just like different frames draw out different aspects of a picture while the picture remains the same (*Reframing*). An example of reframing came in my own life after the birth of our third child. My wife looked up at me and said, "The honeymoon's not over, there are just more people on it." Her wit and play at the time made me realize that our family life was still manageable and fun. Regardless, an important aim of pretend and play methods is to give clients unique opportunities to engage in activities they may be unable or unwilling to do otherwise. Learning to engage clients in these activities is an achievable goal that counseling can foster through behavioral, cognitive, and affective means.

Humor

The use of humor in counseling is not utilized as much as it could be due to the fact that counselors see the therapeutic process as completely serious (Gladding, 2015b). However, humor occurs in counseling, and its deliberate use is premised on several ideas. First, humor is associated with positive wellness (Howlett, 2003). Research has indicated that involvement in humor has a therapeutic effect on one's overall health (Cousins, 1979; Fry, 1991; Greenstein & Holland, 2015; Meggert, 2009). Humor, particularly when it is accompanied by laughter, creates physiological, psychological, and social changes. The skeletal muscles become more relaxed, breathing changes, and the brain releases endorphins, the body's natural painkillers that are positive to well-being (Abrami, 2009; Witmer, 1985). Clients who are able to laugh at themselves or their situations are able to positively take charge of their lives (Markham & Palmer, 1998; Mosak, 1987). Humor seems to be a factor in increasing attention spans, improving comprehension, and promoting recall, all of which are crucial to fostering mental health (R. A. Berk, 2003). Humor is negatively correlated with worry (Kelly, 2002). In his book *Anatomy of an Illness,* Norman Cousins (1979) illustrated how laughter helped him eliminate physical pain and bring him healing pleasure. Cousins's book has led others to playfully credit him as the founder of "ho-ho-holistic health."

A second rationale for using humor in counseling is that it can distance clients from too much subjectivity and enhance the vision clients have of themselves and the environment. A sense of humor is "connected with one's sense of selfhood" (May, 1953, p. 52). Unconscious urges and repressed thoughts become conscious and expressed (D. A. Henderson & Thompson, 2016). Clients basically gain an "aha" experience from their "ha-ha" perspective and achieve insight into problems that have heretofore perplexed them (Mosak, 1987; Mosak & Maniacci, 2011). Often, the first slightly funny moment in counseling sparks the beginning of an emotional breakthrough and the start of resolution. People's abilities to "break free of symptoms with exaggeration and humor is an illustration of self-detachment" (Burke, 1989, p. 281). It allows clients to observe a situation from a distance. May (1953) wrote, "One cannot laugh when in an anxious panic . . . hence the accepted belief in folklore that to be able to laugh in times of danger is a sign of courage" (p. 54). It is in such crises that opportunities for genuine heroism are created as individuals realize that their situations may be serious but they are not hopeless (Watzlawick, 1983).

Third, humor is an excellent predictor of creativity. It is expressed in many forms: laughter, comedy, kidding, joking, mimicking, and teasing (Robinson, 1978). A comic such as Woody Allen achieved success due to his ability to see ordinary relationships in extraordinary ways by making light of them or viewing them from different angles such as in his movies *Annie Hall, Midnight in Paris,* or *Take the Money and Run* (Lax, 1975). Successful clients and counselors are similarly creative (but not nearly as neurotic as Woody Allen) in their perceptions of people and issues. Thus, they achieve an ability to laugh as well as cry.

A fourth rationale for using the art of humor in counseling is past research. It has been only recently that the concept

Creative Reflection

When have you had a moment of insight when laughing? Try to recall the particulars of the situation and why your laughter led you to seeing yourself and the world more insightfully.

of humor "has been taken seriously as a subject worthy of scientific investigation" (G. R. Newton & Dowd, 1990, p. 668). Yet, many studies show promising aspects of humor that make it relevant for counseling (Markham & Palmer, 1998; Meggert, 2009). For instance, humor helps initiate and promote communication in social relationships and increases the likeability of those who use it (Kane, Suls, & Tedeschi, 1977; Martineau, 1972). Couples who share a similar sense of humor are significantly more attracted to each other than those who do not (Murstein & Brust, 1985). In addition, managers and job candidates who are seen as possessing a good sense of humor are more likely to be viewed positively (Duncan, 1985; Machan, 1987). Indeed, humor correlates with problem-solving ability, and it may be used to probe into difficult subject areas, diffuse anger, and circumvent resistance (W. J. Adams, 1974; Gladding & Kezar, 1978; Haig, 1986).

Practice of the Use of Play and Humor in Counseling

Play

Play approaches to counseling have traditionally been directed at children under the age of 12 years who have limited cognitive and verbal abilities. As such, play has often been structured as *play therapy*, which Schaefer (1995) defined as "an interpersonal process wherein a trained therapist systematically applies the curative powers of play to help clients resolve their psychological difficulties" (p. 3). Play therapy is used in a wide variety of settings ranging from those involving the treatment of developmentally related problems to those involving the treatment of dysfunctional behavior (Y.-J. Shen, 2008). International associations and conferences specialize in play therapy. Within play therapy are a number of theories, among the most prominent of them being those that are child centered, psychoanalytic, cognitive behavioral, Jungian, gestalt, filial, Adlerian, Eriksonian, developmental, dynamic, ecosystemic, and strategic (Crenshaw, & Stewart, 2014; O'Connor & Braverman, 2009). *Whew!*

Play may also be used successfully in situations outside of formal play therapy sessions and with adults and adolescents (Gallo-Lopez

& Schaefer, 2005; Schaefer, 2003; Webb, 2015). Many individuals, regardless of age, have trouble expressing their feelings or attitudes verbally or artistically but can express themselves in play through manipulative materials such as puppets, toys, Play-Doh, or clay (Drummond et al., 2016; Glover, 1999). In these situations, play becomes a projective technique, and counselors observe clients in distraction-free situations with selective materials such as matchbox cars, dolls, or artistic materials. Those who use such media in creative and fun ways are most likely to be successful in resolving developmental dilemmas and situational aspects of their lives.

Two primary ways play is manifested in counseling are through the use of sand play (a play therapy process) and a variety of different games. Sand play is the more highly developed of these two procedures and is appropriate for children as young as 2 years old and with adults of all ages (Allan, 2008). Games are universal, fluid, and diverse in nature. Based on needs and knowledge, counselors and clients are entrusted to discern which types of play are to be used and how they will be incorporated into any level of counseling.

Sand Play

The British pediatrician Margaret Lowenfeld (1939, 1979) is credited with the initial establishment of the counseling technique known as *sand play*, which she called the *world technique*. The method was refined by the Swiss Jungian analyst Dora Kalff (1981), who formulated theoretical principles and began training practitioners. Kalff centered her ideas on the importance of a healthy ego and the repairing of impaired ego functions for children who experienced trauma early in their development. In sand play, clients have the opportunity to resolve traumas through externalizing their fantasies and by developing a sense of relationship and control over inner impulses (Kaduson & Schaefer, 2015). The approach is essentially a nonverbal mediator between the unconscious and the outer reality of participants (Richards, Pillay, & Fritz, 2012).

The basic equipment in sand play includes two sand trays of approximately 20 × 30 × 3 inches (approximately 50 × 76 × 8 cm), one of which contains dry sand and the other wet sand. The trays are waterproof, and the insides are painted blue to simulate water when the sand is pushed back. In addition to this environment, numerous miniature toys and objects are made available to children in categories including people, buildings, animals, vehicles, vegetation, structures, natural objects, and symbolic objects such as wishing wells (Kalff, Turner, & Kaliff, 2003; Orton, 1997; Schweiger & Cashwell, 2003).

The process of sand play begins when counselors invite clients to play with the sand and to choose from the assortment of miniatures (Allan, 2008). In this process of invitation, a safe, protected, and nonjudgmental environment is offered. Counselors witness clients' symbolic working through of issues and offer encouragement and support through a consistent presence.

People move through predictable stages in the enactments they create, at least in Western societies. The three most dominant are (a) chaos, (b) struggle, and (c) resolution. To capture the essence of how clients are progressing, many counselors either photograph or sketch the outcomes of each play therapy session. These pictures are later reviewed with individual clients. A typical pattern of treatment in the United States is around 8 to 10 sessions. However, sand play is international, and what is done, how it is done, and how long therapy lasts vary. For instance, in Japan, sand play therapy is called *hakoniwa*, and it makes use of nonverbal communication and concrete activity in ways that differ from those just described (Enns & Kasai, 2003).

Games

The appeal of games covers the life span. "Board games appear to have been a part of the human experience since the beginning of history" (Livesay, 2008, p. 198), with the oldest known board game found in Jordan dating back to approximately 5870 BCE. Games seem to be an innate part of being human. Some healthy games are made up spontaneously and last only a brief time. For instance, my children made up numerous games with tennis balls when they were young. The games were usually played only once or twice and were soon forgotten. They were called by various names, such as wall ball, step ball, and roof ball. The common denominator of the games was they were fun and engaging.

Besides being fun and engaging, most games have rules. The main two types of games with rules are "table games (dominos, cards, dice and board games) and physical games (hide and seek, jump rope, ball games of various types)" (Smilansky & Shefatya, 1990, p. 2). From childhood games of Candy Land, jacks, and fox and hounds to adulthood games of Monopoly, basketball, and chess, there are always people willing to participate and abide by the rules. Playing games is inviting, exciting, and enjoyable for most individuals. Games challenge people's wits and afford them an opportunity to do something with others besides connect in conversation that may not be challenging (Jourard & Landsman, 1980).

An example of a counselor who has used games creatively and therapeutically in counseling is Fatos Erkman, a professor at Bogazici University in Istanbul, Turkey. While she was active as a clinician, Erkman worked with a preadolescent girl from a poor family who was not very cooperative. To get the girl to open up and be cooperative, Erkman played a game of billiards with her. The girl was good at billiards; Erkman was not as skilled although she tried hard. The end result was that the girl won, and with it the power difference that had seemed so huge previously faded. The result was that the relationship between the two individuals grew (personal communication, May 24, 2010).

Humor

In a more spontaneous way than play, the introduction of humor into counseling can originate from counselors or clients, depending on readiness and timing. Counselors from any theoretical position are frequently quite effective with clients if they introduce a measured amount of humor into their sessions. Humor at selective points in the counseling process helps promote joining and breaks down clients' resistance (Markham & Palmer, 1998; Minuchin & Fishman, 1981). To be effective in such circumstances, however, humor must be culturally congruous and spontaneous (Vereen, Butler, Williams, Darg, & Downing, 2006). For example, if counselors humorously point out their own faults or weaknesses as appropriate, clients usually feel more open and comfortable. This type of gentle self-effacement is associated with strong and admired personalities, including Abraham Lincoln, who when accused of being two-faced in a debate joked that if he was, he would not be wearing the face he had. Similarly, blues singer Eddie "Cleanhead" Vinson in a self-effacing manner referred to his baldness as proof that he was so desirable that women had rubbed his hair away (J. J. Moreno, 1987). In counseling, subtle humor might come out if a counselor who misunderstood or misinterpreted a remark paused and said, "Let's try again. I really did not hear what you were saying. Let me make sure these things (pointing to his or her ears and pretending to adjust them) are more receptive this time."

Humor is almost always unexpected and acts as an atypical way of structuring a seriously sanctioned relationship by altering the way individuals or families view distress (Beier, 1966). Witmer (1985) observed that, "Psychologically, humor overrides negative emotions, dissipating them at least for the time being, and then [leads] to perceptual changes in . . . thinking" (p. 169). The result is a refined atmosphere in which "people can consider themselves more objectively than if they are 'out of control'" (Barton & Alexander, 1981, p. 431).

Humor may be used by a counselor if done so respectfully and if the use of humor helps strengthen a therapeutic relationship (Middleton, 2007). One of the outstanding proponents of the use of humor in counseling has been Albert Ellis. His rational emotive behavior therapy approach advocates the use of humor to help clients understand their absurd and self-defeating behaviors more clearly. From this perspective, humor may take many forms, but most often it is manifested in the use of "paradoxical intention, evocative language, irony, wit, cartoons, and rational humorous songs" (Ellis, 1986b, p. 34). The last technique—rational humorous songs—is an especially creative and enjoyable contribution to helping. Ellis (1981) recommended that his clients sing these songs on a regular basis to allow them to laugh at themselves and see their situations more realistically. Although some of the songs contain offensive language, some of them do not, and all of them are imbued with a large amount of fun. One such song is "Whine, Whine, Whine" sung to the tune of the Yale Whiffenpoof song (composed by a Harvard man in 1896). The lyrics are as follows:

> I cannot have all of my wishes filled—
> Whine, whine, whine!
> I cannot have every frustration stilled—
> Whine, whine, whine!
> Life really owes me the things that I miss,
> Fate has to grant me eternal bliss!
> And if I must settle for less than this—
> Whine, whine, whine!
> (Ellis, 1977–1993; reprinted with permission of the Albert Ellis Institute)

Existentialists such as Viktor E. Frankl (1985) and Rollo May (1953) also used humor in their counseling and the theories they created. These theorists/practitioners used humor to help their clients gain increased self-awareness in their lives and identify what they could do to become less anxious and more accepting of themselves and situations. Humor in these existential traditions today takes the form of present-oriented storytelling in which counselors ask clients to try to see the absurdity in a situation as if they were someone from a different culture or planet. Thus, people who are anxious about meeting other people might make up a story or enact a minidrama depicting themselves as nervous and upset to the point of silliness. In addition, anxious people might say nonsense syllables to new acquaintances, such as "abba dabba yabba yo," or simply stare at their own shoes. In a parallel way, existential counselors in the tradition of May and Frankl might share their own stories about comparable situations to those of clients to illustrate pertinent points. These brief stories often have funny endings that may or may not be true, such as the counselor relating that he or she got to a point of desperation about being anxious and then decided that instead of thinking about being anxious anymore resolved instead to go get a cup of coffee because it was more stimulating.

At other times, clients are asked to focus on historical or projected humorous moments in their lives. This exercise helps clients concentrate on an area they have usually forgotten or neglected. Once clients begin to see funny aspects of their lives depicted, they are no longer able to be so serious or overinvolved in current difficulties. In such cases, humor enlightens clients, and they leave these sessions as transformed people. For example, a client who had become depressed over the unalterable loss of an opportunity in young adulthood took on a more optimistic attitude by making up a joke about the end of his life, at which time he was being held accountable for the choices he has made. When asked in the afterlife what he had learned from all his suffering over the years, the client replied, "I'll never do that again."

Humor is an excellent tool for making or emphasizing a point in a therapeutic or educational setting. Most individuals remember amusing stories more easily than

prosaic facts. For example, in illustrating the concept of making changes in life, I often tell my students the following true and humorous story:

> As a novice counselor I once had to make a telephone call from a pay phone. The cost of a call in those days was a dime, and all I had was a quarter. I wondered if I would get 15 cents back if I deposited the quarter into the coin slot. As I was thinking, I noticed that the phone company had written above the coin receiver these words, "This phone does not give change," to which a dissatisfied customer had scribbled below, "It doesn't even try!"

The point of the story, that change is difficult and frequently has to be made alone, is enhanced by the punch line at the end. It helps students remember that despite their best efforts, some individuals will not move past their current state of being "stuck" no matter how well intentioned the counselor may be (Meier & Davis, 2011).

Using humor also results in uniting people who share a common experience. Bonding is encouraged by the employment of almost all the creative arts, but humor is especially powerful because of the enjoyment with which it is associated. Examples of the effect of humor on bonding continually emerge at college class reunions when former classmates remind each other of fun times. They are also present when a group speaking one language, such as Italian, listens for the first time to someone speaking a similar language, such as Spanish. In such moments, differences and similarities are exaggerated and group identities solidified (Arieti, 1976).

Play and Humor in Counseling With Specific Populations

Play and humor differ across the life span and among various cultures (Maples et al., 2001). Thus, there are no universal jokes or playful behaviors that appeal to everyone. For example, adults prefer structured games such as baseball or football much more than children, who engage in solitary or parallel play in a free-form fashion. Puns (humorous plays on words) are not understood by young children but may be relished among adults. On a cultural level, the British and French often find slapstick humor such as that displayed by co-medians Jerry Lewis and Monty Python funnier than do Americans. Likewise, in the 1987 movie *Good Morning, Vietnam* the humor of Robin Williams as a radio talk show host was embraced by troops in the field during the Vietnam conflict but hated by the military hierarchy. Despite personal and cultural differences, play and humor have many applications with various groups.

Children

Play

One of the most direct ways that children express their feelings is through play. Brenner (1997) wrote, "Children who cope effectively with stress are able to enjoy play. They become involved. They smile and laugh and their bodies are relaxed. They use play to symboli-cally reenact their problems, solving them and overcoming imagined aggressors" (p. 175). Therefore, play environments are often used to assess the mental health of children because children feel com-fortable in them (Drummond et al., 2016). Through play, children overcome barriers that may impede good mental health. "Play is a healing and growth process that children are able to use naturally and independently" (Cochran, 1996, p. 288). Overall, "imaginative play in young children . . . appears to be a manifestation and expression of the human tendency to create, transcend the immediate, and be aware of the possible" (Shmukler, 1985, p. 39).

The creativity, energy, and awareness that are part of the nature of play are the basis for structured activities that incorporate play. Through play, children are provided with the opportunity to develop and practice more productive behaviors that may be applied to everyday life (C. Campbell, 1993). For example, Robert P. Bowman (2004) developed an experiential exercise called Test Buster Pep Rally to help children (in Grades 1 to 6) overcome test anxiety in a playful manner. Material in the test buster kit comes in the form of songs, chants, and supportive group activities. Through participation in a test buster rally, children learn to overcome anxieties about tests by essentially playing through their fears. In line with R. P. Bowman's ideas, Cochran (1996) suggested that play can be used to help culturally diverse children overcome edu-cational and social barriers in schools, thereby achieving greater success and self-esteem. For example, in the anger ball activity, a child's anger is released by hitting a ball that momentarily represents something or someone the child has anger toward (*Anger Ball*).

Virginia Axline (1947, 1967) found that when children are en-couraged to own their emotions in an accepting and unstructured environment that involves the use of play, they grow and become more positive in their relationships with others. Axline thus set up situations in which children were free to act out their fantasies in a trusting relationship with a nonjudgmental counselor. These environments allowed children to safely expose their innermost thoughts and feelings in symbolic ways, and these expressions could later be interpreted and treated. This child-centered play therapy approach has been used in a number of ways since its inception, including in the successful treatment of abused children (Scott, Burlingame, Starling, Porter, & Lilly, 2003; J. White & Allers, 1994) as well as in the treatment of childhood enuresis and encopresis (Cuddy-Casey, 1997). In child-centered play therapy, it is the child and not the problem that is the point of focus (Landreth, 1993).

Play has also been used to work therapeutically with special populations of children, such as those with Down's syndrome. For example, Play-Doh has been used as an entertaining medium "for emotional expression on a basic level" (O'Doherty, 1989, p. 174). Participants may orchestrate angry sounds when pounding the Play-Doh, and whining sounds may accompany the squeezing of the material (*Play-Doh Expression*). Dry, clean materials should be used with these children to heighten their curiosity and promote learning.

An interesting example of this approach is found in the paper-and-box stimulus reported by O'Doherty (1989). In this experience, a large packing box filled with various types of paper is kept in the counselor's office, and children are allowed to climb in it and play. The idea behind the box and the games it spontaneously inspires is that through this medium children encounter the creation of rapport, the skill of reciprocity, and the art of pretend. By fixing the box with multiple entrances and exits, counselors can heighten play and social interaction among these children (*Paper and Box Stimulus*).

In general, children enjoy game activities that can have an educational as well as a fun side to them. These activities add reinforcement to counseling sessions. Games are safe and relatively nonthreatening. In addition, "game play avoids an overuse of 'talk therapy,' which may force the child into acting like a miniature adult" (Friedberg, 1996, p. 17). Several games are appropriate for children. One of the earliest was the Talking, Feeling, and Doing Game (R. A. Gardner, 1983), during which children are interviewed in the context of a game with a game board, dice, and movement along squares from start to finish. Children are encouraged to talk and acknowledge their emotions and actions in a positive and productive way. This game is "won" by moving a game piece to the finish square and gaining greater insight into oneself (*Talking, Feeling, and Doing Game*).

Several newer games for children by Berthold Berg that are based on cognitive behavioral theory include the Assertion Game (B. Berg, 1986), the Anger Control Game (B. Berg, 1989), the Anxiety Management Game (B. Berg, 1990a), the Depression Management Game (B. Berg, 1990b), and the Self-Control Game (B. Berg, 1990c). In addition, Brad Erford (2000) created children's games revolving around major issues children face. These games are titled Conflict Resolution, Studying Skillfully, Social Skills, Good Grief, Understanding Anger, Solving Problems, Self-Concept, and Changing Families. Erford's games, like most others, involve a playing board, different color cards, interesting icons to move around, and dice. Ann Vernon (2006a) also developed an emotional educational curriculum for children in Grades 1 through 6 that is presented in the form of games. Several other commercial publishers, such as Childswork/Childsplay (http://www.childswork.com/), have produced interesting and informative games for children in addition to games dealing with a plethora of topics, such as bullying, trauma, divorce, impulsivity, stress, and feelings.

Humor

Humor has a powerful effect when used in counseling children.

> Whether deliberate or spontaneous, humor can add creativity and insight to counseling sessions. Humor is a valuable therapeutic adjunct to making assessments, forming a therapeutic bond, helping children develop social skills, encouraging catharsis, addressing resistance, reframing maladaptive beliefs, and replacing rigid, self-absorbed perspectives. (R. G. Berg, Parr, Bradley, & Berry, 2009, p. 225)

Humor provides a way for children to cope and to make their environments safe. In addition, humor sometimes enhances rapport and builds trust between adult therapists and children (Kilgore, 2003). Humor may also help in the healing process of children recovering from trauma (D. W. Alexander, 1999). With children, humor can take many forms, including storytelling, use of puppets, and word games. Although much humor for children is specific to the environments in which they live, humor has the wonderful ability to transcend cultures. For instance, Herring and Meggert (1994) found humor to be a useful counseling strategy when working with Native American children because of the emphasis on humor among the various tribes of this population.

One of the ways to foster cathartic laughter in children is to "exaggerate routine actions and expressions" (O'Doherty, 1989, p. 175). Children seem to enjoy seeing many of their daily situations mimicked. Humor creates a distancing effect and gives children a clearer perspective on what they are doing and how they and others look in social interactions.

R. G. Berg et al. (2009, pp. 228–229) gave excellent examples of some types of humor

---

Creative Reflection

What games did you enjoy playing as a child? What lessons, if any, did you learn from the games? How do those lessons affect your life now?

that are appropriate for children besides exaggeration. These include the following:

1. The unexpected, for example, a riddle such as "What is clear on the outside and gray on the inside?"—An elephant in a sandwich bag.
2. Incongruity, which is composed of the impossible and improbable, such as "What question can never be answered by 'yes'"?—"Are you asleep?"
3. Word play, in which the double meaning of a word is highlighted, such as "How many people work here?"—About half.
4. Nonverbal and slapstick humor, which involves voice tone, facial expression, body movement, and props.
5. Retrospective humor, in which children may laugh at their earlier behaviors, such as a child who says at the end of counseling, "Boy, I was really a screaming weenie when I first came to see you."

Marriage and family therapist Cloe Madanes (1981) illustrated how having fun in a serious situation can eliminate dysfunctional behavior. In one case, for example, a boy pretended to have a temper tantrum, and his mother pretended to comfort him. Although the enactment was "just pretend," the boy and his mother had fun together, and the temper tantrum behavior disappeared after that. Basically, humor is more physically displayed in young children and more verbally and intellectually manifested in older children (Figley & Kiser, 2013).

Adolescents

Play

Play activities are a natural for use with adolescents (Gallo-Lopez & Schaefer, 2005; Nickerson & O'Laughlin, 1983). Most counselors who work with this age group include play activities for their clients. In hospital settings, play with teenagers may center on the "use of toys, amputation dolls, clay, and checkers" (Keith & Whitaker, 1991, p. 109). It may also include the use of video games, basketball, volleyball, and games that involve eye–hand motor skills and a sense of achievement or teamwork. An interesting game created for high school freshmen is called Frustration (Teeter, Teeter, & Papai, 1976). In this group game, entering students are exposed to some of the hazards of high school and the effects that chance circumstances may have on their lives. They may draw a card that places them in a class with exceptionally bright or mediocre students, or they may find that in a school assembly they are seated next to either a popular or an unpopular classmate. If they choose to think about such situations while playing the game, they have gained insight and understanding about themselves as well as their upcoming environment (*Frustration*).

One of the most frequently used types of play with adolescents is an Outward Bound experience in which teenagers are challenged to individually and collectively overcome a number of obstacles in a wilderness setting (Bacon, 1984). In such a program, the activities themselves become physical metaphors that help bring isolated individuals together as a unit. Often an act of play in the midst of adventure will help solidify the connectedness that increases everyone's sense of their own human qualities as well as those qualities in others.

For situations in which an outdoor experience is not possible, Vernon (2006b) developed an emotional education curriculum for adolescents in Grades 7 through 12. This curriculum, similar to her curriculum for younger children mentioned previously, is presented in the form of games that engage adolescents in learning while they are having fun. Such simulations make it possible to help teens develop their individual and group skills in an educational setting. Sand tray group counseling may be used with preadolescents and adolescents as well (Draper, Ritter, & Willingham, 2003; Flahive & Ray, 2007). In this type of experience, adolescents create in sand trays their own little worlds to reenact real-life events and help them open up to others. The result is improved self-esteem, peer relationships, and academic achievement (Y.-P. Shen & Armstrong, 2008).

Humor

Often adolescents, in the words of Cyndi Lauper, "just want to have fun." They do this by teasing, mimicking, or acting out. Although such light moments may be enjoyed individually and collectively, it is crucial to make sure that fun and laughter are used positively and that the topics that inspire the laughter are adequately addressed. One way to do this is to work with librarians to keep popular and prosocial humor on display at schools and in community settings. These books, periodicals, and even cartoons, such as *Zits* or *LuAnn*, can be the subject of guidance lessons or other public presentations.

Another way to work with teenagers is to have them make up skits that address in humorous ways subjects they have concern over, such as the environment, war, dating, and drugs. A type of cooperative stunt night activity can be the result of such an effort in schools, and the skits can be videotaped and shown to participants again at a party following the event (*Skits*). Through a combination of action and process involving humor such as the ones described here, teenagers gain a sense of empowerment and empathy that gives them more freedom to constructively operate within societal boundaries.

Creative Reflection

When have you ever been in a skit or a play? What did you learn from doing your part in the production? What did you learn from observing or interacting with others?

Adults

Play

Adult development is usually conceptualized in terms of intimacy and generativity issues (Erikson, 1963; Gilligan, 1982). In both domains, the concept of play is seldom stressed. Perhaps this is because "free play is as natural to adults as balancing a checkbook is to children" (Glover, 1999, p. 383). However, Liebmann (2004) stated that adults "need to develop a sense of play, which can give them a much-needed 'space' away from the constraints of normal living, and helps them to renew their capacities for tackling life's problems and opportunities" (p. 13).

Two of the best playful counseling techniques for adults that are often humorous include shame attacks and singing humorous rational songs. Both approaches have qualities that exemplify the philosophy of their originator, Albert Ellis (1977), who advocated that therapeutic interventions can and should be fun at times. As noted previously, in shame attacks, people are encouraged to display behaviors they have been previously fearful of enacting to see that the world does not collapse or fall apart if they make a mistake or do not get their desired outcome. For example, a person might ask for a glass of water in a restaurant without ordering food or might purposely fall down at a shopping mall and see what happens (*Shame Attacks*).

With humorous rational songs, clients play with words and thoughts in a way that makes many of their problems less serious and therefore resolvable (Watzlawick, 1983). Ellis has written numerous songs to familiar tunes, but creative individuals can also write their own words or music (*Humorous Rational Songs*). For example, to the tune "I've Been Working on the Railroad," a client once wrote the following:

> I've been harvesting my problems
>   all the live-long day
> I've been gathering up my problems
>   just to pass the time away
> Can't you see my problems growing
>   like tall stalks of corn
> Can't you hear me as I'm shouting:
>   "Oh, I'm so forlorn!"

Regardless of the artistic nature of play by adults, actions that encourage playfulness can be essential in helping them gain perspective. Counseling with a playful quality is healthy and helpful for adults who are often squeezed between too many demands and inadequate time or resources. Play, especially role plays, can also be instructive in helping novice counselors "actively learn about the issues and challenges of the counseling process" (Rabinowitz, 1997, p. 216) (*Role Plays*).

Humor

Most adults appreciate good humor and are open to laughter. They even appreciate a counseling joke such as the following:

Question: How many counselors does it take to change a light bulb?
Answer: Just one, but the light bulb really has to want to change!

Some adults, especially those who are depressed, can be therapeutically helped through experiencing amusement pertaining to their life situations (Corey, 2013; Ellis, 1977). Thus, humor is an excellent approach to use with these individuals. Counselors, too, often improve their mental health by looking on the humorous side of serious situations at times (Gladding, 2009, 2014).

Most humor with adults in counseling takes the form of verbal exchanges and is often couched as an exaggeration, such as saying to someone who just got fired again for insubordination, "You certainly have gotten to be an expert at shooting yourself in the foot. I admire a good shot, but you may be too good. I wonder how we can work together to help you be less competent in this area?" A danger exists in that exaggerations may become sarcastic, but the best exaggerations contain a good mixture of truth and sensitivity.

In addition to verbalizing, adults may be helped by humor through vocalizing, such as asking a group to laugh and keep laughing whether anything is funny or not. When the counselor laughs with the group in various ways, from that of a little child to the belly laugh of Santa Claus, group members are given permission to act and feel differently, and they are shown through example how to do so.

Older Clients

Play

Little work has been done on how to use play with older people. Nevertheless, older people are diverse in their enjoyment of different forms of playfulness and fun. Because play sometimes depends on physical mobility, older adults may be confined to activities that involve less strenuous exertion, such as blowing bubbles; bouncing balloons; playing sensory awareness games; or participating in sedentary interactions with cards, checkers, or dominos (Mayers & Griffin, 1990). However, many older adults enjoy the same playful events as do other age groups. Regardless, play is helpful in maintaining health and vigor within this population, and the types of play used are quite varied.

One fun example of play used in groups is known as passive–active (Fisher, 1989). Part of a group is passive and the other part active. The active members make statues out of the passive members (within reason), but the passive members may come alive at any time, and likewise the active members may become passive at any time. The enjoyment of this type of play is found in creating the statues and in the element of surprise. It is important for counselors to make sure that the entire group does not become active or passive all at once (*Passive–Active*).

Humor

Humor is much appreciated by many older people, and the wit of clients at advanced ages is often quite keen (Nahemow, 1986). One general advantage older persons have over other age groups is their appreciation of more diverse forms of humor because they have more experiences from which to draw. Certain themes are joked about more than others, such as sexuality, wisdom, and death. Laughter and humor often help older adults cope with life's stressors and losses (Monahan, 2015; Westburg, 2003).

In addition to verbally encouraging and using humor, nonverbal actions on the part of counselors who work with older populations can bring out the best and the lightest within members when warranted. For instance, if an older person takes the role of a doormat in a relationship with others, a counselor might literally have the client lie down and act out this helpless part (Raber, 1987). Such humorous enactments create an impression on clients by using fun and laughter so that they are put in positions of change (Watzlawick, 1983).

Groups

Play

Play can be used in groups in many ways, but one of the best and most structured is in the form of games, if they are not overused. Games can make individuals in groups more aware of themselves and others. Elizabeth E. Mintz (1971) devised a number of games based on gestalt therapy. One of these is Name Game, in which two individuals carry on a conversation using only their names and no other words (*Name Game*). Another is a variation of the Name Game called *Yes No*, in which two individuals have a similar conversation, but in this case only the words *yes* and *no* can be used.

In addition to the gestalt literature, pragmatic practitioners such as Pfeiffer and Jones (1980) have devised group games in the form of exercises that are helpful in moving groups along to appropriate stages of development. These games can be gimmicky if not implemented with purpose and theoretical knowledge. However, in the hands of skilled practitioners, they are stimulating and provide opportunities for personal growth and interpersonal interaction that would otherwise fail to take place.

Overall, conducting group

> play sessions with adults is a powerful and exciting experience. Each session is different. . . . Once people allow themselves to sit on the floor and engage in "child's play," they open themselves to experiences and expressions that are outside their awareness. . . . The unconscious is tapped and finds concrete expression in the structures or scenes created. (Bruner, 2000, p. 336)

Humor

Humor also may have a positive effect on groups. Groups that last frequently contain a humorous component (Gladding, 2016; Scogin & Pollio, 1980). Humor gives members a shared history and a bonding experience and often helps them look forward to group sessions. In addition, it eases tensions, distills hostility, and promotes creativity and positive communication (R. A. Baron, 1974; G. A. Fine, 1977; LaGaipa, 1977; Murstein & Brust, 1985). Groups able to laugh at their failures will be able to take risks together, will be prone to communicate openly and without fear, will be sensitive to the membership needs of the participants, and will be open to change (R. W. Napier & Gershenfeld, 2004).

Overall, the lighter moments in a group help enlighten and enliven the group process when they are expressed in humorous ways. At such times everyone in the group wins by having fun and feeling more connected. For example, if a group is stuck in a stagnant stage during which members talk only on a superficial level, the group leader may urge members to communicate only on that level and in as nonsensical a way as possible. Thus, one person may talk to the group about the weather while another describes the latest fashions. In such situations, group members begin to have fun with their surface conversations and kid each other about topics such as windy moments or long hemlines. The point is that such silliness can be a road to realness and risk taking by group members as they gradually cast off their limited roles and discuss topics that are of genuine concern to them.

Humor within groups can be cultivated by taking advantage of paradoxes within the group, discrepancies, the unpredictable, the unanticipated, universal truths, the absurd, the familiar, and the memorable (R. W. Napier & Gershenfeld, 2004). Humor is a way of helping group members resolve difficulties within themselves, differences they have with others, and outside situations. For instance, with regard to dealing with the death of a parent, J. Moore and Herlihy (1993) found that students they worked with not only needed to talk about their grief but were also helped when they learned to recognize and laugh appropriately at humorous moments in the grief process. In short, group leaders need to use humor in a nonhostile way and help their members see the lighter moments of intense situations. Groups that develop in this way are more harmonious, and as a result individual tolerance is fostered.

Families and Couples

Play

American society has an adage that states the "family that plays together stays together." The saying has an intuitive appeal but is too simple. Although playing can be fun and bonding, it has to be fair and based on a win–win format to be therapeutic. In game theory, a fundamental distinction is made between two types of games that occur in human interaction. The first is a *zero-sum game* in which if one person wins another loses. Zero-sum games set up competitive situations and may be necessary in some situations such as sports that have the goal of crowning a champion, such as football or basketball. The second type of game is a *non-zero-sum game* and is based on the principle that "losses and gains do not cancel each other out. This means that their sum may lie above or below zero" (Watzlawick, 1983, p. 118). In such games everyone may win or lose simultaneously.

Intimate human relationships are always non-zero-sum situations; if one member of a couple or family gains self-esteem by putting down another member, then everyone loses. Often couple and family members do not realize this aspect of deep relationships, and they discount each other and make life difficult for themselves by playing zero-sum games. In healthy and functional marital and familial relationships, it is vital to establish fairness, tolerance, and trust. "Without them, the game becomes a game without end" (Watzlawick, 1983, p. 121). Counselors who work with couples and families have opportunities to help them learn to avoid zero-sum games by setting up cooperative situations inside and outside of counseling sessions in which the good of everyone is promoted at no one's cost. An example of this cooperation is sharing household tasks so that everyone gets a chance to relax and time is gained for family unity activities such as picnics and recreational outings.

A way to help parents and children learn how to improve their relationships is called *filial therapy* (B. Guerney, 1982; L. Guerney & Guerney, 1989; VanFleet, 2014). In this procedure, based on person-centered theory, parents of young children meet in groups to learn how to conduct play sessions with their own children. The idea is to break down communication barriers and feelings that get in the way of parent–child communication while creating positive perceptions and experiences. Filial therapy focuses on two programs: child relationship enhancement therapy and parenting skills training. Separately or together, they help families and individuals gain more feelings of self-worth and competence.

Play (the use of toys, art, drama, or games) may also be included as a child's medium for communication in family counseling sessions (Lund, Zimmerman, & Haddock, 2002). When it is, children are treated as equally important family members with valuable information to share. Play has an as-if quality and opens the door "to creativity that allows families to tell new and different stories" (Lund et al., p. 447).

Creative Reflection

Think of the healthiest couples you know. How do they relate to one another? Are they more cooperative than competitive? What do they do for each other?

Humor

In addition to play and games, humor is frequently used in family counseling. Satir and Bitter (1991) wrote,

> By deliberately understating or overstating a perception, humor clarifies intent, nudges a family member in a new direction, or encourages a little movement or change. . . . It serves as a strengthening agent for families, giving them a new way to experience their joint difficulties. (p. 33)

Veteran family therapists such as Salvador Minuchin and Charles Fishman (1981) use humor as a way of joining with families and helping everyone relax in the opening moments of the counseling process. "Part of the process of joining is to arrive with the family at that point where humor replaces helplessness and despair" (Morawetz & Walker, 1984, p. 61). An example of this occurred once with the experiential therapist Virginia Satir: A mother brought her 8-year-old child in for treatment because he was still eating with his fingers. The mother worried that her son would continue this bad habit and at age 21 would embarrass himself at important social gatherings. Satir's response in the opening session was to look at the mother with a little disbelief and say in an incredulous way, "You mean in 13 years, he won't learn this?" Her response caused both women to laugh, and the mother called back 16 years later to inform Satir of her son's success as a psychologist (Satir & Bitter, 1991).

The use of humor with families is a very personal thing (Barker & Chang, 2013), and it depends on the counselor's skills in reading verbal and nonverbal messages and in timing an appropriate witty response. If presented well, humor may relieve tension at any point of the counseling process, such as when a completely disorganized spouse who is the subject of complaint is described as a person who gives the organized spouse "a wonderful opportunity . . . to learn patience!" (Carter & Orfanidis, 1976, p. 200). Overall, using healthy humor during family counseling can increase the number of positive experiences a couple or family shares (Eckstein, Junkins, & McBrien, 2003). As such, humor serves as a means of strengthening relationships and helping individuals, couples, and families gain greater awareness of situations, self, and others (Gladding, 2015a; McBrien, 1993).

Play and Humor in Counseling With Other Creative Arts

Play and humor appear in many forms. Silly songs, absurd actions, structured activities, jokes, and stories have already been mentioned. In addition to these primarily verbal and musical forms, play and humor are found in combination with other creative arts, such as drama and visual arts in the form of cartoons.

Humor and Drama

Humor and drama are displayed in many ways. Since ancient times, comedies have been a favorite form of entertainment for humankind. In modern times, this type of play continues to be popular as witnessed by the number of comedy clubs in most major cities as well as the number of television shows that are situational comedies or comically oriented. On any given night, American television hosts a variety of comic entertainers from the legendary, gentle humor of *The Tonight Show* to the outrageous skits of *Saturday Night Live*. A great majority of the historically most frequently aired television productions have centered on comic themes, such as *I Love Lucy, M*A*S*H, The Jeffersons, Friends, Seinfeld, Modern Family, Hot in Cleveland,* and *The Big Bang Theory.* Regardless of the form, humor segments are geared toward helping viewers take themselves and the world less seriously.

Counselors as a group are avid comedy consumers because of the power humorous play has in helping them to switch gears in life and enjoy it to the fullest. Some counselors make good use of humor and play with it constructively. One easy way to become involved in using humor is to assign clients a homework task of watching certain television shows or attending a specific comedy performance. This type of assignment must be tailored to the individual taste of the client and is usually not a first-session type of intervention. One way it can be encouraged is to have clients buy or rent certain comic videos and see the material in the privacy of their homes or to view select works with clients in a counseling session. In either case, processing the material afterward is a must.

A second way comic drama can be used in counseling is through enactment, such as mime or clowning. Both mime and clowning take the form of nonverbal but humorous entertainment. They have excellent potential for stirring up emotions that are lighthearted and serious. Professional mimes such as Marcel Marceau can be watched before an actual enactment is attempted. The advantage of humorous mime in counseling is that it is both entertaining and capable of uncovering important unresolved issues. Humorous mime can be used with groups as well as with individuals. It helps clients feel their emotions fully; and when the mime is completed, these clients may be more verbal than usual. The same is true for clowning. Carp (1998) noted, "The clown with its archetypal power, multicultural history, crazy wisdom, hilarious antics, and paradoxical nature is the quintessential character to guide the individual on a healing journey" (p. 254). Principles of clown therapy (or therapeutic clowning) as well as goals and objectives have been well laid out by Carp, as have games/exercises used by clowns and the development of a clown character. Clown techniques can be conceptualized in drama therapy terms, although therapeutic clowning (as described by Patch Adams and others) grew up separate and apart from drama therapy (Pendzik & Raviv, 2011).

Play and Visual Arts

Some comic strips and cartoons have a universal appeal because of their subject matter and focus. Comic strips and cartoons are concrete in conveying a visual message. In counseling, they can be used to illustrate points that either counselors

Creative Reflection

How much humor do you need in your daily life to keep you balanced and emotionally healthy? How do you get it, that is, through television, movies, reading, going to plays?

or clients need to consider. The cartoon in Figure 21, created by Nels Goud and Tom McCain, illustrates this point by showing the

Figure 21 The Counselor's World
Note. Reprinted with permission of Nels Goud and Tom McCain.

demands counselors often face on a daily basis. It conveys this message in a way that words alone could not.

David and Tim Fenell have also illustrated situations in family therapy that show the nature of this endeavor for counselors and consumers. Like Goud and McCain, they get to the essence of relationships in families mainly by picturing the serious in a funny but frank manner (see Figure 22).

Besides being viewed informally, this form of humor can also be used in counseling in the following ways (O'Brien, Johnson, & Miller, 1978). First, counselors can give clients an anthology of selected cartoons or comic strips with the idea that they will be discussed in relationship to clients' problems. Through such a process, counselors hope clients will reconceptualize their concerns in a humorous way.

A second method of using cartoons and comic strips is as homework. Clients are given cartoons they are to study and bring back for discussion in the next session. The main difference between this method and the previous one is that more time is given for reflection on clients' situations.

A third way of using comic strips and cartoons in counseling is for clients to find comic strips and cartoons that relate to their situations and bring them to counseling sessions for discussion.

A fourth way of using this creative art in counseling is to have clients either fill in the ballooned part of cartoon scenes or draw their own picture or strip. In either case, clients reveal essential information about themselves that can be used in sessions as a mechanism for understanding and change.

NOW, WHAT SEEMS TO BE THE PROBLEM?

Figure 22 Now What Seems to Be the Problem?
Note. Reprinted with permission of Timothy and David Fenell.

Finally, anthologies of cartoons, such as the *Therapeutic Cartoons for Kids* series by David Craig (n.d.), can be used to help counselors relate to children at various ages. These books are probably the easiest to use because their focus is on cartoons that can help children be better in school and community settings.

Summary

This chapter has emphasized that although counseling is not a play or a comic activity, various forms of play and humor can be used in a therapeutic way with children, adolescents, adults, older persons, groups, and couples/families. Play is especially powerful in helping clients gain perspective on their situations and in devising appropriate and creative strategies by which to address these concerns. It helps clients rehearse, gain mastery over themselves and their environments, and become integrated on verbal and nonverbal levels. Play may help in establishing rapport and in understanding personal, group, and family dynamics as well. By humanizing counseling into a workable, enjoyable, and productive experience, "the play's the thing" and may capture the imagination of clients and counselors. As such, it may help them ultimately to work in a theory-based, fun, and nonthreatening environment in which understanding and change may occur regardless of age or cultural differences.

Likewise, humor can be used in counseling sessions to help clients and counselors gain insight into and perspective on their situations. Humor is an art with regard to its content and timing. In counseling, humor can be used to probe difficult subject areas, diffuse anger, circumvent resistance, and make the counselor more likable and effective. It is important that the type of humor used in counseling not be hostile. When effective, it helps to promote physiological, psychological, and social changes, thus fostering more positive mental health and alleviating pain (Borcherdt, 2002; Goldin & Bordan, 1999; Goldin et al., 2006). Different forms of humor appeal to various populations, and what may be funny to one individual at a particular age and stage in life may not seem humorous to someone else in another circumstance (Maples et al., 2001). Counselor sensitivity is essential to understanding the choice and timing of actions.

Overall, play and humor are resources for most counselors. Using these modalities in a sensitive and sensible manner has the potential for great impact.

Exercises

1. Many introductory counseling exercises are playful and humorous by, for instance, having individuals pretend to be animals representative of themselves and then actually to behave like themselves. Invite members of a group with whom you work to

begin a session by acting as if they were a significant historical figure. They should play their parts for at least 15 minutes, after which they should inform others of their role and as a group talk about what they learned from the experience about themselves and others that can help them in their daily functioning.

2. Think of a development situation that individuals in society usually experience, for example, going to school, beginning a career, getting married, or having children. Based on your knowledge of these events, devise a board game with dice (similar to the game Monopoly) for clients to play. The idea of the game is to learn about particular situations, not to compete. Try the game out with colleagues, and then after you have made refinements, use it in your counseling setting as appropriate.

3. Consult local and national periodicals and websites to find what comic materials are most widely read. Sample as many of these as you can, and record your feelings about the humor they convey, whether positive, negative, or neutral. Make a presentation to your colleagues on fun that can be used in counseling.

Chapter 9

Animal-Assisted Therapy in Counseling, Therapeutic Horticulture, and Wilderness/Nature Therapy

Eli

As an old dog, he has survived
*   the marriage of his master to a Nutmeg woman,*
*   the first clumsy steps of sandy-haired toddlers,*
*   and the crises of moves around eastern states.*
So in the gentle first light of morning
*   he rolls leisurely in piles of yesterday's clothes*
*   left over from last night's baths by little boys.*
Then slowly, with a slight limp.
*   he enters his daily routine,*
*   approaching the kitchen at the breakfast rush hour*
*   to quietly consume spilled cereal*
*   and dodge congested foot traffic.*
Sure of his place in a system of change
*   he lays down to sleep on an air vent.*
A family grows around him.

—Gladding, 1989

Ecotherapy is an umbrella term for a gathering of techniques and practices that lead to circles of mutual healing between the human mind and the natural world from which it evolved. It includes animal-assisted therapy in counseling, therapeutic horticulture, and wilderness/nature excursions, which are sometimes called adventure experiences in counseling (Chalquist, 2009). These therapies differ from traditional creative arts approaches because the client is introduced to another living organism in therapy sessions. These helping and healing experiences also are unique in the settings in which they take place and in the activities they contain.

Animal-assisted therapy in counseling (AAT-C) includes the use of small animals such as dogs, cats, rabbits, or birds, as well as large animals such as dolphins (dolphin-assisted therapy [DAT]; Dilts, Trompisch, & Bergquist, 2011) or horses (equine-assisted counseling [EAC]; Trotter, 2012), in a therapeutic setting either inside or outside a counselor's office (Chandler, 2012). Therapeutic horticulture, which is gardening with a social and healing purpose in mind, also takes place in either an indoor or an outdoor environment. It requires commitment, imagination, measured risks, and an appreciation for nature (Yasukawa, 2015). However, working with plants, especially if it involves arranging or rearranging flowers or working with small trees, such as in bonsai (an umbrella term for all miniature trees in containers or pots), is usually done in a controlled environment. Wilderness/nature therapy is exactly what it sounds like. Traditional counseling techniques are used in an outdoor setting that may incorporate adventure-based activities or simply an immersion experience in a natural setting.

A common link between all of these counseling approaches is unpredictability. It is virtually impossible to say with certainty how an animal will act all of the time, how a plant will develop and grow, or how a person will react to nature or an outdoor challenge. The good news is that a fairly narrow range of behaviors will likely be seen if animals have been properly trained, plants have been appropriately nourished, and people have been suitably prepared.

Another link between AAT-C, therapeutic horticulture, and wilderness/nature therapy is care and attention. Animals, plants, and people are dependent on the counselors for direction, upkeep, updates, and ultimately their well-being. Thus, counselors must be concerned with these living helpers and in many cases take on additional responsibilities to ensure that no suffering comes to their clients or to the animals, plants, or environments incorporated in these therapies.

Creative Reflection

When have you found comfort or relief from petting an animal, working with a plant, or just being in nature? What was it about the experience that changed you? How long did this feeling last? What did you learn from the experience?

In this chapter, I explore the multidimensional premises behind the power of animals, plants, and nature in life as well as the practical use of animals, plants, and nature in counseling. I distinguish between animal-assisted therapy, horticulture therapy, and nature/wilderness therapy. In addition, I explain and illustrate how these therapeutic approaches can be used with a variety of populations (e.g., from children to adults) and in various settings (e.g., from trauma units to the disabled). The use of animal-assisted therapy, horticulture therapy, and nature/wilderness therapy with other creative arts (e.g., play therapy and with a variety of theories) is also discussed.

Premise of the Use of Animals, Plants, and the Wilderness/Nature in Counseling

Animals

The ability of animals to help people overcome illness or mental disorders is not a new idea (A. H. Fine, 2010). It has a long and strong history. As early as the 1800s, Florence Nightingale is reported to have said, "A small pet animal is often an excellent companion for the sick." Animals have assisted humans over the millennia in many formal and informal ways.

One of the earliest recorded uses of pet animals in therapy occurred in Belgium in the Middle Ages. Pets and people were rehabilitated together, with pets providing a part of the natural therapy for the humans. The York Retreat, a residential center in England and one of the first institutions known for working humanely with mentally ill individuals, was established in 1792. It incorporated both birds and rabbits in the treatment of its patients (Parenti, Foreman, Meade, & Wirth, 2013). In outpatient therapy, a little known early proponent of animal-assisted therapy was Sigmund Freud, who occasionally used his dog Jo-Fi to calm patients down during sessions (Coren & Walker, 1997).

Boris M. Levinson was the first professionally trained clinician to formally introduce and document the way companion animals could hasten the development of rapport between therapist and patient, thereby increasing the likelihood of patient motivation. He called his approach *pet-oriented psychotherapy* and wrote a book about it in 1969. It was the first work to document the power of animals in psychotherapy (B. M. Levinson & Mallon, 1997).

Animal-assisted therapy in counseling utilizes the human–animal bond in goal-directed interventions as part of the counseling process. It incorporates specially trained and evaluated animals as therapeutic agents. Not every animal can work in a therapeutic setting (Chandler,

2012). The ideal canine candidate, for example, must be
even-tempered, patient, and
obedient. The idea is that the
bond between animals and
humans may help clients, especially children or adolescents,
relax and be more open while
promoting self-esteem and
good feelings. Strong memories
often remain for clients who
interact with therapy animals.

Plants/Horticulture

The practice of using plants therapeutically (horticultural therapy) dates back to the courts of the ancient Egyptian pharaohs, who prescribed walks in the palace gardens for those who were mentally disturbed (S. Davis, 2003). It has progressed since then to "an 1800s belief that working in the agricultural fields could benefit mental patients, to the use of gardening as an activity and a therapy for physical rehabilita-tion in the early 1900s, to the presence of many types and programs in the 2000s" (Haller, 2006, p. 2). Many individuals relate better to living but less active forms of life than animals, even if they are not initially aware of it. These individuals need to have interactions in life situations, and many are drawn to life that generates from the soil.

Horticulture therapy takes many forms and depends on the abili-ties and interests of those engaged in it. Activities include everything from giving a person a plant to take care of to inviting interested participants to partake in multigenerational gardening projects. The emphasis is on process, not product (Kampfe, 2015). If successful, the use of horticulture in therapy results in increased interpersonal interaction, reduced stress, positive feedback from others, and a sense that one is doing something worthwhile.

Wilderness/Nature Therapy

Wilderness therapy is a specialized modality within adventure-based counseling (Fletcher & Hinkle, 2002). Wilderness therapy can be defined as using traditional counseling techniques in an outdoor setting that incorporates adventure-based activities (Gass, Gillis, & Russell, 2012; N. R. Hill, 2007). It is based on maximizing the client's tendency to spontaneously self-disclose in environments outside a counselor's office (N. R. Hill, 2007). The approach was initially used with at-risk adolescents, especially delinquent adolescent boys resistant to treat-ment in traditional counseling settings, and was based on the Outward Bound model introduced by Kurt Hahn (Bandoroff & Scherer, 1994). Wilderness therapy is now used with a variety of clients, including those who are resistant to counseling and those who simply love the outdoors. Analysis indicates that prior to wilderness therapy treatment, females are more likely to have participated in self-harming behaviors and suicide attempts, whereas males are more likely to have been significantly involved with criminal activity (Bettmann, Tucker, Tracy, & Parry, 2014).

Creative Reflection

Most people have had an inspiring time with nature, even if they live in a city. Think of when you saw a sunrise or sunset that moved you or had an encounter with a natural phenomenon such as the ocean or wildlife. How did you feel after the experience? How did it affect your life with others?

Nature therapy is a related type of therapeutic approach to wilderness therapy. It is a "nature-oriented form" of expressive art therapy that is less active in form, scope, or substance than wilderness therapy (R. Berger & Tiry, 2012). This innovative approach reconnects people to nature to help them restore their connection to self and others, but it uses exposure to rather than immersion in nature. The focus is on widening people's sense of belonging to something greater than themselves, and it uses nature as both the background and the catalyst in doing so.

Practice of Using Animals, Horticulture, and the Wilderness/Nature in Counseling

Counseling is often thought of as an interpersonal, one-on-one therapeutic experience, and indeed most counseling sessions fit that description. However, a significant minority of clients need something different, and including animals, plants, or wilderness/nature experiences may be appropriate. Horticulture therapy activities can be adapted for use with preschool children, older adults, and intergenerational groups. The goals for these activities, among other things, include participation, self-motivation, and fun (Predny & Reif, 2004).

Animals

Although the term *animal-assisted therapy in counseling* is relatively new, its practice is widely applicable across a variety of mental health settings. It consists of 18 techniques and 10 intentions (D. M. O'Callaghan & Chandler, 2011). Some of the techniques include encouraging the client to play with the animal during the session, having the client ask the therapy animal to perform tricks (such as "sit down"), and encouraging the client to make up stories involving the therapy animal. Some of the intentions include building rapport, enhancing the client's self-confidence, and encouraging the sharing of feelings.

AAT-C models specific behaviors to enhance client social skills and to encourage clients to share feelings. Individuals who benefit most from AAT-C often lack positive attachments to others. Clients with unmet attachment needs and attachment insecurity may be especially attracted to and responsive to this type of therapy (Zilcha-Mano, Mikulincer, & Shaver, 2011). The common core of AAT-C are the unique skills and competencies of the handlers of the animal, their highly developed relationship with the animal, their knowledge of and ability to implement counseling theories with the animal, and their impact on the therapeutic process of helping others with the assistance of the animal (Stewart, Chang, & Rice, 2013).

In animal-assisted therapy in counseling, the amount and kind of interaction between a client and the animal involved varies from placid observation to energetic interaction. For clients who are extremely shy or nervous, observation of what the animal does and when may be the norm. For clients who are more hyper or manic in nature, cuddling or playing games with the animal may be prevalent. In both cases and those in between, clients often talk to the counselor through what they say to or about the animal. For example, "Your dog is so frisky. She reminds me of how outgoing I used to be before my heart got broken." This client is talking about the dog but relating the animal's actions to a personal psychological situation, having been hurt in a romantic relationship, that continues to affect his or her functioning. The information is revealed because of the presence of the dog and its behavior in the room and might be far more difficult to uncover using traditional therapy methods.

Overall, AAT-C may encourage clients to develop care, empathy, and trust as they see the working partnership between the animal and the counselor. These feelings may generalize to others over time. Indeed, AAT-C has been found to increase positive social behaviors and decrease behavior problems, enhance self-esteem, lessen depression and anxiety, and intensify client motivation to participate in counseling (Chandler, Portrie-Bethke, Minton, Fernando, & O'Callaghan, 2010). The presence of a therapy animal in group settings (e.g., skilled nursing facilities, hospitals, schools, or residential facilities) can have a healthy effect not only on clients or patients but on staff and visitors as well (L. S. Shelton, Leeman, & O'Hara, 2011; Stewart & Chang, 2015). Middle-schoolers rated an AAT-C dog high in the three necessary and sufficient Rogerian counseling

Creative Reflection

When I was a young professional and single, I used to come home at the end of the day and tell my dog everything that had happened. Of course, the dog did not understand a word I said, but I felt better afterward, especially if I patted the dog or gave him a hug. When have you "talked" to an animal or interacted with one by hugging it? How did you feel afterward?

traits of unconditional positive regard, empathy, and congruence (Jenkins, Laux, Ritchie, & Tucker-Gail, 2014).

In addition to promoting relationships, AAT-C is seen as an intervention that can promote safety and physical health as well as mental health. An excellent website to learn of the many benefits of animal-assisted therapy and the reasons it is a powerful therapeutic force in counseling is Animal Assisted Therapy International (http://aatinternational.com/).

Plants/Horticulture

Ralph Waldo Emerson is purported to have said, "All my hurts my garden spade can heal." Emerson, like so many others of his day and ours, realized that digging in the soil and growing plants relieves tension and promotes mental health. It can lower blood pressure, reduce oxygen consumption, increase alpha brain wave activity, and engender a feeling of calm (Doherty, 2009). In recent years, that realization has been at least partially captured in a number of books and articles.

One of the most useful and general books in the field of therapeutic horticulture is *Health Through Horticulture: Indoor Gardening Activity Plans* (Rothert, Nelson, & Coakley, 2011). Based on a program developed by the Horticultural Therapy Services Department of the Chicago Botanic Gardens, it explains 20 activities appropriate for all ages and stages of life. Each lesson lays out the materials needed for the activity and the step-by-step process for participants. For example, the first lesson, on spider plants, describes how plants propagate through such means as seeds, cuttings, or runners. Participants actively handle the plants, but they also talk about what they have learned from the lesson and how it applies to their life and to society. Other lessons focus on growing healthy indoor plants, growing colorful leaves, and winter holiday center pieces.

Another excellent "how-to" book in the field is Janice Hoetker Doherty's (2009) *A Calendar Year of Horticulture Therapy*. The ideas in the book were conceived by Doherty when her husband was in a war zone and she was the sole parent of their three young children. Later, when under less stress, Doherty was able to share these ideas, which can be used by a wide variety of people in multiple ways. The book contains 12 months of horticultural projects, with an "essay" each month "to chase the blues away." As she says, everyone can be helped to some degree by being involved with plants and horticultural procedures.

Another book applicable to a wide audience is *Growing With Gardening: A Twelve-Month*

Creative Reflection

Many children have school experiences that involve planting seeds and watching them grow in different environments. Think of a time such an experience happened to you or to someone you know. What were the results? What was learned?

Guide for Therapy, Recreation, and Education (B. Moore, 1989). Although not as new as the other books just cited, the content is fresh, specific, and relevant. *Growing With Gardening* also has activities to try for every month of the year. Forms such as "Your planting calendar" can be copied, and advice on "skills to learn" (such as watering and fertilizing) are pertinent for anyone wanting to be successful when working with plants. Overall this book is a classic.

Most professional therapeutic horticulturalists belong to the American Horticultural Therapy Association (AHTA). In 2015, the association defined a horticultural therapist as someone with the following experience and skills:

- Has a minimum of a bachelor's degree in horticultural therapy, or the minimum of a bachelor's degree with additional coursework in plant science, human science, and horticultural therapy.
- Has completed a 480-hour internship in horticultural therapy.
- Is professionally registered as a horticultural therapist with the American Horticultural Therapy Association as an HTR, Horticultural Therapist—Registered.

Horticulture therapy is a treatment modality that utilized horticultural activities to meet the specific therapeutic or rehabilitation goals of participants with a focus on maximizing social, cognitive, physical, and psychological functioning and enhancing general health and wellness (Haller, 2006). A really strong aspect of therapeutic horticulture is that it requires a minimum investment in time and resources yet yields rich dividends.

Wilderness/Nature

Wilderness therapy focuses primarily on working with delinquent or troubled adolescents in a wilderness area (i.e., a natural area not inhabited by humans). The idea behind the approach is that in a challenging environment, adolescents must change their behaviors to meet the obstacles they face; they cannot rely on previous dysfunctional habits. As they change their habits and ways of thinking, their identity changes, and they become more fully functional individuals. They learn from nature, from the group with whom they camp, and from their own experiences. These troubled youths become more interpersonally competent and gain a sense of accomplishment (Paquette & Vitaro, 2014).

Until recently there were few theoretical underpinnings for this therapeutic approach. Much of the effectiveness of the approach was based on the power of metaphors to increase the transfer of learning from the therapeutic experiences to other domains of the client's life. By reframing actions engaged in during the wilderness experience, the client can see these actions as being representative of challenges in other aspects of life (Hartford, 2011). Overall, empirical evidence has demonstrated the effectiveness of wilderness therapy (Rutko & Gillespie, 2013).

The use of nature by itself, without the overnight camping and activities found in wilderness therapy, has also been effective in helping a wide range of people cope with mental health issues and physical ailments. A natural setting provides new elements to explore such as sticks, rocks, trails, and creeks. This type of exploration can create a more positive mood for everyone involved. Nature therapy is built on three theories:

Creative Reflection

Should every therapeutic approach in counseling be generated from a theory? Why or why not? What are the advantages and disadvantages of having a counseling approach based on a theory?

- the *biophilia hypothesis,* which proposes that humans have an evolutionary relationship with nature that is linked to our biology, psychology, and identity;
- the *attentive restorative theory,* which proposes that under the right conditions, such as diversity and scope, the natural environment has a restorative effect on us; and
- the *psychoevolutionary theory of stress reduction,* which states that visual properties of natural environments, such as complexity and depth, evoke automatic positive affect and parasympathic physiological responses with associated feelings of calmness, relaxedness, pleasantness, and fasciation (M. Jordan, 2015).

Use of Animals, Plants, and the Wilderness/Nature in Counseling With Specific Populations

Animal-assisted therapy, therapeutic horticulture, and experiences in the wilderness and nature can positively influence the mental health and therapeutic experiences of a diverse range of client populations across a wide variety of treatment settings. Some uses for these therapies with specific populations are described in the following sections.

Animal-Assisted Therapy With College Students

Three major problems faced by college students are anxiety, stress, and loneliness. To help alleviate these maladies, Stewart, Chang, and Jaynes (2013) conducted a series of informal

Creative Reflection

How do you feel when you see wildfires, floods, or other destructive forces ravaging natural areas? What do these emotions tell you about your values? How do these values relate to counseling?

outreach programs they called Therapy Dog Nights. Twice a week for 2 hours each, the lead author and her therapy dog were stationed in the common area of a popular residence hall. Students were invited to drop by and interact with her, the dog, or with other students. The intervention was effective in reducing student self-reported anxiety and loneliness. Interaction with the dog was identified as the most influential aspect of the intervention. According to these authors, AAT-C outreach interventions may be an efficient and effective way for university and college counseling centers to meet the growing demands of their students because most counseling centers are not adding staff.

Making physical contact with a dog or a cat can be beneficial even among college students who may not feel stressed. Although no physical change was found in this study while students held the animals, students' diastolic pressure decreased immediately afterward (Somervill, Kruglikova, Robertson, Hanson, & MacLin, 2008).

Animal-Assisted Therapy With Trauma Victims and Those With Mental Disorders

Animal-assisted therapy is an effective treatment for people who have experienced trauma. Much of the work in this area has been focused on veterans, especially on the impact of service dogs on the lives and mental health of U.S. military veterans diagnosed with PTSD (Rose, Aikena, & McColl, 2014). When animal-assisted activities were offered, as opposed to lectures on stress management, patients in a mental hospital who received the animal-assisted activities reported significant decreases in measures of depression, anxiety, and pain when compared with the lecture or control groups (Nepps, Stewart, & Bruckno, 2014). A conservative meta-analysis of 21 studies of individuals with a variety of mental disorders found that AAT-C improved overall social functioning and had a moderate effect on depression, anxiety, and behavioral disturbances (Virués-Ortega, Pastor-Barriuso, Castellote, Población, & Pedro-Cuesta, 2012).

In a study of three groups that evaluated the effectiveness of particular interventions on trauma symptoms for children who had been sexually abused, two groups incorporated variations of animal-assisted therapy into the otherwise similar protocols of all three groups. A total of 153 children ages 7 to 17 participated. Children in the two groups that included therapy dogs showed signifi-

Creative Reflection

Young children are often comforted when they are given stuffed animals, such as beanie babies or teddy bears. Do you think stuffed animals can be as effective as real animals in providing relief to children? Do you think stuffed animals can be effective with adults as well? What makes you think so? What anecdotal or research evidence do you have?

cant decreases in trauma symptoms including anxiety, depression, anger, PTSD, dissociation, and sexual concerns when compared with the third group (Dietz, Davis, & Pennings, 2012).

Animal-Assisted Therapy With Psychiatric Patients Using Farm Animals

In a unique and first of its kind study, a Norwegian group used farm animals to study the effects of AAT on anxiety and depression among psychiatric patients. Using a controlled protocol and follow-up registration, the researchers found that anxiety decreased in the treatment group between the baseline and follow-up periods as well as in the postintervention period when compared with the controls. Depression decreased between baseline and the 6-month follow-up in both treatment and control groups, but there were no significant differences in depression scores between the treatment and control groups at any time points. However, a significant reduction in depression was found in the treatment group during the intervention, and the posttreatment period indicated a positive effect of the intervention on the depression level. Not surprisingly, the patients in the study who showed the largest reduction in depression scores during the intervention reported the largest increase in coping ability, self-esteem, and extroversion (Berget, Ekeberg, Pedersen, & Braastad, 2011).

Therapeutic Horticulture With Adults

Therapeutic horticulture has been used with a wide variety of populations, especially adults. One of the earlier experiments showing the power of horticulture was conducted by Langer and Rodin (1976). They gave nursing home residents a plant to keep in their rooms. Half of the residents took care of the plant themselves, and nursing home staff cared for the other plants. The simple act of caring for the plant resulted in better psychological and physical health for the residents.

Since Langer and Rodin's (1976) work, dozens of research papers have followed describing the benefits of therapeutic horticultural. Ten papers published in England since 2003 reported positive effects of gardening as a mental health intervention, including reduced symptoms of depression and anxiety. Participants have described a range of benefits across emotional, social, vocational, physical, and spiritual domains (Clatworthy, Hinds, & Camic, 2013). M. T. Gonzalez, Hartig, Patil, Martinsen, and Kirkevold (2011) used horticulture with five small groups of depressed clients over a 12-week period. Intervention consisted of "ordinary and easy gardening activities" in urban farm settings. Data was collected prior to, during, immediately after, and 3 months following the intervention. Various assessments and inventories were utilized. All mental health variables showed significant positive change that persisted at the 3-month follow-up. This intervention increased participants' social activity as well.

Likewise, L. M. Baker (2009) found indirect benefits for adult clients engaged in horticulture. These included being in the sunlight for those with depression and sleep disorders, as well as the visual and physical stimulation involved in work-

ing with plants. In addition, horticulture promoted self-expression and creativity in clients, provided them with a sense of focus and purpose, nurtured new skills, and even connected people with the cycle of life (which helped in their own adjustment to life events). Overall, working in the soil with plants increased clients' confidence and self-esteem through goal completion and skill acquisition, along with decreasing stress, anger, and aggression.

Therapeutic Horticulture With People With Disablities and Their Caregivers

In working with individuals with dementia and physical limitations, Kwack, Relf, and Randolph (2004) found the best garden activities were dependent on the people's strength, physical ability, clinical condition, and personal preferences. Well-designed garden activities reduced participants' frustrations with gardening and gave them a wide range of therapeutic benefits that increased self-esteem, success, and self-confidence.

In addition to working in the soil, a Taiwan study with 19 grief caregivers found nature appreciation relieved individual grief and stress (Lin, Lin, & Li, 2014). Although technically not horticulture, just seeing plants growing, whether domestic or wild, may have a therapeutic impact on people.

Therapeutic Horticulture With Posttraumatic Growth Populations

The use of horticulture with posttraumatic growth groups is a productive way of helping participants, especially veterans and others seeking to get past a trauma (Wise, 2015). Posttraumatic growth emphasizes undergoing significant "life-changing" shifts in thinking that contribute to a personal process of change that is deeply meaningful. It is characterized by decreased reactivity to past events and more appreciation of life, even simple life, such as that found in many plants, especially the emerging growth of young vegetation.

Nature Experiences With Children

Natural environments play an important role in the healthy development of children and adolescents. Children who live near green spaces and participate in school recess activities have been found to be healthier and have more learning-related behaviors (e.g., attention and communication skills) than children who do not have access to these advantages.

Natural environments play an important role in learning, development, and adjustment (Flom, Johnson, Hubbart, & Reidt, 2011).

Wilderness Therapy With Adolescent Girls

The effect on and the effectiveness of wilderness therapy on adolescent girls is mixed. To find out why, Gerrard (2014) conducted a qualitative study using a sample of adolescent girls who had been through the program. The girls who benefited had a positive response to a wilderness setting; enjoyed learning survival skills; and had positive changes in their lives, behaviors, and identity development. The girls who did not think they benefited greatly reported negative responses to specific staff members and therapists, depending on the approach utilized by these individuals. They also reported feeling trapped.

Wilderness Therapy With Young Adults (18–28)

Although not as common as working with adolescents (14–17), wilderness therapy has been used with young adults experiencing cancer, grief, and sexual abuse. Time away in a new environment (the wilderness) allowed deviant clients to rethink their previous behaviors as well as separating them from their negative peer group, drugs, or other opportunities for dangerous or self-destructive behaviors. The wilderness is often viewed as a magical place, a place of simplicity free from the distractions and stimulation of civilization, where people can begin to work through the various issues they have been struggling with or avoiding in their lives (Hoag, Massey, Roberts, & Logan, 2013). It appears to work in this way for those alienated from others or misguided in their actions.

Wilderness therapy has also been offered to young adults with insecure attachment styles and who have difficulty being close to or trusting others, including members of their families. These individuals use deactivating strategies, denying attachment needs and avoiding intimacy and close relationships. In wilderness programs, these behaviors are often displayed through isolation, excessive demonstrations of independence, superficial interpersonal connections, and extreme acting-out behaviors. These actions keep others at a comfortable emotional distance. In working with young adults in such a setting, efforts are made to help them feel more secure and to connect them with their families (Bettmann & Jasperson, 2008). Much research still needs to be done on the uses of wilderness therapy with young adults, but the impact of this treatment is promising.

Animal-Assisted Therapy, Horticulture Therapy, and Nature Therapy With Other Creative Arts

Although at first blush it would appear that animal-assisted therapy and therapeutic horticulture would not be compatible with other creative arts therapies, these ways of working with clients have been combined with other mainstream and adjunct approaches. A few of these combination therapies are described in the following sections.

Animal-Assisted Therapy With Play Therapy

A sterling example of combining AAT-C with another modality is animal-assisted play therapy. The primary advocate for this combination is Rise VanFleet (Sori & Hughes, 2014). She states that a key similarity between filial and animal therapy, especially for children, is play. The reciprocal respect between the human and the animal is vital, and that relationship can be used in making this treatment appropriate over the lifetime because the underlying foundation for this approach is attachment theory.

Animal-Assisted Therapy With Mainstream Counseling Theories

In addition to play therapy, AAT-C can be combined with a number of other mainstream counseling theories, including person-centered counseling, cognitive behavior counseling, behavioral counseling, gestalt, psychoanalysis, solution-focused brief therapy, and Adlerian therapy. A counselor's theoretical model and intervention techniques account for about 15% of a successful therapeutic outcome, so application of AAT-C may be more effective when counselors understand how AAT-C fits with the major premises of their guiding theories (Chandler et al., 2010). For instance, person-centered counseling is a nondirective approach to helping, and this theory and AAT-C match up well on techniques such as building rapport, enhancing trust, facilitating feelings of safety, reflecting feelings, and client insight. With gestalt counseling, AAT-C matches up well in facilitating self-discovery and sensory awareness. Clients may also find it easier to share their distress or concerns with the therapy animal in the presence of the counselor.

Therapeutic Horticulture With Behavioral and Person-Centered Counseling

As a group, horticultural therapists favor a theoretical approach in their work with clients. Two of the main theories that are pervasive from a counseling perspective are behavioral and person-centered approaches. Behavioral theories stress doing as a way of bringing about psychosocial change. Thus, they stress that clients in horticulture therapy be planting, pruning, or otherwise working on their plant(s). Counselors who are person-centered do not discount the importance of being active in working with plants. However, they go a step further in emphasizing techniques that include respect for client individuality, encouragement of creativity, allowing for mistakes, active listening, client autonomy, and attempting to understand the whole person.

Nature Therapy With Play Therapy

Peterson and Boswell (2015) have proposed that play therapy be conducted in natural surroundings. They point to research that indicates physical and emotional benefits emerge related to health and well-being when people are exposed to and interact with natural environments: "Significant reductions in stress and depressive symptoms, along with increases in the ability to focus on tasks and an increase in self-esteem and self-concept have been found" (p. 63).

Creative Reflection

Play therapy is a theoretical approach to counseling that differs from the use of the creative arts in counseling. Does it surprise you that play therapy can be used with both animal-assisted therapy in counseling and nature therapy? What does this information tell you about play therapy as a theoretical approach?

Summary

Animal-assisted therapy in counseling, therapeutic horticulture, and wilderness/nature therapy are three excellent ways of working with clients who may be detached, depressed, anxious, self-centered, or alienated from themselves or others. These therapies are unique in bringing a third living entity into the counseling process in the form of animals or plants that are usually seen as nonthreatening and inviting. The nonverbal nature of these entities elicits interactions and comments from clients and requires counselors to pay close attention to relations between the two.

AAT-C, therapeutic horticulture, and wilderness/nature therapy have potential for helping clients, especially when combined with mainstream counseling theories, but these approaches are not appropriate for all clients. Some people have a fear of animals, do not like getting their hands dirty, or have a phobia connected with the outdoors. However, when practiced with the appropriate education and training, these creative arts approaches to counseling have the potential to affect the therapeutic experience of a diverse range of clients across a wide variety of settings in a highly positive manner.

Exercises

1. In small groups of five, ask classmates to talk about their favorite pet when they were growing up or now. What was/is special about that animal? What did it (does it) give to individuals in its environment? What are some favorite memories? Allow 5 to 10 minutes for each animal story. Then have the leader of each group ask each person in the group to talk about his or her feel-

ings about the pet. Note similarities and differences, especially the importance of the animal to the family or to the person telling the story.

2. Visit a farm or an urban garden. Interview the farmer or gardener about their experience in growing different vegetables. Observe what the interviewee tells you about the process and what he or she likes best and least.

3. Visit a local park or natural resource nearby. What attracts you most about the scenery? Notice how you feel in this environment as opposed to the privacy of your house or apartment. What is different? How? What do you wish there were more of? What do you wish there was less of? What does this experience tell you about yourself in relationship to nature?

Chapter 10

Trends in Counseling and the Creative Arts

The Launching

Amid a cascade of thoughts
reflections flow and like a river
weave a path through changing vistas
where there is room and time for growth.
At dusk I ponder the journey's end
and in the spirit of transformation
I quietly launch forth frail ideas
into waters filled with hope and turmoil.
Conscious I may never see
their final form or outcome
yet knowing inside, peacefully,
that others will keep the best on course.

—Gladding, 1991e/2003

It is difficult to predict the future and distinguish between trends and fads. Nevertheless, it is important to plan ahead and to focus on the probable and possible (e.g., Brooks & Gerstein, 1990). In examining the future of counseling, several articles point toward new directions in the field both in the United States and in the world (e.g., Dryden, Mearns, & Thorne, 2000; Gale & Austin, 2003; D. Kaplan & Gladding, 2011). In this chapter, five of these emerging developments are briefly discussed: research, education, identity, interdisciplinary efforts, and technology. Each of these topics will affect not only counseling as a whole but also creative arts therapists and counselors who use the creative arts therapeutically. In all probability, these trends will dominate counseling in the future. Collectively, they will most likely have an impact that will change the way the creative arts in counseling are practiced in specific settings and with special populations. They will also probably change the way the creative arts in counseling are viewed by both the public and professional counselors.

Research

One of the most pressing needs confronting counseling and the creative arts therapies is the generation of research (Leavy, 2015). This need stems from the demands of the public, professional associations, licensure boards, insurance companies, and clinicians. Counselors who use the creative arts in their work must be accountable to their clients and to others connected with mental health services. They must be able to answer questions such as

1. How does improvement produced by creative arts methods compare with those produced by other methods?
2. Is one creative art therapy approach superior to another?
3. What client characteristics are related to maximal outcome with creative arts methods in a counseling context? (Mazza, 1993)

If the creative arts in counseling are to be uniformly respected, they must merit appreciation based on more than anecdotal testimony (Gladding, 2013; Malchiodi, 2005). In essence, to be used therapeutically, the creative arts need to go "beyond riding piggyback" (Lerner, 1992, p. 45) on the already established schools, theories, and research of other behavioral sciences.

Yet, conducting research on the effectiveness of the creative arts in counseling is not easy (Leavy, 2015). One of the frustrations with counseling research in the creative arts is the difficulty of controlling or isolating variables that promote or hinder client growth. Traditional research requires that practitioners demonstrate how a factor, such as a particular piece of music or a specific movement exercise, makes a difference in the treatment of clients. This problem is not particular to the creative arts, and every counseling approach has to address how its main techniques make an impact on the outcome of the therapeutic process (Kirschenbaum & Henderson, 1989; Sheperis, Daniels, & Young, 2010).

For some of the creative arts associated with research-based theories, the problem of empirical validation is not a high hurdle. For example, imagery has a long history of research connected to a number of theories (Marks, 1995; Watts & Trusty, 2003), including a strong link with behaviorism. That connection began in the early days of psychology and became especially prominent in the 1950s through the work of Joseph Wolpe's (1958) reciprocal inhibition model (M. H. Palmer, 2002). In more recent times, research by Arnold A. Lazarus (1982; Lazarus & Shaughnessy, 2002) and professionals in career counseling (Skovholt et al., 1989) have been notable. These studies have shown that imagery is an effective approach to helping people change or consider work options.

Likewise, humor has an affiliation with cognitive behavioral theories, such as rational emotive behavior therapy, and has a record of proven effectiveness (Ellis, 1986a; Raskin, 2009). Similarly, music has a historical link to medicine and medical research. Therefore, it is not surprising that researchers studying musical interventions have found that physical health and well-being and immune function are improved in the therapeutic process when music is used (MacIntosh, 2003; Wheeler, 2015). One of the creative arts, writing, has had a wealth of empirical data generated in recent years supporting its role in mental and physical health (e.g., R. S. Campbell & Pennebaker, 2003; Pennebaker, 2004; Pennebaker & Chung, 2007; Pennebaker, Mehl, & Niederhoffer, 2003). However, there is still considerable work to be completed to determine the influence of select creative arts on the field of counseling used either separately or in combination. One aspect that hinders faster development of research in this area is the lack of tradition among counselors who use the creative arts for investigating their effects.

Nevertheless, McNiff (1986) believed the creative arts have an advantage in generating research due to the fact that they are not "exclusively identified with either art or science" (p. 281). McNiff goes on to state that because the creative arts are broad and encompass arts, psychology, education, religion, philosophy, and psychiatry, varied, cooperative, innovative, and interdisciplinary research is essential and may be forthcoming. Indeed, Rossiter (1992) suggested that because creative arts therapies share much in terms of processes and products, collaborative approaches to researching them may be possible and quite productive.

Creative Reflection

Investigate recent research into one of the primary creative arts such as music or drawing. What new data support using this art form in prevention or intervention?

For those conducting research on the process and outcome of using the creative arts in counseling, new discoveries are emerging that may become a part of the field of assessment as a whole. The challenges of finding proper procedures and of being innovative are the primary obstacles facing scientific practitioners in the field. One way around this difficulty is for researchers to develop methods of investigation that do not necessarily follow empirical research traditions (Politsky, 1995). It will probably take a number of years before such models of inquiry are formulated, but Mitroff and Kilmann (1978) noted that, based on Jungian typology, four outer manifestations for research are associated with the processes of thinking and feeling. First, two thinking typologies exist: the analytic scientist and the conceptual theorist. Both analytic scientists and conceptual theorists seek to explain things in scientific, technical, and theoretical terms apart from human needs or concerns. They are quantitative scientific practitioners. Opposite these thinking types are primary feeling typologies: the conceptual humanist and the particular humanist. Feeling investigators are particularly sensitive to individual differences. These researchers aim toward qualitative investigations.

While waiting for the development of more sophisticated research methods, creative arts therapists and counselors who use the arts will have to rely on tried methods. Books such as *Beginning Research in the Arts Therapies: A Practical Guide* (Ansdell & Pavlicevic, 2001) and *Art-Based Research* (Barone & Eisner, 2012) offer a wealth of pragmatic ways to approach research in this area. One such method is single-case research designs. According to D. Aldridge (1994), "These designs are appropriate for the development of research hypotheses, testing those hypotheses in daily clinical practice, and refining clinical techniques" (p. 333). Most appropriately, single-case research allows for the assessment of individual development and significant incidents in a therapeutic relationship (Kazdin, 2010).

Another group-oriented method is the Structural Analysis of Movement Sessions (SAMS), which "is a system of observation and research of groups-in-action" (Sandel & Johnson, 1996, p. 15). Using SAMS, creative arts clinicians, especially dance and movement specialists, can study how groups as a whole and members individually influence one another. They can also assess the relationship between spatial arrangements and action tasks.

A third method of research is a more traditional comparison between experimental and control groups being offered different treatments, such as verbal versus art therapy (Shechtman & Perl-Dekel, 2000). Through this type of design, similarities and differences between treatment groups may be discovered and incorporated into practice. Further, there are research methods such as surveys and interviews. Although these methods have their flaws, as do any self-report research methods, it appears that they are yielding some interesting results, such as school counselors reporting the use of creative arts activities more in counseling with Asian American students than with Caucasian American students (Yeh, 2001). These interventions may include journal writing, drawing, poetry therapy, and music therapy, and they may be used because counselors consider nonverbal means of emotional expression to be less threatening to students from Asian American cultures.

Education

Although individuals can educate and enrich themselves through practicing the creative arts on self-imposed daylong retreats guided by resource books such as *Wild Heart Dancing* (Sobel, 1994), most people take more formal and group-oriented routes. Since the 1970s, several educational programs have been established for those who wish to specialize in the creative arts in counseling. Some of these programs, such as the one sponsored by the Appalachian Expressive Arts Collective at Appalachian State University, are interdisciplinary in nature and offer an emphasis within a master's program in counseling (Atkins et al., 2003). Other educational programs are more focused on a particular art form and have grown as a specialty. For example, in 1967, only 1 program in art therapy existed in the United States. By 1989, there were 17 approved programs regulated by the American Art Therapy Association (AATA; Levick, 1989). In 2010, the number of AATA-approved master's programs grew to 33.

Other associations devoted to the creative arts of music, dance/ movement, drama, and poetry have likewise established training and educational centers that are either university affiliated or freestanding. The facilities and faculties connected with such programs are devoted to providing systematic information to new practitioners in a cohesive and comprehensive manner. Yet, educational endeavors in the creative arts therapies face several difficulties. Some of the major problems for the creative arts therapies have been identified as follows (D. R. Johnson, 1989, p. 1):

1. How should the educational tasks of clinical practice, research, and theoretical scholarship be distributed among undergraduate, master's, and doctoral programs?
2. What are the essential skills required of creative arts therapists, and what methods of training (e.g., didactic, experiential, research, internship, and thesis) should be used to promote competencies in these skills?
3. How can those who wish to become creative arts therapists "maintain an integrated identity amidst the competing influences of . . . more established fields" such as "education, psychology, counseling, marriage and family therapy, and professional art or music schools" (p. 1), in which training programs in the creative arts in counseling are presently housed?

As with other professions, there are no easy answers to these problematic questions. Some of the solutions depend on the developmental stages of particular creative arts and their history. For example, with regard to the distribution of knowledge, most of the creative arts approaches require advanced degrees. In addition, most of the creative arts therapies have one accrediting body that constantly reviews and updates educational standards.

Indirectly addressing the second question raised by D. R. Johnson about competencies, Levick (1989) stated that "knowledge transcends program orientation" (p. 58). Disorders and issues that are part of all counseling programs must be addressed in therapeutic creative arts programs. Educational institutions offering degrees in creative arts therapies must give their recipients the best of both the art and science of helping. Degrees in the field must address treatment of disorders described in the *Diagnostic and Statistical Manual of Mental Disorders* (5th ed.; American Psychiatric Association, 2013) and the International Statisical Classification of Diseases and Related Health Problems (10th rev.; World Health Organization, 2007).

Further, focusing on the third issue that D. R. Johnson raised about the unique identities of professions, it should be noted that some of the creative arts approaches have been subsumed under other professional disciplines such as psychology, counseling, marriage and family therapy, and medicine. For instance, "the art therapy profession has been almost exclusively tied to the medical model" (McNiff, 1997, p. 40). Professionals who use the creative arts in these recognized areas of mental health services do not mind their identities being conveyed as psychologists, counselors, marriage and family therapists, or physicians, but graduates of programs with degrees specifically in creative arts therapies are sensitive to this type of labeling. Considerable effort has been made by such graduates to be recognized as a unique force in the umbrella structure of mental health service providers. In recent years the federal government, through the Department of Labor, has included art therapy and music therapy in the Occupational Information Network (O*NET Online Consortium, which has replaced the *Dictionary of Occupational Titles* and can be accessed at http://online.onetcenter. org/). Furthermore, these two specialties are listed as related professions under occupational therapy in the *Occupation Outlook Handbook.* (http://www.bls.gov/ooh/)

Overall, the state of education in the creative arts therapies is in flux. A general trend seems to be that more and better standards are being established for those who are interested in obtaining degrees or certifica-

Creative Reflection

Do a quick Internet search of institutions that grant degrees in one or more of the creative arts therapies in which you are interested. Where are they located? What do they convey that their graduates are able to do or are doing?

tion in these areas. Music, art, and dance/movement seem to be the most advanced of the special artistic approaches with regard to formatting comprehensive curricula. However, it will only be through the continued establishment of strong educational programs and growing numbers of practitioners that identity issues will be resolved.

Identity

Almost all effective treatment procedures have common elements. The arts in counseling are no exception. According to Summer (1997), "The similarities in music, art, dance/movement, drama, psychodrama, and poetry" as therapeutic ways of working have commonalties and overlap "in theory, research, clinical practice, education, standards, and ethics of practice" (p. 77). Among the most common qualities they share are "attention to verbal and nonverbal expression, symbolism, use of sensory modes, vision, order, and balance" (Mazza, 1988, p. 485). Websites such as the International Expressive Arts Therapy Association (IEATA; http://www.ieata.org) list all of the major arts therapies (visual arts, movement, drama, music, writing, and other creative processes) and include them in their conferences.

Two aspects of the arts in counseling unite them regardless of anything else. These aspects are expressed in a "commonality of form and pattern" (D. Aldridge, Brandt, & Wohler, 1990, p. 189). With regard to form, the arts "are based on verbs and doing is important" (D. Aldridge et al., 1990, p. 193). This feature is quite different from scientific inquiry, which is premised on empirical data and stresses nouns (Bateson, 1978). In inquiry, there is talk about a dynamic but not enactment. The second crucial quality of the therapeutic arts is the pattern they display, which emphasizes creativity as much as or more than catharsis. This type of expression has the power not only to heal but also to enhance. Creative arts in counseling concentrate on going beyond emotional release to the process of building self-concepts that are stronger and more congruent than before in recipients of these services.

This commonality of form and pattern both unites and frustrates those allied with the use of the creative arts in counseling. On one hand, this common bond promotes the continued growth of the NCCATA (http://www.nccata.org/) and the ACC (http://www.creativecounselor.org/), which are two of the most prevalent umbrella organizations for those who wish to learn more about or promote the creative arts in counseling. On the other hand, the central features that unite the arts are the very qualities that different art therapy groups measure themselves against and stress to emphasize the uniqueness of their disciplines.

Different associations have specific identities that relate to their names, purpose, and emphasis. The creative arts in counseling are no exception. More than half a dozen major arts groups have formed to promote the arts or an art form in counseling. All of them stress knowledge, skill, training, and supervision as being of paramount importance. Among the best known of these groups are the following:

Creative Reflection

Examine one or more of the websites just listed. What is your impression? Does the website draw you in? How much detail is presented and how?

American Art Therapy Association (AATA)
  http://www.arttherapy.org/
American Dance Therapy Association (ADTA)
  http://www.adta.org/
American Music Therapy Association (AMTA)
  http://www.musictherapy.org/
American Society of Group Psychotherapy and Psychodrama (ASGPP)
  http://www.asgpp.org/
Association for Creativity in Counseling (ACC)
  http://www.creativecounselor.org/
Association for Play Therapy (APT)
  http://www.a4pt.org/
Center for Play Therapy
  http://cpt.unt.edu/
International Expressive Arts Therapy Association (IEATA)
  http://www.ieata.org/
National Association for Poetry Therapy (NAPT)
  http://www.poetrytherapy.org/
National Coalition of Creative Arts Therapies Associations (NCCATA)
  http://www.nccata.org/
North American Drama Therapy Association (NADTA)
  http://www.nadta.org/

The NCCATA is the super coalition association of art therapies (composed of representatives from art therapy, dance/movement therapy, drama therapy, music therapy, poetry therapy, and psychodrama). Since 1985, it has become increasingly active in publicizing the benefits of the creative arts therapies to other helping specialists and to the general public.

Interdisciplinary Efforts

A popular television snack food commercial in 1990s began by saying, "Some things just were not made to go together, like poetry and power tools." The scene then focused on a man trying to read poetry while another man cut his way through a room with a power saw. It is an unforgettable scene, and the commercial is effective in illustrating its point. Although some combinations do not complement each other or synergize into a more powerful gestalt than each one taken separately, such is usually not the case with the creative arts in counseling and therapy. In fact, most creative arts harmonize well with one another, such as poetry and music or imagery and movement (Heppner et al., 1994).

A major trend in using the creative arts in counseling is to use them in concert with one another. The metaphor for this type of collaboration of art forms is opera. In an opera, all of the arts are combined: "the drama of the story, the poetry of the libretto, the artistic design of the setting, and the theatric direction of the performers—musicians, singers, and dancers" (Summer, 1997, p. 77).

The history of education in the creative arts in counseling attests to their interrelated nature. Among the first graduate master's degrees in the field was an umbrella program encompassing art, dance, and music therapy at Hahnemann University in 1976 (now Drexel University, formerly known as Allegheny University of the Health Sciences; Levick, 1989). This program continues today, and students can specialize in any of the three creative arts approaches. At the end of their program, however, they are all awarded a master of arts degree, or having earned a master's advanced degree, students may obtain a PhD in creative arts therapies. In a similar type of arrangement, Lesley College in Massachusetts, the California Institute for Integral Studies, and Concordia University in Montreal offer interdisciplinary master's degree programs. Such programs offer students "an opportunity to broaden their artistic horizons and to deepen their sense of themselves as creative people" (Watkins, 1990, p. A17).

The type of programs just described provide a chance for those enrolled to become more aware of their senses and their talents. The programs help increase their flexibility and social skills. Basically, interdisciplinary programs put people together who might not meet each other otherwise and help them talk and collaborate in ways that are personally and professionally enriching. The professional community fostered in such interdisciplinary programs is reflected in other efforts too, such as the publication of the journal *Arts in Psychotherapy,* the *Journal of Creativity and Mental Health,* and programs sponsored by NCCATA and ACC. The common aspect of these collaborative endeavors is the inclusiveness in their content, membership, and commitment.

Numerous other illustrations exist of interdisciplinary arts-based counseling procedures. One of the most powerful examples of the integration of several creative arts therapies is an assessment procedure used at West Oak Hospital in Houston, Texas. Practitioners of art therapy, movement therapy, and music therapy pool their talents to determine if a physician-referred client is an appropriate candidate for any of these treatment procedures. The assessment takes two sessions in which all the creative arts therapists meet together as a team (as opposed to six individually conducted sessions as was previously the case). During this time, sample work in each of the specialty areas is solicited from the client. Then the team makes a recommendation about which creative arts approach, if any, to use. The advantages of this procedure are many, including "one modality may help present an aspect of the patient not elsewhere seen" (Pulliam, Somerville, Prebluda, & Warja-Danielsson, 1988, p. 77).

> ## Creative Reflection
>
> Examine a copy or copies of *Arts in Psychotherapy* or the *Journal of Creativity and Mental Health*. What is your impression of the articles each of these journals publishes? How much integration of the creative arts do you see in these periodicals?

Another example of the interdisciplinary approach to using the creative arts in counseling is a gender role workshop in which extensive use has been made of the creative arts such as guided imagery, movies, music, and music videos to underscore and "promote participants' learning in both the cognitive and affective domains" (O'Neil & Carroll, 1988, p. 193). For example, when discussing family socialization and life, workshop leaders used film clips from the movies *On Golden Pond* (Rydell & Thompson, 1981) and *Ordinary People* (Schwary, Redford, & Guest, 1980). In addition, they showed the Motown anniversary video (de Passe, 1983) and played music from recording artists Marvin Gaye ("What's Going On") and Diana Ross ("Missing You"). Although it might be argued that these creative arts were adjunctive or tangential to the total workshop, the leaders of this experience and the participants did not rate these aspects of learning in such a manner.

In recent years, there has been a movement toward the integration of the creative arts with one another in a therapeutic sense as well as a focus on integrating the creative arts into other cultural settings, such as educational environments. In such surroundings, the creative arts may help students express through an activity their emotions, thoughts, and values in a way that is therapeutic and not stigmatizing (Wengrower, 2001). Thus, students may work on "their weaknesses and ways of coping with them, while at the same time uncovering [their] strengths. This has a positive effect on self-image" (Wengrower, 2001, p. 114).

Technology

> ## Creative Reflection
>
> When have you seen or experienced the creative arts being used in combination to educate or illustrate a point, for example, in a classroom or a seminar? How did you enjoy the combined effect? What would the experience have been like if only one of the creative arts had been used?

The creative arts, like the helping professions in general, have been affected by technology. Computers, in particular, have made a difference in the accessibility of the creative arts to individuals and society at large (Evans, 2012). The art forms that have probably been most affected are those involving music, writing, and drama. However, creative arts therapists have shared the visual arts with clients and others through technological means.

In scriptotherapy, clients may now write out their thoughts and feelings on the Internet in blogs or other formats, and counselors may respond in between more formally arranged sessions (L'Abate & Sweeney, 2011; Wright, 2002). The process may be not only therapeutic but also lifesaving depending on the client's state of mind (J. K. Miller & Gergen, 1998). In drama role playing, integrating video and computer simulations into group work practice is now occurring (Smokowski, 2003). In this process, models may be taped demonstrating desired skills, and computer simulations may be programmed demonstrating certain behaviors. Such a procedure decreases resistance in clients and makes them more open to the possibility of change. In music therapy, clients may take "sound baths" of 20 minutes or so to calm them down or to energize them with music suggested by their counselor or music they find appealing (http://www.holisticonline.com/stress/stress_music-therapy.htm). Those who do this may download or stream music from a variety of Internet sites and program their computers, tablets, phones, or other technology devices accordingly. In art therapy too, computers may be utilized as a creative medium using graphics pads and other art-based programs and software (R. G. Johnson, 2002). Computer art therapy is a growing field (http://www.computerarttherapy.com/). Overall, there is still much to research on the use of technology with regard to the creative arts and counseling. However, it is more likely than less that technology-based tools will play an increased role in the way the creative arts are used therapeutically in the future.

Practitioners and clients can pick up information on each of the art forms covered in this book on any number of Internet websites. Most creative arts therapies associations now make use of technology by at least having a home page on the World Wide Web. Many clinicians who use the arts in counseling construct websites as well (e.g., John Fox's Institute for Poetic Medicine; http://www.poeticmedicine.com/). Some are better than others. By spending some time on the Internet, you as a counselor can find and inform others about appropriate information on the uses of the creative arts in counseling. The following sites are examples of what is available on the Internet and is not an endorsement of any site, materials, or persons. It is best to first visit the sites of professional creative arts therapies associations before visiting the sites of individual or group therapists.

General Creative Arts and Art Therapies Websites

http://www.nccata.org/

The National Coalition of Creative Arts Therapies Associations (NCCATA) maintains this home page that includes information on all of the creative arts therapies that are members of NCCATA.

http://www.creativecounselor.org/

This is the home page of the Association for Creativity in Counseling (ACC). It is not an arts therapy association, but much of the material on the page and many of the publications of ACC relate to arts therapies.

Music Therapy Websites

http://www.musictherapy.org/

This site is the home page of the American Music Therapy Association and provides information on how music therapy is used in a variety of settings with different populations.

http://www.musictherapy.ca/

The Canadian Association for Music Therapy hosts this page, which gives a history of music therapy. It tells what happens in a session and explains how music is used therapeutically.

Dance and Movement Websites

http://www.adta.org

This page is the home of the American Dance Therapy Association. It describes how dance and movement therapy is effective and details the areas in which this method is frequently used.

http://dmtinfo.blogspot.com/

This website is home to the Dance Movement Therapy Association in Canada (DMTAC) and provides information on the association's activities.

Visual Art Therapy Websites

http://www.arttherapy.org/

This is the home page of the American Art Therapy Association. It includes a definition of art therapy, resources, a code of ethics, and information on the annual conference of the American Art Therapy Association.

http://canadianarttherapy.org/

This site host the Canadian Art Therapy Association. It provides information about art therapy in Canada.

Poetry Therapy and Bibliotherapy Websites

http://www.poetrytherapy.org/

This is the website for the National Association for Poetry Therapy, which gives the definition and history of poetry therapy and provides information and resources on the uses of writing as a therapeutic modality.

Drama and Psychodrama Websites

http://www.nadta.org

This is the home page of the North American Drama Therapy Association and is filled with pertinent information on the uses of drama therapy.

http://www.asgpp.org/

> This site is the home page of the American Society of Group Psychotherapy and Psychodrama. It describes the purpose of the association and what group psychotherapy, psychodrama, and sociometry are.

Play Therapy Websites

http://cpt.unt.edu/

> This is the home page for the Center for Play Therapy at the University of North Texas. It describes the programs, products, and services offered there.

http://www.playtherapy.org/

> This is the home page of Play Therapy International, which provides a list of books and articles on play therapy and other international professional resources and contacts.

Humor Therapy Websites

http://www.humormatters.com/

> This is the website of Dr. Steven Sultanoff and is dedicated to educating, informing, and helping its visitors locate resources for learning about humor, health, and healing.

http://www.aath.org/

> The Association for Applied and Therapeutic Humor website is the home for humor and laughter professionals. It includes suggested resources concerning therapeutic humor and information on its speakers' bureau and annual conference.

http://www.patchadams.org/

> This website is the home of the Gesundheith Institute run by Patch Adams. It contains information on Patch Adams and the actitives of the institute.

Animal-Assisted Therapy in Counseling Website

https://www.pdresources.org/uploads/course/e0682.pdf

> At first glance this website appears to be a course syllabus for a 2-hour continuing education unit (CEU) professional development course offered by Lois Jean Brady. However, it is much more than that. The site contains a wealth of information on the historical and contemporary use of animals in therapeutic settings and gives the advantages and drawbacks of using specific animals.

Therapeutic Horticulture Website

http://ahta.org/

> This website is the home of the American Horticultural Therapy Association. It contains links to valuable resouces on the use of plants in therapy.

Wilderness and Nature Therapy Websites

There are numerous wilderness and nature therapy websites but no official association website.

Summary

The creative arts in counseling are currently undergoing a transition that promises to be long term, multifaceted, and productive. Major efforts are under way on a grassroots and a national level to have the creative arts therapies recognized as professions in a more positive way. These efforts include attempts to

- upgrade research,
- strengthen educational standards,
- mold better identities for creative arts therapies individually and collectively,
- become more interdisciplinary with regard to practice, and
- promote and make accessible the creative arts therapies through the use of computers and technology, especially by means of websites.

These five trends will be important in the future as more research is conducted on the use of artistic endeavors in counseling and more refined theories and techniques in the creative arts therapies are generated. Efforts supporting empirical and pragmatic aspects of the creative arts in counseling have the potential to lead to recognition of creative arts approaches in interdisciplinary counseling endeavors and in state licensure or national certification. Educational programs in the creative arts therapies and the incorporation of the creative arts in counseling will most likely continue to evolve. Promotion of the creative arts therapies will also continue, and the use of computers and technology will become increasingly important in highlighting achievements in the creative arts.

Outside of the previously mentioned efforts, counselors who enjoy being creative will, in the spirit of the pioneers of the counseling profession, most likely be artistic in their endeavors to help people change, heal, and achieve an integrated whole. The extent to which formal artistic therapies grow and develop is important to these clinicians and to the helping professions. Approaches and creative techniques that work must go beyond intuition and be empirically supported. In the future, counseling will most likely continue to be an artistic practice with a scientific base, and the creative arts should remain a part of it (Rosenthal, 2002).

Creative Reflection

If you were designing a website to promote the use of the creative arts in counseling, what would you feature most prominently? Why? How?

Exercises

1. If you were to research one of the creative arts, which one would you choose? How would you go about studying its effectiveness in counseling settings? Do you think animal-assisted therapy, horticulture therapy, and wilderness/nature therapy differ drastically from other creative arts therapies? How? How are they also the same?
2. How has technology helped counselors access the creative arts and creative arts activities? How has technology hindered the development of creativity in counselors and other helping professionals?
3. What are creative arts therapists doing to become recognized as core mental health professionals? What are the arguments for granting them professional licensure? What are the arguments against granting them professional licensure?

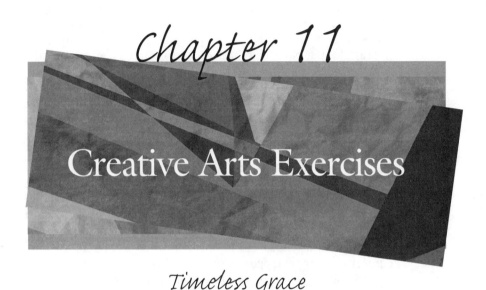

Chapter 11

Creative Arts Exercises

Timeless Grace

At 5 a.m. I ponder
  the magic of the morning and your smile
The day will be long
  and before I'm consumed
    with endless tasks both mundane and worthwhile,
      I focus on the cycle of time and you.
The hues of the dawn are a light gold and pink
  but will give way to a bright blue and white
You beam forth now with radiance
  but will change with the afternoon light
I am helpless to transform the sunrise
  I cannot alter the look on your face
So I sit back, take in the moment,
  and rejoice in your timeless grace.

—Gladding, 2010

Sometimes books contain information that is primarily theoretical or descriptive but not pragmatic. Much of this book is integrative, containing both, but this chapter contains a compilation of many of the creative arts exercises described throughout the text—136 to be exact. It is a quick guide for the busy practitioner who may have skipped over parts of a chapter or simply forgotten some of the information provided. Specific creative arts exercises that may be used in counseling and that were mentioned in more than a fleeting way are briefly described here again under the particular chapter in the text in which they were covered. Most activites covered in Chapter 9 on the uses of animals, plants, and the wilderness/nature are a bit different from activities in Chapters 2–8 in that they are more implied in the chapter than spelled out, not as manipulative, and may take longer to implement.

When considering using any of these exercises, think of the SCAMPER model (Substitute, Combine, Adopt/Adapt, Modify, Put to other uses, Eliminate, Rearrange/Reserve) outlined in Chapter 1. Remember that in using the creative arts it is vital to think about your rationale for using a specific exercise at a particular time, the readiness of the person or group you might use the exercise with, and your own comfort and proficiency as someone using the activity. When in doubt about the appropriateness of what you are going to do with a creative activity, do not do anything! That is, do not do anything you are uncomfortable with or unsure of until you have received training, supervision, or monitoring in the activity in which you wish to engage or have others engage in. Ethics always must take priority in any therapeutic setting, and the ethics codes of most counseling and therapy associations state that professionals should only practice in those areas in which they have expertise and competence.

That being said, the following pages contain the aforementioned material.

Creative Arts Activities—Music

1. *Mindful Music Listening.* A process in which clients, especially with depression, use mindfulness skills while listening to music to notice, label, discuss, and learn to manage their emotions. Possible advantages include greater client self-awareness and emotional regulation as well as a strengthened counselor–client relationship. (Chapter 2, page 30)
2. *Creating Emotional States.* In this activity, clients are asked to bring in a MP3 player with some type of music they enjoy and are asked what part of the music arouses them the most, for example, the rhythm, the melody, the lyrics (if there are any), or some combination of the three. This exercise is particularly appropriate for clients who claim not to have feelings. (Chapter 2, page 31)

3. *Counselor-Selected Music.* In this exercise, counselors select a piece of music they think will speak to a client's situation. The client is then asked to listen to the rhythm and lyrics (if any) of the music and to visualize a color that goes with it. After the song is finished, the client may respond by talking about the experience, drawing, or even moving to show what he or she got out of the exercise. (Chapter 2, page 31)
4. *Listening to Ethnic Music.* In this activity, clients listen to unfamiliar music (i.e., music identified with a particular culture or subculture other than their own). The clients then are asked to react to the music and talk about how the rhythm of the music is like or unlike the beat of their lives. This activity helps make clients aware of the rhythm of the life they lead as well as the rhythm of the life of others. (Chapter 2, page 31)
5. *Improvisation.* This activity can be initiated by asking clients who play an instrument to do variations on a musical theme. In these cases—and in others in which clients understand musical improvisation—clients can play and alter melodies (i.e., make them faster, slower, or more pronounced). The results of such transactions can then be discussed; for example, what varied themes does the client play in life? Discussion of the improvisation may also be left alone. In the latter situation, the process of creating and developing a relationship with the client is seen as therapeutic in and of itself. (Chapter 2, page 32)
6. *Composing Music.* Counselors may request or encourage musically inclined clients to compose a piece of music through which they can represent themselves, whether they write it down or not. At the next session, clients literally make music first and then talk about the experiences of composing and performing afterward. In some cases, musically inclined counselors may compose and play music to represent themselves to clients. Such a process, whether unilateral or reciprocal in nature, assists clients in realizing the universal power that a musical composition can generate. (Chapter 2, pages 32–33)
7. *Music and Guidance Lessons.* Music is often a primary ingredient in teaching guidance lessons. One technique uses music to express feelings. For example, DeLucia-Waack (2001) wrote a hands-on manual for counselors that offers a creative way through music to help children of divorce learn new coping skills. R. P. Bowman (2004) did the same with the subject of test anxiety. Through music, children are helped to understand and overcome the crisis of divorce and test anxiety and develop in healthy ways. In another guidance approach, Gerler (1982) recommended that a counselor and music teacher work together to devise a game in which children are teamed in groups of four and instructed to create musical ways to express feelings without words or lyrics. Through these musical exercises, children learn the power of music and something about the world of grown-ups and themselves. (Chapter 2, page 34)

8. *Learning Songs in Guidance Lessons.* When songs are used in guidance classes, the following procedure is helpful: (a) Introduce the words of a song as a poem. (b) Chant the words in rhythm. (c) Practice chanting words for 3 or 4 minutes per class period until students memorize them. (d) After students know and understand the words, play the song (prerecorded music is fine to use). (e) Keep a double-spaced copy of the words before the children when they sing, with the verses separated from the refrain. (Chapter 2, page 34)

9. *Internal Body and Neighborhood Sounds.* One way of breaking through clients' shells of isolation therapeutically with music is by playing sounds familiar to them, such as internal body sounds (e.g., a stomach growling or a heart beating) or having them listen to neighborhood sounds. Once rapport is established in this manner, rhythmic activities and rhythm instruments such as sticks and tambourines can be used to engage clients, especially children, and gradually draw them into social relationships with others. (Chapter 2, page 35)

10. *Song Writing.* To foster a preventative and therapeutic process, counselors skilled in music can work with clients, especially adolescents, using a number of song-writing techniques, "including changing the words to familiar songs, filling in the blanks of edited familiar songs, vocal improvisation, adding new verses to known songs, parodying familiar songs, and using natural rhythms of speech as a starting point" (Goldstein, 1990, p. 119). In so doing, clients realize for the first time or anew the importance of words in relationships. (Chapter 2, pages 36–37)

11. *Music and Physical and Mental Health List.* Music promotes both physical and mental health through inspiration and distraction. Counselors can make a list of songs in both categories and have clients do the same. Then when there are either physical or mental difficulties, the music can be turned on. (Chapter 2, page 37)

12. *Reminiscence or Present-Oriented Social Groups.* Music is one of the keys to encouraging the discussion of past or present feelings and thoughts about events, such as learning, romance, loss, and family life. In such situations, music is played that revolves around a particular theme, such as the importance of home or family. This activity usually takes place after the group as a whole has warmed up by participating in a brief sing-along of familiar songs that include their own accompaniment of clapping and foot tapping. This approach has been found to be effective in helping reduce depressive symptoms in older people (ages 73 to 94 years) with dementia. (Chapter 2, page 39)

13. *Music and Families/Couples.* Music may be beneficial to families or couples because of its ability to evoke feelings and promote cooperation. Feelings are often rekindled by playing music associated with earlier developmental stages. If a family or couple has experienced contentment or positive affect at a

previous stage, the music of that time may ignite memories that help individuals within these systems remember specific behaviors that were helpful in achieving harmony. Such events, once triggered, can aid the family or couple in generating helpful behaviors and positively reinforcing each other. (Chapter 2, pages 39–40)

14. *Music and Groups.* Music can be especially powerful in a group at its beginning or end. Select music can help set an upbeat or sedate tone when clients first enter the group room. For example, beginning a group through drumming is a unique way to jump-start conversations about group dynamics and each person's role in them. Likewise, during termination, select music or music activities can help instill in clients a sense of closure and can promote integration. (Chapter 2, pages 40–41)

15. *Music, Families, and Ill Member.* Music can serve to promote closeness within families who have members who are sick through group singing, lyric analysis, and reminiscences. This type of bonding enhances the quality of life for family members both inside and outside of the hospital and helps establish better communication patterns and firmer support systems. In the process, anxiety and tension are lessened and intimacy is promoted. Religious faith may be increased through playing and singing religious music if the family is so inclined. In the process of making music, patients bring feelings into consciousness without any immediate verbal labels being attached to their emotions. This active intervention uses clients' strength and creativity to cope and maintain coherence. (Chapter 2, pages 41–42)

16. *Music and Counselor Supervision.* Counselor supervision may be enhanced through bringing music into the process. This procedure may be implemented by having counseling students listen to music outside of class that demonstrates certain concepts, or by bringing lyrical or nonlyrical music into the class that elicits specific emotions or ideas the instructor wants to convey. (Chapter 2, pages 43–44)

17. *Music Autobiography.* In this creative endeavor, clients represent their lives through sound. For instance, someone who has spent a lifetime living by the ocean may splash a hand in water with a certain rhythm; and someone who has lived in an arid region may clap rocks together in a unique way. Completing a music autobiography may also involve connecting bits of lyrical or nonlyrical music together. The effect is particularly powerful if there are verses and a refrain. (Chapter 2, page 46)

18. *Storytelling and Music.* Music may be used to enhance the background of a story. Such pieces set a mood and stir up emotions that would not occur without such an accompaniment. (Chapter 2, page 46)

Creative Arts Activities—Dance/Movement

1. *Home Spot.* In this nonverbal experience, individuals are asked to join hands or put their arms around each other's shoulders. Then they pick out a spot in the room to which they wish to take the group, without telling anyone. Finally, they begin trying to move the group toward the spot they have selected (Jacobs et al., 2016). The ongoing group dynamics are the primary focus of the exercise as group members struggle with issues of power and persuasion in a 2- to 5-minute time span. After the struggle that inevitably comes with the exercise, group members talk to each other about the specifics as well as the general nature of the "dance" they just went through and what it can mean to the life of the group and to their own individual lives. (Chapter 3, page 57)

2. *Walking.* In this activity, clients walk in a circle at their normal pace and cadence. After they have a feel for how they walk, they are asked to walk faster than usual and then to walk in slow motion. Walking is then linked to feelings so that the clients walk as if they were tired, happy, or sad. After this experience, clients are instructed to act as if they were walking on or through different terrain, including a desert, a mountain, mud, ice, water, and even silly substances such as peanut butter, whipped cream, yogurt, and cornflakes. After the walk is completed (usually by pretending to walk through a grassy meadow), clients and their counselors talk about what the experiences were like and what different environments that clients live in are like. Ways of "walking"—that is, moving in different environments—are emphasized. This movement exercise was originally designed for children, but it may be used with individuals of any age. (Chapter 3, page 58)

3. *Locomotion.* The idea of the locomotion exercise is to have clients see how many different movements they can make to get from one place to another (e.g., jumping, running, and skipping). They can then combine movements and even do the same movements with a partner. Afterward, the feelings involved with these movements are processed. The idea that there are a number of ways to get from one point to another is discussed. (Chapter 3, page 58)

4. *Robot.* Clients pretend they can only move or talk as a robot does. They become stiff-limbed and monotone. Halfway into the exercise they become human again. After the exercise, they work with their group leader or counselor and talk about the robot-to-human experience. How did being so stiff and flat affect them? What are the advantages and disadvantages of being flexible? Although initially designed for children, this movement exercise can be used with individuals of any age. (Chapter 3, page 58)

5. *Bodywork.* Any nonverbal activity in which adults actively participate. It makes use of props and gestalt-type experiences to help individuals become more aware of their body and emotions. Many individuals, particularly men, are able to release repressed feelings such as fear, anger, hurt, or joy through bodywork. Women benefit from bodywork too. Through this method, they come to a clearer understanding of their own boundaries and are thus able to be more caring of themselves. Self and nonself distinctions gained through bodywork facilitate better intra- and interpersonal relationships. (Chapter 3, page 61)

6. *Evaluation of Progress.* In this experience, clients are asked to stand up and position themselves according to how much progress they have made during counseling. A line is drawn representing where counseling started, and a goal line is also drawn, with clients placing themselves in between. Such a procedure may be especially powerful for clients who have become resistant to counseling or who are concrete thinkers and need to visualize their progress. The complementary drawing exercise to this movement experience is an idealized and unfinished "Roadmap" of life. (Chapter 3, page 62)

7. *Feeling Pulled.* Clients often have forces in their lives that impede their progress in reaching goals. In this experience, created by Ed E. Jacobs (1992), a client is asked to start moving toward his or her goals with the counselor holding onto the client's arm and pulling him or her backward. The right amount of tug is agreed to by the client. The counseling session then turns to identifying what forces with what levels of power are inhibiting the client. (Chapter 3, pages 62–63)

8. *Circles.* When clients do the same thing over and over, they fail to make progress. In circles, clients are asked to walk around in the same direction a number of times to get a better feel for what doing the same thing again and again is like. It is hoped this realization leads to insight and new directions for the therapy. (Chapter 3, page 63)

9. *Movement Between Chairs.* The premise behind this activity, also created by Ed E. Jacobs (1992), is that clients sometimes need to experience their vacillation with regard to decisions they have discussed but failed to make. In movement between chairs, clients are asked to simply move continuously between two or more chairs that represent decisions they could make. They are not to speak, unless at the end of bouncing back and forth between chairs (which should go on a minimum of 2 to 3 minutes) they have something new to say. (Chapter 3, page 63)

10. *Train Station.* This movement exercise, originated by Playfair, is an icebreaking exercise used in an initial meeting of a group. The group is divided in two, with half of the group designated to be the greeters and the other half the passengers. The group is then given the following instructions: Each greeter has just received a phone call from his or her best friend from early childhood. It has now been a number of years since they saw each other, but the former best friend is to arrive in a few hours at the train station in the city where the greeter now lives. The greeter is so excited that after agreeing to meet the friend, he or she hangs up the phone without thinking to ask what the person who called looks like. Lacking this information, the greeter goes to the train station at the designated hour and decides that the best strategy in this situation is to move slowly but with enthusiasm toward the group of passengers now arriving. With arms waving, the group of greeters move slowly toward the passengers, who all display similar behaviors. As each greeter gets to a passenger, looks are exchanged, but then both realize this is not the right person. Both look away and toward another person in the immediate area who also turns out not to be the right person. This activity continues until all the greeters and passengers have passed each other. Participants then are given a chance to voice how they experienced the exercise. The leader of the group tells them that nothing they ever do in the group will be as embarrassing as this. (Chapter 3, pages 63–64)

11. *Hand Dialog.* In this exercise, two individuals are partners. They are seated and then instructed to improvise dances with their hands with one person initially leading and the other following. They put their hands together and may choose to keep their eyes open, but they are encouraged to close their eyes to get the full impact of this nonverbal experience. Participants may use their fingers, palms, or both in doing their dance. Likewise, they may use the front or back of their hands. After they have danced with their hands for 60 to 90 seconds, the leader instructs them to switch positions from leader to follower. When the dance is finished, time is set aside for discussions between pairs and then the group as a whole about feelings and emotions associated with what they have been through and how such affect is expressed nonverbally. (Chapter 3, page 64)

12. *Shadows.* This exercise involves one person imitating another in a follow-the-leader style. Sometimes it is done in silence, but it is not unusual to have Shadows occur to music. The type of music chosen can help encourage interaction and break down inhibitions. After the event, participants talk about their experience in groups of two, four, eight, and then in the group as a whole. This type of movement opens individuals up for more awareness and gives them a common experience as a basis for sharing. (Chapter 3, pages 64–65)

13. *Family Choreography.* In this movement exercise, different members of a family stage a moment in time in the family's life. Then specific movements are given to each player and repeated until members of the family get a feel for the interconnectedness of the family members' lives together. (Chapter 3, page 65; Chapter 4, page 87)

14. *Enactment.* In this experience, the counselor directs family members to show how they are stuck in dysfunctional behaviors, such as an inability to resolve arguments, and to demonstrate what happens during each step. This type of direction takes the involuntary nature away from the action in which the family members are trapped and places it in the hands of the counselor. Therefore, even if the family members do not resolve their disputes, their relationships with each other change. They have to try another (it is hoped more positive) way of settling their disputes because of the power they have given the counselor to direct their old, nonproductive patterns. (Chapter 3, page 65)

15. *Paradox.* A type of reverse enactment in which the counselor tells clients they cannot do something, such as change, or the counselor instructs clients to go slow. The results are either that clients obey and move differently under the counselor's direction or they rebel and change to resist the counselor's instructions. Change in patterns and movement of clients is the end product. (Chapter 3, page 65)

16. *Adverbs.* One member of a group leaves the room and the others decide on an adverb (a word ending in "ly," such as warmly, slowly). When the member returns, he or she asks designated members to act out a task in a way that reflects the chosen adverb, and the member tries to guess what it is. (Chapter 3, page 67)

17. *Chair Game.* Group members decide on a famous person while one member of the group is out of the room. When that person returns, he or she is treated like the famous person by others in the group until he or she guesses that person's identity. (Chapter 3, page 67)

18. *Areas.* The room is marked off into different feeling areas, such as sad, bored, happy, and angry. Each member of the group spends time in these areas and tries to embody that emotion. Then members reassemble and talk about how each experience felt. (Chapter 3, page 67)

19. *Environments.* A group exercise in which the group breaks into two teams, and each creates an environment for the other, such as the surface of the moon or a tropical jungle. After going through or participating in the environment, the teams reassemble and talk about the experience and how it relates to their lives. (Chapter 3, page 67)

20. *Milling-Around*. In this exercise, individuals simply walk around and participate with others as instructed by the leader—for example, by making or not making eye contact, by touching or not touching each other with shoulders or elbows. The idea is to assess how comfortable each member feels moving in a certain manner. The entire exercise is brief (about 2 to 5 minutes) and is processed with the group leader for as long as needed afterward. (Chapter 3, page 69)

Creative Arts Activities—Imagery

1. *Saying Good-Bye, Getting Closure*. Abraham H. Maslow (1991) advocated imagining the death of someone for whom a person cares and thinking as vividly as possible about what would be truly lost and about what one would most grieve. After clients imagine in this way, Maslow advocated a shift in thinking to how to conduct a complete good-bye and how to best preserve the memory of the person. Another technique he proposed was imagining oneself dying and in the process vividly seeing and saying good-bye to the people one loves best. (Chapter 4, page 78)

2. *Symbolically Re-Create a Problematic Life Situation*. Individuals are to imagine a problematic life situation happening to them. Then they verbalize any thoughts that come to mind. Verbalization is an especially useful way of uncovering specific thoughts associated with particular events. This technique is especially helpful during the assessment stage of counseling to uncover thoughts associated with events of which a person may not be initially aware. (Chapter 4, page 78)

3. *Systematic Desensitization*. Clients are asked to construct a hierarchy of different situations that trouble them, starting with those that are mildly disturbing and working up to those that cause major concern. They are then instructed to clearly picture each situation as they work up the hierarchy with the counselor and to simultaneously relax. The idea behind this method is that being relaxed and anxious are incompatible responses (i.e., reciprocal inhibition) and that clients can be taught to become relaxed in the presence of a situation that previously was bothersome. In other words, one emotion (relaxation or pleasure) is used to counteract another (anxiety), with imagery playing a major role in the process. (Chapter 4, pages 78–79)

4. *Incorporating Pain Into One's Life Rather Than Fighting It*. This type of incorporation can occur through dissociation (imagining the hurt outside of the body), fantasy (fantasizing that one is suffering for a good cause), imagining numbness, and focusing on sensations (studying what the feelings are like). (Chapter 4, page 79)

5. *Imagining Games for Children.* In this exercise, a teacher or parent reads a passage to children from a structured exercise book, such as Richard de Mille's (1967) *Put Your Mother on the Ceiling* or Joseph E. Shorr's (1977) *Go See the Movie in Your Head.* The children then visualize the scene. These types of imagery games at their best create divergent thinking, motivate and challenge children, and bring fun into the lives of those involved. They foster freedom in a constructive way not otherwise possible. When done properly, imagery games are interspersed with reality-based exercises, which promotes an appreciation for imagery and reality within young children. (Chapter 4, page 80)

6. *Through Loving Eyes.* This exercise is used with elementary school children who have low self-esteem. It is valuable in enhancing their self-concept. In this procedure, children look at themselves through the eyes of a special person. Children then pretend to be artists, and in this role they draw special people in their lives who love them. After the drawings are finished (just one drawing per child), the children pretend to be the special people whom they have drawn and to see themselves through loving eyes. Then they reassociate back into their own bodies and bring back with them loving feelings from the experience. (Chapter 4, page 80)

7. *Relationship and Sexual Imagery.* Imagery about sexual fantasies may be used therapeutically to enhance a couple's sex life under the direction of a licensed sex therapist. This is part of a treatment for relationship problems devised by Masters and Johnson (1970). (Chapter 4, page 81)

8. *Problem-Solving Daydreams.* Images generated by daydreaming on how to solve a problem can be used to help adolescents and adults anticipate and productively respond ahead of time to developmental situations they expect to face. (Chapter 4, page 81)

9. *Depression and Imagery.* Clients are asked to imagine something that makes them angry and are taught how to gain control over the imaging process (rather than being a victim of it) and the feelings associated with certain symbols. Similarly, they may learn socially gratifying imagery and positive imagery procedures and use these methods to temporarily or permanently combat depressive thoughts. The use of imagery as a visual art form, especially in combination with verbal directive techniques, often produces extensive and long-lasting improvements. It enhances the effectiveness of verbal cognitions in altering unpleasant moods. (Chapter 4, pages 81–82)

10. *Relaxed Imagery Trips for Older Adults.* Guided imagery exercises can be used to help those who are growing older take relaxed trips in time either to a place they long to go or back to a place they

have enjoyed before. These imaginary trips are followed with a process session. Individuals who have traveled in their minds come back to the counselor or a group setting and share their experiences in verbal or nonverbal forms, such as talking or drawing. (Chapter 4, page 82)

11. *Enhancing Group Process Through Imagery.* Imagery can be used to enhance the group process in almost any stage, but it may be especially powerful in the adjourning stage. For instance, during this stage, where the focus is on closure and anticipation, group members may give each other good-bye gifts in the form of future visions for themselves and others. (Chapter 4, page 83)

12. *Common Object.* In this fantasy exercise, members of a group are encouraged to imagine themselves as a common object, such as a piece of luggage or a ladder. They are then asked to describe what their lives would be like and how they would feel if they were indeed that object. For example, as a piece of luggage, a group member might have an active life of travel and feel both exhilarated and exhausted. When talking about the common object, members are encouraged to stay in the present tense. They end up talking about themselves in many ways and seeing their lives differently as a result of projection and fantasy. (Chapter 4, pages 83–84)

13. *Occupational/Career Daydreams.* Although daydreams and fantasies do not guarantee a dream will come true, such processes are instrumental in helping individuals contemplate new possibilities, try out new options, and make more informed life-planning decisions. Clients keep track of their daydreams about careers and discuss these unsolicited fantasies with the counselor in future meetings. (Chapter 4, page 85)

14. *Transition From Graduate to Colleague Status.* In this process, counselor supervisors set up a ritual in which students are guided through an imagery exercise that confirms that they are now ready to leave their graduate status behind and join the ranks of professional counselors. At the end of the imagery experience, they are presented with smooth stones that metaphorically represent their transition from rough neophyte learners to polished professionals. The stones are reminders of the words in the exercise and communicate to the new counselors that they are ready to embark on their professional journey. (Chapter 4, pages 85–86)

15. *Career Imagery Card Sort.* Clients are asked to sort 150 cards with career titles into five piles. During sorting, clients are asked to reflect on how the occupation matches up with their daydreams. Afterward, clients pick an occupation of high interest to them based on their daydreams and are taken on a guided fantasy of a day in that specific occupation. (Chapter 4, page 86)

16. *Family Choreography.* Family choreography is an outgrowth of family sculpting; people in a family are arranged in various physical positions in space that represents their relationships to each other at a particular moment in time. Then a family situation (past, present, or future) is silently enacted using repetitive motions. Family choreography is like a videotape, whereas family sculpting is like a photograph. (Chapter 4, pages 86–87)

17. *Guided Imagery and Music.* Trainers have used the largo movements of baroque instrumental music, with their strong, regular bass-line rhythms of about 60 beats per minute, to help athletes envision winning performance. Any type of music will promote mental imagery as long as the listener finds it relaxing. Guided imagery and music can also be used in the treatment of people with rheumatoid arthritis. (Chapter 4, page 87)

18. *Mailbox.* The client is instructed to take 12 to 24 photographs of a mailbox from as many angles as possible and to bring the photos to the next counseling session mounted on poster board. The counselor and the client then discuss the task and examine the pictures. In this process the client usually discovers that just as a mailbox can be viewed from many angles, so can other situations. A client is then freed by this analogy exercise to devise novel images for his or her own life. (Chapter 4, page 88)

19. *Draw in the Air What You See in Your Mind.* This technique, which may seem silly at first, helps clients put body movement to an image and reinforces their mental picture of it through simple motor movements. (Chapter 4, page 88)

Creative Arts Exercises—Visual Art

1. *Sun, Cloud, Tree.* The client is asked to make two drawings of these three elements: a sun, a cloud, and a tree. An equal amount of space is devoted to each drawing. In the second drawing, the client is asked to make one of the elements either larger or smaller. The participant is encouraged to recognize that if one thing changes, even slightly, everything changes. (Chapter 1, page 16)

2. *Body Outline Drawings.* A person lies spread out on the floor, and the outline of his or her body is traced on butcher paper. After the drawings are completed, individuals decorate them literally and figuratively. Sometimes in this latter process, clients, especially children, reveal directly or indirectly troublesome aspects of their lives that can later be discussed. (Chapter 5, page 98)

3. *Serial Drawings.* Portrayals or sketches of any object, such as a tree, an animal, or a scene, are drawn by a client multiple times over multiple sessions after the counselor requests the client to initially draw a picture. The idea behind the use of serial drawings

is that through them clients will symbolically represent themselves and their problems. By working in a positive transference manner that involves a talk component to complement the visual element, a positive self-concept may emerge, and behavior change occurs. (Chapter 5, page 98)

4. *Visual Journaling.* Visual journaling is essentially keeping an art diary. This type of diary contains both images, usually drawings, and words. Like a traditional diary, the contents may be a rough draft that may later become finished artwork, and the materials in the journal are meant to document day-to-day experiences, activities, and emotions. Often they are autobiographical. (Chapter 5, pages 98–99)

5. *Altered Books.* Clients are asked to choose a book and change (altering) it in a variety of ways. Anything goes: People draw, paint, collage, overwrite, or even destroy pages as a form of artistic self-expression. Rather than working with a sketchbook or journal with blank white pages, the nature of the book itself provides a stimulus for creative journaling. Old hard-cover books are best for use as future altered books. (Chapter 5, page 99)

6. *Phototherapy.* This exercise presents a way to capture and express feelings and ideas in a visual-symbolic form across the life span. It has many similarities to art therapy and works particularly well for people who find other visual arts too demanding or too risky to try. *Active phototherapy* involves photos taken by a client that represent a feeling the client has or photos that the client thinks represent him or her. After the photos are taken and mounted on a poster board or in a scrapbook, the counselor and client talk about them and about ways change may come about. In *passive photography*, the client mounts on poster board or in a scrapbook representative pictures of him- or herself taken from a photo album or a popular publication that show how life has been for the person. Themes are identified and discussed. Ways of altering these themes are then pursued if appropriate. (Chapter 5, page 100)

7. *Draw a Circle.* Clients, usually children, are asked to draw a circle and then to color different parts of the circle to represent various feelings they have about themselves, such as smart, dumb, good, or bad. Drawing in such a manner helps these individuals become more aware of how they see themselves. It also opens up concrete avenues for them to use in talking about their feelings. (Chapter 5, page 103)

8. *Rosebush.* A counselor who meets on a regular basis with a person, usually a child, asks the individual to draw a rosebush every time he or she meets with the counselor. In this process, which takes place over an extended period of time (at least 10 sessions), a therapeutic alliance and rapport are developed between the counselor and the person, and a sanctuary where growth, development, and healing can occur is created. The

rosebush is symbolic of the child's mental health, and changes in the drawings indicate positive movement or distress within the child. (Chapter 5, pages 103–104)

9. *Family Drawing and Storytelling.* This procedure is used as part of a larger process and usually with children under the age of 10 to help the counselor find out more about family dynamics. It has four steps: (a) Children draw their families, including themselves, on a sheet of white paper. (b) They make up a story of what the family is doing in the picture. (c) They draw on a separate sheet of paper any family member that may have been left out of the original picture (e.g., a divorced parent or a family pet). (d) After all of the drawings are photocopied and cut out, children (on a one-to-one basis) tell the counselor stories about small-group family interactions, using the cutouts as symbolic representations. (Chapter 5, page 104)

10. *Draw Pictures of Various Careers.* This procedure is often used with children to promote their awareness of various occupations, but it also can be used with adolescents and young adults. In the exercise, clients are encouraged to think about their vocational futures. They then draw what they believe certain vocations to be like. The drawings are then discussed with the counselor with regard to their accuracy and the feel the client has about working in such an environment. (Chapter 5, page 105)

11. *Draw a Bridge.* The client is asked to draw a bridge representing where the client is now on one side and how the client will be when counseling is completed on the other side. In talking with the counselor, the client tries to answer these questions: What are the obstacles in the way of getting from one side of the bridge to another? What are the steps that need to be accomplished to complete the journey? (Chapter 5, page 106)

12. *Draw Yourself in a Scene 15 Years From Now.* In this exercise, the client is asked to envision where he or she may be in 15 years. What goals are in the future? What will the client need to do to reach his or her destination? (Chapter 5, page 106)

13. *Draw and Paint Troublesome Dreams and Daydreams.* This process may be used with clients of almost any age, although it is most often used with adolescents and young adults. By drawing and painting a dream or daydream, the covert nature of the dream or daydream becomes more overt, and clients are able to see what they are facing in a concrete manner. Clients who participate in this activity gain a mastery over the dream or daydream content. (Chapter 5, pages 107–108)

14. *Group Mural.* In this exercise long pieces of paper are hung on walls, and various art materials are distributed. Clients, especially in a group, are instructed to draw feelings they have about themselves or the group. Counselors then work with the group

and the individuals in it on what they have drawn and how it relates to the mission of the group and to them as members of the group. (Chapter 5, page 108)

15. *Clay Piece Group.* In this exercise, clients work in a structured small circle on individual clay pieces that represent who they are with clay the counselor has given them. This exercise may be used as an icebreaker to start a group. Group leaders encourage members to tell the group about their work, what it represents, and how they are like or unlike it. (Chapter 5, page 108)

16. *Classic Paintings.* This type of artwork can arouse feeling responses that may lead to reflections on issues clients have repressed or want to talk about. Classic paintings, whether abstract or realistic, may stimulate clients, especially adults, to verbally reflect on or write about what is troubling or difficult in their lives. Classic paintings may be used with individuals or with groups as a starting place for fostering insight and promoting growth in almost any stage of counseling but particularly the working stage. Viewing such paintings and writing about them may also be a powerful homework assignment. (Chapter 5, page 109)

17. *Feeling Tapestry.* With clients who have many feelings especially connected with a difficult and unresolved situation, a feeling tapestry may be created. The tapestry, which is completed all at once or over a series of sessions, is made up of drawings clients make about emotions they have about themselves or challenges they face. Once the feelings are recognized visually, clients and counselors work on them to either lessen their potency or overcome them. (Chapter 5, page 109)

18. *Life Path and Career Road Map.* In this exercise, clients map out their lives either personally or professionally. They draw out the directions, that is, the roads that lead to specific destinations. The idea in this visual art exercise is to give clients free rein to evaluate the factors that have influenced or will most heavily influence them and then symbolize these events and people in a form that allows them to see the past, present, and future all together. In such an experience, clients can get a feel for what may lie ahead if they do not think through their plans. (Chapter 5, pages 109–110)

19. *Windows.* In this experience, a person is asked to draw a window and then to draw scenery in the window, either looking from the outside in (i.e., interiors) or from the inside out (i.e., landscapes). The type of window drawn and the view are then discussed by the counselor and the client, especially with regard to issues and directions in life (e.g., whether the person is focusing inwardly or outwardly). There is no one

correct way to focus. The drawing is simply meant to bring the client into greater awareness. (Chapter 5, page 110)

20. *Balloons.* Each member of a group is given a sheet of paper with his or her name on it and a drawing of a bunch of balloons. Members of the group then pass their papers to the right around the group, and other members of the group write or draw a kindness or good quality about the person on one of the balloons. They continue passing the papers and writing or drawing on them until each sheet is returned to its owner. This is an excellent way to end a group. (Chapter 5, page 113)

21. *Rainbow.* In this exercise, a brightly colored rainbow is made with every group member's name on a stripe. As the group leader reads each person's name, other group members call out strengths of that person, which the leader writes down or symbolically draws on that person's stripe. This is an excellent multicultural exercise and a good way to end a group. (Chapter 5, page 113)

22. *Joint Family Scribble.* Individual members of a family are asked to make scribbles. Then they are instructed to incorporate their scribbles into a unified picture. Counselors look for cooperation or competition in making the unified picture and how each family member contributes to the picture. When the picture is finished, the counselor and family talk about it and the process the family went through to complete it. (Chapter 5, page 114)

23. *Concurrent Family Drawing/Conjoint Family Drawing.* In the concurrent family drawing exercise, each member of the family is instructed to "Draw a picture as you see yourself as a family." Members draw a picture by themselves and then discuss the finished product with the rest of the family. A general discussion is then conducted on how the pictures overlap and how they differ, as well as how the family would like to see themselves. In the conjoint drawing exercise, the family works as a unit to produce just one picture of who they are as a family, and the counselor observes cooperation or competition with regard to doing the drawing. That dynamic and the drawing itself are then discussed with the family. (Chapter 5, page 114)

24. *Concurrent or Conjoint Family Holiday Drawing.* This drawing exercise is a variation on the regular concurrent/conjoint family drawing but is centered around a holiday theme. (Chapter 5, page 114)

25. *Symbolic Drawing of Family Life Space.* In this exercise, the counselor draws a large circle and instructs the family to draw everything that represents aspects of the family, including members in relationship to each other, inside the circle. People and institutions that are not a part of the family are drawn outside the circle. As with the other visual art exercises, the results of this procedure often get individuals within families talking to each other in new ways. (Chapter 5, page 114)

26. *Kinetic Family Drawing.* This is one of the most widely used projective methods in the world for evaluating an individual's perception of his or her family in context, and clinicians need specialized training to administer it. In this test, an individual (often a child) is asked to "draw everyone in the family doing something." In analyzing the drawing, the examiner looks for who is present and who is omitted or given a substitute. The size of the figures is important, as well as their position, distance, and interaction with one another. (Chapter 5, page 114)

27. *Relational Drawings.* In this method, the counselor gives a couple the following homework assignment with an example.

> I would like each of you to make a drawing of your partner. Make your drawing in a metaphorical image, as you experience your partner. You can choose an animal, a house, a landscape, a person, whatever you find most appropriate to express how you experience your partner. . . . When you have made the drawing of your partner, you draw yourself on the same paper, also in a metaphorical image, as you experience yourself in relation to your partner. Let me give you an example. . . . Then I tell them that I might, for instance, make a drawing of my wife as a soccer ball. I then would draw this soccer ball on the paper and then I would ask myself, if she is a soccer ball, what would I be? Would I be the grass on which the ball rests? Would I be the soccer player kicking the ball? Would I be the pump inflating the ball? Would I be the goal? Or the referee? Then I choose an image, and I draw it on the paper. (Rober, 2009, p. 120)

When the couple returns, the emphasis of the session is on what happens around the drawings, not the drawings themselves. In particular, the focus of the therapist is on the client's hesitations and the client's surprises. The respectful dialog of the counselor with the partners about the drawing is central. (Chapter 5, page 115)

28. *Counselor Drawings.* To challenge a client's perception of a situation or make it more of a problem that can be worked on, a counselor may make a drawing of what he or she perceives a client's difficulty is. For instance, if a client states that a problem is so large it cannot be overcome and yet solid evidence shows the contrary, the counselor might draw two pictures. Both would be of a mountain, with the first mountain much higher and steeper than the second. After the drawings are made, the counselor may tell the client that he or she sees the difficulty that has been presented more like the second drawing. This process is a visual reframing of a problem, which becomes more solvable if the client changes his or her perception. (Chapter 5, pages 116–117).

29. *Visual Art With Literature.* Clients read a poem, a short story, or a novel and then draw main events or characters as they perceived them from their readings. This exercise may be especially exciting for preadolescents and adolescents. It gives them a paper trail of images by which to remember a story and an experience. It helps them visually remember main points in the literature that relate to them. (Chapter 5, page 118)

30. *Illustrated Text About Difficult Situations.* Clients are asked to make a book about their difficult situations that shows their feelings but that contains words as well. For example, participants could create a *Pain Getting Better Book* in and through which they can objectify their pain through drawings and simultaneously be helped to tap their inner resources. This type of book both empowers participants and helps them discover the best within themselves. (Chapter 5, page 119)

Creative Arts Exercises—Literature

1. *5-Minute Writing Sprint.* This writing exercise is used to help clients who think they cannot write to do so. Clients are asked to do this exercise usually outside of a counseling session for homework, although it may be used in a session. Before beginning, clients find a place to write, a consistent time to write, and bring with them paper and two pencils or pen (in case one breaks or runs out of ink). Limited time is one of the crucial elements in this exercise. Before beginning to write, a timer is set to go off after 5 minutes, so the client does not have to continually keep track of time. Then the client begins writing about anything he or she wishes. The only rules are that the writing instrument (i.e., the pencil or pen) has to constantly be in motion. If words do not come to mind, the writer doodles or scribbles on the paper in a motion that is similar to writing and that is continuous. When the timer goes off, the person stops writing even if in midsentence.

    This approach to writing is practical; most clients can find 5 minutes to devote to writing. In doing this exercise, I like to have clients write one day and read and reflect on what they have written the next. This practice helps clients stay motivated to write and gives them an opportunity to process what they are writing. (Chapter 6, page 130)

2. *Word Cluster.* This writing exercise revolves around a central word, such as *anger, anxiety,* or *distress.* The word leads clients to branch out from the original word to people, places, times, or situations associated with the word. When the association is finished, the client discusses ways of constructively dealing with the intensity of the emotions and thoughts that may have arisen. (Chapter 6, page 130)

3. *Character Sketch.* Clients loosen up their writing skills (and their thought processes) simultaneously by writing a character sketch on someone they find interesting. When such an exercise is done, clients have a good opportunity to compare themselves with the admired person in a positive way. (Chapter 6, pages 130–131)

4. *Letters From the Future.* This is a letter-writing exercise that may be used as an intervention to help sexual abuse survivors develop a sense of empowerment and control over their lives. In the process, victims of sexual abuse develop a future orientation in which they perceive themselves as strong and competent individuals who possess the resources needed to manage the influence of past abuse experience. In doing so, they externalize their problems, create new realities, and identify solutions to their situations. Then they write therapeutic letters to themselves that can be used during a session or afterward. The letters can take many forms, such as "strength through suffering," "personal accomplishment," "older, wiser self," and "rainy day" correspondence. These letters serve as a vehicle to self-exploration and the creation of change. (Chapter 6, page 131)

5. *Rewriting a Story.* Rewriting is an emphasis of solution-focused counselors. A key to solution-focused work is for counselors to help clients find exceptions to the stories they tell or write. These exceptions are then examined and expanded to create new stories and break old, repetitive, nonproductive patterns of behavior. The idea is based on the philosophy of constructivism, which states that reality is a reflection of observation and experience, not an objective entity. (Chapter 6, page 132)

6. *Interactive Journaling.* In this literary exercise, individual clients or members of a group share personal thoughts about themselves and what is going on in their lives with the counselor or other group members. These types of journals foster growth, and in a group they allow members to affirm and support each other altruistically and to deepen their understanding of self and others.

   Common forms of journal work include the following:

   a. *The Period Log.* Individuals are encouraged to define a recent period of their lives, reflect on their experiences and life events during that period, and record their feelings, impressions, and descriptions.

   b. *The Daily Log.* This form of writing closely resembles a diary and serves as a running record of the person's subjective experience of daily life.

   c. *The Stepping Stones.* The most significant points of movement in a person's life are listed in this type of journal. These points can help individuals see overall patterns and unconscious goals and motivations.

d. *The Dream Log.* This log is used to keep a record of dreams and dream themes and patterns that may be shared with the counselor individually or in a group.

e. *Twilight Images.* Thoughts and images that occur just before falling asleep are recorded in this type of writing. (Chapter 6, pages 135–136)

7. *Autobiography.* In this writing exercise, clients express what has been important in their lives, emphasize likes and dislikes, identify values, describe interests and aspirations, acknowledge successes and failures, and recall meaningful personal relationships. Such an experience, especially for emotionally mature clients, can be thought-provoking, insightful, and a stimulus for action. The experience can also relieve tension. (Chapter 6, pages 136–137)

8. *Memory Book.* A memory book includes narratives such as stories, anecdotes, and poetry as well as songs, photographs, and genograms. It is a way of passing traditions, values, and norms on from one generation to another and may be done physically or digitally. It is a powerful way of psychotherapeutically working with clients and significant others who have terminal illnesses. (Chapter 6, page 138)

9. *Mutual Storytelling.* This is a verbal means of written expression. This approach, devised by Richard A. Gardner (1971), involves a counselor and client who participate in telling a story together. The counselor begins the story with a phrase such as "Once upon a time" and tailors his or her initial remarks to parallel the present situation of the client. The story is then turned over to the client for telling. The counselor intervenes only when the client becomes stuck or asks for help, at which point the counselor adds neutral descriptive material or asks a question. The idea behind this activity is for the client to really hear and attempt to resolve areas in life that are presently troubling him or her. (Chapter 6, pages 139–140)

10. *Co-Story-Ing.* This is a modification of R. A. Gardner's mutual storytelling method in which counselors work with children to write their stories instead of just telling stories. This is particularly helpful with children who are not developmentally ready for talk therapies. The advantage of writing stories down is that they can be revisited and refined. Furthermore, insight sometimes does not come until after a story is written or talked about. Co-story-ing is a five-stage process that involves acceptance and affirmation of children's responses. The stages are preparation (gathering of materials), explanation (of what is to be done), composition (writing of the story), ending-reflection (completion of the task), and expanding alternatives (in which the story is revisited and can be altered). (Chapter 6, page 140)

11. *Therapeutic Fairy Tale.* In this written exercise, clients are asked to participate in a pretend experience for a limited time. Specifically, they are asked to imagine and then do the following: (a) Set up a scene far from the here and now in time and place. (b) Within this setting, include a problem or a predicament. (c) Include a solution to the problem that is positive and pleasing. (d) Write their story within a 6- to 10-minute time period. Tales begin with "Once upon a time" because that is how all fairy tales begin, but after this standard opening clients are on their own. After the tale is written, clients share their stories either individually or in a group setting, depending on the counseling format. Particular attention is paid to how thorough the fairy tale is, the qualities of the main characters, the nature of the pleasing and positive ending and what it depends on (e.g., skill, chance, luck), and the type of language used in creating the story. It is stressed to participants after this exercise that the limited amount of time is symbolic of life in general; they do not have unlimited time to work on life issues. (Chapter 6, pages 142–143)

12. *Writing the Wrongs to Make Them Right.* In this procedure, clients write out the wrong or disconcerting experiences they have had in life (e.g., unexpected death of a loved one, divorce, loss of physical or mental abilities). After the wrong has been described, clients write the situation right by not changing the facts but by simply writing out what they learned from the experiences and how they have benefited or been made right (or better) from it. (Chapter 6, pages 144–145)

13. *Life Review.* This writing process is targeted toward older adults. It involves having a person write his or her autobiography using family albums, old letters, personal memories, and interviews with others to gather and integrate life experiences into a meaningful whole. Ideally, this effort produces wisdom and satisfaction while alleviating pain and regrets. (Chapter 6, page 145)

14. *Reaction Readings.* In group work with older people, residents in nursing homes, and residents in other long-term care facilities, the group members read poems aloud together (i.e., a choral reading). They "then react to the content of the poems with their own knowledge, opinion, emotion, and imagination" (Asmuth, 1995, p. 415). The residents become their own audience of their own performance and are stimulated emotionally and intellectually. Furthermore, their self-concepts and cohesiveness as a group improve. (Chapter 6, page 145)

15. *Poems as a Group Catalyst.* This process, which can be used as an icebreaker, involves having the group leader read a nondidactic poem—such as those by Langston Hughes, Maya Angelou, James Dickey, or A. R. Ammons—to group participants after they have been through a series of warm-up exercises. Each person in the group is asked to identify with an image in the poem and then talk about how this image represents his or her. For example, a person might identify with grass and talk about how his or her life is growing. (Chapter 6, page 146)

16. *Closing Poems.* In this written exercise, group participants write couplets or lines about what they have learned in the group. The lines are then linked together in an interactive way that results in a collaborative poem. The poem may begin with the line "Today I learned in the group" or "Through this group experience I learned." A good ending line is "Now I am moving on." Such a procedure requires everyone's participation. It is usually an effective way to terminate a group experience permanently, or in the case of open-ended groups, to close the group for that session. (Chapter 6, page 146)

17. *Music and Writing.* Music helps stir up feelings and words that otherwise would remain dormant. For example, John Denver's song "Poems, Prayers, and Promises" can be played as a backdrop for a writing exercise titled "What I Believe In," in which participants write about their most important values and how they are expressed. Special effects tapes, such as sounds of the wind, a waterfall, or a crackling fire, may be useful in setting a type of atmosphere conducive to reading or writing too. (Chapter 6, page 149)

18. *Personal Logo and Story.* In this exercise, a logo is developed through playing with doodles until a symbol emerges that feels just right for the participant. A story is then written to accompany the art and is shared with the counselor or in a group. (Chapter 6, page 150)

19. *Lines of Feelings.* Clients are asked to draw and color lines that represent their feelings about certain situations or people. The lines vary in length and shape, but often jagged, rough lines in red or orange are used to signify anger or discontent, whereas smooth, flowing lines in blues and greens are more often used to display calmness and contentment. After the lines are drawn, clients can expand on them by writing about what the lines represent, how it feels to draw them, or to whom or what they are directed. (Chapter 4, page 89; Chapter 5, page 120; Chapter 6, page 150)

Creative Arts Activities—Drama

1. *Role Playing.* In this dramatic exercise, clients enact scenes or situations they would otherwise describe. In the gestalt form of role playing, clients are directed to role-play all aspects of a situation they would otherwise describe. (Chapter 7, page 164)

2. *Empty Chair.* In this activity, two chairs are used: a hot seat for people who want to work and an empty chair into which troublesome emotions may be projected. Clients who choose to work using this gestalt method reflect and project emotions onto the empty chair as needed and talk with the polar parts of themselves until some integrated resolution results. Use of the personal noun "I" is encouraged in this type of transaction to increase a sense of personal responsibility. (The empty chair technique should only be used after a counselor has mastered gestalt theory and therapy and should initially be supervised by another experienced clinician.) (Chapter 7, pages 164–165)

3. *Shame Attack.* In a shame attack, an activity originated in rational emotive behavior therapy by Albert Ellis, clients are encouraged to display behaviors they have been previously fearful of enacting, to see that the world does not collapse or fall apart if they make a mistake or do not get their desired outcome. For example, a person might ask for a glass of water in a restaurant without ordering food or might purposely fall down at a shopping mall and see what happens. (Chapter 7, page 165; Chapter 8, page 191)

4. *Acting "as if."* In this activity, clients discuss how they would like to behave. Then they are instructed to act as if they were the person they wish to be. This technique is often met with protests because clients think they are being phony, but stress is lowered when individuals involved know they are simply acting and that their new behaviors in effect are no different from trying on new clothes to see how well they fit and feel. (Chapter 7, pages 165–166)

5. *Family Puppet Interview.* In this drama technique, children make up stories about the family using puppets. These stories often highlight conflicts and alliances within families but may be of limited usefulness. (Asking direct questions to young children is often more productive in obtaining information.) (Chapter 7, page 166)

6. *Hamlet Dilemma.* This approach works on both an experiential and a cognitive level. It is used with adolescents who first warm up by reading or viewing a video version of *Hamlet* and then examining the wants and needs of each character. This is followed by a role play in groups of three, in which one student plays the protagonist and is flanked by the other two students, whose roles are that of revenge and caution, action and inaction. In these role plays, which last 15 minutes, each of the flanking actors tries passionately to persuade the prince (or princess) to choose his or her point of view. After time is called, the protagonist shares with the others in the group thoughts and feelings that emerged during his or her decision making. The process is repeated until each of the trio (and ultimately everyone in a group) has an opportunity to actively participate as the protagonist. (Chapter 7, pages 167–168)

7. *Playback Theatre.* This is a formal type of videodrama that involves self-disclosure of audience members' personal stories. The disclosure is followed by an improvised dramatization of the audience members' stories by a director and players who have been trained in the art of improvisational theater. Playback seeks to enter the world of tellers and artistically reflect the essence of their narrative through a moment-to-moment improvisation. It is through the artistic expression of the players' representation of the story that the audience can internalize their empathic feelings. Playback Theatre was developed to promote healing and social connection; it was not necessarily designed as a drama therapy intervention. (Chapter 7, page 168)

8. *Spouse Situation Inventory*. This inventory is composed of 24 representative problem situation vignettes that women of alcoholic partners confront. The vignettes are read individually by a woman who pretends that the administrator of the inventory is her partner. The woman pretends to say and do exactly what she would with her partner in the situation. Her response is evaluated, and in the process the woman has an opportunity to learn how effective her reaction is and what else she might say or do. (Chapter 7, pages 169–170)

9. *Family Sculpting*. In this silent but dramatic activity, members of a family are asked to arrange one another as a living statue. They are given the chance to actively and concretely convey their impressions of the family in a nonverbal yet potent manner by having different family members assume certain poses or postures. Sometimes their positioning is exaggerated, but the point is not lost on anyone as to how that family member and family dynamics are seen through the eyes of the person doing the arranging of the family. Because the process involves all members of the family unit, it enables the family to work with the counselor in a collaborative fashion. Sometimes sculpting is used to disengage family members from emotional experiences and facilitate insight into past and present situations. At other times it is used to bring about an affective experience that will unblock unexpressed emotions. Sculpting is usually appropriate at any time during the treatment of a family because it stimulates interaction and promotes insight. At a minimum, sculpting should include (a) selecting a sculptor; (b) choosing sculpture content (event, problem, or process); (c) sculpting individual members of the family unit; (d) detailing the sculpture; (e) adding the sculptor into the scene; (f) choosing to give the sculpture a descriptive title, a resolution, or a ritualistic motion; (g) sculpting other relevant situations until a pattern emerges; (h) deroling and debriefing all involved; and (i) processing the results. (Chapter 4, page 87; Chapter 7, pages 171–172)

10. *Pictorial Dramatization*. In this exercise, clients draw pictures of an important moment, person, conflict, or fantasy. These pictures reveal inner feelings and give important data on self-esteem. Clients go on to act out short pantomimes or improvisational scenes based on the pictures. By doing so, they see and feel simultaneously and become more aware of themselves and their environments. (Chapter 7, page 173)

11. *Enacting the Poem "Autobiography in Five Short Chapters"* (P. Nelson, 1993). Instead of reading this poem (which is often read in addiction groups), participants enact it in a group setting, playing the roles of the protagonist, the narrator, the director, trees on a street, and a hole in the sidewalk. The protagonist

goes from accidentally falling in a hole to walking down another street. People who enact the poem or participate in such an enactment through supportive roles get a feel for what the poem is conveying in a more meaningful way than through just reading it. (Chapter 7, page 173)

Creative Arts Activities—Play and Humor

1. *Reframing.* In reframing, a situation does not change, it is simply described differently and seen in a more positive light. Thus, reframing is like putting different frames on a picture. Each of the frames draws out different aspects of the picture, but the picture remains the same. For example, a child who misbehaves a lot may be said to be "incorrigible." By changing the frame, the same child could be described as "naughty." Reframing the picture of the child makes working toward a solution possible. Reframing can be used by a counselor with almost any situation to help move toward resolution. (Chapter 8, page 178)
2. *Anger Ball.* In this activity, a client's anger is released by hitting a ball that momentarily represents something or someone the person has anger toward. This action is better than hitting someone, but it is like catharsis in that it is only the first step in moving past anger and into resolution. (Chapter 8, page 186)
3. *Play-Doh Expression.* Play-Doh may be used as an entertaining medium for emotional expression on a basic level. In this play activity, clients may orchestrate angry sounds when pounding the Play-Doh and make whining sounds while squeezing the material. Dry, clean materials should always be used, and it should be remembered that this activity only produces a catharsis and not a resolution to the feeling involved. (Chapter 8, page 187)
4. *Paper and Box Stimulus.* A large packing box filled with various types of paper is kept in the counselor's office, and children (up to preteens) are allowed to climb in it and play. The idea behind the box and the games it spontaneously inspires is that through this medium children encounter the creation of rapport, the skill of reciprocity, and the art of pretend. By fixing the box with multiple entrances and exits, counselors can heighten play and social interaction among these children. (Chapter 8, page 187)
5. *Talking, Feeling, and Doing Game.* This is a commercially produced game in which children are interviewed about their feelings. The game includes a game board, dice, and movement along squares from start to finish. Children are encouraged to talk and acknowledge their emotions and actions in a positive and productive way. This game is "won" by moving a game piece to the finish square and gaining greater insight into oneself. (Chapter 8, page 187)

6. *Frustration.* This is a group game for adolescents made up by Teeter, Teeter, and Papai in 1976. In this game, entering students are exposed to some of the hazards of high school and the effects that chance circumstances may have on their lives. They may draw a card that places them in a class with exceptionally bright or mediocre students, or they may find that in a school assembly they are seated next to either a popular or an unpopular classmate. If they choose to think about such situations while playing the game, they have gained insight and understanding about themselves as well as their upcoming environment. (Although the original game is dated, creative counselors can use the idea to create a similar game and use it in group guidance classes.) (Chapter 8, page 189)

7. *Skits.* Often overlooked as a way to creatively address issues, skits humorously address subjects that clients, especially adolescents and young adults, have concern over, such as the environment, war, dating, and drugs. A type of cooperative skit activity can be the result of such an effort in educational settings. At such a time, skits can be videotaped and shown to participants again. From skits, teens and young adults gain a sense of empowerment and empathy that gives them more freedom to constructively operate within societal boundaries. (Chapter 8, page 190)

8. *Humorous Rational Songs.* In this musical activity, originated by Albert Ellis, clients put new words and thoughts to a familiar tune in the form of lyrics. In doing so, they make many of their problems less serious and more resolvable. (Chapter 8, page 191)

9. *Role Plays.* This involves an activity in which a role, usually not one familiar to the client, is assumed and actively played, such as being assertive. In the process, if the role play is successful, the client learns more about issues and challenges of being seen or cast in a certain way. (Chapter 8, page 191)

10. *Passive–Active.* This movement activity can be used with any age group as a warm-up exercise. It requires part of a group to be passive and the other part active. The active members make statues out of the passive members (within reason), but the passive members may come alive at any time, and likewise the active members may become passive at any time. The enjoyment of this type of play activity is found in creating the statues and in the element of surprise. As a warm up, this activity can go on for around 5 minutes. It is important for counselors to make sure that the entire group does not become active or passive all at once. (Chapter 8, pages 192–193)

11. *Name Game.* This is a playful and humorous game in which two individuals carry on a conversation using only their names and no other words. A variation of Name Game is called *Yes No*, in which two individuals have a similar conversation, but in this case only the words *yes* and *no* can be used. (Chapter 8, page 193)

Creative Arts Activities—Animals, Horticulture, and Nature

Note. These exercises do not appear in Chapter 9
but have been created as complements to the chapter.

1. *Animal Interaction.* Think of a popular animal, such as a dog or horse, with which you have had some experiential interactions. What did you learn from interacting with the animal? How did you feel after the experience? If the experience was extensive, what were your favorite memories, and what did you learn about life from the animal?

2. *Calming Touch.* Practice petting your own pet or a pet of someone you know. Gauge how calm you feel afterward on a scale of 1 to 10?

3. *Finding Out.* Interview a mental health professional who uses an animal as an assistant in his or her therapy or counseling. Ask the professional about significant therapeutic experiences regarding the animal and how they conduct sessions differently when the animal is not present.

4. *Lessons From Stories About Animals.* What were your favorite stories or books involving people and animals when you were a child or adolescent? What lessons were implied or apparent in the stories about the relationship between the species? What relevance do those lessons have in your life now?

5. *Plant and Life Stages.* Almost everyone has grown a plant from a seed, whether it be vegetables or flowers. Think back on your own experience (or interview someone about theirs if you have never done this). How did the experience increase empathy or understanding of life for you or the person involved? Has this experience influenced your interactions with or appreciation of plant life or how you see different stages of life?

6. *Lessons From Plants.* Interview someone who makes all or part of their livelihood from planting or working with plants (e.g., a florist or a farmer). Ask them how they enjoy their work and what lessons from plants they can apply to people or themselves.

7. *Impressions From Nature.* Take a hike for approximately an hour in a natural area, such as a local, state, or federal park. Record your impressions and feelings immediately. What aspects of what you saw impressed you most? What were your thoughts and feelings about these features? How do they differ from how you usually think and feel about your environment?

8. *Wilderness Therapy and Change.* Interview someone who conducts wilderness therapy or someone who has been involved in wilderness therapy. What changes do they notice about those who are participants? What changes do they notice about themselves during or after a wilderness experience?

9. *Feelings From Environments.* Spend half an hour or more in a natural habitat. What do you notice most in the environment? What do you notice most about yourself as you are affected by the environment? What are your feelings regarding the habitat? If possible, have a habitat experience of this type for 5 days in a row. Quickly record your thoughts and feelings after each experience.

References

Abell, S. C. (1998). The use of poetry in play therapy: A logical integration. *Arts in Psychotherapy, 25*, 45–49.

Abraham, I. L., Neundorfer, M. M., & Terris, E. A. (1993). Effects of focused visual imagery on cognition and depression among nursing home residents. *Journal of Mental Imagery, 17*, 61–76.

Abrami, L. M. (2009). The healing power of humor in logotherapy. *International Forum for Logotherapy, 32*, 7–12.

Achterberg, J., & Lawlis, G. F. (1984). *Imagery and disease*. Champaign, IL: Institute for Personality and Ability Testing.

Adams, K. (1998). *The way of the journal* (2nd ed.). Lutherville, MD: Sidran.

Adams, W. J. (1974). The use of sexual humor in teaching human sexuality at the university level. *The Family Coordinator, 23*, 365–368.

Adamson, E. (1984). *Art as healing*. London, England: Conventure.

Adler, A. (1963). *The practice and theory of individual psychotherapy* (P. Radin, Trans.). Patterson, NJ: Littlefield, Adams. (Original work published 1924)

Alberti, R. E., & Emmons, M. L. (2008). *Your perfect right* (9th ed.). Atascadero, CA: Impact.

Aldridge, D. (1989). A phenomenological comparison of the organization of music and the self. *Arts in Psychotherapy, 16*, 91–97.

Aldridge, D. (1994). Single-case research designs for the creative art therapist. *Arts in Psychotherapy, 21*, 333–342.

Aldridge, D., Brandt, G., & Wohler, D. (1990). Toward a common language among the creative art therapies. *Arts in Psychotherapy, 17*, 189–195.

Aldridge, D., Gustorff, D., & Neugebauer, L. (1995). A preliminary study of creative music therapy in the treatment of children with developmental delay. *Arts in Psychotherapy, 22*, 189–205.

Aldridge, G. (1996). "A walk through Paris": The development of melodic expression in music therapy with a breast-cancer patient. *Arts in Psychotherapy, 23*, 207–223.

Alesandrini, K. L. (1985). Imagery research with adults: Implications for education. In A. S. Sheikh & K. S. Sheikh (Eds.), *Imagery in education* (pp. 199–221). Farmingdale, NY: Baywood.

Alexander, D. W. (1999). *Children changed by trauma: A healing guide.* Oakland, CA: New Harbinger.

Alexander, M. (2000). Cinemeducation: Teaching family systems through the movies. *Families, Systems, and Health: The Journal of Collaborative Family Health Care, 18,* 455–467.

Allan, J. (1978). Serial drawing: A therapeutic approach with young children. *Canadian Counsellor, 12,* 223–228.

Allan, J. (2008). *Inscapes of the child's world.* New York, NY: Continuum International Publishing Group.

Allan, J., & Brown, K. (1993). Jungian play therapy in elementary schools. *Elementary School Guidance and Counseling, 28,* 30–41.

Allan, J., & Crandall, J. (1986). The rosebush: A visualization strategy for possible identification of child abuse. *Elementary School Guidance and Counseling, 21,* 44–51.

Allport, G. W. (1955). *Becoming: Basic considerations for a psychology of personality.* New Haven, CT: Yale University Press.

Alvarado, V. I., & Cavazos, L. J. (2006/2007). Allegories and symbols in counseling. *Journal of Creativity in Mental Health, 2,* 51–59.

Alvares, T. S. (1998). Healing through imagery: Gabriel's and Maria's journeys. *Arts in Psychotherapy, 25,* 313–322.

Alvarez, N., & Mearns, J. (2014). The benefits of writing and performing in the spoken word poetry community. *Arts in Psychotherapy, 41,* 263–268.

Alyami, A. M. S. (2015). The role of art therapy in counterterrorism: The Saudi experience. *Arts in Psychotherapy, 44,* 1–10.

American Art Therapy Association. (2010). *About the American Art Therapy Association.* Retrieved from http://www.americanarttherapyassociation.org/aata-aboutus.html

American Dance Therapy Association. (2015). *About dance/movement therapy.* Retrieved from http://www.adta.org/About_DMT

American Music Therapy Association. (2010a). *Frequently asked questions about music therapy.* Retrieved from http://www.musictherapy.org/faq/

American Music Therapy Association. (2010b). *Music therapy makes a difference.* Retrieved from http://www.musictherapy.org/faq/#267

American Psychiatric Association (2013). *Diagnostic and statistical manual of mental disorders* (5th ed.). Arlington, VA: Author.

Amerikaner, M., Schauble, P., & Ziller, R. (1980). Images: The use of photographs in personal counseling. *Personnel and Guidance Journal, 59,* 68–73.

Anderson, A. N., Kennedy, H., DeWitt, P., Anderson, E., & Wambold, M. Z. (2014). Dance/movement therapy impacts mood states of adolescents in a psychiatric hospital. *Arts in Psychotherapy, 41,* 257–262.

Ansdell, G., & Pavlicevic, M. (2001). *Beginning research in the arts therapies: A practical guide.* Philadelphia, PA: Jessica Kingsley.

Anser-Self, K., & Feyissa, A. (2002). The use of poetry in psychoeducational groups with multicultural-multilingual clients. *Journal for Specialists in Group Work, 27,* 136–160.

Aoki, T. (2000). Review on studies of collage therapy. *Japanese Journal of Counseling Science, 33,* 323–333.

Appleton, V. (2001). Avenues of hope: Art therapy and the resolution of trauma. *Art Therapy, 18,* 6–13.

Appleton, V. E., & Dykeman, C. (1996). Using art in group counseling with Native American youth. *Journal for Specialists in Group Work, 21,* 224–231.

Arbuthnott, K. D., Arbuthnott, D. W., & Rossiter, L. (2001). Guided imagery and memory: Implications for psychotherapists. *Journal of Counseling Psychology, 48,* 123–132.

Arieti, S. (1976). *Creativity: The magic synthesis.* New York, NY: Basic Books.

Arnheim, R. (1990). The artist as healer. *Arts in Psychotherapy, 17,* 1–4.

Arnheim, R. (1994). Artistry in retardation. *Arts in Psychotherapy, 21,* 329–332.

Ashen, A. (1977). *Psycheye: Self-analytic consciousness.* New York, NY: Brandon House.

Ashida, S. (2000). The effect of reminiscence music therapy sessions on changes in depressive symptoms in elderly persons with dementia. *Journal of Music Therapy, 37,* 170–182.

Ashley, F. B., & Crenan, M. (1993). Dance: The movement activity for the elderly. *Nursing Homes, 42,* 50–51.

Asmuth, M. V. (1995). Reaction reading: A tool for providing fantasy imagery for long-term care facility residents. *Gerontologist, 35,* 415–419.

Atchison, D. (2001). Sharing feelings through clay. In H. G. Kaduson & C. E. Schaefer (Eds.), *101 more favorite play therapy techniques* (pp. 111–114). Northvale, NJ: Jason Aronson.

Atkins, S., Adams, M., McKinney, C., McKinney, H., Rose, L., Wentworth, J., & Wentworth, J. (2003). *Expressive arts therapy.* Boone, NC: Parkway.

Atterburg, C., Sorg, J., & Larson, A. (1983). Aerobic dancing in a long-term care facility. *Physical and Occupational Therapy in Geriatrics, 2,* 71–73.

Avrahami, D. (2005). Visual art therapy's unique contribution to the treatment of post-traumatic stress disorder. *Journal of Trauma and Dissociation, 64,* 5–37.

Avrahami, E. (2003). Cognitive-behavioral approach in psychodrama: Discussion and example from addiction treatment. *Arts in Psychotherapy, 30,* 209–216.

Axline, V. (1947). *Play therapy.* Boston, MA: Houghton-Mifflin.

Axline, V. (1967). *Dibs in search of self.* New York, NY: Ballantine.

Bacon, S. (1984). *The conscious use of metaphor in Outward Bound.* Denver, CO: Outward Bound School.

Bailey, L. M. (1984). The use of songs in music therapy with cancer patients and their family. *Music Therapy, 4,* 5–17.

Baker, E. K. (2003). *Caring for ourselves: A therapist's guide to personal and professional well-being.* Washington, DC: American Psychological Association.

Baker, L. M. (2009). Nature's pervading influence: A therapy of growth. *International Journal of Disability, Development and Education, 56*(1), 93–96.

Baker, S. B. (1982). The use of music with autistic children. *Journal of Psychosocial Nursing and Mental Health Services, 20,* 31–34.

Ballard, M. B. (2012). The family life cycle and critical transitions: Utilizing cinematherapy to facilitate understanding and increase communication. *Journal of Creativity in Mental Health, 7,* 141–152.

Bandler, R., & Grinder, J. (1975). *The structure of magic.* Palo Alto, CA: Science & Behavior Books.

Bandoroff, S., & Scherer, D. G. (1994). Wilderness family therapy: An innovative treatment approach for problem youth. *Journal of Child and Family Studies, 3,* 175–191.

Bandura, A. (1977). *Social learning theory.* Upper Saddle River, NJ: Prentice-Hall.

Barbour, J. (1991, March 27). Doctors who become writers. *Winston-Salem Journal,* pp. W1, W4.

Barker, P. (1985). *Using metaphors in psychotherapy.* New York, NY: Brunner/Mazel.

Barker, P., & Chang, J. (2013). *Basic family therapy* (6th ed.). New York, NY: Oxford University Press.

Baron, P. (1991). Fighting cancer with images. In H. Wadeson, J. Durkin, & D. Perach (Eds.), *Advances in art therapy* (pp. 148–168). New York, NY: Wiley.

Baron, R. A. (1974). The aggressive-inhibiting influence of nonhostile humor. *Journal of Experimental Social Psychology, 10,* 23–33.

Barone, T., & Eisner, E. W. (2012). *Art-based research.* Los Angeles, CA: Sage.

Bartlett, J. R. (2003, July/August). Storytelling through the ages. *ASCA School Counselor,* 11–14.

Barton, C., & Alexander, J. E. (1981). Functional family therapy. In A. S. Gurman & D. P. Kniskern (Eds.), *Handbook of family therapy* (pp. 403–443). New York, NY: Brunner/Mazel.

Bateson, G. (1978). *Steps to an ecology of mind.* London, England: Paladin.

Baum, F. L. (2000). *The wonderful wizard of Oz.* New York, NY: Hill. (Original work published 1900)

Beale, A. V., & Scott, P. C. (2001). Bullybusters: Using drama to empower students to take a stand against bullying behavior. *Professional School Counseling, 4,* 300–305.

Beaudry, I. D. (1997). Reconfiguring identity. *Arts in Psychotherapy, 24,* 51–57.

Beaulieu, J. (1987). *Music and sound in the healing arts: An energy approach.* New York, NY: Station Hill.

Becker, K., Reiser, M., Lambert, S., & Covello, C. (2014). Photovoice: Conducting community-based participatory research and advocacy in mental health. *Journal of Creativity in Mental Health, 9,* 188–209.

Behrends, A., Müller, S., & Dziobek, I. (2012). Moving in and out of synchrony: A concept for a new intervention fostering empathy through interactional movement and dance. *Arts in Psychotherapy, 39,* 107–116.

Beier, E. (1966). *The silent language of psychotherapy.* Chicago, IL: Aldine.

Berg, B. (1986). *The Assertion Game.* Dayton, OH: Cognitive Counseling Resources.

Berg, B. (1989). *The Anger Control Game*. Dayton, OH: Cognitive Counseling Resources.

Berg, B. (1990a). *The Anxiety Management Game*. Dayton, OH: Cognitive Counseling Resources.

Berg, B. (1990b). *The Depression Management Game*. Dayton, OH: Cognitive Counseling Resources.

Berg, B. (1990c). *The Self-Control Game*. Dayton, OH: Cognitive Counseling Resources.

Berg, R. G., Parr, G., Bradley, L. J., & Berry, J. J. (2009). Humor: A therapeutic intervention for child counseling. *Journal of Creativity in Mental Health, 4,* 225–236.

Berger, A. (1988). Working through grief by writing poetry. *Journal of Poetry Therapy, 1,* 11–19.

Berger, A., & Giovan, M. (1990). Poetic interventions with forensic patients. *Journal of Poetry Therapy, 4,* 83–92.

Berger, R., & Tiry, M. (2012). The enchanting forest and the healing sand—Nature therapy with people coping with psychiatric difficulties. *Arts in Psychotherapy, 39*(5), 412–416.

Berget, B., Ekeberg, O., Pedersen, I., & Braastad, B. O. (2011). Animal-assisted therapy with farm animals for persons with psychiatric disorders: Effects on anxiety and depression, a randomized controlled trial. *Occupational Therapy in Mental Health, 27,* 50–64.

Berk, L. E. (2013). *Child development* (9th ed.). Upper Saddle River, NJ: Pearson.

Berk, R. A. (2002). *Humor as an instructional defibrillator: Evidence-based techniques in teaching and assessment*. Sterling, VA: Stylus.

Berk, R. A. (2003). *Professors are from Mars®, students are from Snickers®.* Sterling, VA: Stylus.

Berne, E. (1964). *Games people play*. New York, NY: Grove.

Bernstein, R. E., Ablow, J. C., Maloney, K. C., & Nigg, J. T. (2014). Piloting play write: Feasibility and efficacy of a playwriting intervention for at-risk adolescents. *Journal of Creativity in Mental Health, 9,* 446–467.

Berry, J. (1987). *Every kid's guide to handling feelings*. Chicago, IL: Children's Press.

Best, P. A. (2000). Theoretical diversity and clinical collaboration: Reflections by a dance/movement therapist. *Arts in Psychotherapy, 27,* 197–211.

Bettleheim, B. (1976). *The uses of enchantment: The meaning and importance of fairy tales*. New York, NY: Knopf.

Bettmann, J. E., & Jasperson, R. A. (2008). Adults in wilderness treatment: A unique application of attachment theory and research. *Clinical Social Work Journal, 36,* 51–61.

Bettmann, J. E., Tucker, A. R., Tracy, J., & Parry, K. J. (2014). An exploration of gender, client history, and functioning in wilderness therapy participants. *Residential Treatment for Children & Youth, 31,* 155–170.

Bing, E. (1970). The conjoint family drawing. *Family Process, 9,* 173–194.

Black, J., & Enns, G. (1998). *Better boundaries: Owning and treasuring your life*. New York, NY: Harbinger.

Blatner, A. (1995). Psychodrama. In R. J. Corsini & D. Wedding (Eds.), *Current psychotherapies* (5th ed., pp. 399–408). Itasca, IL: Peacock.

Blatner, A. (1996). *Acting in: Practical application of psychodramatic methods* (3rd ed.). New York, NY: Springer.

Blatner, A. (1997). Psychodrama: The state of the art. *Arts in Psychotherapy, 24*, 23–30.

Blatner, A. (2001). Psychodramatic methods in psychotherapy. In D. J. Wiener (Ed.), *Beyond talk therapy* (pp. 125–143). Washington, DC: American Psychological Association.

Blatner, A. (2004). *Foundations of psychodrama: History, theory, and practice* (4th ed.). New York, NY: Springer.

Blatner, A., & Wiener, D. (Eds.). (2007). *Interactive and improvisational drama: Varieties of applied theater and performance*. Lincoln, NE: iUniverse.

Block, B. A. (2001). The psychological cultural relational model applied to therapeutic, educational adolescent dance programs. *Arts in Psychotherapy, 28*, 117–123.

Blomdahl, C., Gunnarsson, A. B., Guregård, S., & Björklund, A. (2013). A realist review of art therapy for clients with depression. *Arts in Psychotherapy, 40*, 322–330.

Blood, P., & Patterson, A. (Eds.). (1992). *Rise up singing: The group singing songbook*. Bethlehem, PA: Sing Out.

Bolles, R. N. (2016). *What color is your parachute? 2010: A practical manual for job-hunters and career-changers*. Berkeley, CA: Ten Speed Press.

Bonny, H. L. (1987). Music: The language of immediacy. *Arts in Psychotherapy, 14*, 255–261.

Bonny, H. L. (1997). The state of the art of music therapy. *Arts in Psychotherapy, 24*, 65–73.

Borcherdt, B. (2002). Humor and its contributions to mental health. *Journal of Rational-Emotive & Cognitive-Behavior Therapy, 20*, 247–257.

Borders, S. G., & Naylor, A. P. (1993). *Children talking about books*. Phoenix, AZ: Oryx.

Borgmann, E. (2002). Art therapy with three women diagnosed with cancer. *Arts in Psychotherapy, 29*, 245–251.

Bornmann, B. A., & Crossman, A. M. (2011). Playback Theatre: Effects on students' views of aggression and empathy within a forensic context. *Arts in Psychotherapy, 38*, 164–168.

Botello, R. K., & Krout, R. E. (2008). Music therapy assessment of automatic thoughts: Developing a cognitive–behavioral application of improvisation to assess couple communication. *Music Therapy Perspectives, 26*, 51–55.

Bourne, E. J. (2015). *The anxiety and phobia workbook* (6th ed.). Oakland, CA: New Harbinger.

Bowen, C. A., & Rosal, M. L. (1989). The use of art therapy to reduce the maladaptive behaviors of a mentally retarded adult. *Arts in Psychotherapy, 16*, 211–218.

Bowman, D. O., Sauers, R. J., & Judice, R. P. (1996). Exploration of sexual identity through poetry therapy. *Journal of Poetry Therapy, 10*, 19–26.

Bowman, R. P. (1987). Approaches for counseling children through music. *Elementary School Guidance and Counseling, 21,* 284–291.

Bowman, R. P. (2004). *Test buster pep rally* (2nd ed.). Chapin, SC: Youthlight.

Bowman, T. (1994). Using poetry, fiction, and essays to help people face shattered dreams. *Journal of Poetry Therapy, 8,* 81–89.

Bradley, L. J., Whiting, P., Hendricks, B., Parr, G., & Jones, E. G., Jr. (2008). The use of expressive techniques in counseling. *Journal of Creativity in Mental Health, 3,* 44–57.

Brand, A. (1987). Writing as counseling. *Elementary School Guidance and Counseling, 21,* 266–275.

Bräuninger, I. (2012a). Dance movement therapy group intervention in stress treatment: A randomized controlled trial (RCT). *Arts in Psychotherapy, 39,* 443–450.

Bräuninger, I. (2012b). The efficacy of dance movement therapy group on improvement of quality of life: A randomized controlled trial. *Arts in Psychotherapy, 39,* 296–303.

Brenner, A. (1997). *Helping children cope with stress.* San Francisco, CA: Jossey-Bass.

Brillantes-Evangelista, G. (2013). An evaluation of visual arts and poetry as therapeutic interventions with abused adolescents. *Arts in Psychotherapy, 40,* 71–84.

Brodsky, W., & Niedorf, H. (1986). "Songs from the heart": New paths to greater maturity. *Arts in Psychotherapy, 13,* 333–341.

Brody, E., Goldspinner, J., Green, K., Leventhal, R., & Porcino, J. (2003). *Spinning tales, weaving hope.* Gabriola Island, British Columbia, Canada: New Society.

Brooke, S. L. (1995). Art therapy: An approach to working with sexual abuse survivors. *Arts in Psychotherapy, 22,* 447–466.

Brooks, D. K., Jr., & Gerstein, L. H. (1990). Counselor credentialing and interprofessional collaboration. *Journal of Counseling & Development, 68,* 477–484.

Brown, A., & Latimir, M. (2001). Between images and thoughts: An art psychotherapy group for sexually abused adolescent girls. In J. Murphy (Ed.), *Art therapy with young survivors of sexual abuse: Lost for words* (pp. 184–200). New York, NY: Brunner-Routledge.

Brown, H. J., Jr. (2000). *Life's little instruction book* (Rev. ed.). Nashville, TN: Thomas Nelson.

Brown, J. M. (2001). Towards a culturally centered music therapy practice. *Canadian Journal of Music Therapy, 8,* 11–24.

Brown, N. W. (2006/2007). The therapeutic use of fairy tales with adults in group therapy. *Journal of Creativity in Mental Health, 2,* 89–96.

Brownell, A. J. (1981). Counseling men through bodywork. *Personnel and Guidance Journal, 60,* 252–255.

Bruneaua, L., & Pehrsson, D.-E. (2014). The process of therapeutic reading: Opening doors for counselor development. *Journal of Creativity in Mental Health, 9,* 346–365.

Bruner, K. S. (2000). Group play with adults. *Arts in Psychotherapy, 27,* 333–338.

Bruscia, K. E. (1987). *Improvisational models of music therapy.* Springfield, IL: Charles C Thomas.

Bruscia, K., Dileo, C., Shultis, C., & Dennery, K. (2009). Expectations of hospitalized cancer and cardiac patients regarding the medical and psycho-therapeutic benefits of music therapy. *Arts in Psychotherapy, 36,* 239–244.

Buck, J. (1948). The H-T-P test. *Journal of Clinical Psychology, 4,* 151–159.

Bunney, J. (1979). Dance therapy: An overview. In P. B. Hallen (Ed.), *The use of the creative arts in therapy* (pp. 24–26). Washington, DC: American Psychiatric Association.

Bunt, L., & Hoskyns, S. (2002). Practicalities and basic principles of music therapy. In L. Bunt & S. Hoskyns (Eds.), *The handbook of music therapy* (pp. 27–53). New York, NY: Brunner-Routledge.

Burke, J. F. (1989). *Contemporary approaches to psychotherapy and counseling.* Pacific Grove, CA: Brooks/Cole.

Burkholder, J. P., Grout, D. J., & Palisca, C. V. (2015). *A history of Western music* (9th ed.). New York, NY: Norton.

Burleigh, L. R., & Beutler, L. E. (1997). A critical analysis of two creative arts therapies. *Arts in Psychotherapy, 23,* 375–381.

Burns, D. D. (1999). *Feeling good: The new mood therapy* (2nd ed.). New York, NY: Avon/HarperCollins.

Burns, S. T. (2008). Utilizing fictional stories when counseling adults. *Journal of Creativity in Mental Health, 3,* 441–454.

Buser, J. K., Buser, T. J., Gladding, S. T., & Wilkerson, J. (2011). The creative counselor: Using the SCAMPER model in counselor training. *Journal of Creativity in Mental Health, 6,* 256–273.

Bushong, D. J. (2002). Good music/bad music: Extant literature on popular music media and antisocial behavior. *Music Therapy Perspectives, 20,* 69–79.

Cadrin, L. (2005/2006). Dying well. *Journal of the Association for Music and Imagery, 10,* 1–25.

Camilleri, V. (2002). Community building through drumming. *Arts in Psychotherapy, 29,* 261–264.

Campbell, C. (1993). Play: The fabric of elementary school counseling programs. *Elementary School Guidance and Counseling, 28,* 10–16.

Campbell, D. (1974). *If you don't know where you're going, you'll probably end up somewhere else.* Niles, IL: Argus Communications.

Campbell, J. (1949). *The hero with a thousand faces.* New York, NY: Pantheon.

Campbell, R. S., & Pennebaker, J. W. (2003). The secret life of pronouns: Flexibility in writing style and physical health. *Psychological Science, 14,* 60–65.

Capacchione, L. (2001). *The creative journal: The art of finding yourself.* Pompton Plains, NJ: New Page Books.

Carkhuff, R. R. (2010). *The art of helping* (9th ed.). Amherst, MA: Human Resources Development.

Carmichael, K. (2000). Using a metaphor in working with disaster survivors. *Journal for Specialists in Group Work, 25,* 7–15.

Carp, C. E. (1998). Clown therapy: The creation of a clown character as a treatment intervention. *Arts in Psychotherapy, 25,* 245–255.

Carroll, M. R. (1970). Silence is the heart's size. *Personnel and Guidance Journal, 48*, 546–551.

Carson, D. K. (1999). The importance of creativity in family therapy: A preliminary consideration. *The Family Journal: Counseling and Therapy for Couples and Families, 7*, 326–334.

Carson, D. K., & Becker, K. W. (2003). *Creativity in mental health practice.* New York, NY: Haworth.

Carter, E. A., & Orfanidis, M. M. (1976). Family therapy with one person and the family therapist's own family. In P. J. Guerin Jr. (Ed.), *Family therapy* (pp. 193–219). New York, NY: Gardner.

Cassity, M. (1981). The influence of a socially valued skill on peer acceptance in a music therapy group. *Journal of Music Therapy, 18*, 148–154.

Casson, J. (1996). Archetypal splitting: Drama, therapy, and psychodrama. *Arts in Psychotherapy, 23*, 307–309.

Castenada, C. (1972). *Journey to Ixtlan: The lessons of Don Juan.* New York, NY: Simon & Schuster.

Cavanagh, M. E. (1982). *The counseling experience.* Pacific Grove, CA: Brooks/Cole.

Chace, M. (1967, November). Music in dance therapy. *Music Journal, 25,* 25, 27.

Chaiklin, S., & Wengrower, H. (Eds.). (2016). *The art and science of dance/movement therapy: Life is dance* (2nd ed.). New York, NY: Routledge.

Chalquist, C. (2009). A look at the ecotherapy research evidence. *Ecopsychology, 1*(2), 64–74.

Chamberlain, D., Heaps, D., & Robert, I. (2008). Bibliotherapy and information prescriptions: A summary of the published evidence-base and recommendations from past and ongoing Books on Prescription projects. *Journal of Psychiatric and Mental Health Nursing, 15*, 24–36.

Chan, D. W. (2001). Reframing student counseling from the multiple-intelligences perspective: Integrating talent development and personal growth. *Asian Journal of Counseling, 8*, 69–86.

Chance, S. (1988). Loss and resolution. *Journal of Poetry Therapy, 2,* 93–98.

Chandler, C. K. (2012). *Animal-assisted therapy in counseling* (2nd ed.). New York, NY: Routledge.

Chandler, C. K., Portrie-Bethke, T. L., Minton, C. A. B., Fernando, D. M., & O'Callaghan, D. M. (2010). Matching animal-assisted therapy techniques and intentions with counseling guiding theories. *Journal of Mental Health Counseling, 32*, 354–374.

Chavis, G. G. (1986). The use of poetry for clients dealing with family issues. *Arts in Psychotherapy, 13*, 121–128.

Chavis, G. G. (1987). *Family: Stories from the interior.* St. Paul, MN: Graywolf.

Cheek, J. R., Bradley, L. J., Parr, G., & Lan, W. (2003). Using music therapy techniques to treat teacher burnout. *Journal of Mental Health Counseling, 25*, 204–217.

Chen, M., Noosbond, J., & Bruce, M. (1998). Therapeutic documents in group counseling: An active change agent. *Journal of Counseling & Development, 76*, 404–411.

Chiefetz, D. (1977). Activities. In B. Zavatsky & R. Padgett (Eds.), *The whole word catalogue 2* (pp. 176–180). New York, NY: Teachers & Writers Collaborative.

Childers, J. H., Jr. (1989). Looking at yourself through loving eyes. *Elementary School Guidance and Counseling, 23,* 204–209.

Childers, J. H., Jr., & Burcky, W. D. (1984). The jogging group: A positive wellness strategy. *AMHCA Journal, 6,* 118–125.

Christenberry, W. (1991). *Of time and places.* Albuquerque: University of New Mexico Press.

Christenbury, L., Beale, A. V., & Patch, S. S. (1996). Interactive bibliocounseling: Recent fiction and nonfiction for adolescents and their counselors. *The School Counselor, 44,* 133–145.

Clarkson, G. (1994). Creative music therapy and facilitated communication: New ways of reaching students with autism. *Preventing School Failure, 38,* 31–33.

Clarkson, P., & Cavicchia, S. (2014). *Gestalt counseling in action* (4th ed.). Thousand Oaks, CA: Sage.

Clatworthy, J., Hinds, J., & Camic, P. M. (2013). Gardening as a mental health intervention: A review. *Mental Health Review Journal, 18*(4), 214–225.

Clifton, L. (1991). *Quilting.* Brockport, NY: BOA Editions.

Cochran, J. L. (1996). Using play and art therapy to help culturally diverse students overcome barriers to school success. *The School Counselor, 43,* 287–298.

Cohen, G. D. (2000). *The creative age.* New York, NY: Avon.

Cohen, G. D. (2005). *The mature mind: The positive power of the aging brain.* New York, NY: Basic Books.

Cohen-Liebman, M. S. (1999). Draw and tell: Drawings within the context of child sexual abuse investigations. *Arts in Psychotherapy, 26,* 185–194.

Cohn, R. (1984). Resolving issues of separation through art. *Arts in Psychotherapy, 11,* 29–35.

Collins, D. (1991, March 12). "Big dance" awaiting deacons. *Winston-Salem Journal,* p. C1.

Collins, K. S., Furman, R., & Langer, C. L. (2006). Poetry therapy as a tool of cognitively based practice. *Arts in Psychotherapy, 33,* 180–187.

Comfort, C. E. (1985). Published pictures as psychotherapeutic tools. *Arts in Psychotherapy, 12,* 245–256.

Conley, D. (1994). *If you believe in you* [Cassette recording]. New Rochelle, NY: Treehouse.

Constantine, L. (1978). Family sculpture and relationship mapping techniques. *Journal of Marriage and Family Counseling, 4,* 13–23.

Constantino, G., Malgady, R., & Rogler, L. (1986). Cuento therapy: A culturally sensitive modality for Puerto Rican children. *Journal of Consulting and Clinical Psychology, 54,* 639–645.

Conyne, R., & Bemak, F. (2004). *Journeys to professional excellence: Lessons from leading counselor educators and practitioners.* Alexandria, VA: American Counseling Association.

Cook, E. L., & Silverman, M. J. (2013). Effects of music therapy on spirituality with patients on a medical oncology/hematology unit: A mixed-methods approach. *Arts in Psychotherapy, 40,* 239–244.

Coren, S., & Walker, J. (1997). *What do dogs know?* New York, NY: Free Press.

Corey, G. (2010). *Creating your professional path: Lessons from my journey.* Alexandria, VA: American Counseling Association.

Corey, G. (2013). *Theory and practice of counseling and psychotherapy* (9th ed.). Pacific Grove, CA: Brooks/Cole.

Cormier, R. (1986). *The chocolate war.* New York, NY: Bantam Books.

Cormier, R. (1991). *After the first death.* New York, NY: Bantam Books.

Cormier, R. (1996). *I am the cheese.* New York, NY: Bantam Books.

Corsini, R. J. (Ed.). (2001). *Handbook of innovative therapy* (2nd ed.). New York, NY: Wiley.

Cortina, M. A., & Fazel, M. (2015). The art room: An evaluation of a targeted school-based group intervention for students with emotional and behavioural difficulties. *Arts in Psychotherapy, 42,* 35–40.

Costello, M., Phelps, L., & Wilczenski, F. (1994). Children and military conflict: Current issues and treatment implications. *The School Counselor, 41,* 220–225.

Costin, C. (2007). *The eating disorder sourcebook* (3rd ed.). New York, NY: McGraw-Hill.

Coughlin, E. K. (1990, May 23). Renewed appreciation of connections between body and mind stimulate researchers to harness healing power of the arts. *Chronicle of Higher Education,* pp. A6, A9.

Coughlin, E. K. (1991, February 13). A Cinderella story: Research on children's books takes on new life as a field of literary study. *Chronicle of Higher Education,* pp. A5–A7.

Cousins, N. (1979). *Anatomy of an illness as perceived by the patient.* New York, NY: Norton.

Coven, A. B., Ellington, D. B., & Van Hull, K. G. (1996). The use of gestalt psychodrama in group counseling. In S. T. Gladding (Ed.), *New developments in group counseling* (pp. 17–19). Greensboro, NC: ERIC/CASS.

Covington, H. (2001). Therapeutic music for patients with psychiatric disorders. *Holistic Nursing Practice, 15,* 59–69.

Cowles, J. (1997). Lessons from *The Little Prince*: Therapeutic relationships with children. *Professional School Counseling, 1,* 57–60.

Cox, A. M., & Albert, D. H. (2003). *The healing heart—Families.* Gabriola Island, British Columbia, Canada: New Society.

Crabbs, M. A., Crabbs, S. K., & Wayman, J. (1986). Making the most of music: An interview with Joe Wayman. *Elementary School Guidance and Counseling, 20,* 240–245.

Craig, D. (n.d.). *Therapeutic Cartoons for Kids series.* Retrieved from http://www.any-book-in-print.com/cartoon_bks/cartoon_bks.htm

Crandell, S. (2007). *Thinking about tomorrow: Reinventing yourself at midlife.* New York, NY: Warner Wellness.

Crenshaw, D. A., & Stewart, A. L. (Eds.). (2014). *Play therapy: A comprehensive guide to theory and practice.* New York, NY: Guilford Press.

Creskey, M. N. (1988). Processing possible selves in possible worlds through poetry. *Journal of Poetry Therapy, 1,* 207–220.

Crocker, J. W., & Wroblewiski, M. (1975). Using recreational games in counseling. *Personnel and Guidance Journal, 53,* 453–458.

Csikszentmihalyi, M. (1996). *Creativity.* New York, NY: HarperCollins.

Cuddy-Casey, M. (1997). A case study using a child-centered play therapy approach to treat enuresis and encopresis. *Elementary School Guidance and Counseling, 31,* 220–225.

Cudney, M. R. (1975). *Self-defeating characters.* Kalamazoo, MI: Life Giving Enterprises.

Cupal, D. D., & Brewer, B. W. (2001). Effects of relaxation and guided imagery on knee strength, reinjury anxiety, and pain following anterior cruciate ligament reconstruction. *Rehabilitation Psychology, 46,* 28–43.

Dallin, B. (1986). Art break: A 2-day expressive therapy program using art and psychodrama to further the termination process. *Arts in Psychotherapy, 13,* 137–142.

Dansby, G. (2003, September 6). *It's a WRAP!* Paper presented at the annual conference of the Southern Association for Counselor Education and Supervision, Chattanooga, TN.

Dattilo, J., & Rusch, F. (2012). Teaching problem solving to promote self-determined leisure engagement. *Therapeutic Recreation Journal, 46,* 91–105.

Davis, J., & Brown, C. (2000). Mental imagery: In what form and for what purpose is it utilized by counselor trainees? *Journal of Mental Imagery, 24,* 73–82.

Davis, K. M. (2008). Teaching a course in creative approaches in counseling with children and adolescents. *Journal of Creativity in Mental Health, 3,* 220–232.

Davis, S. (2003). Development of the profession of horticultural therapy. In S. Simons & M. Straus (Eds.), *Horticulture as therapy: Principles and practice.* Binghamton, NY: Haworth.

Day, N. (1989). *Survivor* [Cassette recording]. Pittsburgh, PA: Author.

DeLucia-Waack, J. L. (2001). *Using music in children of divorce groups: A session-by-session manual for counselors.* Alexandria, VA: American Counseling Association.

DeLucia-Waack, J. L., & Gellman, R. A. (2007). The efficacy of using music in children of divorce groups: Impact on anxiety, depression, and irrational beliefs about divorce. *Group Dynamics: Theory, Research, and Practice, 11,* 272–282.

DeLucia-Waack, J. L., & Gerrity, D. (2001). Effective group work for elementary school-age children whose parents are divorcing. *The Family Journal: Counseling and Therapy for Couples and Families, 9,* 273–284.

de Mille, R. (1967). *Put your mother on the ceiling.* New York, NY: Penguin Books.

de Morais, A. H., Dalécio, M. A. N., Vizmann, S., de Carvalho Bueno, V. L. R., Roecker, S., Salvagioni, D. A. J., & Morais, G. J. E. (2014). Effect on scores of depression and anxiety in psychiatric patients after clay work in a day hospital. *Arts in Psychotherapy, 41*, 205–210.

de Passe, S. (Writer/Producer). (1983). *Motown 25: Yesterday, today, forever* [Motion picture]. United States: MGM Studios.

Dequine, E., & Pearson-Davis, S. (1983). Videotaped improvisational drama with emotionally disturbed adolescents: A pilot study. *Arts in Psychotherapy, 10*, 15–21.

Dermer, S. B., & Hutchings, J. B. (2000). Utilizing movies in family therapy: Applications for individuals, couples, and families. *American Journal of Family Therapy, 28*, 163–180.

de Saint-Exupéry, A. (1943). *The little prince* (R. Howard, Trans.). San Diego, CA: Harcourt.

de Tord, P., & Bräuninger, I. (2015). Grounding: Theoretical application and practice in dance movement therapy. *Arts in Psychotherapy, 43*, 16–22.

Dietz, T. J., Davis, D., & Pennings, J. (2012). Evaluating animal-assisted therapy in group treatment for child sexual abuse. *Journal of Child Sexual Abuse, 21*, 665–683.

Dilts, R., Trompisch, N., & Bergquist, T. M. (2011). Dolphin-assisted therapy for children with special needs: A pilot study. *Journal of Creativity in Mental Health, 6*, 56–68.

Dingfelder, S. F. (2010, April). Dance, dance, evolution. *Monitor on Psychology*, 40–45.

Dingle, G. A., Kelly, P. J., Flynn, L. M., & Baker, F. A. (2015). The influence of music on emotions and cravings in clients in addiction treatment: A study of two clinical samples. *Arts in Psychotherapy, 45*, 18–25.

Dittmann, M. (2003, July/August). Digging beneath the surface. *Monitor on Psychology*, p. 76.

Dobson, R. L., Bray, M. A., Kehle, T., Theodore, L. A., & Peck, H. L. (2005). Relaxation and guided imagery as an intervention for children with asthma: A replication. *Psychology in the Schools, 42*, 707–720.

Dogan, T. (2010). The effects of psychodrama on young adult's attachment styles. *Arts in Psychotherapy, 37*, 112–119.

Doherty, J. H. (2009). *A calendar year of horticultural therapy*. Boynton Beach, FL: Lilyflower Publishing.

Dollarhide, C. T. (2003, July/August). Cinematherapy: Making media work for you. *The School Counselor, 42*(6), 16–17.

Dosamantes-Beaudry, I. (1999). Divergent cultural self-construals: Implications for the practice of dance/movement therapy. *Arts in Psychotherapy, 26*, 225–231.

Dosamantes-Beaudry, I. (2001). A psychoanalytically informed application of dance/movement therapy. In D. J. Wiener (Ed.), *Beyond talk therapy* (pp. 245–262). Washington, DC: American Psychological Association.

Draper, K., Ritter, K., & Willingham, E. (2003). Sand tray group counseling with adolescents. *Journal for Specialists in Group Work, 28*, 244–260.

Dreyer, S. S. (1992). *The best of bookfinder: A guide to children's literature about interests and concerns of youth aged 2–18.* Circle Pines, MN: American Guidance Service.

Dr. Seuss. (1976). *Yertle the turtle and other stories.* New York, NY: Random House. (Original work published 1950)

Drummond, R. J., Sheperis, C., & Jones, K. D. (2016). *Appraisal procedures for counselors and helping professionals* (8th ed.). Upper Saddle River, NJ: Pearson.

Dryden, W., Mearns, D., & Thorne, B. (2000). Counselling in the United Kingdom: Past, present, and future. *British Journal of Guidance and Counselling, 28,* 467–483.

Duffey, T. (2015, June 18). *Creativity in counseling: Fostering effective and resilient counseling practice collaboratively.* Presentation made at the American Counseling Association/Asia Pacific Counseling Conference.

Duffey, T., Lumadue, C., & Woods, S. (2001). A musical chronology and the emerging life song. *The Family Journal: Counseling and Therapy for Couples and Families, 9,* 398–406.

Duffey, T., Somody, C., & Clifford, S. (2006/2007). Conversations with my father: Adapting a musical chronology and the emerging life song with older adults. *Journal of Creativity in Mental Health, 2,* 45–63.

Dufrene, P. M., & Coleman, V. D. (1994). Art and healing for Native American Indians. *Journal of Multicultural Counseling and Development, 22,* 145–152.

Duggan, D. (1981). Dance therapy. In R. J. Corsini (Ed.), *Handbook of innovative psychotherapies* (pp. 229–240). New York, NY: Wiley.

Duncan, W. J. (1985). The superiority theory of humor at work: Joking relationships as indicators of formal and informal status patterns in small, task-oriented groups. *Small Group Behavior, 16,* 556–564.

Dunne, P. B. (1988). Drama therapy techniques in one-to-one treatment with disturbed children and adolescents. *Arts in Psychotherapy, 15,* 139–149.

Eberle, R. F. (1971). *SCAMPER: Games for imagination development.* Buffalo, NY: DOK.

Eckhardt, K. J., & Dinsmore, J. A. (2012). Mindful music listening as a potential treatment for depression. *Journal of Creativity in Mental Health, 7,* 175–186.

Eckstein, D., Junkins, E., & McBrien, R. (2003). Ha, ha, ha: Improving couple and family healthy humor. *The Family Journal: Counseling and Therapy for Couples and Families, 11,* 301–305.

Edwards, D. (1999). *How to handle a hard-to-handle kid.* Minneapolis, MN: Free Spirit Press.

Edwards, D., & Mullis, F. (2001). Creating a sense of belonging to build safe schools. *Journal of Individual Psychology, 57,* 196–203.

Eisenstein-Naveh, A. R. (2001). Therapy: The use of task, imagery, and symbolism to connect the inner and outer worlds. *The Family Journal: Counseling and Therapy for Couples and Families, 9,* 314–324.

Elligan, D. (2004). *Rap therapy: A practical guide for communicating with youth and young adults through rap music.* New York, NY: Kensington.

Ellis, A. (1977). Fun as psychotherapy. In A. Ellis & R. Grieger (Eds.), *Handbook of rational-emotive therapy* (pp. 262–270). New York, NY: Springer.

Ellis, A. (1977–1993). *A garland of rational songs.* New York, NY: Albert Ellis Institute.

Ellis, A. (1981). The use of rational humorous songs in psychotherapy. *Voices, 16,* 29–36.

Ellis, A. (1986a). Discomfort anxiety: A new cognitive behavioral construct. In A. Ellis & R. Grieger (Eds.), *Handbook of rational-emotive therapy* (Vol. 2, pp. 105–120). New York, NY: Springer.

Ellis, A. (1986b). Rational-emotive therapy and cognitive behavior therapy: Similarities and differences. In A. Ellis & R. Grieger (Eds.), *Handbook of rational-emotive therapy* (Vol. 2, pp. 31–45). New York, NY: Springer.

Ellis, A. (1988). *How to stubbornly refuse to make yourself miserable about anything—Yes, anything!* Secaucus, NJ: Lyle Stuart.

Ellis, A., & Dryden, W. (1997). *The practice of rational emotive behavior therapy* (2nd ed.). New York, NY: Springer.

Emunah, R. (1985). Drama therapy and adolescent resistance. *Arts in Psychotherapy, 12,* 71–80.

Emunah, R. (1989). Dramatic enactment in the training of drama therapists. *Arts in Psychotherapy, 16,* 29–36.

Emunah, R. (1990). Expression and expansion in adolescence: The significance of creative arts therapy. *Arts in Psychotherapy, 17,* 101–107.

Emunah, R. (2001). Drama therapy in action. In D. J. Wiener (Ed.), *Beyond talk therapy* (pp. 99–123). Washington, DC: American Psychological Association.

Enns, C. Z. (2001). Some reflections on imagery and psychotherapy implications. *Journal of Counseling Psychology, 48,* 136–139.

Enns, C. Z., & Kasai, M. (2003). Hakoniwa: Japanese sand play therapy. *The Counseling Psychologist, 31,* 93–112.

Erford, B. (2000). *Counseling innovation games: Conflict resolution, studying skillfully, social skills, good grief, understanding anger, solving problems, self-concept, and changing families.* Shrewsbury, PA: Author.

Erikson, E. H. (1963). *Childhood and society* (2nd ed.). New York, NY: Norton.

Erikson, E. H. (1968). *Identity: Youth and crisis.* New York, NY: Norton.

Erikson, E. H. (1975). *Life history and the historical moment.* New York, NY: Norton.

Esfandiari, N., & Mansouri, S. (2014). The effect of listening to light and heavy music on reducing the symptoms of depression among female students. *Arts in Psychotherapy, 41,* 211–213.

Esman, A. H. (1988). Art and psychopathology: The message of outsider art. *American Journal of Art Therapy, 27,* 13–21.

Evans, S. (2012). Using computer technology in expressive arts therapy practice: A proposal for increased use. *Journal of Creativity in Mental Health, 7,* 49–63.

Fagen, T. (1982). Music therapy in the treatment of anxiety and fear in terminal pediatric patients. *Music Therapy, 2,* 13–23.

Fair, C. D., Connor, L., Albright, J., Wise, E., & Jones, K. (2012). "I'm positive, I have something to say": Assessing the impact of a creative writing group for adolescents living with HIV. *Arts in Psychotherapy, 39,* 383–389.

Farr, M. (1997). The role of dance/movement therapy in treating at-risk African American adolescents. *Arts in Psychotherapy, 24,* 183–191.

Feder, E., & Feder, B. (1981). *The expressive arts therapies.* Upper Saddle River, NJ: Prentice-Hall.

Feldman, N. (2008). Assisting children in the creation of new life performances: Expanding possibilities for social and emotional development. *Child and Adolescent Social Work Journal, 25,* 85–97.

Figley, C. R. (1986). *Trauma and its wake.* New York, NY: Brunner/Mazel.

Figley, C. R., & Kiser, L. (2013). *Helping traumatized families* (2nd ed.). New York, NY: Routledge.

Fine, A. H. (Ed.). (2010). *Handbook on animal-assisted therapy: Theoretical foundations and guidelines for practice* (3rd ed.). San Diego, CA: Academic Press.

Fine, G. A. (1977). Humor in situ: The role of humor in small group culture. In A. J. Chapman & H. C. Foot (Eds.), *It's a funny thing, humor* (pp. 315–318). New York, NY: Pergamon.

Finn, C. A. (2003). Helping students cope with loss: Incorporating art into group counseling. *Journal for Specialists in Group Work, 28,* 155–165.

Fisher, P. P. (1989). *Creative movement for older adults.* New York, NY: Human Sciences.

Flahive, M., & Ray, D. (2007). Effect of group sandtray therapy with pre-adolescents in a school setting. *Journal for Specialists in Group Work, 32,* 362–382.

Flake, C. L. (1988). A systems approach: The foundation of a quality environment. In M. H. Brown (Ed.), *Quality environments for young children.* Champaign, IL: Stipes.

Flanigen, D. (Director). (2002). Concrete angel [Music video]. In Martina McBride (Performer), *Greatest hits.* Nashville, TN: RCA Records.

Fleming, W. (1994). *Arts and ideas* (9th ed.). New York, NY: Harcourt Brace.

Fleshman, B., & Fryear, J. L. (1981). *The arts in therapy.* Chicago, IL: Nelson-Hall.

Fletcher, T. B., & Hinkle, J. S. (2002). Adventure based counseling: An innovation in counseling. *Journal of Counseling & Development, 80,* 277–285.

Flom, B., Johnson, C., Hubbart, J., & Reidt, D. (2011). The natural school counselor: Using nature to promote mental health in school. *Journal of Creativity in Mental Health, 6,* 118–131.

Foley, V. D. (1989). Family therapy. In R. J. Corsini & D. Wedding (Eds.), *Current psychotherapies* (4th ed., pp. 455–500). Itasca, IL: Peacock.

Forrester, A. M. (2000). Role-playing and dramatic improvisation as an assessment tool. *Arts in Psychotherapy, 27,* 235–240.

France, M. H., Cadieux, J., & Allen, E. (1995). Letter therapy: A model for enhancing counseling intervention. *Journal of Counseling & Development, 73,* 317–318.

Frank, A. (2003). *The diary of Anne Frank: The revised critical edition*. New York, NY: Doubleday. (Original work published 1947)

Frank, J. D. (1978). *Effective ingredients of successful psychotherapy*. New York, NY: Brunner/Mazel.

Frankenfelder, M. T. (1988). For later days—A fulfillment. *Arts in Psychotherapy, 15*, 251–254.

Frankl, V. E. (1985). Paradoxical intention. In G. R. Weeks (Ed.), *Promoting change through paradoxical therapy* (pp. 99–110). Homewood, IL: Dow Jones-Irwin.

Franklin, E. (2006). *Inner focus, outer strength: Using imagery and exercise for health, strength, and beauty*. Hightstown, NJ: Elysian Editions/ Princeton Book.

Franzke, E. (1989). *Fairy tales in psychotherapy: The creative use of old and new tales*. New York, NY: Hogrefe & Huber.

Fredenburg, H. A., & Silverman, M. J. (2014). Effects of cognitive-behavioral music therapy on fatigue in patients in a blood and marrow transplantation unit: A mixed-method pilot study. *Arts in Psychotherapy, 41*, 433–444.

Freud, S. (1953). The interpretation of dreams. In J. Strachey (Ed. & Trans.), *The standard edition of the complete psychological works of Sigmund Freud* (Vol. 4, pp. 1–310). London, England: Hogarth Press. (Original work published 1900)

Freud, S. (1961). The ego and the id. In J. Strachey (Ed. & Trans.), *The standard edition of the complete psychological works of Sigmund Freud* (Vol. 19, pp. 3–66). London, England: Hogarth Press. (Original work published 1923)

Friedberg, R. D. (1996). Cognitive–behavioral games and workbooks: Tips for school counselors. *Elementary School Guidance and Counseling, 31*, 11–19.

Friedman, E. H. (1984, January/February). The play's the thing. *Family Therapy Networker*, 24–29.

Fry, W., Jr. (1991, April). *Laughter for the health of it: Search for humor research*. Paper presented at the annual conference of the Humor Project, Saratoga Springs, NY.

Furman, L. (1990). Video therapy: An alternative for the treatment of adolescents. *Arts in Psychotherapy, 17*, 165–169.

Gale, A. U., & Austin, B. D. (2003). Professionalism's challenges to professional counselors' collective identity. *Journal of Counseling & Development, 81*, 3–10.

Gallo-Lopez, L., & Schaefer, C. E. (Eds.). (2005). *Play therapy with adolescents*. Lanham, MD: Jason Aronson.

Gardner, J. (1993). Runaway with words: Teaching poetry to at-risk teens. *Journal of Poetry Therapy, 6*, 213–227.

Gardner, R. A. (1971). *Therapeutic communication with children: The mutual storytelling technique in child psychotherapy*. New York, NY: Jason Aronson.

Gardner, R. A. (1983). The Talking, Feeling, and Doing Game. In C. E. Schaefer & K. J. O'Connor (Eds.), *Handbook of play therapy* (pp. 259–273). New York, NY: Wiley.

Garland, J., & Garland, C. (2001). *Life review in health and social care.* Philadelphia, PA: Brunner Routledge.

Gass, M. A., Gillis, H. L., & Russell, K. C. (2012). *Adventure therapy: Theory, research, and practice.* New York, NY: Routledge.

Gawain, S. (1978). *Creative visualization.* San Rafael, CA: New World Library.

Geddes, M., & Medway, J. (1977). The symbolic drawing of family life space. *Family Process, 16,* 219–228.

Geller, S. K., Kwaplen, A., Phillips, E. K., Wiggers, T. T., Jordan, K., & Marcellino, I. (1986). "Artbreak": Innovation in student life programming. *Journal of College Student Personnel, 27,* 229–233.

Gerber, J. (1994). The use of art therapy in juvenile sex offender specific treatment. *Arts in Psychotherapy, 21,* 367–374.

Gerler, E. R., Jr. (1982). *Counseling the young learner.* Upper Saddle River, NJ: Prentice-Hall.

Gerrard, L. L. (2014). Women and their woods: Reflections on adolescence and wilderness therapy experiences. *Dissertation Abstracts International: Section BE: The Sciences and Engineering, 75*(6-B)(E).

Gfeller, K. (1988). Musical components and styles preferred by young adults for aerobic fitness activities. *Journal of Music Therapy, 25,* 28–43.

Gfeller, K. E. (2002a). Music as communication. In R. F. Unkefer & M. H. Thaut (Eds.), *Music therapy in the treatment of adults with mental disorders: Theoretical bases and clinical interventions* (2nd ed., pp. 42–59). St. Louis, MO: MMB Music.

Gfeller, K. E. (2002b). Music as therapeutic agent: Historical and sociocultural perspectives. In R. F. Unkefer & M. H. Thaut (Eds.), *Music therapy in the treatment of adults with mental disorders: Theoretical bases and clinical interventions* (2nd ed., pp. 60–67). St. Louis, MO: MMB Music.

Gibson, R. L., & Mitchell, M. H. (2008). *Introduction to counseling and guidance* (7th ed.) Upper Saddle River, NJ: Pearson.

Gilbert, J. P. (1977). Music therapy perspectives on death and dying. *Journal of Music Therapy, 14,* 165–171.

Gilligan, C. (1982). *In a different voice: Psychological theory and women's development.* Cambridge, MA: Harvard University Press.

Ginicola, M., Smith, C., & Trzaska, J. (2012). Counseling through images: Using photography to guide the counseling process and achieve treatment goals. *Journal of Creativity in Mental Health, 7,* 310–329.

Gladding, S. T. (1974). Without applause. *Personnel and Guidance Journal, 52,* 586.

Gladding, S. T. (1975). Twilight. *Personnel and Guidance Journal, 53,* 230. (Rev. 2003)

Gladding, S. T. (1985). Counseling and the creative arts. *Counseling and Human Development, 18,* 1–12.

Gladding, S. T. (1988, April). *Counseling as an art: The use of the expressive arts in counseling.* Paper presented at the conference of the American Association for Counseling and Development, Chicago, IL.

Gladding, S. T. (1989). *Eli.* Unpublished manuscript.

Gladding, S. T. (1990a). *In lines through time.* Unpublished manuscript. (Rev. 2003)

Gladding, S. T. (1990b). Journey. *Journal of Humanistic Education and Development, 28,* 142.

Gladding, S. T. (1991a). *Dance street.* Unpublished manuscript. (Rev. 2003)

Gladding, S. T. (1991b). *An image of Timothy.* Unpublished manuscript. (Rev. 2010)

Gladding, S. T. (1991c). *In acceptance.* Unpublished manuscript. (Rev. 2010)

Gladding, S. T. (1991d). *Harmony.* Unpublished manuscript. (Rev. 2003)

Gladding, S. T. (1991e). *The launching.* Unpublished manuscript. (Rev. 2003)

Gladding, S. T. (1991f, April). *The well practitioner.* Paper presented at the annual conference of the American Counseling Association, Reno, NV.

Gladding, S. T. (1993). The therapeutic use of play in counseling: An overview. *Journal of Humanistic Counseling and Development, 31,* 106–115.

Gladding, S. T. (1995). Creativity in counseling. *Counseling and Human Development, 28,* 1–12.

Gladding, S. T. (2008). The impact of creativity in counseling. *Journal of Creativity in Mental Health, 3,* 97–104.

Gladding, S. T. (2009). *Becoming a counselor: The light, the bright, and the serious* (2nd ed.). Alexandria, VA: American Counseling Association.

Gladding, S. T. (2010). *Timeless grace.* Unpublished manuscript.

Gladding, S. T. (2012). Art in counseling. In C. A. Malchiodi (Ed.), *Handbook of art therapy* (2nd ed., pp. 263–274). New York, NY: Guilford Press.

Gladding, S. T. (2013). *Counseling: A comprehensive profession* (7th ed.). Upper Saddle River, NJ: Pearson.

Gladding, S. T. (2014, September 22). *Some fun and funny facts about wellness: How humor adds to your health.* Keynote address at the Louisiana Counseling Association Conference, New Orleans, LA.

Gladding, S. T. (2015a). *Family therapy: History, theory, and practice* (6th ed.). Upper Saddle River, NJ: Pearson.

Gladding, S. T. (2015b, March 13). *Humor in counseling: Maximizing a therapeutic tool.* Paper presented at American Counseling Association Conference, Orlando, FL.

Gladding, S. T. (2016). *Groups: A counseling specialty* (6th ed.). Upper Saddle River, NJ: Pearson.

Gladding, S. T., Bentley, P., & Flannery, B. (2003, February). *The impact of lyrics on your life.* Paper presented at the conference of the North Carolina Counseling Association, Charlotte, NC.

Gladding, S. T., & Gladding, C. T. (1991). The ABCs of bibliotherapy. *The School Counselor, 39,* 7–13.

Gladding, S. T., & Heape, S. (1987). Popular music as a poetic metaphor in family therapy. *American Journal of Social Psychiatry, 7,* 109–111.

Gladding, S. T., & Henderson, D. A. (2000). Creativity and family counseling: The SCAMPER model as a template for promoting creative processes. *The Family Journal: Counseling and Therapy for Couples and Families, 8,* 245–249.

Gladding, S. T., & Kezar, E. F. (1978). Humor in teaching family life education: Advantages of use and guidelines for preventing abuse. *Family Life Educator, 9,* 10–11.

Gladding, S. T., Newsome, D., Henderson, D. A., & Binkley, E. (2008). The lyrics of hurting and healing: Finding words that are revealing. *Journal of Creativity in Mental Health, 3,* 212–219.

Gladding, S. T., & Wallace, M. J. D. (2010). The potency and power of counseling stories. *Journal of Creativity in Mental Health, 5,* 15–24.

Glover, N. M. (1999). Play therapy and art therapy for substance abuse clients who have a history of incest victimization. *Journal of Substance Abuse Treatment, 16,* 381–387.

Goessling, K., & Doyle, C. (2009). Thru the Lenz: Participatory action research, photography, and creative process in an urban high school. *Journal of Creativity in Mental Health, 4,* 343–365.

Gold, J. (1988). The value of fiction as therapeutic recreation and developmental mediator: A theoretical framework. *Journal of Poetry Therapy, 1,* 135–148.

Golden, L. (2001). Creative writing as therapy. *The Family Journal: Counseling and Therapy for Couples and Families, 9,* 201–202.

Golden, W. L. (1986). Rational-emotive hypnotherapy: Principles and techniques. In A. Ellis & R. Grieger (Eds.), *Handbook of rational-emotive therapy* (Vol. 2, pp. 281–291). New York, NY: Springer.

Goldin, E., & Bordan, T. (1999). The use of humor in counseling: The laughing cure. *Journal of Counseling & Development, 77,* 405–410.

Goldin, E., Bordan, T., Araoz, D. L., Gladding, S. T., Kaplan, D., Krumboltz, J., & Lararus, A. (2006). Humor in counseling: Leaders perspective. *Journal of Counseling & Development, 84,* 397–405.

Goldstein, S. L. (1990). A songwriting assessment for hopelessness in depressed adolescents: A review of the literature and a pilot study. *Arts in Psychotherapy, 17,* 117–124.

Gonzalez, M. T., Hartig, T., Patil, G. G., Martinsen, E. W., & Kirkevold, M. (2011). A prospective study of group cohesiveness in therapeutic horticulture for clinical depression. *International Journal of Mental Health Nursing, 20,* 119–129.

Gonzalez, T., & Hayes, B. G. (2009). Rap music in school counseling based on Don Elligan's rap therapy. *Journal of Creativity in Mental Health, 4,* 161–172.

Good, D. A., & Rosal, M. L. (1999, March). *Interweaving art therapy into group work.* Paper presented at the annual conference of the American Counseling Association, San Diego, CA.

Goodhill, S. W. (1987). Dance and movement therapy with abused children. *Arts in Psychotherapy, 14,* 59–68.

Gordon, D. (1978). *Therapeutic metaphors.* Cupertino, CA: META.

Gorelick, K. (1987a). Greek tragedy and ancient healing: Poems as theater and Asclepian temple in miniature. *Journal of Poetry Therapy, 1,* 38–43.

Gorelick, K. (1987b). Poetry therapy as therapeutic ritual in treating traumas from the past. *American Journal of Social Psychiatry, 7,* 93–95.

Gorelick, K., & Lerner, A. (1997, May). *Choice or chance: Choosing and using literature.* Paper presented at the annual conference of the National Association for Poetry Therapy, Cleveland, OH.

Gosciewski, F. W. (1975). Photo counseling. *Personnel and Guidance Journal, 53,* 600–604.

Gottman, J. (1995). *Why marriages succeed or fail: And how you can make yours last.* New York, NY: Simon & Schuster.

Goud, N. (2010). *Self-exploration.* Indianapolis, IN: Dutch Gold Press.

Gramaglia, C., Abbate-Daga, G., Amianto, F., Brustolin, A., Campisi, S., De-Bacco, C., & Fassino, S. (2011). Cinematherapy in the day hospital treatment of patients with eating disorders. Case study and clinical considerations. *Arts in Psychotherapy, 38,* 261–266.

Grason, S. (2005). *Journalution: Journaling to awaken your inner voice, heal your life, and manifest your dreams.* Novato, CA: New World Library.

Greenberg, I. A. (1974). Moreno: Psychodrama and the group process. In I. A. Greenberg (Ed.), *Psychodrama: Theory and therapy* (pp. 11–28). New York, NY: Behavioral.

Greenstein, M., & Holland, J. (2015). *Lighter as we go: Virtues, character strengths, and aging.* New York, NY: Oxford University Press.

Grigsby, J. P. (1987). The use of imagery in the treatment of posttraumatic stress disorder. *Journal of Nervous and Mental Disease, 175,* 55–59.

Grothe, M. (2008). *I never met a metaphor I didn't like.* New York, NY: HarperCollins.

Guerin, P. J., Jr. (1976). The use of the arts in family therapy: I never sang for my father. In P. J. Guerin Jr. (Ed.), *Family therapy: Theory and practice* (pp. 480–500). New York, NY: Gardner.

Guerney, B. (1982). Filial therapy: Description and rationale. In G. L. Landreth (Ed.), *Play therapy* (pp. 342–353). Springfield, IL: Charles C Thomas.

Guerney, L., & Guerney, B. (1989). Child relationship enhancement: Family therapy and parent education. *Person Centered Review, 4,* 344–357.

Guli, L. A., Semrud-Clikeman, M., Lerner, M. D., & Britton, N. (2013). Social Competence Intervention Program (SCIP): A pilot study of a creative drama program for youth with social difficulties. *Arts in Psychotherapy, 40,* 37–44.

Gunnison, H., & Renick, T. E. (1985). Using fantasy-imagery and relaxation techniques. *Journal of Counseling & Development, 64,* 79–80.

Gunsberg, A. (1988). Improvised musical play: A strategy for fostering social play between developmentally delayed and nondelayed preschool children. *Journal of Music Therapy, 25,* 178–191.

Gussak, D. (2009). Comparing the effectiveness of art therapy on depression and locus of control of male and female inmates. *Arts in Psychotherapy, 36,* 202–207.

Gutiérrez, E. O. F., & Camarena, V. A. T. (2015). Music therapy in generalized anxiety disorder. *Arts in Psychotherapy, 44,* 19–24.

Haboush, A., Floyd, M., Caron, J., LaSota, M., & Alvarez, K. (2006). Ballroom dance lessons for geriatric depression: An exploratory study. *Arts in Psychotherapy, 33,* 89–97.

Hadley, R. T., Hadley, W. H., Dickens, V., & Jordon, E. G. (2001). Music therapy: A treatment modality for special-needs populations. *International Journal for the Advancement of Counselling, 23,* 215–221.

Hageman, M. B., & Gladding, S. T. (1983). The art of career exploration: Occupational sex-role stereotyping among elementary school children. *Elementary School Guidance and Counseling, 17,* 280–287.

Hagood, M. M. (2000). *The use of art in counseling child and adult survivors of sexual abuse.* Philadelphia, PA: Jessica Kingsley.

Haig, R. A. (1986). Therapeutic uses of humor. *American Journal of Psychotherapy, 40,* 543–553.

Haight, B. K., & Haight, B. S. (2008). *The handbook of structured life review.* Baltimore, MD: Health Professional Press.

Hakvoort, L., & Bogaerts, S. (2013). Theoretical foundations and workable assumptions for cognitive behavioral music therapy in forensic psychiatry. *Arts in Psychotherapy, 40,* 192–200.

Haley, J. (1978). *Leaving home.* New York, NY: McGraw-Hill.

Hall, E., Hall, C., Stradling, P., & Young, D. (2006). *Guided imagery: Creative interventions in counseling and psychotherapy.* Thousand Oaks, CA: Sage.

Haller, H. L. (2006). The framework. In H. L. Haller & C. L. Kramer (Eds.), *Horticultural therapy methods* (p. 2). Binghamton, NY: Haworth.

Hammer, T. R. (2009). Controlling images, media, and women's development: A review of the literature. *Journal of Creativity in Mental Health, 4,* 202–216.

Hammond, L. C., & Gantt, L. (1998). Using art in counseling: Ethical considerations. *Journal of Counseling & Development, 76,* 271–276.

Hannaford, M. J., & Hannaford, J. (1979). *Counselor under construction.* Atlanta, GA: Author.

Hanser, S. B. (1988). Controversy in music listening/stress reduction research. *Arts in Psychotherapy, 15,* 211–217.

Harjo, J. (1983). *She had some horses.* New York, NY: Thunder's Mouth.

Harper, B. L. (1985). Say it, review it, enhance it with a song. *Elementary School Guidance and Counseling, 19,* 218–221.

Harter, S. L. (2007). Visual art making for therapist growth and self-care. *Journal of Constructivist Psychology, 20,* 167–182.

Hartford, G. (2011). Practical implications for the development of applied metaphor in adventure therapy. *Journal of Adventure Education & Outdoor Learning, 11,* 145–160.

Hartung, P. J., & Subich, L. M. (2010). *Developing self in work and career: Concepts, cases, and contexts.* Washington, DC: American Psychological Association.

Hays, D. G., Forman, J., & Sikes, A. (2009). Using artwork and photography to explore adolescent females' perceptions of dating relationships. *Journal of Creativity in Mental Health, 4,* 295–307.

Heimes, S. (2011). State of poetry therapy research (review). *Arts in Psychotherapy, 38,* 1–8.

Heller, G. N. (1985, November). *Ideas, initiatives, and implementations: Music therapy in America, 1789–1848.* Paper presented at the joint conference of the National Coalition of Arts Therapy Associations, New York, NY.

Heller, P. O. (2009). *Word arts collage: A poetry therapy memoir.* Columbus, OH: Pudding House.

Henderson, D. A., & Gladding, S. T. (1998). The creative arts in counseling: A multicultural perspective. *Arts in Psychotherapy, 25,* 183–187.

Henderson, D. A., & Thompson, C. L. (2016). *Counseling children* (8th ed.). Pacific Grove, CA: Brooks/Cole.

Henderson, P., Rosen, D., & Mascaro, N. (2007). Empirical study on the healing nature of mandalas. *Psychology of Aesthetics, Creativity, and the Arts, 1,* 148–154.

Hendricks, K. T. (1982). Transpersonal movement therapy. In G. Hendricks & B. Weinhold (Eds.), *Transpersonal approaches to counseling and psychotherapy* (pp. 165–187). Denver, CO: Love.

Hendrix, H. (2008). *Getting the love you want: A guide for couples* (20th anniversary ed.). New York, NY: Holt.

Heninger, O. E. (1987). Poetry generated by stillbirth and live birth: Transgenerational sharing of grief and joy. *Journal of Poetry Therapy, 1,* 14–22.

Heppner, M. J., O'Brien, K. M., Hinkelman, J. M., & Humphrey, C. A. (1994). Shifting the paradigm: The use of creativity in career counseling. *Journal of Career Development, 21,* 77–86.

Herring, R. D., & Meggert, S. S. (1994). The use of humor as a counselor strategy with Native American Indian children. *Elementary School Guidance and Counseling, 28,* 67–78.

Herrmann, U. (1995). A Trojan horse of clay: Art therapy in a residential school for the blind. *Arts in Psychotherapy, 22,* 229–234.

Hesley, J. W., & Hesley, J. G. (2001). *Rent two films and let's talk in the morning: Using popular movies in psychotherapy* (2nd ed.). New York, NY: Wiley.

Hill, L. (1992). Fairy tales: Visions for problem resolution for eating disorders. *Journal of Counseling & Development, 70,* 584–587.

Hill, N. R. (2007). Wilderness therapy as a treatment modality for at-risk youth: A primer for mental health counselors. *Journal of Mental Health Counseling, 29*(4), 338–349.

Hiltebrand, E. (1999). Coping with cancer through image manipulation. In C. Malchiodi (Ed.), *Medical art therapy with adults* (pp. 113–135). Philadelphia, PA: Jessica Kingsley.

Hoag, M. J., Massey, K. E., Roberts, S. D., & Logan, P. (2013). Efficacy of wilderness therapy for young adults: A first look. *Residential Treatment for Children & Youth, 30,* 294–305.

Hodas, G. R. (1991). Using original music to explore gender and sexuality with adolescents. *Journal of Poetry Therapy, 4,* 205–220.

Hodas, G. (1993). *Stretch yourself? Songs for coping* [Cassette recording with user's guide]. Philadelphia, PA: Second Chance.

Hodas, G. R. (1994). Reversing narratives of failure through music and verse in therapy. *The Family Journal: Counseling and Therapy for Couples and Families, 2,* 199–207.

Hodges, D. (1993). For every season . . . art and poetry therapy with terminally ill patients. *Journal of Poetry Therapy, 7,* 21–43.

Hoffman, L. W. (1983). Imagery and metaphors in couple therapy. *Family Therapy, 10,* 141–156.

Hoffman, R. M. (2008). Letter writing: A tool for counselor educators. *Journal of Creativity in Mental Health, 3,* 345–356.

Holland, J. L. (1985). *The self-directed search: A guide to educational and vocational planning.* Odessa, FL: Psychological Assessment Resources.

Horwitz, E. B., Kowalski, J., & Anderberg, U. M. (2010). Theater for, by and with fibromyalgia patients: Evaluation of emotional expression using video interpretation. *Arts in Psychotherapy, 37,* 13–19.

Hoskins, M. (1985, April). *Therapeutic fairy tales.* Paper presented at the annual conference of the National Association of Poetry Therapy, Chicago, IL.

Howard, J. (1990). *Margaret Mead: A life.* New York, NY: Random House.

Howe, J. W., Burgess, A. W., & McCormack, A. (1987). Adolescent runaways and their drawings. *Arts in Psychotherapy, 14,* 35–40.

Howlett, D. (2003, March 4). It hurts not to laugh. *USA Today,* p. 9D.

Hudson, P. E. (2002, Fall). Best practices: Thinking outside the book with children and adolescents. *Interaction, 6*(1), 2–3.

Hug, E. (1997). Current trends in psychodrama: Eclectic and analytic dimensions. *Arts in Psychotherapy, 24,* 31–35.

Hughes, J. N. (1988). Interviewing children. In J. M. Dillard & R. R. Reilly (Eds.), *Strategic interviewing* (pp. 90–113). Columbus, OH: Merrill.

Humphrey, S. M. (2005). *Dare to dream! 25 extraordinary lives.* New York, NY: Prometheus Books.

Huss, E., & Sarid, O. (2014). Visually transforming artwork and guided imagery as a way to reduce work related stress: A quantitative pilot study. *Arts in Psychotherapy, 41,* 409–412.

Hynes, A. M., & Hynes-Berry, M. (1986). *Bibliotherapy: The interactive process.* Boulder, CO: Westview.

Ingalls, Z. (1997, February 28). A professor of medicine discovers the healing power of poetry. *Chronicle of Higher Education,* pp. B8, B9.

Ingram, M. A. (2003, June). *A poetic voice for a diverse world.* Keynote address presented at the annual conference of the American School Counselor Association, St. Louis, MO.

Irwin, E. C. (1987). Drama: The play's the thing. *Elementary School Guidance and Counseling, 21,* 276–283.

Irwin, E. C., & Malloy, E. (1975). Family puppet interview. *Family Process, 14,* 179–191.

Ishiyama, F. I., & Westwood, M. J. (1992). Enhancing client-validating communication: Helping discouraged clients in cross-cultural adjustment. *Journal of Multicultural Counseling and Development, 20,* 50–63.

Jaaniste, J., Linnell, S., Ollerton, R. L., & Slewa-Younan, S. (2015). Drama therapy with older people with dementia—Does it improve quality of life? *Arts in Psychotherapy, 43,* 40–48.

Jack, S. J., & Ronan, K. R. (2008). Bibliotherapy: Practice and research. *School Psychology International, 29,* 161–182.

Jackson, S. A. (2001). Using bibliotherapy with clients. *Journal of Individual Psychology, 57,* 289–297.

Jacobi, E. M., & Eisenberg, G. M. (2001/2002). The efficacy of guided imagery and music (GIM) in the treatment of rheumatoid arthritis. *Journal of the Association for Music and Imagery, 18,* 57–74.

Jacobs, E. E. (1992). *Creative counseling techniques: An illustrated guide.* Odessa, FL: Psychological Assessment Resources.

Jacobs, E. E., Schimmel, C. J., Masson, R. L., & Harvill, R. L. (2016). *Group counseling* (5th ed.). Belmont, CA: Thomson Brooks/Cole.

James, M., & Johnson, D. (1996). Drama therapy in the treatment of combat related posttraumatic stress disorder. *Arts in Psychotherapy, 23,* 383–395.

James, M., & Jongeward, D. (1971). *Born to win.* Reading, MA: Addison-Wesley.

James, R. K., & Myer, R. (1987). Puppets: The elementary school counselor's right or left arm. *Elementary School Guidance and Counseling, 21,* 292–299.

Jenkins, C. D., Laux, J. M., Ritchie, M. H., & Tucker-Gail, K. (2014). Animal-assisted therapy and Rogers' core components among middle school students receiving counseling services: A descriptive study. *Journal of Creativity in Mental Health, 9,* 174–187.

Jennings, B., & Vance, D. (2002). The short-term effects of music therapy on different types of agitation in adults with Alzheimer's. *Activities, Adaptation, and Aging, 26,* 27–33.

Johnson, D. R. (1982). Principles and techniques of drama therapy. *Arts in Psychotherapy, 9,* 83–90.

Johnson, D. R. (1986). The developmental method in drama therapy: Group treatment with the elderly. *Arts in Psychotherapy, 13,* 17–33.

Johnson, D. R. (1989). Introduction to the special issue on education and training in the creative arts therapies. *Arts in Psychotherapy, 16,* 1–3.

Johnson, D. R., & Eicher, V. (1990). The use of dramatic activities to facilitate dance therapy with adolescents. *Arts in Psychotherapy, 17,* 157–164.

Johnson, D. R., & Emunah, R. (Eds.). (2009). *Current approaches to drama therapy* (2nd ed.). Springfield, IL: Charles C Thomas.

Johnson, D. W., & Johnson, F. P. (2014). *Joining together* (11th ed.). Upper Saddle River, NJ: Pearson.

Johnson, E. (1981). The role of objective and concrete feedback in self-concept treatment of juvenile delinquents in music therapy. *Journal of Music Therapy, 18,* 137–147.

Johnson, R. G. (2002). High tech play therapy. In C. E. Schaefer & D. Cangelosi (Eds.), *Play therapy techniques* (2nd ed., pp. 365–371). Northvale, NJ: Jason Aronson.

Jordan, K. (2001). Family art therapy: The joint family holiday drawing. *The Family Journal: Counseling and Therapy for Couples and Families, 9,* 52–54.

Jordan, M. (2015). *Nature and therapy.* New York, NY: Routledge.

Joshua, J. M., & DiMenna, D. (2000). *Read two books and let's talk next week.* New York, NY: Wiley.

Jourard, S. M. (1971). *The transparent self* (Rev. ed.). New York, NY: Van Nostrand Reinhold.

Jourard, S. M., & Landsman, T. (1980). *Healthy personality* (4th ed.). New York, NY: Macmillan.

Jung, C. G. (1933). *Modern man in search of a soul.* New York, NY: Harcourt, Brace & World.

Jung, C. G. (1953). The structure of the unconscious (R. F. C. Hull, Trans.). In *The collected works of Carl Jung: Vol. 7. Two essays on analytical psychology* (pp. 263–290). Princeton, NJ: Princeton University Press.

Jung, C. G. (1954). *The collected works of Carl Jung: Vol. 16. The practice of psychotherapy* (R. F. C. Hull, Trans.). Princeton, NJ: Princeton University Press.

Jung, C. G. (1963). *Memories, dreams, reflections* (A. Jaffe, Ed., & R. C. Winston, Trans.). New York, NY: Random House.

Jung, C. G. (1964). *Man and his symbols* (M. L. Franz, Ed.). Garden City, NY: Doubleday.

Jung, C. G. (1968). *The collected works of Carl Jung: Vol. 8. The structure and dynamics of the psyche* (R. F. C. Hull, Trans.). Princeton, NJ: Princeton University Press.

Justice, R. W. (1994). Music therapy interventions for people with eating disorders in an inpatient setting. *Music Therapy, 12,* 104–110.

Kaduson, H. G., & Schaefer, C. E. (Eds.). (2015). *Short-term play therapy for children* (3rd ed.). New York, NY: Guilford Press.

Kahn, B. B. (1999). Art therapy with adolescents: Making it work for school counselors. *Professional School Counseling, 2,* 291–298.

Kaiser, D. H. (1996). Indications of attachment security in a drawing task. *Arts in Psychotherapy, 23,* 333–340.

Kalff, D. M. (1981). *Sand play: A psychotherapeutic approach to the psyche.* Boston, MA: Sigo.

Kalff, D. M., Turner, B. A., & Kalff, M. (2003). *Sandplay: A psychotherapeutic approach to the psyche.* Cloverdale, CA: Temenos Press.

Kalish-Weiss, B. I. (1988). Born blind and visually handicapped infants: Movement psychotherapy and assessment. *Arts in Psychotherapy, 15,* 101–108.

Kaminsky, M. (1974). *What's inside you, it shines out of you.* New York, NY: Horizon.

Kampfe, C. (2003, March). *Parallels between creative dance and creative counseling.* Paper presented at the annual conference of the American Counseling Association, Anaheim, CA.

Kampfe, C. M. (2015). *Counseling older people: Opportunities and challenges.* Alexandria, VA: American Counseling Association.

Kanchier, C. (1997, February). Using intuition in career decision making. *Counseling Today,* pp. 14, 16.

Kane, T. R., Suls, J., & Tedeschi, J. T. (1977). Humor as a tool of social interaction. In A. J. Chapman & M. C. Foot (Eds.), *It's a funny thing, humor* (pp. 13–16). New York, NY: Pergamon.

Kaplan, D., & Gladding, S. T. (2011). A vision for the future of counseling: The 20/20 principles for unifying and strengthening the profession. *Journal of Counseling & Development, 89,* 367–372.

Kaplan, D. M., Tarvydas, V. M., & Gladding, S. T. (2014). 20/20: A vision for the future of counseling: The new consensus definition of counseling. *Journal of Counseling & Development, 92,* 366–372.

Kaplan, F. F. (1994). The imagery and expression of anger: An initial study. *Art Therapy, 11,* 139–143.

Karpman, S. (1968). Fairy tales and script drama analysis. *Transactional Analysis Bulletin, 7,* 38–43.

Kaslow, N. J., & Eicher, V. W. (1988). Body image therapy: A combined creative arts therapy and verbal psychotherapy approach. *Arts in Psychotherapy, 15,* 177–188.

Kazdin, A. E. (2010). *Single-case research designs: Methods for clinical and applied settings.* New York, NY: Oxford University Press.

Kedem-Tahar, E., & Felix-Kellermann, P. (1996). Psychodrama and drama therapy: A comparison. *Arts in Psychotherapy, 23,* 27–36.

Keith, D. V., & Whitaker, C. A. (1991). Experiential/symbolic family therapy. In A. M. Horne & J. L. Passmore (Eds.), *Family counseling and therapy* (2nd ed., pp. 108–140). Itasca, IL: Peacock.

Kelly, W. E. (2002). An investigation of worry and sense of humor. *Journal of Psychology, 136,* 657–666.

Kelsch, D., & Emry, K. (2003, June). *Sharing the counseling program vision: Bibliotherapy using established language arts curriculum.* Paper presented at the annual conference of the American School Counselor Association, St. Louis, MO.

Kennedy, A. (2008, November). Creating connections, crafting wellness. *Counseling Today,* 34–38.

Kennedy, H., Reed, K., & Wamboldt, M. Z. (2014). Staff perceptions of complementary and alternative therapy integration into a child and adolescent psychiatry program. *Arts in Psychotherapy, 41,* 21–26.

Kersting, K. (2003, November). What exactly is creativity? *Monitor on Psychology,* 40–41.

Kestenbaum, C. J. (1985). The creative process in child psychotherapy. *American Journal of Psychotherapy, 39,* 479–489.

Kiepe, M.-S., Stöckigt, B., & Keil, T. (2012). Effects of dance therapy and ballroom dances on physical and mental illnesses: A systematic review. *Arts in Psychotherapy, 39,* 404–411.

Kilgore, L. (2003). Humor in clinical therapy with children. In A. J. Klein (Ed.), *Humor in children's lives: A guidebook for practitioners* (pp. 33–46). Westport, CT: Praeger.

Kim, J. K., & Suh, J. H. (2013). Children's kinetic family drawings and their internalizing problem behaviors. *Arts in Psychotherapy, 40,* 206–214.

Kim, S., Kim, G., & Ki, J. (2014). Effects of group art therapy combined with breath meditation on the subjective well-being of depressed and anxious adolescents. *Arts in Psychotherapy, 41,* 519–526.

Kimbel, T. M., & Protivnak, J. J. (2010). For those about to rock (with your high school students), we salute you: School counselors using music interventions. *Journal of Creativity in Mental Health, 5,* 25–38.

Kincade, E. A., & Evans, K. M. (1996). Counseling theories, process, and interventions in a multicultural context. In J. L. DeLucia-Waack (Ed.), *Multicultural counseling competencies: Implications for training and practice* (pp. 89–112). Alexandria, VA: American Counseling Association.

Kipper, D. A., Green, D. J., & Prorak, A. (2010). The relationship among spontaneity, impulsivity, and creativity. *Journal of Creativity in Mental Health, 5,* 39–53.

Kirschenbaum, H., & Henderson, V. L. (Eds.). (1989). *The Carl Rogers reader.* Boston, MA: Houghton Mifflin.

Klasfeld, M. (Director). (2007). When you're gone [Music video]. In Arvil Lavigne (Performer), *The best damn thing.* Nashville, TN: RCA Records.

Kleinke, C. L. (2002). *Coping with life challenges* (2nd ed.). Long Grove, IL: Waveland Press.

Klinger, E. (1987). The power of daydreams. *Psychology Today, 21,* 36–39, 42–44.

Koch, K. (1970). *Wishes, lies, and dreams.* New York, NY: Harper & Row.

Koch, K. (1977). *I never told anybody: Teaching poetry writing in a nursing home.* New York, NY: Random House.

Koch, S., & Brauninger, S. (2006). International dance/movement therapy research: Recent findings and perspectives. *American Journal of Dance Therapy, 28,* 127–136.

Koch, S., Kunz, T., Lykou, S., & Cruz, R. (2014). Effects of dance movement therapy and dance on health-related psychological outcomes: A meta-analysis. *Arts in Psychotherapy, 41,* 46–64.

Koch, S., & Weidinger-von der Recke, B. (2009). Traumatised refugees: An integrated dance and verbal therapy approach. *Arts in Psychotherapy, 36,* 289–296.

Koestler, A. (1964). *The act of creation.* New York, NY: Macmillan.

Kolodzey, J. (1983, January). Poetry: The latest word in healing. *Prevention, 35,* 62–68.

Kottler, J. A. (2006). *Divine madness: Ten stories of creative struggle.* San Francisco, CA: Jossey-Bass.

Kottler, J. A. (2010). *On being a therapist* (4th ed.). San Francisco, CA: Jossey-Bass.

Kottman, T., & Johnson, V. (1993). Adlerian play therapy: A tool for school counselors. *Elementary School Guidance and Counseling, 28,* 42–51.

Kramer, E. (1971). *Art as therapy with children.* New York, NY: Schocken.

Kramer, S. (Producer/Director), & Rose, W. (Writer). (1967). *Guess who's coming to dinner* [Motion picture]. United States: Columbia Pictures.

Kress, V., Adamson, N., Demarco, C., Paylo, M. J., & Zoldan, C. A. (2015). The use of guided imagery as an intervention in addressing non-suicidal self-injury. *Journal of Creativity in Mental Health, 8,* 35–47.

Kress, V. E., Hoffman, R., & Thomas, A. M. (2008). Letters from the future: The use of therapeutic letter writing in counseling sexual abuse survivors. *Journal of Creativity in Mental Health, 3,* 105–118.

Krueger, D. W., & Schofield, E. (1986). Dance and movement therapy of eating disordered patients: A model. *Arts in Psychotherapy, 13,* 323–331.

Kwack, H., Relf, P. D., & Rudolph, J. (2004). Adapting garden activities for overcoming difficulties of individuals with dementia and physical limitations. *Activities, Adaptation & Aging, 29*(1), 1–13.

Kwiatkowska, H. Y. (1967). Family art therapy. *Family Process, 6,* 37–55.

Kwiatkowska, H. Y. (1978). *Family therapy and evaluation through art.* Springfield, IL: Charles C Thomas.

L'Abate, L. (1992). *Programmed writing: A psychotherapeutic approach for individuals, couples, and families.* Pacific Grove, CA: Brooks/Cole.

L'Abate, L., Ganahl, G., & Hansen, J. C. (1986). *Methods of family therapy.* Upper Saddle River, NJ: Prentice-Hall.

L'Abate, L., & Sweeney, L. (2011). *Research on writing approaches in mental health.* Bingley, West Yorkshire, England: Emerald Group Publishing.

LaGaipa, J. (1977). The effects of humor on the flow of social conversation. In A. J. Chapman & H. C. Foot (Eds.), *It's a funny thing, humor* (pp. 421–427). New York, NY: Pergamon.

Lai, N.-H., & Tsai, H.-H. (2014). Practicing psychodrama in Chinese culture. *Arts in Psychotherapy, 41,* 386–390.

Lai, Y. (1999). Effects of music listening on depressed women in Taiwan. *Issues in Mental Health Nursing, 20,* 229–246.

Lampropoulos, G. K., Kazantis, K., & Deane, F. P. (2004). Psychologists' use of motion pictures. *Professional Psychologist: Research and Practice, 35,* 345–351.

Lampropoulos, G. K., & Spengler, P. M. (2005). Helping and change without traditional therapy: Commonalities and opportunities. *Counselling Psychology Quarterly, 18,* 47–59.

Landreth, G. L. (1993). Child-centered play therapy. *Elementary School Guidance and Counseling, 28,* 17–29.

Landy, R. J. (1991). The dramatic basis of role theory. *Arts in Psychotherapy, 18,* 29–41.

Landy, R. J. (1997). Drama therapy: The state of the art. *Arts in Psychotherapy, 24,* 5–11.

Landy, R. J. (2001). *New essays in drama therapy: Unfinished business.* Springfield, IL: Charles C Thomas.

Landy, R. J. (2006). The future of drama therapy. *Arts in Psychotherapy, 33,* 135–142.

Langer, E. J., & Rodin, J. (1976). The effects of choice and enhanced personal responsibility for the aged: A field experiment in an institutional setting. *Journal of Personality and Social Psychology, 34*(2), 191–198.

Lankton, C. H., & Lankton, S. R. (1989). *Tales of enchantment: Goal-oriented metaphors for adults and children in therapy.* New York, NY: Brunner/Mazel.

Lankton, S. R., & Lankton, C. H. (1983). *The answer within: A clinical framework of Ericksonian hypnotherapy.* New York, NY: Brunner/Mazel.

Lasseter, J., Privette, G., Brown, C., & Duer, J. (1989). Dance as a treatment approach with a multidisabled child: Implications for school counseling. *The School Counselor, 36,* 310–315.

Lax, E. (1975). *On being funny: Woody Allen and comedy.* New York, NY: Manor.

Lazarus, A. A. (1977). *In the mind's eye.* New York, NY: Rawson.

Lazarus, A. A. (1982). *Personal enrichment through imagery* [Audiotape]. New York, NY: BMA Audio Cassettes.

Lazarus, A. A. (2000). Multimodal therapy. In R. J. Corsini & D. Wedding (Eds.), *Current psychotherapy* (6th ed., pp. 340–374). Itasca, IL: Peacock.

Lazarus, A. A., & Shaughnessy, M. F. (2002). An interview with Arnold A. Lazarus. *North American Journal of Psychology, 4,* 171–182.

Leary, D. E. (1992). William James and the art of human understanding. *American Psychologist, 47,* 152–160.

Leavy, P. (2015). Method meets art (2nd ed.). New York: NY: Guilford Press.

Leedy, J. (1985). *Poetry as healer.* New York, NY: Vanguard.

LeLieuvre, R. B. (1998). "Goodnight Saigon": Music, fiction, poetry, and film in readjustment group counseling. *Professional Psychology: Research and Practice, 29,* 74–78.

Lent, J. (2009). Journaling enters the 21st century: The use of therapeutic blogs in counseling. *Journal of Creativity in Mental Health, 4,* 68–73.

Lepore, S. J., & Smyth, J. M. (2003). *The writing cure: How expressive writing promotes health and emotional well-being.* Washington, DC: American Psychological Association.

Lerer, S. (2008). *Children's literature: A reader from Aesop to Harry Potter.* Chicago, IL: University of Chicago Press.

Lerner, A. (1988). Poetry therapy corner. *Journal of Poetry Therapy, 2,* 118–120.

Lerner, A. (1992). Poetry therapy corner. *Journal of Poetry Therapy, 6,* 45–48.

Lerner, A. (1994). *Poetry in the therapeutic experience.* St. Louis, MO: MMB Music.

Lerner, A. (1997). A look at poetry therapy. *Arts and Psychotherapy, 24,* 81–89.

Lerner, A., & Mahlendorf, U. (Eds.). (1991). *Life guidance through literature.* Chicago, IL: American Library Association.

Lessner, J. W. (1974). The poem as catalyst in group counseling. *Personnel and Guidance Journal, 53,* 33–38.

Levick, M. F. (1989). On the road to educating the creative arts therapist. *Arts in Psychotherapy, 16,* 57–60.

Levine, S. K. (1996). The expressive body: A fragmented totality. *Arts in Psychotherapy, 23,* 131–136.

Levinson, B. M., & Mallon, G. P. (1997). *Pet-oriented child psychotherapy* (2nd ed.). Springfield, IL: Charles C Thomas.

Levinson, D. J., Darrow, C. N., Klein, E. B., Levinson, M. H., & McKee, B. (1978). *The seasons of a man's life.* New York, NY: Knopf.

Levitt, H., Korman, Y., & Angus, L. (2000). A metaphor analysis in treatments of depression: Metaphor as a marker of change. *Counselling Psychology Quarterly, 13,* 23–35.

Levy, F. J. (1988). Introduction. In F. J. Levy (Ed.), *Dance movement therapy* (pp. 1–16). Reston, VA: American Alliance for Health, Physical Education, Recreation, and Dance.

Levy, I., & Keum, B. T-H. (2014). Hip-hop emotional exploration in men. *Journal of Poetry Therapy, 27*(4), 217–233.

Levy, T. M. (1987). Brief family therapy: Clinical assumptions and techniques. In P. A. Keller & S. R. Heyman (Eds.), *Innovations in clinical practice: A source book* (pp. 63–77). Sarasota, FL: Professional Resource Exchange.

Lewis, P. (1997). Multiculturalism and globalism in the arts in psychotherapy. *Arts in Psychotherapy, 24,* 123–127.

Liebmann, M. (2004). *Art therapy for groups* (2nd ed.). New York, NY: Routledge.

Lin, Y.-J., Lin, C.-Y., & Li, Y.-C. (2014). Planting hope in loss and grief: Self-care applications of horticultural therapy for grief caregivers in Taiwan. *Death Studies, 38*(9), 603–611.

Lindbergh, A. M. (1975). *Gift from the sea.* New York, NY: Pantheon. (Original work published 1955)

Lindner, E. C. (1982). Dance as a therapeutic intervention for the elderly. *Educational Gerontology, 8,* 167–174.

Linesch, D. (2001). Art making in family therapy. In D. J. Weiner (Ed.), *Beyond talk therapy* (pp. 225–243). Washington, DC: American Psychological Association.

Lingerman, H. (1995). *The healing energies of music.* Wheaton, IL: Theosophical Publishing House.

Livesay, H. (2008). Passing go in the game of life: Board games in therapeutic play. In L. C. Rubin (Ed.), *Popular culture in counseling, psychotherapy, and play-based interventions* (pp. 197–224). New York, NY: Springer.

Loewenthal, D. (2013). Talking pictures therapy as brief therapy in a school setting. *Journal of Creativity in Mental Health, 8,* 21–34.

Louden-Gerber, G., & Duffey, T. (2008). Synthesizing the Enneagram through music. *Journal of Creativity in Mental Health, 3,* 320–329.

Lowenfeld, M. (1939). The world pictures of children. *British Journal of Medical Psychology, 18,* 65–73.

Lowenfeld, M. (1979). *The world technique.* London, England: Allen & Unwin.

Lowry, D. T., & Towles, D. E. (1989). Soap opera portrayals of sex, contraception, and sexually transmitted diseases. *Journal of Communication, 39,* 76–83.

Lubart, T. I. (1999). Creativity across cultures. In R. J. Sternberg (Ed.), *Handbook of creativity* (pp. 339–350). New York, NY: Cambridge University Press.

Lund, L. K., Zimmerman, T. S., & Haddock, S. A. (2002). The theory, structure, and techniques for the inclusion of children in family therapy: A literature review. *Journal of Marital and Family Therapy, 28,* 445–454.

Luria, A. (1968). *The mind of mnemonist.* New York, NY: Basic Books.

Lyddon, W., Clay, A., & Sparks, C. (2001). Metaphor and change in counseling. *Journal of Counseling & Development, 79,* 269–274.

Machan, D. (1987, November 2). What's black and blue and floats in the Monongahela River? *Forbes,* 216–220.

Machover, K. (1949). *Personality projection in the drawing of the human figure.* Springfield, IL: Charles C Thomas.

MacIntosh, H. B. (2003). Sounds of healing: Music in group work with survivors of sexual abuse. *Arts in Psychotherapy, 30,* 17–23.

MacKay, B. (1987). Uncovering buried roles through face painting and storytelling. *Arts in Psychotherapy, 14,* 201–208.

MacKay, B. (1989). Drama therapy with female victims of assault. *Arts in Psychotherapy, 16,* 293–300.

Madanes, C. (1981). *Strategic family therapy.* San Francisco, CA: Jossey-Bass.

Makin, S. R. (1994). *A consumer's guide to art therapy.* Springfield, IL: Charles C Thomas.

Malchiodi, C. A. (2005). Expressive therapies. In C. A. Malchiodi (Ed.), *Expressive therapies* (pp. 1–15). New York, NY: Guilford Press.

Malchiodi, C. (2010a, June 15). Cool art therapy intervention #4: Visual journaling. *Psychology Today.* Retrieved from http://www.psychologytoday.com/blog/the-healing-arts/201006/cool-art-therapy-intervention-4-visual-journaling

Malchiodi, C. (2010b, June 15). Cool art therapy intervention #6: Mandala drawing. *Psychology Today.* Retrieved from http://www.psychologytoday.com/blog/the-healing-arts/201003/cool-art-therapy-intervention-6-mandala-drawing

Malchiodi, C. A. (Ed.). (2012). *Handbook of art therapy* (2nd ed.). New York, NY: Guilford Press.

Mandsager, N., Newsome, D., & Glass, S. (1997, February). *Music as metaphor.* Paper presented at the annual conference of the North Carolina Counseling Association, Greensboro, NC.

Manning, T. M. (1987). Aggression depicted in abused children's drawings. *Arts in Psychotherapy, 14,* 15–24.

Mansfield, B. (2003, July 1). 12-year-old's song stirs charts, listeners' hearts. *USA Today,* p. 3D.

Manz, C. C., & Neck, C. P. (2013). *Mastering self-leadership: Empowering yourself for personal excellence* (6th ed.). Upper Saddle River, NJ: Prentice-Hall.

Maples, M. F., Dupey, P., Torres-Rivera, E., Phan, L. T., Vereen, L., & Garrett, M. T. (2001). Ethnic diversity and the use of humor in counseling: Appropriate or inappropriate? *Journal of Counseling & Development, 79,* 53–60.

Markert, L. F., & Healy, C. C. (1983). The effects of poetry and lyrics on work values. *Journal of Career Education, 10,* 104–110.

Markham, K. D., & Palmer, K. E. (1998, February). *Songs you know by heart.* Poster session presented at the annual conference of the North Carolina Counseling Association, Greensboro, NC.

Marks, D. F. (1995). New directions for mental imagery research. *Journal of Mental Imagery, 19,* 153–167.

Martin, R. A. (2007). *The psychology of humor: An integrated approach.* Burlington, MA: Academic Press.

Martineau, W. H. (1972). A model of the social function of humor. In J. H. Goldstein & P. E. McGhee (Eds.), *The psychology of humor* (pp. 101–125). New York, NY: Academic Press.

Martz, L. L. (1962). *The poetry of meditation.* New Haven, CT: Yale University Press.

Maslow, A. H. (1968). *Toward a psychology of being* (2nd ed.). New York, NY: Van Nostrand Reinhold.

Maslow, A. H. (1991). Experiential exercises for gratitude. *Journal of Humanistic Education and Development, 29,* 121–122.

Mason-Luckey, B., & Sandel, S. L. (1985). Intergenerational movement therapy: A leadership challenge. *Arts in Psychotherapy, 12,* 257–262.

Masserman, J. H. (1986). Poetry as music. *Arts in Psychotherapy, 13,* 61–67.

Masters, W. H., & Johnson, V. E. (1970). *Human sexual inadequacy.* Boston, MA: Little, Brown.

Mateos-Moreno, D., & Atencia-Doña, L. (2013). Effect of a combined dance/movement and music therapy on young adults diagnosed with severe autism. *Arts in Psychotherapy, 40,* 465–472.

Maultsby, M. C., Jr. (1977). *Rational-emotive imagery.* In A. Ellis & R. Grieger (Eds.), *Handbook of rational-emotive therapy* (pp. 225–230). New York, NY: Springer.

Maultsby, M. C., Jr. (1990). *Rational behavior therapy.* Appleton, WI: Rational Self-Help Aids.

May, R. (1953). *Man's search for himself.* New York, NY: Norton.

May, R. (1969). *Love and will.* New York, NY: Norton.

May, R. (1975). *The courage to create.* New York, NY: Norton.

Mayers, K. (1995). Songwriting with traumatized children. *Arts in Psychotherapy, 22,* 495–498.

Mayers, K., & Griffin, M. (1990). The play project: Use of stimulus objects with demented patients. *Journal of Gerontological Nursing, 16,* 32–37.

Mazza, N. (1986). Poetry and popular music in social work education: The liberal arts perspective. *Arts in Psychotherapy, 13,* 293–299.

Mazza, N. (1988). Poetry and popular music as adjunctive psychotherapy techniques. In P. A. Keller & S. R. Heyman (Eds.), *Innovations in clinical practice: A source book* (Vol. 7, pp. 485–494). Sarasota, FL: Professional Resource Exchange.

Mazza, N. (1993). Poetry therapy: Toward a research agenda for the 1990s. *Arts in Psychotherapy, 20,* 51–59.

Mazza, N. (2003). *Poetry therapy: Theory and practice.* New York, NY: Brunner-Routledge.

Mazza, N. F., & Hayton, C. J. (2013). Poetry therapy: An investigation of a multidimensional clinical model. *Arts in Psychotherapy, 40,* 53–60.

McBrien, R. J. (1993). Laughing together: Humor as encouragement in couples counseling. *Individual Psychology, 49,* 419–427.

McClary, R. (2007). Healing the psyche through music, myth, and ritual. *Psychology of Aesthetics, Creativity and the Arts, 1,* 155–159.

McClure, B. A., Merrill, E., & Russo, T. R. (1994). Seeing clients with an artist's eye: Perceptual simulation exercises. *Simulation and Gaming, 25,* 51–60.

McConeghey, H. (2003). *Art and soul.* Putnam, CT: Spring Publications.

McDonnell, L. (1984). Music therapy with trauma patients on a pediatric service. *Music Therapy, 4,* 55–63.

McFerran, K. S., & Saarikallio, S. (2014). Depending on music to feel better: Being conscious of responsibility when appropriating the power of music. *Arts in Psychotherapy, 41,* 89–97.

McKay, M., Davis, M., & Fanning, P. (1981). *Thoughts and feelings: The art of cognitive stress intervention.* Richmond, CA: New Harbinger.

McKee, J. E., Presbury, J., Benson, J., Echterling, L. G., Cowen, E., & Marchal, J. (2003, September 6). *A four-step approach to expanding metaphorical horizons in counseling.* Paper presented at the annual conference of the Southern Association for Counselor Education and Supervision, Chattanooga, TN.

McNiff, S. (1986). Freedom of research and artistic inquiry. *Arts in Psychotherapy, 13,* 279–284.

McNiff, S. (1997). Art therapy: A spectrum of partnerships. *Arts in Psychotherapy, 24,* 37–44.

Meekums, B. (2000). *Creative group therapy for women survivors of child sexual abuse.* London, England: Jessica Kingsley.

Meekums, B., & Daniel, J. (2011). Arts with offenders: A literature synthesis. *Arts in Psychotherapy, 38,* 229–238.

Meekums, B., Vaverniece, L., Majore-Dusele, I., & Rasnacs, O. (2012). Dance movement therapy for obese women with emotional eating: A controlled pilot study. *Arts in Psychotherapy, 39,* 126–133.

Meggert, S. S. (2009). *Creative humor at work.* New York, NY: University Press of America.

Meier, S. T., & Davis, S. R. (2011). *The elements of counseling* (7th ed.). Belmont, CA: Brooks/Cole.

Mellou, E. (1995). Review of the relationship between dramatic play and creativity in young children. *Early Child Development and Care, 112,* 85–107.

Memory, B. C. (2002, June 14). *Healthy vibrations: Use of music with at-risk children and teens.* Paper presented at the Summer Institute for Helping Professions, East Carolina University, Greenville, NC.

Menninger Foundation. (1986). *Art therapy: The healing vision.* Topeka, KS: Author.

Mercer, A., Warson, E., & Zhao, J. (2010). Visual journaling: An intervention to influence stress, anxiety, and affect levels in medical students. *Arts in Psychotherapy, 37,* 143–148.

Mercer, L. E. (1993). Self-healing through poetry writing. *Journal of Poetry Therapy, 6,* 161–168.

Metzl, E. S., & Morrell, M. A. (2008). The role of creativity in models of resilience: Theoretical exploration and practical application. *Journal of Creativity in Mental Health, 3,* 303–318.

Meyer, S. (1985). Women and conflict in dance therapy. *Women and Therapy,* *4,* 3–17.

Michel, D. E., & Pinson, J. (2013). *Music therapy in principle and practice* (2nd ed.). Springfield, IL: Charles C Thomas.

Middleton, W. (2007). Gunfire, humour, and psychotherapy. *Australasian Psychiatry, 15,* 148–155.

Miller, J. K., & Gergen, K. J. (1998). Life on the line: The therapeutic potentials of computer-mediated conversation. *Journal of Marital and Family Therapy, 24,* 189–202.

Miller, M. E. (1991, July 16). A dose of sound to ease cancer's pain. *News & Observer* (Raleigh, NC), pp. 1E, 6E.

Miller, R. G. H., & Spence, J. (2013). The impact of breathing and music on stress levels of clients and visitors in a psychiatric emergency room. *Arts in Psychotherapy, 40,* 347–351.

Milliken, R. (2002). Dance/movement therapy as a creative arts therapy approach in prison to the treatment of violence. *Arts in Psychotherapy, 29,* 203–206.

Mills, J. C., & Crowley, R. J. (1986). *Therapeutic metaphors for children and the child within.* New York, NY: Brunner/Mazel.

Mills, L., & Daniluk, J. (2002). Her body speaks: The experience of dance therapy for women survivors of child sexual abuse. *Journal of Counseling & Development, 80,* 77–85.

Minor, A. J., Moody, S. J., Tadlock-Marlo, R., Pender, R., & Person, M. (2013). Music as a medium for cohort development. *Journal of Creativity in Mental Health, 8,* 381–394.

Mintz, E. E. (1971). *Marathon groups: Reality and symbol.* New York, NY: Appleton-Century-Crofts.

Minuchin, S., & Fishman, H. C. (1981). *Family therapy techniques.* Cambridge, MA: Harvard University Press.

Mitoma, J., & Stieber, D. A. (Eds.). (2002). *Envisioning dance: On film and video.* Philadelphia, PA: Routledge.

Mitroff, I. I., & Kilmann, R. H. (1978). *Methodological approaches to social science.* San Francisco, CA: Jossey-Bass.

Mohammadian, Y., Shahidi, S., Mahaki, B., Mohammadi, A. Z., Baghban, A. A., & Zayeri, F. (2011). Evaluating the use of poetry to reduce signs of depression, anxiety and stress in Iranian female students. *Arts in Psychotherapy, 38,* 59–63.

Mohacsy, I. (1995). Nonverbal communication and its place in the therapy session. *Arts in Psychotherapy, 22,* 31–38.

Molina, B., Monteiro-Leitner, J., Gladding, S., Pack-Brown, S., & Whittington-Clark, L. (2003, March 25). *Creative arts across cultures.* Paper presented at the annual conference of the American Counseling Association, Anaheim, CA.

Moller, L. (2013). Project "For Colored Girls:" Breaking the shackles of role deprivation through prison theatre. *Arts in Psychotherapy, 40,* 61–70.

Monahan, K. (2015). The use of humor with older adults aging in place. *Social Work in Mental Health, 13,* 61–69.

Monseau, V. R. (1994). Studying Cormier's protagonists: Achieving power through young adult literature. *ALAN Review, 22,* 31–33.

Moon, C. (1997). Art therapy: Creating the space we will live in. *Arts in Psychotherapy, 24,* 45–49.

Mooney, K. (2000). Focusing on solutions through art: A case study. *Australian and New Zealand Journal of Family Therapy, 21,* 34–41.

Moore, B. (1989). *Growing with gardening: A twelve-month guide for therapy, recreation, and education.* Chapel Hill, NC: University of North Carolina Press.

Moore, J., & Herlihy, B. (1993). Grief groups for students who have had a parent die. *The School Counselor, 41,* 54–59.

Morawetz, A., & Walker, G. (1984). *Brief therapy with single-parent families.* New York, NY: Brunner/Mazel.

Moreno, J. J. (1985). Music play therapy: An integrated approach. *Arts in Psychotherapy, 12,* 17–23.

Moreno, J. J. (1987). The therapeutic role of the blues singer and considerations for the clinical application of the blues form. *Arts in Psychotherapy, 14,* 333–340.

Moreno, J. J. (1988a). Multicultural music therapy: The world music connection. *Journal of Music Therapy, 25,* 17–27.

Moreno, J. J. (1988b). The music therapist: Creative arts therapist and contemporary shaman. *Arts in Psychotherapy, 15,* 271–280.

Moreno, J. J. (1999). Ancient sources and modern applications: The creative arts in psychodrama. *Arts in Psychotherapy, 26,* 95–101.

Moreno, J. L. (1945). *Group psychotherapy: A symposium.* New York, NY: Beacon House.

Moreno, J. L. (1947). The theatre for spontaneity. In *Psychodrama monographs* (No. 4). New York, NY: Beacon House. (Original work published 1923 as Das Stegif Theatre)

Moreno, J. L. (1993). *Who shall survive? Foundations of sociometry, group psychotherapy, and sociodrama.* Roanoke, VA: Royal. (Original work published 1934)

Morgovsky, J. (2003, August 10). *Reading pictures.* Paper presented at the annual conference of the American Psychological Association, Toronto, Ontario, Canada.

Morris, E. (2001). *The rise of Theodore Roosevelt.* New York, NY: Random House.

Morrison, N. C., & Rasp, R. R. (2001). The application of facilitated imagery to marital counseling. In B. J. Brothers (Ed.), *Couples, intimacy issues, and addiction* (pp. 131–151). New York, NY: Haworth Press.

Mosak, H. H. (1987). *Ha ha and aha: The role of humor in psychotherapy.* Muncie, IN: Accelerated Development.

Mosak, H. H., & Maniacci, M. (2011). Adlerian psychotherapy. In R. J. Corsini & D. Wedding (Eds.), *Current psychotherapies* (9th ed., pp. 67–112). Itasca, IL: Peacock.

Mössler, K., Assmus, J., Heldal, T. O., Fuchs K., & Gold, C. (2012). Music therapy techniques as predictors of change in mental health care. *Arts in Psychotherapy, 39*, 333–341.

Mulky, M. (2004). Recreating masculinity: Drama therapy with male survivors of sexual assault. *Arts in Psychotherapy, 31*, 19–38.

Mungas, R., & Silverman, M. J. (2014). Immediate effects of group-based wellness drumming on affective states in university students. *Arts in Psychotherapy, 41*, 287–292.

Murkoff, H., & Mazel, S. (2008). *What to expect when you're expecting* (4th ed.). New York, NY: Workman.

Murstein, B. I., & Brust, R. G. (1985). Humor and interpersonal attraction. *Journal of Personality Assessment, 49*, 637–640.

Music an effective tool in HIV prevention, researcher finds. (2003, July 2). *Ascribe Newswire*. Retrieved from http://PsycPORT.com

Myers, J. E. (1989). *Infusing gerontological counseling in counselor preparation*. Alexandria, VA: American Counseling Association.

Myers, J. E. (1998). Bibliotherapy and DCT: Co-constructing the therapeutic metaphor. *Journal of Counseling & Development, 76*, 243–250.

Myrick, R. D., & Myrick, L. S. (1993). Guided imagery: From mystical to practical. *Elementary School Guidance and Counseling, 28*, 62–70.

Nadeau, R. (1984). Using the visual arts to expand personal creativity. In B. Warren (Ed.), *Using the creative arts in therapy* (pp. 61–86). Cambridge, MA: Brookline.

Nahemow, L. (1986). Humor as a database for the study of aging. In L. Nahemow, K. A. McCluskey-Fawcett, & P. E. McGhee (Eds.), *Humor and aging* (pp. 3–26). New York, NY: Academic Press.

Napier, A. Y. (1990). *The fragile bond*. New York, NY: HarperCollins.

Napier, A. Y., & Whitaker, C. A. (1978). *The family crucible*. New York, NY: Bantam Books.

Napier, R. W., & Gershenfeld, M. K. (2004). *Groups: Theory and experience* (7th ed.). Boston, MA: Houghton-Mifflin.

Narita, J. (1996). *Coming into passion: Song for a sansei* [Play]. San Francisco, CA: Author.

Naumberg, M. (1966). *Dynamically oriented art therapy*. New York, NY: Grune & Stratton.

Neck, C. P., Stewart, G. L., & Manz, C. C. (1995). Thought self-leadership as a framework for enhancing the performance of performance appraisers. *Journal of Applied Behavioral Science, 31*, 278–302.

Neilsen, P., King, R., & Baker, F. (Eds.). (2016). *Creative arts in counseling and mental health*. Los Angeles, CA: Sage.

Nelson, L., & Finneran, L. (2006). *Drama and the adolescent journey: Warm-ups and activities to address teen issues*. Portsmouth, NH: Heinemann Drama.

Nelson, P. (1993). *There's a hole in my sidewalk*. Hillsboro, OR: Beyond Words.

Nelson, R. (1996). *Incident at Crystal Lake*. Huntington, WV: Aegina Press.

Nelson, R. (1997). *In the land of choice*. Huntington, WV: Aegina Press.

Nepps, P., Stewart, C. N., & Bruckno, S. R. (2014). Animal-assisted activity: Effects of a complementary intervention program on psychological and physiological variables. *Journal of Evidence-Based Complementary & Alternative Medicine, 19*(3), 211–215.

Ness, M. E. (1989). The use of humorous journal articles in counselor training. *Counselor Education and Supervision, 29,* 35–43.

Newcomb, N. S. (1994). Music: A powerful resource for the elementary school counselor. *Elementary School Guidance and Counseling, 29,* 150–155.

Newton, A. K. (1995). Silver screens and silver linings: Using theater to explore feelings and issues. *Gifted Child Today, 18*(2), 14–19.

Newton, F. B. (1976). How may I understand you? Let me count the ways. *Personnel and Guidance Journal, 54,* 257–260.

Newton, G. R., & Dowd, E. T. (1990). Effect of client sense of humor and paradoxical interventions on test anxiety. *Journal of Counseling & Development, 68,* 668–672.

Nichols, M. (2013). *Family therapy: Concepts and methods* (10th ed.). Upper Saddle River, NJ: Pearson.

Nichols, M., & Fellenberg, S. (2000). The effective use of enactments in family therapy: A discovery-oriented process study. *Journal of Marital and Family Therapy, 26,* 143–152.

Nicholson, J. I., & Pearson, Q. M. (2003). Helping children cope with fears: Using children's literature in classroom guidance. *Professional School Counseling, 7,* 15–19.

Nickerson, E. T., & O'Laughlin, K. S. (1983). The therapeutic use of games. In C. E. Schaefer & K. J. O'Connor (Eds.), *Handbook of play therapy* (pp. 174–187). New York, NY: Wiley.

Norcross, J. C., Campbell, L. F., Grohol, J. M., Santrock, J. W., Selagea, F., & Sommer, R. (2013). *Self-help that works* (4th ed.). New York, NY: Oxford University Press.

Nordoff, P., & Robbins, C. (1977). *Creative music therapy.* New York, NY: John Day.

O'Brien, C. R., Johnson, J., & Miller, B. (1978). Cartooning in counseling. *Personnel and Guidance Journal, 57,* 55–56.

O'Callaghan, C., & Grocke, D. (2009). Lyric analysis research in music therapy: Rationales, methods and representations. *Arts in Psychotherapy, 36,* 320–328.

O'Callaghan, D. M., & Chandler, C. K. (2011). An exploratory study of animal-assisted interventions utilized by mental health professionals. *Journal of Creativity in Mental Health, 6,* 90–104.

O'Connor, K. J., & Braverman, L. M. (Eds.). (2009). *Play therapy theory and practice: Comparing theories and techniques* (2nd ed.). New York, NY: Wiley.

O'Doherty, S. (1989). Play and drama therapy with the Down's syndrome child. *Arts in Psychotherapy, 16,* 171–178.

Ohanian, V. (2002). Imagery rescripting within cognitive behavior therapy for bulimia nervosa: An illustrative case report. *International Journal of Eating Disorders, 31,* 352–357.

Ohrt, J. H., Foster, J. M., Hutchinson, T. S., & Ieva, K. P. (2009). Using music videos to enhance empathy in counselors-in-training. *Journal of Creativity in Mental Health, 4,* 320–333.

Okun, B. F., & Kantrowitz, R. E. (2015). *Effective helping* (8th ed.). Belmont, CA: Brooks/Cole.

Omizo, M. M., & Omizo, S. A. (1989). Art activities to improve self-esteem among native Hawaiian children. *Journal of Humanistic Education and Development, 27,* 167–176.

O'Neil, J. M., & Carroll, M. R. (1988). A gender role workshop focused on sexism, gender role conflict, and gender role journey. *Journal of Counseling & Development, 67,* 193–197.

O'Neill, B. (1997, May). *The unconstraining voice: The poetics of well-being.* Keynote address presented at the annual conference of the National Association for Poetry Therapy, Cleveland, OH.

Oppawsky, J. (2001). Using drawings when working with adults in therapy. *Journal of Psychotherapy in Independent Practice, 2,* 49–61.

Orkbi, H., Bar, N., & Eliakim, L. (2014). The effect of drama-based group therapy on aspects of mental illness stigma. *Arts in Psychotherapy, 41,* 458–466.

Orton, G. L. (1997). *Strategies for counseling with children and their parents.* Pacific Grove, CA: Brooks/Cole.

Osborn, C. (1989). Reminiscence: When the past eases the present. *Journal of Gerontological Nursing, 15,* 6–12.

Ostertag, J. (2002). Unspoken stories: Music therapy with abused children. *Canadian Journal of Music Therapy, 9,* 10–29.

Ostlund, D. R., & Kinnier, R. T. (1997). Values of youth: Messages from the most popular songs of four decades. *Journal of Humanistic Counseling, Education and Development, 36,* 83–91.

Owens, G. (1986). Music therapy in France. *Arts in Psychotherapy, 13,* 301–305.

Painter, W. M. (1989). *Musical story hours: Using music with storytelling and puppetry.* Hamden, CT: Library Professional.

Palmer, A. (2003, July/August). Violent song lyrics may lead to violent behavior. *Monitor on Psychology, 34*(7), 25.

Palmer, M. H. (2002). A description of a rapid desensitization procedure. *Behavior Therapist, 25,* 171.

Papp, P. (1976). Family choreography. In P. Guerin Jr. (Ed.), *Family therapy: Theory and practice* (pp. 465–479). New York, NY: Gardner.

Papp, P. (1982). Staging reciprocal metaphors in a couples group. *Family Process, 21,* 453–467.

Paquette, J., & Vitaro, F. (2014). Wilderness therapy, interpersonal skills and accomplishment motivation: Impact analysis on antisocial behavior and socioprofessional status. *Residential Treatment for Children & Youth, 31,* 230–252.

Pardeck, J. T., & Pardeck, J. A. (1993). *Bibliotherapy: A clinical approach for helping children.* Landhorne, PA: Gordon & Breach.

Pare, T. J., Shannon, B., & Dustin, T. (1996). The use of guided imagery in family of origin group therapy. *Canadian Journal of Counselling, 30,* 42–54.

Parenti, L., Foreman, A., Meade, B. J., & Wirth, O. (2013). A revised taxonomy of assisted animals. *Journal of Rehabilitation Research and Development, 50*(6), 745–756.

Parker-Pope, T. (2015, January 19). Writing your way to happiness. *New York Times.* Retrieved from http://well.blogs.nytimes.com/2015/01/19/writing-your-way-to-happiness/

Parr, G., Haberstroh, S., & Kottler, J. (2000). Interactive journal writing as an adjunct in group work. *Journal for Specialists in Group Work, 25,* 229–242.

Pasiali, V. (2013). A clinical case study of family-based music therapy. *Journal of Creativity in Mental Health, 8,* 249–264.

Payne, H. (2006). *Dance movement therapy: Theory, research, and practice* (2nd ed.). New York, NY: Routledge.

Pearson, Q. M. (2002, October). *Bringing the client into the classroom using popular music and poetry.* Paper presented at the conference of the Association for Counselor Education and Supervision, Park City, UT.

Pearson, Q. M. (2003). Polished rocks: A culminating guided imagery for counselor interns. *Journal of Humanistic Counseling, Education and Development, 42,* 116–120.

Peck, M. S. (1978). *The road less traveled.* New York, NY: Simon & Schuster.

Pehrsson, D. E. (2006/2007). Co-story-ing: Collaborative story writing with children who fear. *Journal of Creativity in Mental Health, 2,* 85–91.

Pehrsson, D. E., Allen, V. P., Folger, W. A., McMillen, P., & Lowe, I. (2007). Bibliotherapy with adolescents experiencing a divorce. *The Family Journal: Counseling and Therapy for Couples and Families, 15,* 409–414.

Pehrsson, D. E., & McMillen, P. (2005). A bibliotherapy evaluation tool: Grounding counselors in the therapeutic use of literature. *Arts in Psychotherapy, 32,* 47–59.

Pendzik, S., & Raviv, A. (2011). Therapeutic clowning and drama therapy: A family resemblance. *Arts in Psychotherapy, 38,* 267–275.

Pennebaker, J. W. (1990). *Opening up: The healing power of confiding in others.* New York, NY: Avon Books.

Pennebaker, J. W. (1997). Writing about emotional experiences as a therapeutic process. *Psychological Science, 8,* 162–165.

Pennebaker, J. W. (2004). *Writing to heal: A guided journal for recovering from trauma and emotional upheaval.* New York, NY: New Harbinger.

Pennebaker, J. W., & Chung, C. K. (2007). Expressive writing, emotional upheavals, and health. In H. S. Friedman & R. C. Silver (Eds), *Foundations of Health Psychology* (pp. 263–284). New York, NY: Oxford University Press.

Pennebaker, J. W., Mehl, M. R., & Niederhoffer, K. G. (2003). Psychological aspects of natural language use: Our words, our selves. *Annual Review of Psychology, 54,* 547–577.

Perakis, C. R. (1992). Prescriptive literature: Story and lyric as therapy. *Journal of Poetry Therapy, 6,* 95–100.

Perls, F. S. (1969). *Gestalt therapy verbatim.* Moab, UT: Real People.

Perls, F. S. (1970). Four lectures. In J. Fagan & I. L. Shepherd (Eds.), *Gestalt therapy now* (pp. 14–38). New York, NY: Harper & Row.

Perls, F. S., Hefferline, R. F., & Goodman, P. (1951). *Gestalt therapy*. New York, NY: Dell.

Peters, J. S. (2001). *Music therapy: An introduction* (2nd ed.). Springfield, IL: Charles C Thomas.

Peterson, D., & Boswell, J. N. (2015). Play therapy in a natural setting: A case example. *Journal of Creativity in Mental Health, 10*, 62–67.

Pfeiffer, D. C., & Jones, J. E. (1980). *A handbook of structured experiences for human relations training* (Vol. 7). San Diego, CA: University Associates.

Pierce, L. (2014). The integrative power of dance/movement therapy: Implications for the treatment of dissociation and developmental trauma. *Arts in Psychotherapy, 41*, 7–15.

Piercy, F. P., Sprenkle, D. H., & Wetchler, J. L. (1997). *Family therapy sourcebook* (2nd ed.). New York, NY: Guilford Press.

Pillay, Y. (2009). The use of digital narratives to enhance counseling and psychotherapy. *Journal of Creativity in Mental Health, 4*, 32–41.

Pincus, D., & Sheikh, A. A. (2009). *Imagery for pain relief: A scientifically grounded guidebook for clinicians*. New York, NY: Routledge.

Pink, D. (2006). *A whole new mind*. New York, NY: Penguin.

Piper, W. (1972). *The little engine that could*. New York, NY: Grosset & Dunlap. (Original work published 1930)

Pittman, F. (1989, October). *The secret passions of men*. Paper presented at the annual conference of the American Association for Marriage and Family Therapy, San Francisco, CA.

Plach, T. (1996). *The creative use of music in group therapy*. Springfield, IL: Charles C Thomas.

Politsky, R. H. (1995). Toward a typology of research in the creative arts therapies. *Arts in Psychotherapy, 22*, 307–314.

Pope, K. S., Singer, J. L., & Rosenberg, L. C. (1984). Sex, fantasy and imagination: Scientific research and clinical applications. In A. A. Sheikh (Ed.), *Imagination and healing* (pp. 197–210). Farmingdale, NY: Baywood.

Potkay, C. R. (1974). Teaching abnormal psychology concepts using popular song lyrics. *Teaching of Psychology, 9*, 233–234.

Potocek, J., & Wilder, V. N. (1989). Art/movement psychotherapy in the treatment of the chemically dependent patient. *Arts in Psychotherapy, 16*, 99–103.

Potter, B. (1972). *The tale of Peter Rabbit*. New York, NY: Dover. (Original work published 1902)

Powell, M. L., Newgent, R. A., & Lee, S. M. (2006). Group cinematherapy: Using metaphor to enhance adolescent self-esteem. *Arts in Psychotherapy, 33*, 247–253.

Pratt, R. R. (2004). Art, dance, and music therapy. *Physical Medicine and Rehabilitation Clinics of North America, 15*, 827–841.

Predny, M. L., & Reif, D. (2004). Horticulture therapy activities for preschool children, elderly adults, and intergenerational groups. *Activities, Adaptation & Aging, 28*, 1–18.

Prinzhorn, H. (1972). *Artistry of the mentally ill*. New York, NY: Springer. (Original work published 1922)

Progoff, I. (1975). *At a journal workshop.* New York, NY: Dialogue House.

Prueter, B. A., & Mezzano, J. (1973). Effect of background music upon initial counseling interaction. *Journal of Music Therapy, 10,* 205–212.

Pulliam, J. C., Somerville, P., Prebluda, J., & Warja-Danielsson, M. (1988). Three heads are better than one: The expressive arts group assessment. *Arts in Psychotherapy, 15,* 71–77.

Punkanen, M., Saarikallio, S., & Luck, G. (2014). Emotions in motion: Short-term group form dance/movement therapy in the treatment of depression: A pilot study. *Arts in Psychotherapy, 41,* 493–497.

Raber, W. C. (1987). The caring role of the nurse in the application of humor therapy to the patient experiencing helplessness. *Clinical Gerontologist, 7,* 3–11.

Rabinowitz, F. E. (1997). Teaching counseling through a semester-long role-play. *Counselor Education and Supervision, 36,* 216–223.

Rainwater, J. (1979). *You're in charge! A guide to becoming your own therapist.* Los Angeles, CA: Guild of Tutors.

Rambo, T. (1996). The use of creative arts in adolescent group therapy. In S. T. Gladding (Ed.), *New developments in group counseling* (pp. 31–33). Greensboro, NC: ERIC/CASS.

Raskin, V. (2009). *The primer of research humor.* New York, NY: Mouton de Gruyter.

Ray, D. C., Perkins, S. R., & Oden, K. (2004). Rosebush fantasy technique with elementary school students. *Professional School Counseling, 7,* 277–282.

Ray, L., Soares, E. J., & Tolchinsky, B. (1988). Explicit lyrics: A content analysis of top 100 songs from the 50s to the 80s. *Speech Communication Annual, 2,* 43–56.

Reiter, S. (1988). The Wizard of Oz in the land of id: A bibliotherapy approach. *Journal of Poetry Therapy, 3,* 149–156.

Renard, S., & Sockel, K. (1987). *Creative drama: Enhancing self-concepts and learning.* Ann Arbor, MI: ERIC/CASS. (ERIC Document Reproduction Service No. ED 345164)

Reynolds, F. (1999). Cognitive behavioral counseling of unresolved grief through the therapeutic adjunct of tapestry making. *Arts in Psychotherapy, 26,* 165–171.

Reynolds, F. (2012). Art therapy after stroke: Evidence and a need for further research. *Arts in Psychotherapy, 39,* 239–244.

Rhyne, J. (1973). *The gestalt art experience.* Belmont, CA: Wadsworth.

Richards, S. D., Pillay, J., & Fritz, E. (2012). The use of sand tray techniques by school counsellors to assist children with emotional and behavioural problems. *Arts in Psychotherapy, 39,* 367–373.

Richardson, A. (1969). *Mental imagery.* London, England: Routledge & Kegan Paul.

Rider, M. S. (1987). Treating chronic disease and pain with music-mediated imagery. *Arts in Psychotherapy, 14,* 113–120.

Riley, S. (1987). The advantages of art therapy in an outpatient clinic. *American Journal of Art Therapy, 26,* 21–29.

Riley, S. (1997, Winter). Children's art and narratives: An opportunity to enhance therapy and a supervisory challenge. *The Supervision Bulletin,* 2–3.

Riley, S. (2003). Using art therapy to address adolescent depression. In C. A. Malchiodi (Ed.), *Handbook of art therapy* (pp. 220–228). New York, NY: Guilford Press.

Rio, R. (2002). Improvisation with the elderly: Moving from creative activities to process-oriented therapy. *Arts in Psychotherapy, 29,* 191–201.

Rio, R. E., & Tenney, K. S. (2002). Music therapy for juvenile offenders in residential treatment. *Music Therapy Perspectives, 20,* 89–97.

Riordan, R. J. (1996). Scriptotherapy: Therapeutic writing as a counseling adjunct. *Journal of Counseling & Development, 74,* 263–269.

Riordan, R. J., & Ketchum, S. B. (1996). Therapeutic correspondence: The usefulness of notes and letters in counseling. *Georgia Journal of Professional Counseling,* 31–40.

Riordan, R. J., Mullis, F., & Nuchow, L. (1996). Organizing for bibliotherapy: The science in the art. *Individual Psychology, 52,* 169–180.

Riordan, R. J., & Wilson, L. S. (1989). Bibliotherapy: Does it work? *Journal of Counseling & Development, 67,* 506–508.

Ritter, M., & Low, K. G. (1996). Effects of dance and movement therapy: A meta-analysis. *Arts in Psychotherapy, 23,* 249–260.

Robbins, J. M., & Pehrsson, D.-E. (2009). Anorexia nervosa: A synthesis of poetic and narrative therapies in the outpatient treatment of young adult women. *Journal of Creativity in Mental Health, 4,* 42–56.

Rober, P. (2009). Relational drawings in couple therapy. *Family Process, 48,* 117–133.

Robinson, V. M. (1978). Humor in nursing. In C. Carlson & B. Blackwell (Eds.), *Behavioral concepts and nursing intervention* (2nd ed., pp. 191–210). Philadelphia, PA: Lippincott.

Rofes, E. E. (Ed.). (1981). *The kids' book of divorce: By, for, and about kids.* Lexington, MA: Lewis.

Rogers, C. R. (1951). *Client-centered therapy.* Boston, MA: Houghton-Mifflin.

Rogers, C. R. (1957). The necessary and sufficient conditions of therapeutic personality change. *Journal of Consulting Psychology, 21,* 95–103.

Rogers, F. (1998). *When a pet dies.* New York, NY: Putnam.

Rogge, R. D., Cobb, R. J., Lawrence, E., Johnson, M. D., & Bradbury, T. N. (2013). Is skills training necessary for the primary prevention of marital distress and dissolution? A 3-year experimental study of three interventions. *Journal of Consulting and Clinical Psychology, 81*(6), 949–996.

Roje, J. (1994). Consciousness as manifested in art: A journey from the concrete to the meaningful. *Arts in Psychotherapy, 21,* 375–385.

Roosa, L. W. (1981). The family drawing/storytelling technique: An approach to assessment of family dynamics. *Elementary School Guidance and Counseling, 15,* 269–272.

Rooyackers, P. (1998). *101 drama games for children.* Alameda, CA: Hunter House.

Rooyackers, P. (2002). *101 more drama games for children.* Alameda, CA: Hunter House.

Rosato, F. D. (2012). *Walking and jogging for health and wellness* (6th ed.). Belmont, CA: Brooks/Cole.

Roscoe, B., Krug, K., & Schmidt, J. (1985). Written form of self-expression utilized by adolescents. *Adolescence, 20,* 841–844.

Rose, S., Aikena, A., & McColl, M. A. (2014). A scoping review of psychological interventions for PTSD in military personnel and veterans. *Military Behavioral Health, 2,* 264–282.

Rosenblatt, J. (1991, February 6). From rock 'n' roll to zydeco: Eclectic archives of popular music at Bowling Green State University. *Chronicle of Higher Education,* pp. B6–B7.

Rosenthal, H. (2002). Samuel T. Gladding on creativity. *Journal of Clinical Activities, Assignments, and Handouts in Psychotherapy Practice, 2,* 23–33.

Rossiter, C. (1992). Commonalities among the creative arts therapies as a basis for research collaboration. *Journal of Poetry Therapy, 5,* 227–235.

Rossiter, C. (1997, May). *Where we're coming from: Cultural understanding through poetry therapy.* Paper presented at the annual conference of the National Association for Poetry Therapy, Cleveland, OH.

Rossiter, C., & Brown, R. (1988). An evaluation of interactive bibliotherapy in a clinical setting. *Journal of Poetry Therapy, 1,* 157–168.

Rossman, M. L. (1984). Imagine health! Imagery in medical self-care. In A. A. Sheikh (Ed.), *Imagination and healing* (pp. 231–258). Farmingdale, NY: Baywood.

Rothert, E. A., Nelson, K., & Coakley, K. (2011). *Health through horticulture: Indoor gardening activity plans.* Chicago, IL: CreateSpace Independent Publishing Platform.

Rubin, J. (1980). Art in counseling: A new avenue. *Counseling and Human Development, 13,* 1–12.

Rubin, J. A. (2010). *Introduction to art therapy: Sources and resources.* New York, NY: Routledge.

Rubin, L. C. (2000). The use of paint-by-number art in therapy. *Arts in Psychotherapy, 27,* 269–272.

Rubin, R. J. (1978). *Using bibliotherapy: A guide to theory and practice.* Phoenix, AZ: Oryx.

Rubinstein, H. (1990). *The Oxford book of marriage.* New York, NY: Oxford University Press.

Rus-Makovec, M., Furlan, M., & Smolej, T. (2015). Experts on comparative literature and addiction specialists in cooperation: A bibliotherapy session in aftercare group therapy for alcohol dependence. *Arts in Psychotherapy, 44,* 25–34.

Russel, J. (1995). Art therapy on a hospital burn unit: A step towards healing and recovery. *Art Therapy, 12,* 38–45.

Russell, L. A. (1992). Comparisons of cognitive, music, and imagery techniques on anxiety reduction with university students. *Journal of College Student Development, 33,* 516–523.

Russell-Chapin, L. A., & Stoner, C. R. (1995). Mental health counselors as consultants for diversity training. *Journal of Mental Health Counseling, 17,* 146–156.

Rutko, E. A., & Gillespie, J. (2013). Where's the wilderness in wilderness therapy? *Journal of Experiential Education, 36,* 218–232.

Ryan, R. M., Lynch, M. E, Vansteenkiste, M., & Deci, E. L. (2011). Motivation and autonomy in counseling, psychotherapy, and behavior change: A look at theory and practice. *The Counseling Psychologist, 39,* 193–260.

Rychtarik, R. G., & McGillicuddy, N. B. (1997). The Spouse Situation Inventory: A role-play measure of coping skills in women with alcoholic partners. *Journal of Family Psychology, 11,* 289–300.

Rydell, M. (Producer), & Thompson, E. (Writer). (1981). *On golden pond* [Motion picture]. United States: ITC Films.

Ryder, P. (1976). Theatre as prison therapy. *Drama Review, 20,* 60–66.

Sandel, S. L., Chaiklin, S., & Lohn, A. (Eds.). (1993). *Foundations of dance/ movement therapy: The life and work of Marian Chace.* Columbia, MD: Marian Chace Memorial Fund of the American Dance Therapy Association.

Sandel, S. L., & Johnson, D. R. (1996). Theoretical foundations of the structural analysis of movement sessions. *Arts in Psychotherapy, 23,* 15–25.

Santos, E. (2014, October 13). Coloring isn't just for kids. It can actually help adults combat stress. *The Huffington Post.* Retrieved from http://www. huffingtonpost.com/2014/10/13/coloring-for-stress_n_5975832.html

Sarid, O., & Huss, E. (2011). Image formation and image transformation. *Arts in Psychotherapy, 38,* 252–255.

Satir, V. (1972). *Peoplemaking.* Palo Alto, CA: Science and Behavior Books.

Satir, V. M., & Bitter, R. (1991). The therapist and family therapy: Satir's human validation process model. In A. M. Horne & J. L. Passmore (Eds.), *Family counseling and therapy* (2nd ed., pp. 13–46). Itasca, IL: Peacock.

Schaefer, C. E. (Ed.). (1995). *The therapeutic powers of play.* Northvale, NJ: Jason Aronson.

Schaefer, C. E. (2003). *Play therapy with adults.* Hoboken, NJ: Wiley.

Schaefer, C. E., & Reid, S. E. (1986). *Game play.* New York, NY: Wiley.

Schieffer, J. L., Boughner, S. R., Coll, K. M., & Christensen, O. J. (2001). Guided imagery combined with music: Encouraging self-actualizing attitudes and behaviors in at-risk community college students. *Journal of College Student Psychotherapy, 15,* 51–69.

Schiff, M., & Frances, A. (1974). Popular music: A training catalyst. *Journal of Music Therapy, 11,* 33–40.

Schimmel, C. J. (2006/2007). Seeing is remembering: The impact of using creative props with children in schools and community agencies. *Journal of Creativity in Mental Health, 2,* 59–74.

Schlender, B., & Tetzeli, R. (2015). *Becoming Steve Jobs: The evolution of a reckless upstart into a visionary leader.* New York, NY: Crown Publishing.

Schmidt, J. A. (1983). Songwriting as a therapeutic procedure. *Music Therapy Perspectives, 1*(2), 4–7.

Schneck, D. J., & Berger, D. S. (2006). *The music effect: Physiology and clinical applications.* London, England: Jessica Kingsley.

Schudson, K. R. (1975). The simple camera in school counseling. *Personnel and Guidance Journal, 54,* 225–226.

Schulberg, C. (1981). *Music therapy source book.* New York, NY: Human Sciences.

Schultz, K. D. (1984). The use of imagery in alleviating depression. In A. A. Sheikh (Ed.), *Imagination and healing* (pp. 129–158). Farmingdale, NY: Baywood.

Schwary, R. (Producer), Redford, R. (Director), & Guest, J. (Writer). (1980). *Ordinary people* [Motion picture]. United States: Paramount Pictures.

Schweiger, W. K., & Cashwell, C. S. (2003, September). *Sand tray therapy.* Paper presented at the annual conference of the Southern Association for Counselor Education and Supervision, Chattanooga, TN

Schweitzer, C. L. S. (2014). Tempo and temperament: A music lesson on the significance of time for the art of pastoral care. *Pastoral Psychology, 63*(5/6), 719–734.

Scogin, F., & Pollio, H. (1980). Targeting and the humorous episode in group process. *Human Relations, 33,* 831–852.

Scott, T. A., Burlingame, G., Starling, M., Porter, C., & Lilly, J. P. (2003). Effects of individual client-centered play therapy on sexually abused children's mood, self-concept, and social competence. *International Journal of Play Therapy, 12,* 7–30.

Seibel, J. (2008). Behind the gates: Dance/movement therapy in a women's prison. *American Journal of Dance Therapy, 30,* 106–109.

Seligman, L. (1985). The art and science of counseling. *American Mental Health Counselors Association Journal, 7,* 2–3.

Sendak, M. (1984). *Where the wild things are.* New York, NY: Harper-Collins.

Shafer, K. S., & Silverman, M. J. (2013). Applying a social learning theoretical framework to music therapy as a prevention and intervention for bullies and victims of bullying. *Arts in Psychotherapy, 40,* 495–500.

Shaffer, W. (1996). Psychodrama technique in the middle school or meanwhile back at Elsinore Castle. In S. T. Gladding (Ed.), *New developments in group counseling* (pp. 35–36). Greensboro, NC: ERIC/CASS.

Sharp, C., Smith, J. V., & Cole, A. (2002). Cinematherapy: Metaphorically promoting therapeutic change. *Counselling Psychology Quarterly, 15,* 269–276.

Shechtman, Z., & Perl-Dekel, O. (2000). A comparison of therapeutic factors in two group treatment modalities: Verbal and art therapy. *Journal for Specialists in Group Work, 23,* 288–304.

Sheikh, A. A. (Ed.). (2002). *Handbook of therapeutic imagery techniques.* Amityville, NY: Baywood.

Sheikh, A. A., Sheikh, K. S., & Moleski, L. M. (1985). The enhancement of imaging ability. In A. A. Sheikh & K. S. Sheikh (Eds.), *Imagery in education* (pp. 223–239). Farmingdale, NY: Baywood.

Shelton, L. S., Leeman, M., & O'Hara, C. (2011). *Introduction to animal assisted therapy in counseling.* Retrieved from http://www.counseling.org/docs/default-source/vistas/vistas_2011_article_55.pdf?sfvrsn=9

Shelton, R. (2003). *No direction home: The life and music of Bob Dylan.* New York, NY: Da Capo Press.

Shen, Y.-J. (2008). Reasons for school counselors' use or nonuse of play therapy: An exploratory study. *Journal of Creativity in Mental Health, 3,* 30–43.

Shen, Y.-P., & Armstrong, S. A. (2008). Impact of group sandtray therapy on the self-esteem of young adolescent girls. *Journal for Specialists in Group Work, 33,* 118–137.

Sheperis, C. J., Daniels, M. H., & Young, J. S, (2010). *Counseling research: Quantitative, qualitative, and mixed results.* Upper Saddle River, NJ: Pearson.

Sheperis, C. J., Hope, K., & Palmer, C. (2003, May). *Family ties: Uniting systems theory and practice through cinematherapy.* Paper presented at the annual conference of the American Counseling Association, Anaheim, CA.

Shinebourne, P., & Smith, P. A. (2010). The communicative power of metaphors: An analysis and interpretation of metaphors in accounts of the experience of addiction. *Psychology and Psychotherapy: Theory, Research and Practice, 83,* 59–73.

Shmukler, D. (1985). Imaginative play: Its implication for the process of education. In A. A. Sheikh & K. S. Sheikh (Eds.), *Imagery in education* (pp. 39–62). Farmingdale, NY: Baywood.

Shorr, J. E. (1977). *Go see the movie in your head.* New York, NY: Popular Library.

Shorr, J. E. (2002). *Psychotherapy through imagery* (2nd ed.). New York, NY: Thieme-Stratton.

Short, A. E. (1992). Music and imagery with physically disabled elderly residents: A GIM adaptation. *Music Therapy, 11,* 65–98.

Siegel, B. S. (1986). *Love, medicine, and miracles.* New York, NY: Harper & Row.

Siegell, M. (1987). Review of the book *Music and Trance*: A theory of the relations between music and possession. *Arts in Psychotherapy, 14,* 183–185.

Silverman, M. J. (2003). The influence of music on the symptoms of psychosis: A meta-analysis. *Journal of Music Therapy, 40,* 27–40.

Silverman, M. J. (2008). Nonverbal communication, music therapy, and autism: A review of literature and case example. *Journal of Creativity in Mental Health, 3,* 3–19.

Singer, J. L. (2006). *Imagery in psychotherapy.* Washington, DC: American Psychological Association.

Sklare, G. B., Sabella, R. A., & Petrosko, J. M. (2003). A preliminary study of the effects of group solution-focused guided imagery on recurring individual problems. *Journal for Specialists in Group Work, 28,* 370–381.

Skovholt, T. M. (1981). *Career imagery card sort.* Minneapolis, MN: University of Minnesota Press.

Skovholt, T. M., Morgan, J. I., & Negron-Cunningham, H. (1989). Mental imagery in career counseling and life planning: A review of research and intervention methods. *Journal of Counseling & Development, 67,* 287–292.

Skovholt, T. M., & Thoen, G. A. (1987). Mental imagery in parenthood decision making. *Journal of Counseling & Development, 65,* 315–316.

Slivka, H. H., & Magill, L. (1986). The conjoint use of social work and music therapy in working with children of cancer patients. *Music Therapy, 6,* 30–40.

Smilansky, S., & Shefatya, L. (1990). *Facilitating play.* Gaithersburg, MD: Psychosocial & Educational.

Smokowski, P. R. (2003). Beyond role-playing: Using technology to enhance modeling and behavioral rehearsal in group work practice. *Journal for Specialists in Group Work, 28,* 9–22.

Smucker, M. R., & Dancu, C. V. (1999). *Cognitive–behavioral treatment for adult survivors of childhood trauma: Imagery rescripting and reprocessing.* Northvale, NJ: Jason Aronson.

Snir, S., & Wiseman, H. (2013). Relationship patterns of connectedness and individuality in couples as expressed in the couple joint drawing method. *Arts in Psychotherapy, 40,* 501–508.

Snow, S. (1996). Fruit of the same tree: A response to Kedem-Tahar and Kellermann's comparison of psychodrama and drama therapy. *Arts in Psychotherapy, 23,* 199–206.

Sobel, E. (1994). *Wild heart dancing.* New York, NY: Bantam Books.

Solomon, G. (1995). *The motion picture prescription: Watch this movie and call me in the morning: 200 movies to help you heal life's problems.* Santa Rosa, CA: Aslan.

Solomon, G. (2002). *Reel therapy: How movies inspire you to overcome life's problems.* Santa Rosa, CA: Aslan.

Somervill, J. W., Kruglikova, Y. A., Robertson, R. L., Hanson, L. M., & MacLin, O. H. (2008). Physiological responses by college students to a dog and a cat: Implications for pet therapy. *North American Journal of Psychology, 10*(3), 519–528.

Sommers-Flanagan, J., & Sommers-Flanagan, R. (2015). *Counseling and psychotherapy theories in context and practice* (2nd ed.). Hoboken, NJ: Wiley.

Sommers-Flanagan, R., Elander, C., & Sommers-Flanagan, J. (2000). *Don't divorce us! Kids' advice to divorcing parents.* Alexandria, VA: American Counseling Association.

Somody, C., & Hobbs, M. (2006/2007). Paper bag books: A creative intervention with elementary school children experiencing high-conflict parental divorce. *Journal of Creativity in Mental Health, 2,* 73–87.

Sori, C. F., & Hughes, J. C. (2014). Animal-assisted play therapy: An interview with Rise VanFleet. *The Family Journal: Counseling and Therapy for Couples and Families, 22,* 350–356.

Stahler, W. (2006/2007). Prayerformance: A drama therapy approach with female prisoners recovering from addiction. *Journal of Creativity in Mental Health, 2,* 3–12.

Stanley, J. D. (1999). *Reading to heal: How to use bibliotherapy in your life.* Boston, MA: Houghton Mifflin.

Star, K. L., & Cox, J. A. (2008). The use of phototherapy in couples and family counseling. *Journal of Creativity in Mental Health, 3,* 373–382.

Stark, A., & Lohn, A. F. (1989). The use of verbalization in dance and movement therapy. *Arts in Psychotherapy, 16,* 105–113.

Staum, M. (1983). Music and rhythmic stimuli in the rehabilitation of gait disorders. *Journal of Music Therapy, 20,* 69–87.

Steinhardt, L. (1985). Freedom within boundaries: Body outline drawings in art therapy with children. *Arts in Psychotherapy, 12,* 25–34.

Stepakoff, S. (2009). From destruction to creation, from silence to speech: Poetry therapy principles and practices for working with suicide grief. *Arts in Psychotherapy, 36,* 105–113.

Stephens, T., Braithwaite, R. L., & Taylor, S. E. (1998). Model for using hip-hop music for small group HIV/AIDS prevention counseling with African American adolescents and young adults. *Patient Education and Counseling, 35,* 127–137.

Stephensen, C., & Baker, F. (2015). Music therapy and mental recovery. In P. Neilsen, R. King, & F. Baker (Eds.), *Creative arts in counseling and mental health* (pp. 95–107). Los Angeles, CA: Sage.

Sternberg, R. J., & Lubart, T. I. (1996). Investing in creativity. *Arts in Psychotherapy, 31,* 677–688.

Stevens, R., & Spears, E. H. (2009). Incorporating photography as a therapeutic tool in counseling. *Journal of Creativity in Mental Health, 4,* 3–16.

Stewart, L., & Chang, C. Y. (2015). Animal-assisted counseling in therapy. *American Counseling Association Practice Brief.* Retrieved from https://www.counseling.org/docs/default-source/practice-briefs/animal-assisted-therapy.pdf

Stewart, L., Chang, C., & Jaynes, A. (2013, May 1). Creature comforts. *Counseling Today.* Retrieved from http://ct.counseling.org/2013/05/creature-comforts

Stewart, L. A., Chang, C. Y., & Rice, R. (2013). Emergent theory and model of practice in animal-assisted therapy in counseling. *Journal of Creativity in Mental Health, 8,* 329–348.

Storr, A. (1992). *Music and the mind.* New York, NY: Free Press.

Straum, M. (1993). A music/nonmusic intervention with homeless children. *Journal of Music Therapy, 36,* 256–262.

Strick, F. L. (2001). The child's own touching rules book. In H. G. Kaduson & C. E. Schaefer (Eds.), *101 more favorite play therapy techniques* (pp. 120–123). Northvale, NJ: Jason Aronson.

Stuart, W. (1997). *Imagery and symbolism in counseling.* London, England: Jessica Kingsley.

Styron, W. (1990). *Darkness visible: A memoir of madness.* New York, NY: Random House.

Summer, L. (1997). Considering the future of music therapy. *Arts in Psychotherapy, 24,* 75–80.

Sweeney, T. J. (2009). *Adlerian counseling: A practitioner's approach* (5th ed.). New York, NY: Routledge.

Sylvia, W. M. (1977). Setting the stage: A counseling playlet. *Elementary School Guidance and Counseling, 12,* 49–54.

Takata, Y. (2002). Supporting by a nurse teacher in a school infirmary using collage therapy. *Psychiatry and Clinical Neurosciences, 56,* 371–379.

Teeter, R., Teeter, T., & Papai, J. (1976). Frustration: A game. *The School Counselor, 23,* 264–270.

Thaut, M. H. (1988). Rhythmic intervention techniques in music therapy with gross motor dysfunctions. *Arts in Psychotherapy, 15,* 127–137.

Thaut, M. H. (2009). *Rhythm, music, and the brain: Scientific foundations and clinical applications.* Philadelphia, PA: Routledge.

Thomson, D. M. (1997). Dance/movement therapy with the dual-diagnosed: A vehicle to the self in the service of recovery. *American Journal of Dance Therapy, 19,* 63–79.

Thoresen, C. E. (1969). Relevance and research in counseling. *Review of Educational Research, 9,* 264.

Tibbetts, T. J., & Stone, B. (1990). Short-term art therapy with seriously emotionally disturbed adolescents. *Arts in Psychotherapy, 17,* 139–146.

Titus, J. E., & Sinacore, A. L. (2013). Art-making and well-being in healthy young adult women. *Arts in Psychotherapy, 40,* 29–36.

Toffoli, G., & Allan, J. (1992). Group guidance for English as a second language students. *The School Counselor, 40,* 136–145.

Toman, S. M., & Rak, C. F. (2000). The use of cinema in the counselor education curriculum: Strategies and outcomes. *Counselor Education and Supervision, 40,* 105–115.

Took, K. J., & Weiss, D. S. (1994). The relationship between heavy metal and rap music and adolescent turmoil: Real or abstract? *Adolescence, 25,* 613–623.

Tortora, S. (2005). *The dancing dialogue: Using the communicative power of movement with young children.* Baltimore, MD: Brookes.

Trim, M., & Gale, T. (2004). *Growing and knowing: A selection guide for children's literature.* Munich, Germany: K. G. Saur.

Tromski, D., & Doston, G. (2003). Interactive drama: A method for experiential multicultural training. *Journal of Multicultural Counseling and Development, 31,* 52–62.

Trotter, K. S. (2012). *Harnessing the power of equine-assisted counseling: Adding animal assisted therapy to your practice.* New York, NY: Routledge.

Trounstein, J. R. (2001). *Shakespeare behind bars: The power of drama in women's prisons.* New York, NY: St. Martin's Press.

Trowbridge, M. M. (1995). Graphic indicators of sexual abuse in children's drawings: A review of the literature. *Arts in Psychotherapy, 22,* 485–494.

Tuckman, B. W., & Jensen, M. A. C. (1977). Stages of small-group development revisited. *Group and Organizational Studies, 2,* 419–427.

Ullman, E., & Dachinger, P. (1996). *Art therapy in theory and practice.* New York, NY: Schocken. (Original work published 1975)

Utay, J., & Miller, M. (2006). Guided imagery as an effective therapeutic technique: A brief review of its history and efficacy research. *Journal of Instructional Psychology, 33,* 40–43.

Utley, A. & Garza, Y. (2011). The therapeutic use of journaling with adolescents. *Journal of Creativity in Mental Health, 6,* 29–41.

Valine, W. J. (1983). Intensifying the group member's experience using the group log. *Journal for Specialists in Group Work, 8,* 101–104.

VanFleet, R. (2014). *Filial therapy: Strengthening parent child relations through play* (3rd ed.). Sarasota, FL: Professional Resources Press.

Vanger, P., Oerter, U., Otto, H., Schmidt, S., & Czogalik, D. (1995). The musical expression of the separation conflict during music therapy. *Arts in Psychotherapy, 22,* 147–154.

Veltman, M. W. M., & Browne, K. D. (2003). Trained raters' evaluation of kinetic family drawings of physically abused children. *Arts in Psychotherapy, 30,* 3–12.

Ventre, M. (1994). Guided imagery and music in process: The interweaving of the archetype of the mother, mandala, and music. *Music Therapy, 12,* 19–38.

Vereen, L. G., Butler, S. K., Williams, F. C., Darg, J. A., & Downing, T. K. E. (2006). The use of humor when counseling African American college students. *Journal of Counseling & Development, 84,* 10–15.

Vernon, A. (2006a). *Thinking, feeling, and behaving: An emotional education curriculum for children (Grades 1–6)* (Rev. ed.). Champaign, IL: Research Press.

Vernon, A. (2006b). *Thinking, feeling, and behaving: An emotional education curriculum for children (Grades 7–12)* (Rev. ed.). Champaign, IL: Research Press.

Vick, R. M. (2012). A brief history of art therapy. In C. A. Malchiodi (Ed.), *Handbook of art therapy* (2nd ed., pp. 5–16). New York, NY: Guilford Press.

Viorst, J. (1976). *Alexander and the terrible, horrible, no good, very bad day.* New York, NY: Simon & Schuster.

Viorst, J. (1998). *Necessary losses.* New York, NY: Simon & Schuster.

Virués-Ortega, J., Pastor-Barriuso, R., Castellote, J. M., Población, A., & Pedro-Cuesta, J. (2012). Effect of animal-assisted therapy on the psychological and functional status of elderly populations and patients with psychiatric disorders: A meta-analysis. *Health Psychology Review, 6,* 197–221.

Volkman, S. (1993). Music therapy and the treatment of trauma-induced dissociative disorders. *Arts in Psychotherapy, 20,* 243–251.

von Rossberg-Gempton, I. E., Dickinson, J., & Poole, G. (1999). Creative dance: Potentiality for enhancing social functioning in frail children and young children. *Arts in Psychotherapy, 26,* 313–327.

Wadeson, H. (1980). *Art psychotherapy.* New York, NY: Wiley.

Wadeson, H. (1987). Pursuit of the image: Painting from poetry in a personal midlife odyssey. *Arts in Psychotherapy, 14,* 177–182.

Wager, K. M. (1987). Prevention programming in mental health: An issue for consideration by music and drama therapists. *Arts in Psychotherapy, 14,* 135–141.

Wald, J. (2003). Clinical art therapy with older adults. In C. A. Malchiodi (Ed.), *Handbook of art therapy* (pp. 294–307). New York, NY: Guilford Press.

Waller, D. (2012). Group art therapy: An interactive approach. In C. A. Malchiodi (Ed.), *Handbook of art therapy* (2nd ed., pp. 353–367). New York, NY: Guilford Press.

Warren, B. (1984). Drama: Using the imagination as a stepping stone for personal growth. In B. Warren (Ed.), *Using the creative arts in therapy* (pp. 131–155). Cambridge, MA: Brookline.

Warren, B. (1993). Introduction. In B. Warren (Ed.), *Using the creative arts in therapy* (pp. 3–8). New York, NY: Routledge.

Wasserman, M. (1988). Poetry as a healing force in later adulthood: The case of Nezahualcoyotl. *Journal of Poetry Therapy, 1,* 221–228.

Watkins, B. T. (1990, September 19). In nontraditional, interdisciplinary study at Columbia College, artists get a chance to broaden their horizons, hone creativity. *Chronicle of Higher Education*, pp. A17, A20.

Watson, J. (1980). Bibliotherapy for abused children. *The School Counselor, 27*, 204–208.

Watts, R. E., & Trusty, J. (2003). Using imagery team members in reflecting "as if." *Journal of Constructivist Psychology, 16*, 335–340.

Watzlawick, P. (1983). *The situation is hopeless, but not serious.* New York, NY: Norton.

Webb, N. B. (Ed.). (2015). *Play therapy with children and adolescents in crisis* (4th ed.). New York, NY: Guilford Press.

Weber, A. M., & Haen, C. (2005). *Clinical application of drama therapy in child and adolescent treatment.* New York, NY: Brunner-Routledge.

Wedding, D., & Neimiec, R. M. (2014). *Movies and mental illness: Using films to understand psychopathology* (4th ed.). Boston, MA: Hogrefe Publishing.

Weinhold, B. K. (1987). Altered states of consciousness: An explorer's guide to inner space. *Counseling and Human Development, 20*, 1–12.

Weiser, J. (1999). *Phototherapy techniques* (2nd ed.). Vancouver, British Columbia, Canada: PhotoTherapy Centre Press.

Weiser, J. (2001). Phototherapy techniques: Using clients' personal snapshots and family photos as counseling and therapy tools. *Afterimage: The Journal of Media Arts and Cultural Criticism, 29*(3), 10–15.

Weiss, J. C. (1999). The role of art therapy in aiding older adults with life transitions. In M. Duffy (Ed.), *Handbook of counseling and psychotherapy with older adults* (pp. 182–196). New York, NY: Wiley.

Wells, N. F. (1988). An individual music therapy assessment procedure for emotionally disturbed young adolescents. *Arts in Psychotherapy, 15*, 47–54.

Wengrower, H. (2001). Arts therapies in educational settings: An intercultural encounter. *Arts in Psychotherapy, 28*, 109–115.

Wenz, K., & McWhirter, J. J. (1990). Enhancing the group experience: Creative writing exercises. *Journal for Specialists in Group Work, 15*, 37–42.

West, J. D., Osborn, C. J., & Bubenzer, D. L. (Eds.). (2003). *Leaders and legacies.* New York, NY: Brunner Routledge.

Westburg, N. G. (2003). Hope, laughter, and humor in residents and staff at an assisted living facility. *Journal of Mental Health Counseling, 25*, 16–32.

Westhenen, N., & Fritz, E. (2014). Creative arts therapy as treatment for child trauma: An overview. *Arts in Psychotherapy, 41*, 527–534.

Wheeler, B. L. (Ed.). (2015). *Music therapy handbook.* New York, NY: Guilford Press.

White, A. (1985). Meaning and effects of listening to popular music: Implications for counseling. *Journal of Counseling & Development, 64*, 65–69.

White, J., & Allers, C. T. (1994). Play therapy with abused children: A review of the literature. *Journal of Counseling & Development, 72*, 390–394.

White, M., & Epston, D. (1990). *Narrative means to therapeutic ends.* New York, NY: Norton.

Wiener, D. J. (2001). Rehearsals for growth: Applying improvisational theater games to relationship therapy. In D. J. Wiener (Ed.), *Beyond talk therapy: Using movement and expressive techniques in clinical practice* (pp. 165–180). Washington, DC: American Psychological Association.

Wigram, T. (2004). *Improvisation: Methods and techniques for music therapy clinicians, educators, and students.* London, England: Jessica Kingsley.

Willey, M. (1993). *The Melinda zone.* New York, NY: Bantam Books.

Williams, C. B., Frame, M. W., & Green, E. (1999). Counseling groups for African American women: A focus on spirituality. *Journal for Specialists in Group Work, 24,* 260–273.

Williams, K., & Lent, J. (2008). Scrapbooking as an intervention for grief recovery with children. *Journal of Creativity in Mental Health, 3,* 455–467.

Williams, M. (1922). *The velveteen rabbit: How toys become real.* New York, NY: Doubleday.

Williamson, M. (2008). *The age of miracles: Embracing the new midlife.* New York, NY: Hay House.

Wilner, K. B. (2001). Core energetics: A therapy on bodily energy and consciousness. In D. J. Wiener (Ed.), *Beyond talk therapy: Using movement and expressive techniques in clinical practice* (pp. 183–203). Washington, DC: American Psychological Association.

Wilson, G. T. (2011). Behavior therapy. In R. J. Corsini & D. Wedding (Eds.), *Current psychotherapies* (9th ed., pp. 235–275). Belmont, CA: Brooks/Cole.

Wilson, J. (Producer), Costner, K. (Producer/Director), & Blake, M. (Writer). (1990). *Dances with wolves* [Motion picture]. United States: Orion Pictures.

Wilson, N. S. (1983). "What can school do for me?": A guidance play. *School Counselor, 30,* 374–380.

Wilson, T. D. (2011). *Redirect: Changing the stories we live by.* New York, NY: Back Bay Books.

Winnicott, D. W. (1974). *Playing and reality.* New York, NY: Pelican.

Wise, J. (2015). *Digging for victory: Horticultural therapy with veterans for post-traumatic growth.* London, England: Karmac Books.

Witmer, J. M. (1985). *Pathways to personal growth.* Muncie, IN: Accelerated Development.

Witmer, J. M., & Young, M. E. (1985). The silent partner: Uses of imagery in counseling. *Journal of Counseling & Development, 64,* 187–190.

Witmer, J. M., & Young, M. E. (1987). Imagery in counseling. *Elementary School Guidance and Counseling, 22,* 5–16.

Wolpe, J. (1958). *Psychotherapy by reciprocal inhibition.* Stanford, CA: Stanford University Press.

Wong, Y. J., & Rochen, A. B. (2009). Potential benefits of expressive writing for male college students with varying degrees of restricted emotionality. *Psychology of Men and Masculinity, 10,* 149–159.

Woodard, S. L. (1995). Counseling disruptive Black elementary school boys. *Journal of Multicultural Counseling and Development, 23,* 21–28.

World Health Organization (2007). *International statistical classification of diseases and related health problems* (10th rev.). Retrieved from http://apps.who.int/classifications/apps/icd/icd10online/

Wright, J. (2002). Online counseling: Learning from writing therapy. *British Journal of Guidance and Counselling, 30,* 285–298.

Wright, J., & Chung, M. C. (2001). Mastery or mystery? Therapeutic writing: A review of the literature. *British Journal of Guidance and Counseling, 29,* 277–291.

Yaniv, D. (2014). Don't just think there, do something: A call for action in psychological science. *Arts in Psychotherapy, 41,* 336–342.

Yasukawa, M. (2015). Horticultural therapy for the cognitive functioning of elderly people with dementia. In I. Soderback. (Ed.), *International handbook of occupational therapy interventions* (2nd ed., pp. 811–824). New York, NY: Springer.

Yeh, C. J. (2001). An exploratory study of school counselors' experiences with and perceptions of Asian American students. *Professional School Counseling, 4,* 349–356.

Yochim, K. (1994). The collaborative poem and inpatient group therapy: A brief report. *Journal of Poetry Therapy, 7,* 145–149.

Yon, R. K. (1984). Expanding human potential through music. In B. Warren (Ed.), *Using the creative arts in therapy* (pp. 106–130). Cambridge, MA: Brookline.

Ziff, K., Pierce, L., Johanson, S., & King, M. (2012). ArtBreak: A creative group counseling program for children. *Journal of Creativity in Mental Health, 7,* 108–121.

Zilcha-Mano, S., Mikulincer, M., & Shaver, P. R. (2011). Pet in the therapy room: An attachment perspective on animal-assisted therapy. *Attachment and Human Development, 6,* 541–561.

Zorn, J. D. (2007). *Listening to music* (5th ed.). Upper Saddle River, NJ: Pearson.

Subject Index

Figures are indicated by "f" following page numbers.

J

N

T

(Continued)

Name Index

A

Abell, S. C., 140
Ablow, J. C., 168
Abraham, I. L., 83
Abrami, L. M., 179
Achterberg, J., 72
Adams, Kay, 124, 129, 130
Adams, P., 197, 231
Adams, W. J., 180
Adamson, E., 108
Adamson, N., 75
Adler, Alfred, 56, 78, 165
Aeschylus, 155
Aesop, 133
Aikena, A., 212
Albert, D. H., 151
Alberti, R. E., 127
Albright, J., 128
Aldridge, D., 25, 33, 222, 225
Aldridge, G., 42
Alesandrini, K. L., 88
Alexander, D. W., 188
Alexander, J. E., 183
Alexander, M., 162
Allan, J., 8, 11, 82, 98, 103, 177–178, 181
Allen, E., 131
Allen, Toby, 19
Allen, V. P., 141
Allen, Woody, 179, 180
Allers, C. T., 187
Allport, G. W., 12, 56, 176
Alvarado, V. I., 137
Alvares, T. S., 72
Alvarez, K., 61

Alvarez, N., 125
Alyami, A. M. S., 112
Amerikaner, M., 106, 151
Ammons, A. R., 146, 256
Anderberg, U. M., 155
Anderson, A. N., 59
Anderson, E., 59
Anderson, Robert, 162
Angelou, Maya, 133, 146
Angus, L., 138
Ansdell, G., 222
Anser-Self, K., 135
Aoki, T., 122
Appleton, V. E., 14, 105
Arbuthnott, D. W., 72
Arbuthnott, K. D., 72
Arieti, S., 11, 176, 185
Aristotle, 5, 125
Armeniox, L. F., 54
Armstrong, S. A., 190
Arnheim, R., 17, 109
Ashen, A., 74
Ashida, S., 39
Ashley, F. B., 61
Ashliman, D. L., 144
Asmuth, M. V., 145, 256
Assmus, J., 28
Astaire, Fred, 50
Atchison, D., 100
Atencia-Doña, L., 45
Atkins, S., 2, 5, 10, 20, 223
Atterburg, C., 62
Austin, B. D., 220
Avrahami, D., 96
Avrahami, E., 165
Axline, V., 178, 186–187

B

Bach, Johann Sebastian, 46
Bacon, S., 190
Bailey, L. M., 41
Baker, E. K., 131
Baker, F. A., 24
Baker, L. M., 214
Baker, S. B., 35
Ballard, M. B., 161
Bandler, R., 75
Bandoroff, S., 206
Bandura, A., 37
Bar, N., 160
Barbour, J., 124
Barker, P., 32, 196
Baron, P., 109
Baron, R. A., 194
Barone, T., 222
Bartlett, J. R., 163
Barton, C., 183
Bateson, G., 225
Baum, F. L., 133
Beale, A. V., 118, 167
Beaudry, I. D., 51
Beaulieu, J., 24, 30
Becker, K. W., 5, 101
Behrends, A., 50, 52
Beier, E., 183
Bemak, F., 149
Bentley, P., 27
Berg, B., 187–188
Berg, Matraca, 44
Berg, R. G., 188
Berger, A., 125, 149
Berger, D. S., 24
Berger, R., 207
Berget, B., 213
Bergman, Ingmar, 162
Bergquist, T. M., 204
Berk, L. E., 166
Berk, R. A., 176, 179
Berne, E., 75, 156
Bernstein, R. E., 168
Berry, J., 126, 188
Best, P. A., 52
Bettleheim, B., 139
Bettmann, J. E., 207, 215
Beutler, L. E., 165
Bing, E., 114
Binkley, E., 27
Bitter, R., 196
Björklund, A., 95
Black, Clint, 44
Black, J., 127
Blake, M., 157

Blatner, A., 9, 154, 157, 159, 160
Block, B. A., 50, 59
Blomdahl, C., 95
Blood, P., 41
Bogaerts, S., 43
Bolles, R. N., 127
Bonny, H. L., 10, 25, 30, 47
Borcherdt, B., 200
Bordan, T., 200
Borders, S. G., 139
Borgmann, E., 109
Bornmann, B. A., 168
Boswell, J. N., 217
Botello, R. K., 40
Boughner, S. R., 87
Bourne, E. J., 143
Bowen, C. A., 109
Bowen, Murray, 148
Bowman, D. O., 147
Bowman, R. P., 34, 186, 237
Bowman, T., 125
Braastad, B. O., 213
Bradbury, T. N., 161
Bradley, L. J., 2, 31, 42–43, 161, 188
Brady, L. J., 231
Brahms, Johannes, 42
Braithwaite, R. L., 41
Brand, A., 140
Brandt, G., 225
Bräuninger, I., 55, 60, 66
Bräuninger, S., 52
Braverman, L. M., 177, 180
Bray, M. A., 73
Brenner, A., 186
Brewer, B. W., 79
Bridges, Robert Seymour, 124
Brillantes-Evangelista, G., 105, 135
Britton, N., 155
Brockovich, Erin, 162
Brodsky, W., 30
Brody, E., 151
Brooke, S. L., 96
Brooks, D. K., Jr., 220
Brown, A., 105
Brown, C., 59, 80
Brown, H. J., Jr., 133
Brown, J. M., 24
Brown, K., 177–178
Brown, N. W., 144
Brown, R., 127
Browne, K. D., 114
Brownell, A. J., 53, 61
Bruce, M., 147
Bruckno, S. R., 212
Bruneaua, L., 128
Bruner, K. S., 193

Bruscia, K. E., 26, 28, 38
Brust, R. G., 180, 194
Bubenzer, D. L., 149
Buck, J., 96
Buddha, 133
Bunney, J., 54
Bunt, L., 29
Burcky, W. D., 60
Burgess, A. W., 95
Burke, J. F., 20, 177, 179
Burkholder, J. P., 6
Burleigh, L. R., 165
Burlingame, G., 187
Burns, D. D., 143
Burns, S. T., 133, 143, 144
Burton, Robert, 7
Buser, J. K., 14
Buser, T. J., 14
Bushong, D. J., 36
Butler, Jerry, 39
Butler, S. K., 183

C

Cadieux, J., 131
Cadrin, L., 87
Camarena, V. A. T., 24
Camic, P. M., 213
Camilleri, V., 40
Campbell, C., 186
Campbell, D., 110
Campbell, J., 154
Campbell, R. S., 221
Campo, Rafael, 124
Capacchione, L., 98
Carkhuff, R. R., 51
Carmichael, K., 133
Caron, J., 61
Carp, C. E., 197
Carroll, M. R., 135, 228
Carson, D. K., 3, 5
Carter, E. A., 196
Carter, Jimmy, 143
Cashwell, C. S., 181
Cassity, M., 36
Casson, J., 158
Castellote, J. M., 212
Castenada, C., 17
Cavanagh, M. E., 3
Cavazos, L. J., 137
Cavicchia, S, 164
Chace, Marian, 54, 55, 66
Chaiklin, S., 50, 52, 54, 56
Chalquist, C., 204
Chamberlain, D., 125–126
Chan, D. W., 17

Chance, S., 144
Chandler, C. K., 204, 205–206, 207, 208, 216
Chang, C., 208, 211
Chang, J., 196
Chapman, J., 40
Chavis, G. G., 126, 134, 146, 148
Cheek, J. R., 42–43
Chekhov, Anton, 124
Chen, M., 147
Chiefetz, D., 58
Childers, J. H., Jr., 60, 80
Christenberry, W., 17
Christenbury, L., 118
Christensen, O. J., 87
Chung, C. K., 221
Chung, M. C., 128
Churchill, Winston, 16
Cicero, 6
Clarkson, G., 42
Clarkson, P., 164
Clatworthy, J., 213
Clay, A., 138
Clifford, S., 38
Clifton, L., 135
Coakley, K., 209
Cobb, R. J., 161
Cochran, J. L., 177, 186
Cohen, G. D., 3, 38
Cohen-Liebman, M. S., 102
Cohn, R., 121
Cole, A., 161
Coleman, V. D., 7, 115
Coll, K. M., 87
Collins, D., 66
Collins, K. S., 149
Comfort, C. E., 97
Confucius, 6, 133
Conley, Dan, 45
Connor, L., 128
Constantine, L., 171
Constantino, G., 13–14
Conyne, R., 149
Cook, E. L., 26
Copeland, Aaron, 27
Coren, S., 205
Corey, G., 149, 192
Cormier, R., 141
Corsini, R. J., 5
Cortina, M. A., 102
Costello, M., 141
Costin, C., 127
Costner, K., 157
Coughlin, E. K., 6, 7, 139
Cousins, N., 178, 179
Covello, C., 101

Eisenstein-Naveh, A. R., 75
Eisner, E. W., 222
Ekeberg, O., 213
Elander, C., 141
Eliakim, L., 160
Elligan, D., 37
Ellington, D. B., 164
Ellis, A., 12, 19, 165, 177, 183, 184,
  191, 192, 221, 258, 261
Emerson, Ralph Waldo, 209
Emmons, M. L., 127
Emry, K., 127, 141, 147
Emunah, R., 59, 154, 157, 159, 168,
  170, 174
Enns, C. Z., 74, 182
Enns, G., 127
Epston, D., 131
Erford, B., 188
Erickson, Milton, 74
Erikson, E. H., 11, 16, 147, 177, 191
Erkman, Fatos, 182
Esfandiari, N., 24
Esman, A. H., 92, 112
Espenak, Liljan, 55, 56
Euripides, 155
Evan, Blanche, 55
Evans, K. M., 115, 136, 137
Evans, S., 228

F

Fagen, T., 41
Fair, C. D., 128
Fanning, P., 79
Farr, M., 59
Fazel, M., 102
Feder, B., 52
Feder, E., 52
Feldman, N., 167
Felix-Kellermann, P., 154, 158, 159
Fellenberg, S., 163, 170
Fernando, D. M., 208
Feyissa, A., 135
Figley, C. R., 72, 189
Fine, A. H., 205
Fine, G. A., 194
Finn, C. A., 102
Finneran, L., 167
Fisher, P. P., 55, 62, 66, 75, 82, 120,
  192
Fishman, H. Charles, 170, 183, 196
Fitzgerald, Paul, 120
Flahive, M., 190
Flake, C. L., 6, 7
Flanigen, D., 47
Flannery, B., 27

Fleming, W., 6
Fleshman, B., 5, 7, 18, 54
Fletcher, T. B., 206
Flom, B., 215
Floyd, M., 61
Flynn, L. M., 24
Foley, V. D., 172
Folger, W. A., 141
Foreman, A., 205
Forman, J., 106
Forrester, A. M., 157
Fosse, Bob, 50
Foster, J. M., 47
Fox, John, 229
Frame, M. W., 44
Framo, James, 148
France, M. H., 131
Frances, A., 43
Frank, J. D., 20
Frankenfelder, M. T., 111
Frankl, V. E., 184
Franklin, E., 82
Franzke, E., 142
Fredenburg, H. A., 42
Freud, S., 4, 8, 52, 56, 76, 95, 125, 205
Friedberg, R. D., 187
Friedman, E. H., 155, 156, 158, 173
Fritz, E., 5, 18, 181
Fry, W., Jr., 179
Fryear, J. L., 5, 7, 18, 54
Fuchs, K., 28
Furlan, M., 125
Furman, L., 168
Furman, R., 149

G

Gale, A. U., 220
Gale, T., 134
Gallo-Lopez, L., 180–181, 189
Ganahl, G., 171
Gandhi, 16, 163
Gantt, L., 121
Gardner, J., 135
Gardner, R. A., 139, 140, 187, 255
Garland, C., 145
Garland, J., 145
Garza, Y., 136
Gass, M. A., 206
Gawain, S., 75
Gaye, Marvin, 228
Gearing, Ashley, 27
Geddes, M., 114
Geller, S. K., 108
Gellman, R. A., 33
Gerber, J., 105

K

L